The **Buddha** Said...

ABOUT THE AUTHOR

The Osho teachings defy categorization, covering everything from the individual quest for meaning to the most urgent social and political issues facing society today. His books are not written but are transcribed from audio and video recordings of extemporaneous talks given to international audiences over a period of 35 years. Osho has been described by the *Sunday Times* in London as one of the "1,000 Makers of the 20th Century" and by American author Tom Robbins as "the most dangerous man since Jesus Christ".

About his own work Osho has said that he is helping to create the conditions for the birth of a new kind of human being. He has often characterized this new human being as "Zorba the Buddha" – capable both of enjoying the earthy pleasures of a Zorba the Greek and the silent serenity of a Gautama Buddha. Running like a thread through all aspects of Osho's work is a vision that encompasses both the timeless wisdom of the East and the highest potential of Western science and technology.

Osho is also known for his revolutionary contribution to the science of inner transformation, with an approach to meditation that acknowledges the accelerated pace of contemporary life. His unique "Active Meditations" are designed to first release the accumulated stresses of body and mind, so that it is easier to experience the thought-free and relaxed state of meditation.

The **Buddha** Said...

meeting the challenge of life's difficulties

OSHO

WATKINS PUBLISHING

LONDON

Distributed in the USA and Canada by Sterling Publishing Co., Inc.
387 Park Avenue South, New York, NY 10016

This edition first published in the UK and USA 2007 by
Watkins Publishing, Sixth Floor, Castle House,
75–76 Wells Street, London W1T 3QH

Reprinted 2007, 2008

Source of the Sutras:
Sermons of a Buddhist Abbot – the Classic of American Buddhism by Soyen Shaku
Introduction by Taitetsu Unno
Three Leaves (Random House USA) published September 2004
ISBN: 0-385-51048-9

Material in this volume has been selected from an original
series of talks entitled "The Discipline of Transcendence".

3 5 7 9 10 8 6 4

Designed by Jerry Goldie
Typeset By Dorchester Typesetting Group
Printed in the UK by CPI William Clowes Ltd, Beccles, NR34 7TL
Library of Congress Cataloging-in-Publication Data Available

ISBN: 978-1-84293-115-8

www.watkinspublishing.co.uk

For information about custom editions, special sales, premium and
corporate purchases, please contact Sterling Special Sales
Department at 800-805-5489 or specialsales@sterlingpub.com

CONTENTS

Chapter 1:

The Most Excellent Way

THE BUDDHA SAID:

To be free from the passions and to be calm, this is the most excellent way. Those who leave their parents, go out of the home, understand the mind, reach the source, and comprehend the immaterial, are called shramanas. *Those who observe the precepts of morality, who are pure and spotless in their behavior, and who exert themselves for the attainment of the fruits of saintship are called arhats.*

Next is the anagamin. *At the end of his life, the spirit of the* anagamin *ascends to the heaven and obtains arhatship.*

Next is the skridagamin. *The* skridagamin *ascends to the heaven (after his death), comes back to the earth once more, and then attains arhatship.*

Next is the srotapanna. *The* srotapanna *dies seven times and is born seven times, when he finally attains arhatship. By the severance of passions is meant that like the limbs severed they are never again made use of.*

Gautama Buddha is like Gourishankar, the highest peak of the Himalayas. He is one of the purest beings, one of the most virgin souls, a rare phenomenon on this earth. The rarity is that Buddha is a scientist of the inner world – a scientist of the spirit. That is a rare combination. To be religious is simple, to be a scientist is simple – but to combine, to synthesize these two polarities is incredible. It is unbelievable, but it has happened.

Buddha is the richest human being that has ever lived; rich in the sense that all the dimensions of life are fulfilled in him. He is not one-dimensional.

There are three approaches towards truth. One is the approach of power, another the approach of beauty, and the third the approach of grandeur.

The scientific approach is the search for power; that's why Lord Bacon said "knowledge is power". Science has made man very powerful, so much so that man can destroy the whole planet earth. For the first time in the history of consciousness man is capable of committing a global suicide, a collective suicide. Science has released tremendous power. Science is continuously searching for more and more power. This too is an approach towards truth, but a partial approach.

Then there are poets, mystics, people with an aesthetic sense. They look at truth as beauty – Jalaluddin Rumi and Rabindranath Tagore and others, who think that beauty is truth. They create art, they create new sources of beauty in the world. The painter, the poet, the dancer, the musician, they are also approaching truth but from a totally different dimension than power.

The poet is not like the scientist. The scientist works with analysis, reason, observation. The poet functions through the heart, trust, love – through the irrational. He has nothing to do with mind and reason.

The greater part of religious people belong to the second dimension. The Sufis, the Bauls – they all belong to the aesthetic approach. Hence so many beautiful mosques, churches, cathedrals, temples like Ajanta and Ellora – they were created by religious people. Whenever religious activity predominates, art is created, music is created, great painting is created; the world becomes a little more beautiful. It doesn't become more powerful, but it becomes more beautiful, more lovely, more worth living.

The third approach is that of grandeur. The old Bible prophets – Moses, Abraham; Islam's prophet Mohammed; Krishna and Ram in Hinduism – their approach is through the dimension of grandeur, through the awe that one feels looking at this vastness of the universe. The Upanishads, the Vedas, they all approach the world of truth through grandeur. They are full of wonder. The universe is unbelievably there, with such grandeur, that you can only bow down before it – nothing else is possible. One simply feels humble, reduced to nothing.

These are the three dimensions ordinarily available to approach truth. The first dimension creates the scientist, the second the artist, and the third the prophets. The rarity of Buddha consists of this – that his approach is a synthesis of all the three, and not only a synthesis but it goes beyond the three.

Buddha is a rationalist. He's not like Jesus and he is not like Krishna – he's absolutely a rationalist. Einstein, Newton or Edison would not find any flaw in his reasoning. Any scientist will be immediately convinced of his truth. His approach is purely logical, he convinces the mind. You cannot find a loophole in him.

Somebody has sent me a beautiful anecdote about a famous actor and atheist, W. C. Fields.

> He was doing a tour of the United States. One day his manager came into his hotel room and was shocked to see him reading a copy of the Gideon Bible.
>
> "Bill!" he said, "What the hell are you doing? I thought you were an atheist."
>
> Fields replied, "Just looking for loopholes, just looking for loopholes."

But you cannot look for a loophole in the Buddha. Yes, you can look for loopholes in Jesus, there are many – because Jesus believes, trusts, he has faith. He is simple like a child. There is no argument within him. The proof exists, but there is no argument for it. His whole being is his proof.

But it is not so with Buddha. You may not be at all in harmony with his heart, you may not believe him at all, you may not look at the proof he is, but you will have to listen to his argument. He has both the proof and the argument. He himself is the proof of what he is saying, but that is not all. If you are not ready to look at him he can force you, he can convince you; he is a rationalist.

Even a man like Bertrand Russell, who was an atheist, purely logical, has said, "Jesus I can fight – with Buddha I start feeling hesitant." He has written a book, *Why I am not a Christian* – a great and argumentative book. Christians have not yet replied to it; his argument still holds. But faced with Buddha he suddenly feels hesitant, he is not so certain of his ground – because Buddha can convince him on his own ground. Buddha is as analytical as Bertrand Russell.

You need not be a religious person to be convinced by Buddha, that's his rarity. You need not believe at all. You need not believe in God, you need not believe in the soul, you need not believe in anything – still you can be with Buddha, and by and by you will come to know about the soul and about godliness also, but those will not be hypotheses.

No belief is required to travel with Buddha. You can come to him with all your skepticism – he accepts and welcomes you, and he says, "Come with me." First he convinces your mind, and once your mind is convinced and you start traveling with him, by and by you start feeling that he has a message which is beyond mind, he has a message which no reason can confine. But first he convinces your reason.

Buddha's approach is suprarational, but not against reason. This has to be understood in the very beginning. It has something to do with the beyond, suprarational, but that suprarational is not against the rational, it is in tune with it. The rational and the suprarational are a continuity; this is the rarity of Buddha.

Krishna says to Arjuna, "Surrender to me." Buddha never says that, he convinces you to surrender. Krishna says, "Surrender to me, then you will be convinced." Buddha says, "Be convinced first, then surrender comes like a shadow. You need not worry about it, don't talk about it at all."

Because of this rational approach he never brings in any concept that cannot be proved. He never talks about God. H. G. Wells has said about Buddha, "He is the most godly and the most godless man in the whole history of man." Yes, it is so – the most godly and most godless. You cannot find a more godly person than Buddha. Every other personality simply fades before him. His luminosity is superb, his being has no comparison, but he does not talk about God.

Because he has never talked about God, many think that Buddha is an atheist – he is not. He has not talked about God because there is no way to talk about God. All talk about God is nonsense. Whatsoever you can say about God is going to be false. It is something that cannot be said.

Other seers also say that nothing can be said about God, but they do say this much, that nothing can be said about God. Buddha is really logical, he will not say even this, because he says, "Even to say that nothing can be said about God, you have said something. If you say, 'God cannot be defined,' you have defined him in a negative way – that he cannot be defined. If you say, 'Nothing can be said,' that too you are saying." Buddha is strictly logical. He will not utter a single word.

Ludwig Wittgenstein, one of the greatest thinkers of this age, one of the greatest of all the ages also, has said, "That which cannot be said must not be said. That which cannot be said, one must be silent thereof." Because to talk something about something that is unutterable is a sacrilege.

Buddha is not an atheist but he never talks about God. That's why I say he is a rarity. He brings many people to godliness – he brought more people than anybody else has. Millions of people were brought to become godly in his presence, but he never uttered the word. Not only God but even the soul, the self – he has no theory about it. He simply says, "I can show you the way to go in. You go in and look." He says, "Buddhas can only indicate the path, they cannot provide you with a philosophy. You are there, go in and see."

One man came to Buddha. He was a great scholar, a sort of professor, had written many books, was known all over the country. Maulingaputta was his name. He said to Buddha, "I have come with a dozen questions and you have to answer them."

Buddha said, "I will answer, but you will have to fulfill a requirement. For one year you will have to be with me in total silence, then I will answer – not before. Right now I can answer, but you will not receive the answers because you are not ready. Whatever I say you will misinterpret because you have too many interpretations crowding your mind. Whatever I say will have to pass through your mind. For one year you just be silent so that you can drop the knowledge. When you are empty, whatsoever you want to ask I will answer, I promise you."

As Buddha was saying this, another of his disciples, Sariputta, started laughing – a mad laughter. Maulingaputta must have felt embarrassed. He said, "What is the matter? Why are you laughing?"

Sariputta said, "I am not laughing at you, I am laughing at myself. This man deceived me also. I had come with many questions and he said, 'Wait for one year,' and I waited. One year has passed. I am laughing because now those questions have disappeared. He goes on asking, 'Now, bring me those questions!' But I cannot bring those questions, they have disappeared. So, Maulingaputta, if you really want your questions to be answered, ask now! Don't wait for one year. This man is deceptive."

Buddha introduced many people, millions of people, to the inner world, but in a very rational way. This is simple – that first you have to become a receiver, first you have to attain to silence; then communion is possible, not before that.

Buddha never used to answer any metaphysical questions. He was always ready to answer any question about method, but he was never ready to answer any question about metaphysics. This is his scientific approach. Science believes in method. Science never answers the "why", it always answers the "how".

If you ask a scientist, "Why does the world exist?" he will say, "I don't know – but I can answer how the world exists." If you ask him, "Why is there water?" he cannot answer; he will just shrug his shoulders. But he can say how the water is there; how much oxygen, how much hydrogen makes the water happen. He can give you the method, the "how", the mechanism. He can show you how to make water, but he cannot show you why.

Buddha never asks any "why" questions, but that doesn't mean that he is an atheist. His approach is very different from other atheists Theists require you to believe, to have faith, to trust. Buddha says, "How can one believe? You are asking the impossible."

Listen to his argument. He says if somebody is doubtful, how can he believe? If the doubt has arisen already, how can he believe? He may repress the doubt, he may enforce the belief, but deep down like a worm the doubt will go on lurking and eating his heart. Sooner or later the belief is bound to collapse, because it is unfounded; there is no foundation to it. In the foundation there is doubt, and on the foundation of doubt you have raised the whole structure of your belief.

Have you watched it? Whenever you believe, deep down there is doubt. What type of belief is this?

Buddha says if there is no doubt then there is no question of belief. Then one simply knows. There is no need for any Krishna to say, "Surrender, then you will believe" – there is no point. If Arjuna has faith, he has it; if he has not, then there is no way to create it. Then at the most Arjuna can play a game of showing, pretending that he believes. But belief cannot be enforced.

For those whose faith is natural, spontaneous, there is no question of faith – they simply believe. They don't know even what belief is. Small children, they simply believe. But once doubt enters, belief becomes impossible. And doubt has to enter; it is part of growth.

Doubt makes one mature. You remain childish unless doubt has penetrated your soul. Unless the fire of doubt starts burning you, you remain immature; you don't know what life is. You start knowing life only by doubting, by being skeptical, by raising questions.

Buddha says faith comes, but not against doubt, not as belief. Faith comes by destroying doubt with argument, by destroying doubt with more doubt, by eliminating doubt through doubt itself. A poison can be destroyed only by a poison – that is Buddha's method. He does not say believe. He says go deep into your doubt, go to the very end, unafraid; don't repress it. Travel the whole path of doubt to the very end, and that very journey will take you beyond it. Because a moment comes when doubt starts doubting itself. That's the ultimate doubt – when doubt doubts doubt itself. That point has to come if you go to the very end. You first doubt belief, you doubt this and that. One day, when everything has been doubted, suddenly a new and ultimate doubt arises – you start doubting doubt.

This is tremendously new in the world of religiousness. Then doubt kills doubt, doubt destroys doubt, and faith is gained. This faith is not against doubt, this faith is beyond doubt. This faith is not opposite to doubt, this faith is the absence of doubt.

Buddha says you will have to become children again, but the path has to go through the world, through many jungles of doubts, arguments, reasonings. And when a person comes back home, attains his original faith, it is totally different. He is not just a child, he is an old man . . . mature, experienced, and yet childlike.

This sutra, "The Sutra of Forty-Two Chapters", has never existed in India. It never existed in Sanskrit or in Pali, but only in Chinese. A certain Emperor

6

Ming of the Han Dynasty, AD 67, invited a few Buddhist masters to China to bring the message of Buddha there. Nobody knows the names of those Buddhist masters, but a group went to China. And the emperor wanted a small anthology of Buddhist sayings to be compiled as a first introduction to the Chinese people.

Buddhist scriptures are so extensive, the Buddhist literature is a world in itself – thousands of scriptures exist. And they go into very great detail, because Buddha believes in logical analysis. He goes to the very root of everything. His analysis is profound and perfect, so he goes very deeply into details. It was difficult. What to translate in a totally new country where nothing like Buddha has ever existed? So these Buddhist masters composed a small anthology of forty-two chapters. They collected sayings from here and there, from this scripture and that, from this sermon and that.

This book was compiled in the style of Confucian analects because it was going to be introduced to a Confucian country – people who had become very well acquainted with the way Confucius talks, with the way Confucian scriptures were made and compiled. People were familiar with Confucius, so the Buddhist masters composed this sutra exactly along the same lines. The analects of Confucius start every sentence, every paragraph with the phrase "The master said . . ." This sutra starts in a similar way – every saying starts with "The Buddha said . . ."

In the beginning of the 20th century scholars used to think that the original must have existed in Sanskrit or Pali; then it disappeared or was lost, and this sutra in Chinese was a translation. That is wrong. This sutra never existed in India. As it is, it never existed. Of course, each saying comes from Buddha, but the whole work is a new work, a new anthology. So that should be remembered.

And that's what makes it such a good basic introduction to the Buddha's world. It is very simple; it contains everything in a very simple way. It is very direct. It is, in essence, the whole of Buddha's message but very succinct, not long and wordy as other Buddhist scriptures are.

THE BUDDHA SAID:

To be free from the passions and to be calm, this is the most excellent way.

Buddha always talks about the way, never about the goal. Because he says, "What to say about the goal? It is futile to talk about it. If you know, you know. If you don't know, there is no way to figure it out before you reach it." He talks only about the way. He has not even a single word for the goal – godliness, Brahman, the truth, the absolute, the Kingdom of God. No, he has not any word for the goal; all he talks about is the way.

To be free from the passions and to be calm, this is the most excellent way.

In this one simple sentence Buddha's whole teaching is present. To be free from the passions and to be calm . . . These are two aspects of one phenomenon, two sides of one coin – to be free from passions and to be calm. You cannot be calm if you are not free from passions, and you cannot be free from passions if you are not calm. They go together, and one has to work for both together.

Why is man so tense? Why is there so much anxiety and anguish? Why is man not calm, collected and centered? So many passions go on pulling you this way and that, pushing you this way and that. You are being pulled in many directions, hence you become fragmentary, you become divided, you become split. You lose your center. You forget completely who you are.

Watch. When you are greedy for money, who are you? You are just a greed for money and nothing else. When you are angry, your ego is hurt, who are you? You are just anger, a wounded ego, nothing else. When you are full of sexual passion, who are you? You are just sexuality, libido, and nothing else. When you are ambitious and you want power, prestige, respectability, who are you? You are simply ambition and nothing else.

Watch, and you will find many passions in you but you will not find who you are – just all those passions pulling you apart, and each passion goes in its own way. If you want money then you will have to sacrifice other passions for it. A person who is mad after money may forget all about sex; it is very easy for a miser to be celibate. In fact, celibacy may be a sort of miserliness. You don't want to share your energy, you don't want to share your sexual energy with anybody; you are a miser.

A person who is politically ambitious can become celibate very easily because his whole passion drives him in one way. A scientist who is too much into his research can forget all about the opposite sex. It is easy; if one passion possesses you completely then you can forget everything else.

It is a well-known fact that scientists are very absent-minded people. Their whole mind goes into one direction, but then they become very poor also. Their field of vision becomes narrower and narrower and narrower. That's what specialization is. A greedy person becomes narrower and narrower. He thinks only about money; he goes on counting money. His whole mind knows only one music and that is that of money; only one love, and that is that of money.

The people who are possessed by one passion are, in a way, integrated. They are not rich, they don't have many dimensions to their being; they have only one taste, but they have a certain integration. They are not split. You will not find this type of person going mad, because they are already mad in one direction, so they are not split. But this happens rarely. Ordinarily a person runs in all the directions.

I have heard:

> A scientist and a gorilla were sent into outer space together. Pinned to the front of the gorilla's spacesuit was an envelope with special instructions in it. Dying of curiosity, the scientist waited until it was the gorilla's turn to sleep so that he could sneak a peek into the envelope.
>
> Very carefully he slit the envelope open and unfolded a single piece of paper that was inside. Printed on it was the following: Don't Forget To Feed The Scientist.

A scientist becomes one-pointed; his life is that of concentration, and a concentrated person attains to a false sort of unity. Ordinarily people are not so concentrated. Meditation is far away – they are not even capable of concentration! Their lives are a hodgepodge, a mess. One hand is going north, one leg is going south, one eye is looking to the east, the other eye is looking to the west. They are going in all directions. This pull and push of many directions takes them apart. They become fragmentary, they lose wholeness. How can you be silent, how can you be calm?

The person who is concentrated also cannot be calm, because his life becomes lopsided. He is just moving in one direction; all other aspects of his life are starved. A scientist doesn't pay attention to what beauty is, what love is. He does not know what poetry is; he is too confined by his mathematical world. He becomes lopsided. So many parts of him are starved, hungry. He cannot be calm. When you are starved, how can you be calm?

The person who is moving in all directions has a little more richness than the specialist, but his richness has a schizophrenia in it; he becomes split. How can you be silent and calm when you have so many masters pulling you in different directions?

These are ordinarily the two types of people, and both are uneasy, deep in turmoil. a state of great disturbance

骚动，混乱

9

THE BUDDHA SAID:

> *To be free from the passions and to be calm, this is the most excellent way*

What is his way?

> *Those who leave their parents, go out of the home, understand the mind, reach the source, and comprehend the immaterial, are called* shramanas.

This word has to be understood, it is very basic – *shramana*. In India, two paths have existed. One is that of the brahmin and the other of the *shramana*. The path of the brahmin is the path of grace. The brahmin believes that by your own efforts, you cannot arrive. Your effort is so small, you are so tiny – how can you possibly know truth by your own efforts? The help of God will be needed, grace will be needed.

The path of the brahmin is the path of grace, so you have to pray. Only when God helps can you move on the path. Unless he wills it, you cannot arrive; there is no possibility for you to move alone. God is necessary, his help is necessary, his hand is needed – unless he takes you above the world, you will be struggling in vain. So for the brahmin, prayer is the path. The brahmin believes in prayer.

The *shramana* is just diametrically opposite. The word *shramana* comes from a root *shram*. *Shram* means "to exert oneself", to make effort. *Shram* means "effort". There is no possibility of any grace, because Buddha never talks about God. Buddha says, you don't know God – how can you pray? To whom are you going to pray? Your prayer will be coming from a deep ignorance. How can you pray to a God you don't know and that you have never seen? What type of communication is possible? You will be just talking to the empty sky. You might as well be talking to yourself! It is mad.

Have you seen mad people talking to themselves – sitting alone and talking to somebody? They are talking to somebody, but everybody can see that there is no one there. They are talking to themselves.

In the rational approach of Buddha, a man praying to God is mad, crazy. What are you doing? Do you know if God exists? If you know, then there is no need to pray. You say that you are praying in order to know God . . . the brahmin says, "We can know God only by prayer, by his help, by his grace."

Now this is absurd, logically absurd. You are moving in a circle. You say, "We can know God only by prayer." Then how can you pray? – because you don't know God yet. And you say, "Only by prayer will we be able to attain his grace."

This is a vicious circle, this is illogical. The flaw in the reasoning is very clear, the loophole is apparent.

This is the problem with the ordinary religious person – he cannot argue. The atheist can destroy your whole argument in a second. Religious people avoid debate because they know they don't have any base from which to argue.

You say, "We are searching for God," and then at the same time you say, "Only through prayer will we be able to search for him." You don't know him yet – prayer is not possible. And if you know him, prayer is not needed. Buddha says only through your own effort, through your own *shrama*, will you achieve godliness. There is no question of any grace. In a way it looks very hard, in another way it seems to be very, very scientific. You are alone here, lost in this forest of the world, and sitting under a tree you are just praying, not knowing to whom you are praying, where the God is, whether he is or not. You may be wasting your time. If there is no God, then . . . ? All the time that you wasted in prayer could have been used to search, to find out.

Buddha says once you understand that you are lost and you have to find your own way and there is no help coming, you become responsible. Prayer is irresponsible. To pray is just to avoid responsibility, to pray is to be lazy. To pray is just an escape. Buddha says effort is needed. It is an insult to pray. So in the Buddhist approach nothing like prayer exists, only meditation. You can meditate, you cannot pray. *Meditation*

This is the difference between meditation and prayer. Prayer needs a belief in God, meditation needs no belief. Meditation is purely scientific. It simply says that there are states of mind where thinking stops. It simply says there are ways to stop the thinking, to drop thinking and to come to a silent state of mind . . . a tranquil, serene state of mind. And it is that state of mind that gives you what truth is, gives you the glimpse, opens the door – but it comes only by your own effort. Each individual is alone and has to work hard – and if you miss, only you will be responsible. If you don't arrive, you cannot blame anybody because there is nobody to blame.

The path of Buddha is the path of the *shramana* – one who believes in his own effort. It looks very austere, arduous. One starts feeling afraid. In our fear we need somebody's help. Even a belief that somewhere some God exists, gives us relief.

I have heard:

> The seasick passenger lying listlessly on his deck chair stopped a passing steward. Pointing into the distance, he said, "Over there – it's land, isn't it?"
>
> "No, sir," replied the steward. "It's the horizon."
>
> "Never mind," sighed the passenger, "it's better than nothing."

But the horizon is nothing. How can it be better than nothing? It only appears to exist, it is not really there. Nothing exists like the horizon; the horizon is just illusory. But even that, to a seasick passenger, seems to be good. It is at least something – better than nothing. Belief, to Buddha, is like the horizon. Your gods are like horizons, mirages. You believe in them because you feel alone. You don't know they exist; you create them because you need them. But your need cannot be a guarantee of their truth. Your need cannot be a guarantee of their reality.

You are in a dark night passing through a forest. You are alone, you need a companion. You can imagine a companion, you can start talking to a companion, you can even start answering as if you are the companion. It will give you an illusion that somebody is there. You can believe in the companion, you can be completely hypnotized by it, but that does not mean that you can create the companion in reality.

People start whistling when they are alone. Passing through a dark night, they start whistling. It helps, it is better than nothing. You listen to your own noise and it gives you the idea that there is somebody else. People start singing; listening to their own voice gives a feeling that somebody else is there. Because you have always listened to others talking, the very sound that you hear gives you a feeling that another person must be there.

But Buddha says that just because you feel a need, reality has no necessity to fulfill it. Reality does not change according to your need. Your need is true – that you are alone and you would like a father figure in the sky, a God. That's why Christians call God "the father"; it is a father figure.

Psychologists will agree with Buddha. They say that the idea of God just reflects a need for a father figure. Every small child has a father – protective, giving a sense of security. One feels absolutely okay because the father is there. Then you grow, then you become mature. Then your father is no longer a protection. Then you know that your father is as weak as you are, then you know your father is as limited as you are. And by and by you see your father is becoming weaker and weaker every day, growing old. Your trust is lost, but the need remains; you need some father figure. You want somewhere to go and talk to your father, who is no longer there. Lost, you create a god, a goddess; you create a father or mother figure. It is your need, certainly – a psychological need – but this need keeps you immature.

Buddha is all for maturity. He says drop all these figures – they don't exist, and even if they did exist this would not be the way to find them. The way is to become calm and quiet. The way is to become so alone and so accepting of one's aloneness that there is no need for anybody's grace. Become so silent and alone that you are fulfilled within your own self, that you are enough unto yourself. Then you will be calm. Then a grace will start happening to you, but it is not a grace coming from God. It is a grace spreading out from your own center. You will become graceful.

Buddha sitting, standing, walking, is grace personified. But this grace is not coming from somewhere else; it is surfacing from his own innermost depths, it is bubbling up from his own center. It is like a flower that has flowered on the tree – it has come out of the tree. It is not a gift from somebody else, it is a growth.

This is the difference between the path of the brahmin and the path of the shramana. On the brahmin's path, truth is a gift, God's gift. On the shramana's path, truth is a growth that happens to you from your own being. It is yours. Truth is not something outside to be discovered, it is something inside to be realized.

Those who leave their parents, go out of the home, understand the mind, reach the source, and comprehend the immaterial, are called shramana.

Now, the definition of the *shramana*. Who is called a *shramana*? Who is really a seeker of truth? Who is making real effort, authentic effort to discover what truth is? The first thing – they leave their parents. Now this is symbolic, don't take it literally. It is symbolic and psychological.

A child lives for nine months in the womb of his mother . . . totally protected, in such a beautiful, warm atmosphere; never again will he be able to find such comfort. No worry, no responsibility – even for breathing. He has no need to breathe himself, the mother breathes for him. He has no worry that he will be left hungry; the mother goes on feeding him. He is so protected, so secure. Psychologists say that in the religious search, people are seeking the same womb again. All their concepts of paradise are nothing but magnified wombs, absolutely comfortable. In the Hindu mythology they say that in heaven there is a tree called *kalpavriksha* – the wish-fulfilling tree. You sit under it, and the moment any desire arises, even before you come to know that it has arisen it will be fulfilled. You think of food and food will be there, instantly. You think of a bed because you are feeling sleepy – instantly the bed will be there. This is what the womb is. The womb is a *kalpataru*, a wish-fulfilling tree. The child never becomes aware of any need. Before he becomes aware it is fulfilled; it is absolutely automatic.

But the child has to leave the womb; it is needed for his growth. Comfort alone can never help you to grow, because there is no challenge. The child has to leave the womb, and the first thing the child will have to do upon leaving the womb is the basis of all survival – he will have to breathe on his own. He will have to make an effort on his own. He is becoming a *shramana*. In the mother's womb he was a brahmin. Everything was happening through grace. Everything was happening, he was not doing anything. But everybody has to come out of the womb. Every brahmin has to become a *shramana*. Buddha says through being a *shramana*, growth is possible.

Then the child by and by grows farther away, farther away from the mother. After birth he will still have to depend on the breast of the mother; then a moment will come when he will no longer depend on the breast either. But still he will depend on the mother to feed him. Then he will go to school. He is going farther away from the mother, he is becoming more and more independent, he is becoming more and more an individual. Then one day he falls in love with another woman and he is cut off from the mother completely.

That's why no mother can ever forgive the woman who has taken away her son. Never – it is impossible for the mother to forgive the woman who has taken away her son . . . it is a deep conflict. But a man becomes really mature when he falls in love with a woman, because then he has turned his back to his mother completely. Now he has turned 180 degrees.

Buddha says that in the psychological world many roots still have to be cut. You should become more and more aware that you may have gone far away from the mother, but you have created psychological mothers. You may have come far away from the father, but then you create a father figure in heaven – God ruling all over the world, the supreme sovereign, and you call him "Father". Again you are trying to become dependent – as if you are afraid of your independence. All these are roots; all the roots have to be cut.

Jesus says somewhere . . . and I suspect that he must have got those ideas from some Buddhist source, because Jesus came five hundred years after Buddha and by that time, Buddhist attitudes had spread all over the Middle East. They had penetrated far into the middle of Asia, they had entered deep into Egypt. Jesus was brought up in Egypt. He must have come to know about these ideas. And there is every possibility that he visited India before he returned to Jerusalem to teach. There are sources that say that he visited the Buddhist university of Nalanda. He must have come to know about the path of the *shramana*, because in his teachings he says a few things that have no traditional source in Jewish ideology.

For example he says, "Unless you hate your father and mother, you cannot become my disciples." Christians always feel embarrassed if you say this. What type of teaching is this? – "Unless you hate your father and mother . . ." And you say that Jesus is love and he has come to teach love to the world? You say that God is love? The teaching seems to be full of hatred – "Hate your mother and father." All the great teachers have said, "Respect your father and mother," and what nonsense – Jesus is saying to hate them?

He must have heard it from some sources outside of Judaism. Those sources can only be Buddhist, because Buddha says: *Those who leave their parents, go out of the home* . . .

Don't take it literally. Don't take Jesus literally either. He is not saying you should hate your father and mother. He is simply saying to cut yourself completely away from the father and mother. He is saying to cut yourself away from security. Become insecure. Free yourself from all dependency. Become independent, become an individual – that's what he is saying.

Jesus is using a very rough language, and Buddha is using cultured language. Jesus was not very well educated; he was a rough man, a carpenter's son. And the Jewish tradition is very rough. The prophets speak in fiery language. Their language looks more political than religious. Buddha was the son of a king – well educated, cultured. Their terminology is different because they are different persons, but the meaning is the same.

One has to leave the parents, one has to leave the home, one has to leave the past. One has to become totally independent, alone . . . trembling in that aloneness, but one has to become alone. One has to become absolutely responsible for oneself, and then only one can understand the mind. If you go on depending on others, your very dependence will not allow you to understand who you are.

Cut all sources, cut yourself away from all relationship. You are left alone, now there is nobody else. You have to see into your own soul, you have to encounter yourself. That is the only way to encounter oneself. Then you reach to the very source of your being, by understanding the mind . . . *and comprehend the immaterial.* *spiritual, intangible.*

See, Buddha does not say comprehend the spiritual. He says comprehend the immaterial. This is the difference. His approach is so rational, he will not assert something in which you can find a loophole. He will not say "the spiritual"; he simply says "the immaterial".

Ask the physicist, he will understand the language of Buddha. The scientist says, "By analyzing the atom we came to electrons." Electrons are just electric particles, almost immaterial. Matter has disappeared, only energy is there. You cannot call it matter, you can only call it im-matter. And then by analyzing the electron they have come to almost emptiness – immaterial emptiness. The physicist will understand the Buddhist terminology.

Buddha reached the same point by analyzing the mind. By analyzing the mind he came to a stage where no thought was there . . . simple emptiness. He calls it "the immaterial". Thought is the inner "material". When you disperse thought and only space remains, it is immaterial.

The same has happened in modern physics. They were analyzing matter in the outside world and they came to the immaterial. Buddha reached the immaterial on his inner journey, and science has reached the immaterial in its outer journey, but both have reached the immaterial. Scientists also will not say that this is spiritual. The scientist can only say this much – that whatever was matter is no longer there. He cannot say what is there. "This much can be said – that whatever we used to think of as matter is no longer there; all that we can say is a denial."

BUDDHA SAYS:

. . . and comprehend the immaterial, they are called shramanas.

Now the categories of *shramanas*:

> *Those who observe the precepts of morality, who are pure and spotless in their behavior, and who exert themselves for the attainment of the fruits of saintship, are called arhats.*

Arhat is the highest state of no-mind. The word arhat means "one who has conquered his enemies". *Ari* means "enemy" and arhat means "one who has conquered the enemy".

Who is the enemy? It is not outside you. The passions, the distractions, the desires, the hatred, jealousy, possessiveness, anger, sexuality – these are the enemies. In one way your mind is the enemy, the root enemy. One who has conquered the mind is called arhat. This is the highest state – one who has come above all the clouds.

Have you sometimes, traveling by air, watched when the airplane goes above the clouds? All the clouds are just below you and you are in the pure, blue sky. That is the inner state of arhat. One goes on penetrating the mind. By and by the clouds of passions are no longer there, they are left far behind, and you are soaring higher and higher into pure space, into the immaterial space. This is the state of arhat.

In Buddhist terminology that is the highest state. What Christians call Christ, Buddha calls arhat. What Jainas call *arihanta* – that word also means the same. Or what Hindus call the *avatara* – Rama, Krishna – that is the same state, the state of arhat.

But Buddha is very scientific in that too. He does not call it *avatara*, because *avatara* means "God descending into the world" – you have to believe in God. In no way does he use any term that contains some presuppositions. He uses simple terms, without any presuppositions.

Next is the anagamin.

Arhat is the highest state, next to it is the *anagamin. Anagamin* means "one who will not come again". He says:

At the end of his life, the spirit of the anagamin *ascends to the heaven and obtains arhatship.*

It is just below the arhat state.

Anagamin – the word means "one who will not come again". Gone, he will be gone. Gone, he will be gone forever, he will not return. He has come to the point of no return. He is just close to being an arhat, he has passed the clouds. Just on the boundary, he is standing on the threshold of being an arhat. Maybe a small clinging has remained in him, and that clinging is with the body. So when he dies, that clinging also disappears. He will not be coming back.

Next is the skridagamin.

Skridagamin means "one who comes back".

The skridagamin *ascends to the heaven and after his death comes back to the earth once more . . .*

Only once. He has still some clinging – very faint, but there are still a few roots and he will be pulled back to another womb again. He is not absolutely desireless. The arhat is absolutely desireless. A *skridagamin* has passed beyond the gross desires, but subtle desires are still there.

What are the gross desires? Desire for money, for power, prestige – these are gross desires. The desire to be free, to be calm, the desire to attain to the ultimate state of arhatship – these are subtle desires, but they are still desires. He will have to come back only once.

Next is the srotapanna.

The word *srotapanna* means "one who has entered into the stream". *Srota* means stream and *apanna* means "one who has entered". *Srotapanna* means "one who has entered the stream". He has just begun his journey on the path. He is no longer worldly – he has become a sannyasin, he has entered the river. Faraway is the ocean, but he has entered the river, he has started. And when the journey is begun, it will end. However far it is, it is not far away.

The real problem is with those who have not even entered into the stream. They are standing on the bank. These are the worldly people, standing on the bank. The sannyasin, the *bhikkhu*, is the one who has entered into the river – knows well that the ocean is far away, but now half the journey is over, just by entering.

Next is the srotapanna. *The* srotapanna *dies seven times and is born seven times, when he finally attains arhatship.*

These are just symbolic, don't take them literally . . . these are just symbolic things. "Seven" does not mean exactly seven. It means many times he will die, many times he will be born, but his face is turned towards the ocean. He has entered into the Ganges and the journey has started.

By the severance of passions is meant that like the limbs severed they are never again made use of.

And Buddha said that by dropping the passions, he means that it is as if somebody cuts off your hand; then you cannot use it. Or somebody takes your eyes out; then you cannot see through them. One who is ready to enter into the stream is one who, on his own, voluntarily drops passions, who says, "I will not use them again."

Remember, this is not repression in the Freudian meaning of the term. One does not repress it, one simply withdraws energy from it. Sex remains there – you do not repress it, you simply don't cooperate any more. The difference is tremendous. When sex is there and you repress it, you fight with it, then you don't go above it – you remain with it. If you fight with it, you are still clinging to it. And if you fight with it you will remain afraid of it.

Buddha says one simply does not cooperate with it. A desire, a sexual desire arises – what will you do? Buddha says you simply watch. Let it be there. It will come and it will go. It will flicker in the mind, will try to attract you; you remain watchful, you don't allow any unconsciousness, otherwise it will enter in you. You simply remain watchful.

Says Buddha, "One has to be just mindful. Then one is like a house where lamps are burning, where lamps are lit – the thieves are afraid to enter. When there are no lamps and the house is dark, then thieves enter easily. The person who has really become mindful is like the house where there is a guard at the door, fully awake, and lamps are lit. It is difficult for the thieves to enter, they cannot gather courage."

The same happens when you are aware – you have a guard. When you are aware, your house is lit with light. Passions cannot enter you. They can come by, they can roam around, they will try to persuade you. But if you simply watch, they will disappear of their own accord – because they live through your cooperation. Don't fight with them and don't indulge in them; just remain aware. Then by and by they will drop like severed limbs.

If you start fighting, you are creating another problem. Instead of being an indulgent person you will become a repressive person. The problem is not solved, only the name is changed.

I have heard:

> A doctor was treating a man who had been brought in paralytically drunk. "If the patient sees green snakes again, give him some of this medicine," he told the nurse.
>
> Later on he came back to find the man raving – but he hadn't been given the medicine. "Didn't I tell you to give him this medicine if he saw green snakes again?" the doctor demanded.
>
> "But he didn't see green snakes," the nurse replied.
>
> "Oh?"
>
> "No, he has been seeing purple frogs."

Now whether you see green snakes or purple frogs makes no difference – you are drunk! There are people who cooperate with their passions and there are people who fight with their passions – but both remain stuck with the passions. One is friendly, another is antagonistic, but both remain involved with the passions, and both are ways of subtle cooperation.

One has to drop out of the relationship. One has to just become a spectator, a watcher. Once you start watching you will become aware of layers and layers of passions. There are many layers. When gross passions are gone, more subtle layers will be found. Our whole life is like an onion. You peel it – another layer; you peel that – another layer, fresher, younger, more alive. But if you go on peeling, a moment comes when just emptiness is left in your hands. That's what Buddha calls nirvana – emptiness. All layers gone.

I have heard:

> The guitarist of a pop group was involved in a car accident and sustained injuries to his head. On arrival at the hospital the doctor ordered that his long, thick hair be completely cut off to enable the extent of the injuries to be seen. A nurse was detailed to undertake the task, and she set to work with a large pair of scissors.
>
> After ten minutes or so she said to the young man, "You went to North Lancaster Comprehensive School when you were younger, didn't you?"

"Yes, I did," answered the youth. "Were you there as well?"

"No," said the nurse, "I'm from London."

"Well, how on earth did you know which school I went to?" queried the young man.

"I have just come to your cap," replied the nurse.

Layers upon layers . . . And the deeper you cut, the more you will find – many things that were missing for many years; you will find your cap! The deeper you go into your mind, the deeper you will go in your childhood. Many things forgotten, lost – again, they are there. Nothing is ever lost, everything goes on accumulating. When you come to a point where you cannot find anything, then you have come to your being. The being is not like a layer; the being is simply space, pure space. The being is simply emptiness.

Buddha calls being "non-being", he calls it *anatta*. Buddha says if you find yourself, then there must be some layer still left. When suddenly you come to a point where you cannot find yourself – you are, and you cannot find yourself – then you have come home. And this can be attained only by effort.

This is his framework. Next we will start moving into his methodology – the ways of meditation, the ways of inner discipline; the ways to transcend the ego, the ways to transcend all. That's why I have called this series of talks "The Discipline of Transcendence". But this is Buddha's framework.

Ordinarily you are standing on the bank. Then you cannot hope, then you are in a hopeless state. If you become a *srotapanna*, if you enter the stream, that's what I call *sannyas*. Through *sannyas* you become a *srotapanna* – you enter the stream, you take courage, you take the jump. It is a quantum leap from the bank into the stream. They are very close, but they are totally different. The bank never goes anywhere. It has no growth, it never moves. It is static, stagnant, stale, dead. And just right there is the flowing river, which is going somewhere.

If your life is not going anywhere, you are standing on the bank. Enter the stream and you start a journey. Your life starts changing, transforming. You begin a transfiguration, a metamorphosis, and each moment new visions open their doors to you. One day the river reaches the ocean. That day you become arhat, you dissolve into the ocean.

First *srotapanna*, then *skridagamin*, then *anagamin*, then *arhata*. These are the states. It is a very scientific framework. From being a worldly person you become *srotapanna* and then your journey has started.

Enough for today.

Chapter 2:

No Prejudice in the Heart

THE BUDDHA SAID:

The homeless shramana *cuts off the passions, frees himself*
of attachments, understands the source of his own mind,
penetrates the deepest doctrine of Buddha, and
comprehends the dhamma, which is immaterial. He has
no prejudice in his heart. He has nothing to hanker after.
He is not hampered by the thought of the way nor is he
entangled in karma. No prejudice, no compulsion, no
discipline, no enlightenment and no going up through the
grades and yet in possession of all honors in itself. This is
called the way.

THE BUDDHA SAID:

Those who shaving their heads and faces become
shramanas *and who receive instruction in the way should*
surrender all worldly possessions and be contented with
whatever they obtain by begging. One meal a day and one
lodging under a tree and neither should be repeated, for
what makes one stupid and irrational are attachments
and the passions.

THE BUDDHA SAID:

There are ten things considered good by all beings, and ten
things evil. Three of them depend upon the body, four
upon the mouth, and three upon thought. Three evil deeds

*depending upon the body are killing, stealing, and
committing adultery. The four depending upon the mouth
are slandering, cursing, lying and flattery. The three
depending upon thought are envy, anger and infatuation.
All these things are against the holy way, and therefore
they are evil. When these evils are not done, there are ten
good deeds.*

The first thing: Buddha emphasizes very much the idea of a homeless wanderer
– the idea of homelessness. It need not be taken literally, but the idea is tremendously significant. If you build a house, if you build a home around you, you
are doing something which is not possible in the nature of things because this
life is a flux. This life is not more than momentary. This life is not stable, not
permanent – we are here only for a few moments. Death is approaching
continuously; we are dying every moment while we are living.

To make this place, this space, a home, is absurd. The home is not possible
here, the home is possible only in eternity. Time cannot be made a home, and if
you try to make a home here then you will be constantly in misery because you
will be fighting against nature; you will be going against what Buddha calls
dhamma.

Dhamma simply means Tao, the way things are. If you want to make a
dream permanent, you will suffer, because dream as such cannot be permanent.
Its very nature is to be non-permanent. In fact, even to repeat the same dream
again is difficult. The dream is illusory, you cannot live in it forever.

To think of a permanent life here on this shore, the shore of time, is stupid.
If you are a little intelligent, if you are a little aware and if you can see all around
you what is happening . . . You were not here one day, and you will not be here
one day again. How can you make a home here? You can stay here as if one stays
overnight in a caravanserai – when the morning comes you have to go. Yes, you
can pitch tents here, but you cannot make a home. You can have shelter, but you
should not become attached to it. You should not call it "my", "mine". The
moment you call anything "mine" you are falling into stupidity.

Nothing belongs to you, nothing can belong to you. One is a homeless
wanderer in the very nature of things. Time is impermanent. Time means the
temporary. Time cannot have any eternal home in it. To make a home in time is
to make a house on the sands, or to make a signature in water – you go on
making it; it goes on disappearing. Buddha says to understand this homeless-

ness is to become a sannyasin. There is no necessity that you leave home. You can leave if you feel good that way, if it fits with your nature. You can leave home, you can literally become a wanderer but it is not a must. You can remain in the home but it is no longer a home for you. You know you don't possess it. You may be using it for a while, but tomorrow you have to go. So don't make a home anywhere – not even in the body, because that body is also continuously disappearing.

If you don't make a home anywhere then you are a sannyasin in spirit – and a sannyasin is never miserable, because misery comes out of attachment. When your attachments are not fulfilled as you wanted them to be, when your expectations are not fulfilled, frustration arises. Frustration is a by-product. If you don't expect, nobody can frustrate you. If you don't want to make a home here, even death cannot frighten you. Nothing can frighten you. If you don't cling to anything, how can you be made miserable? Your clinging creates misery, because you want to cling and in the very nature of things, things are changing; you cannot cling. They are slipping constantly out of your hands, there is no way to cling to them.

You cling to the wife, you cling to the husband, to the children, to the parents, to the friends. You cling to persons, to things, and everything is in a constant flux. You are trying to hold a river in your arms and the river is flowing fast; it is rushing towards some unknown goal – you are frustrated. The wife falls in love with somebody else – you are frustrated. The husband escapes – you are frustrated. The child dies – you are frustrated. The bank fails, goes bankrupt – you are frustrated. The body becomes ill, weak, death starts knocking at the door – you are frustrated. But these frustrations are because of your expectations. You are responsible for them.

If you understand that this place is not a home and you are a homeless wanderer here, a stranger in an unknown land; you have to leave, you have to go . . . if you have penetrated that point, if you have understood it, then you don't make a home anywhere. You become a homeless wanderer, a *parivrajaka*. You may even literally become so; it depends on you.

You may really become a wanderer, or spiritually you may become a wanderer. My own emphasis is not to become literally a wanderer, because what is the point? Buddha's emphasis was not so; let it be clear to you. Buddha has not said what to do, whether to follow him literally or not. Millions followed him literally – they dropped out of their homes, out of their families; they really became *bhikkhus* wandering all over the country, begging. I don't insist on that. If really you understand, then there is no need to do it in such a factual way. Because to me it appears that when a person does not understand the idea completely, only then he literally becomes a wanderer; otherwise there is no need. You can be in the home, you can be with your wife and your children, and yet remain alert that nothing belongs to you; remain alert that you don't fall into attachments; remain alert that if things change you are ready to accept the change, that you will not weep for the spilt milk, that you will not cry, that you will not go crazy and mad.

To me this seems to be more significant than really becoming a wanderer, because that is easier. And if there is no home and if you don't possess anything, then how can you renounce? The very idea of renouncing it makes it clear that somewhere deep in the unconscious you thought that you possessed it, because you can renounce only something which you possess.

How can you renounce? Your wife is not yours – how can you renounce? Your children are not yours – how can you renounce? They don't belong to you, so where is the point to renounce then? You can simply understand that they don't belong to you; that we are strangers – we have met on the way, or we have stayed under the same tree for a few days, but we are strangers.

Understanding it deep in your awareness is enough. My emphasis is to become a spiritual wanderer. There is no need to drag the body like a beggar; just let your spirit be that of a wanderer, and that is enough. Don't create bondage for your spirit.

THE BUDDHA SAID:

The homeless shramana *cuts off the passions . . .*

Passions are our dreams. Passions are our dreams of the future, desires of the future, desires of how things should be. Deep down we are always discontent; whatever is, is not satisfying. We are continuously weaving dreams to change things – to build a better house, to have a better wife, to have a better education, to have more money, to have this, to have that. We are continuously thinking in terms of how to make life better. We go on living in the future which is not.

Living in the future is a dream because it exists not. Living in the future is based on a deep discontent with the present.

So two things have to be understood about passions. One, whatsoever we have we cling to it. Look at the paradox: whatsoever we have we cling to it and still we are not satisfied with it. We are miserable with it so we desire to modify it, to decorate it, to make it better. We continuously cling to that which we have, and we continuously desire that which we don't have, and between these two we are crushed! And this will be so always and always. It was so yesterday, it is so today, it is going to be so tomorrow . . . your whole life. What you have, you will

paradox — contradiction
以是而非的論点 24

cling to so that nobody can take it away, and still you will be miserable with it and you will hope that someday things will be better. A person who lives in passion, in desire, lives a futile life – always miserable, always dreaming. Miserable with reality and dreaming about unreal things.

I have heard:

> "How many fish have you caught?" a passerby asked old Mulla Nasruddin who was fishing off the end of the pier.
>
> "Well," said the old Mulla thoughtfully, "if I catch this one that is nibbling at my bait and two more, I will have three."
>
> This is how human mind goes on dreaming. Our life is short, very short, and our dreams are immense.
>
> Seamus and Bridget met on Rockaway Beach. As they stretched out together on a blanket under the boardwalk, Seamus whispered huskily, "Bridget, I love you."
>
> "But," protested Bridget, "we have only just met!"
>
> "I know," replied Seamus, "but I am only here for the weekend."

Everybody is here only for the weekend. Life is really very short. How is love possible? How can you make a home here? How can you possess anything? Everything is continuously disappearing. You are chasing shadows.

Buddha says:

> *The homeless* shramana *cuts off the passions, frees himself of attachments . . .*

By attachments he means relationships that really don't exist, only you believe that they exist. You are a husband – you believe that a certain relationship exists between you and your wife, but it is just a belief. Have you not observed the fact that even living with a woman for forty, fifty years, she remains a stranger, and you remain a stranger to her? Down the centuries, men have been trying to understand women and the feminine mind, but they have not been able to understand yet. The woman has been trying to understand the mind of the man, yet it remains a mystery. And men and women have lived together for centuries.

Observe it. How can you relate to anybody? The other remains out of your grasp. The other remains other – unreachable. You may touch the periphery, and the other may even pretend that yes, you have related, but we remain alone. Relationship is just make-believe. It helps, it helps in a way. It allows us to feel that we are not alone. It makes life a little more comfortable, but that comfort is

periphery (n) – outer edge

illusory. The other remains the other, and there is no way to penetrate the mystery of the other. We are alone.

When Buddha says "the homeless *shramana* frees himself of all attachments", he means that one comes to see that attachment is not possible here. Attachment is impossible, relationship is impossible. All relationship is just an absurd effort because you cannot reach the other, you cannot touch the center of the other's being. And unless you have touched the center, how can you relate? You don't know the other's soul, you only know the body, actions, attitudes – they are just on the periphery. We meet on the periphery, that is the misery of relationship. We remain on the periphery and we keep on believing in our hope, in our desire, that some day the relationship will really happen and the center will meet the center, the heart will meet the heart, that we will dissolve into one another – but it never happens.

It cannot happen. To become aware of this disturbing reality is difficult because it takes the very ground from underneath your feet. You are left so lonely that you again start believing in old dreams, relationship, this and that. You again start trying to create bridges . . . but you never succeed and have never succeeded. Not that your effort is not enough, not that your skill is not enough, but because in the very nature of things attachment is an impossibility. You are trying to do something that reality does not allow.

Your aloneness is eternal. Buddha says that to understand this aloneness and to remain true to it is the meaning of dropping attachments. Not that you escape from the world, but simply all attachments drop, bridges drop. And this is the beauty – that when all attachments drop, you become more understanding, and your life with others becomes more peaceful . . . because you don't hope. You don't hope for the impossible, you don't expect. Whatsoever happens you feel grateful, and whatsoever does not happen you know it cannot happen. You become, in a deeper way, very accepting. You don't try to force reality to be according to your desires. You start learning how to let go, how to be one and harmonious with the reality itself.

> . . . *understands the source of his own mind, penetrates the deepest doctrine of Buddha . . .*

What is the deepest doctrine of Buddha? Buddha's greatest message is the message of no-self, *anatta* – that is his deepest doctrine. That you have to understand. First he says don't make a home here, then he says don't be attached. Then he says look into yourself – you are not!

First he says the world is illusory, don't make a home here. Then he says attachments are just dreams, drop all attachments from your mind. And then he comes to his deepest doctrine. The doctrine is: now look inside, you are not.

You can exist only with a home, with possessions, with relationships. The "I" is nothing but a combination of all these dreams, a cumulative effect. Dreams of possessing things, dreams of possessing people – relationships, attachment, love, passion, dreams of the future – all these accumulate and become the ego. When you drop all these, suddenly you disappear, and in your disappearance the law starts functioning in its truest way. That is what the Buddha calls the dhamma, the Tao, the ultimate law.

So there are three layers of the ego. The first layer is the world – your house, your car, your bank balance. Second, attachments – your relationships, your affairs, your children, wife, husband, friends, enemies. And the deepest layer, you. And these all are joined together. If you really want to get rid of your ego, you will have to move in a very scientific way. That's what Buddha is doing. First, no home; second, no relationships; third, no self. If you do the two first things, the preliminary things, the third happens automatically – you look inside and you are not there. And when you see that you are not there – there is no entity inside, no substantial entity, you cannot call yourself "I" – you are freed.

This is what liberation is in the Buddhist way. This is what nirvana is. The word nirvana means cessation of the self, arising of a no-self, emptiness . . . the zero experience. Nothing is, only nothing is. Then how can you be disturbed? because now there is nobody to be disturbed. Then how can you die? because now there is nobody to die. How can you be born? because now there is nobody to be born. This nobodyness is tremendously beautiful. It is opening and opening, space and space, with no boundaries.

This is Buddha's concept of reality. It is very difficult to understand. We can understand that ego can be dropped – but the soul!? Then we go on in a subtle way remaining egoistic. Then we call it that subtle ego the soul, the atman.

Buddha is very consistent. He says any idea of yourself, that you can be in some way, is egoistic.

Let me try to explain it to you through modern physics, because modern physics has also come to the same point. Ask the modern scientist; he says matter only appears to be, it is not. If you go deeper into matter, you find only emptiness. It is nothing but emptiness. If you analyze matter, if you keep on dividing the atom, then it disappears. At the ultimate core only emptiness remains . . . only space, pure space. The same analysis Buddha did with the self. What scientists have been doing with matter, Buddha did with mind. And both agree that if analysis goes deep enough, then there is no substance left; all substance disappears. Non-existence is left.

Buddha could not survive in India. India is the oldest country in the world which has believed in the self, the atman. The Upanishads, the Vedas, from Patanjali to Mahavira, everybody has believed in the self. They were all against the ego but they never dared to say that the self is also nothing but a trick of the ego. Buddha dared to assert the ultimate truth. While he was alive, people could tolerate him. His presence was such a powerful presence, his presence was so convincing that they could not deny it, they could not say that what he is saying was against the human mind, absolutely against the human mind. They may have discussed here and there; sometimes a few people came to discuss with him also – "What are you saying? Then what is the point of being liberated if nobody remains? We hope for liberation so that *we* will be liberated."

Buddha's emphasis is that you will never be liberated, because until and unless you die there is no liberation. Liberation is from the self, the self is not liberated. Liberation is from the self itself.

But his presence was very convincing; whatsoever he was saying must be true. His existence was a proof. The grace that had happened to him, the harmony that was surrounding him, the luminousness that was following him wherever he walked, moved . . . the glow. People were puzzled – because this man was saying that there is no self, only tremendous emptiness inside. They could not deny him, but by the time Buddha had gone, they started criticizing, arguing; they started denying. Only five hundred years after Buddha left his body, Buddhism was uprooted from India. People could not believe in such a drastic attitude. Nothing is, the world is illusory, attachments are stupid, and in the final analysis you are not. Then what is the point? If everything is a dream and even the self is a dream, then why should we go into it? Let it be a dream – at least something is there. Why should we make so much effort, so many arduous efforts to achieve just nothingness?

But you have to understand. What Buddha calls nothingness is nothingness from your side – he says nothing remains, nothing of your world, nothing of your relationship, nothing of you – but he is not saying that nothing remains. He is saying nothing remains from your side, and that which remains cannot be expressed. That which is left, there is no way to express it to you, no way to communicate it. Because in whatsoever way it is communicated, it will be mis-understood. If Buddha says, "Yes, the self exists, but the self is a non-ego state," you may nod your head that "yes, we understand." But you don't understand, because the very idea of self carries something of the ego in it: "I am." Howsoever pure, but the "I" remains. Your idea of atman, self, supreme self, Self with a capital S, is nothing but a transfigured ego.

It happened:

> Mulla Nasruddin and the local priest were always fighting and
> arguing and eventually they finished up in the court. After listening
> to evidence from both sides, the magistrate said, "I feel sure that this
> can be settled amicably. Shake hands with each other and say
> something of good will."
>
> The priest shook Nasruddin's hand and said, "I wish for you what
> you wish for me."
>
> "See, Your Honor?" said the Mulla. "He is starting it again!"

He has not said anything, he has simply said, "I wish for you what you wish for
me." But Mulla knows well what he wishes for the other man. He says, "He is
starting it again!" Whatever is said to you will be colored by you.

Buddha remained very pure; he wouldn't allow you to corrupt. He wouldn't
give you even a hint. He simply denied totally, absolutely. He said whatsoever
you know disappears – your world, your love, your attachments, your things,
your relationships, you. You are the center, your world is your periphery. They
all disappear together. It is not possible that you can be saved when your world
is lost. When the periphery, the circumference is lost, the center is also lost. They
go together. When the elephant moves, the tail of the elephant also moves with
it. When your whole world drops, you also drop with it; you are part of it, an
organic part of that dream. But let me remind you – don't misunderstand
Buddha. He was very logical not to say anything about that which remains. He
said, "Come and experience it." He said, "Don't force me to relate it to you lin-
guistically. Let it be existential experience." You disappear but in a way for the
first time you appear. But this appearance is something so totally different from
all your experiences that there is no way to relate it. Whatsoever will be said will
be wrong, because you will interpret it in your own way.

> *The homeless* shramana *cuts off the passions, frees himself of attach-
> ments, understands the source of his own mind, penetrates the deepest
> doctrine of Buddha, and comprehends the* dhamma *which is immaterial.*

This much Buddha allows – that there is a dhamma, a natural law, which is
immaterial. He will not say spiritual; he simply says it is "immaterial". What is
this dhamma? What is this law?

It will be easy if you understand Lao Tzu's concept of Tao, or if you
understand the Vedic concept of *vaidya*. There must be something like a law
that holds everything together. The changing seasons, the moving stars . . . the
whole universe goes on so smoothly; it must have a certain law.

existential experience
relating to human 29 *existence*

The difference has to be understood. Jews, Christians, Mohammedans, Hindus, call that law "God" – they personify it. Buddha is not ready to do that. He says to personify God is to destroy the whole beauty of it, because that is anthropomorphic, anthropocentric attitude. Man thinks of God as if he is just like man – magnified, quantitatively millions of times bigger, but still, like man. Buddha says God is not a person. That's why he never uses the word "God". He talks about dhamma, the law. God is not a person but just a force, an immaterial force. Its nature is more like law than like a person.

That's why in Buddhism, prayer does not exist. You cannot pray to a law; it will be pointless. You cannot pray to the law of gravitation, can you? It will be meaningless. The law cannot listen to your prayer. You can follow the law, and you can be in happy harmony with the law. Or, you can disobey the law and you can suffer. But there is no point in praying to the law. If you go against the law of gravitation you may break a few of your bones, you may have a few fractures. If you follow the law of gravitation, you can avoid the fractures – but what is the point of praying? Sitting before the icon and praying to the Lord – "I am going for a journey, help me" – it is absurd.

Buddha says the universe runs according to a law, not according to a person. His attitude is scientific. Because, he says, a person can be whimsical. You can pray to God and you can persuade him, but that is dangerous. Somebody who is not praying to God may not be able to persuade him. God may be prejudiced – a person is always capable of prejudice. And that's what all the religions say – that if you pray, God will save you; if you pray you will not be miserable. If you don't pray, you will be thrown into hell. To think in these terms about God is human, but very unscientific. That means God enjoys your flattery, your prayers. So if you are a praying person and you go regularly to the church, to the temple, and you read the Gita and the Bible, you recite the Koran, then he will help you; otherwise he will be annoyed by you. If you say, "I don't believe in God," he will be very angry at you. Buddha says this is stupid. God is not a person. You cannot annoy him and you cannot buttress him, you cannot flatter him. You cannot persuade him to your own way; whether you believe in him or not, that doesn't matter.

A law exists beyond your belief. If you follow it, you are happy. If you don't follow it, you become unhappy. Look at the austere beauty of the concept of law. Then the whole question is of a discipline, not of prayer. Understand the law and be in harmony with it. Don't be in a conflict with it, that's all. No need for a temple, no need for a mosque, no need to pray. Just follow your understanding.

Buddha says that whenever you are miserable it is just an indication that you have gone against the law, you have disobeyed the law. Whenever you are in misery, just understand one thing; watch, observe, analyze your situation, diagnose it – you must be going somewhere against the law, you must be in conflict with the law. Buddha says it is not that the law is punishing you; no, that is foolish – how can a law punish you? You are punishing yourself by being against the law. If you go with the law, it is not that the law is rewarding you – how can the law reward you? If you go with it, you are rewarding yourself. The whole responsibility is yours to obey or disobey. If you obey, you live in heaven. If you disobey, you live in hell. Hell is a state of your own mind when you are antagonistic to the law, and heaven is a state of your own mind when you are in harmony.

He has no prejudice in his heart.

Buddha says one who understands the law has no prejudice in his heart.

He has nothing to hanker after. He is not hampered by the thought of the way, nor is he entangled in karma. No prejudice, no compulsion, no discipline, no enlightenment, and no going up through the grades, and yet in possession of all honors in itself – this is called the way.

This is a very revolutionary statement. You cannot come across such a statement in Krishna's assertions, or Jesus' assertions, or Mohammed's. This is tremendously revolutionary. Buddha says a real man of understanding does not even hanker for enlightenment. Because even to desire enlightenment is to desire, and desire is misery. Whether you desire money or you desire satori, whether you desire some person or you desire enlightenment, whether you desire prestige, power, respectability, or you desire dhyana, samadhi, meditation, enlightenment, desire as such is the same. The nature of desire is the same. Desire means desire, and desire brings misery. What you desire is irrelevant – you desire, and that's enough to make you miserable.

Desire means you have moved away from reality, you have moved away from that which is. Desire means you have fallen into the trap of a dream. Desire means you are not here now, you have gone somewhere in the future.

Non-desire is enlightenment – so how can you desire enlightenment? If you desire enlightenment your very desire prevents its happening. You cannot desire enlightenment, you can only understand the nature of desire, and in the light of understanding, desire disappears – as you bring a lamp into a dark room, darkness disappears. Desire is darkness. When you light a candle of understanding, desire disappears. And when there is no desire, there is enlightenment. That's what enlightenment is. Try to understand this. This is one of the things you will need very much.

31

It is very easy to change the object of your desire from worldly things to otherworldly things.

I was in a certain town and I had gone for an evening walk. Just as I was approaching the garden a woman came to me and gave me a booklet. On the booklet there was a beautiful garden on the cover page, and a beautiful bungalow by the side of a spring. Tall trees, and far in the background snow peaks ... I looked inside. Inside, I was surprised to see that it was a propaganda pamphlet printed by some Christian community. In the pamphlet it said, "If you want to have a beautiful house in the garden of God, then follow Jesus. If in the other world you want such a beautiful house then follow Jesus."

Now this type of attitude seems to be very worldly! But this has been the case. Except Buddha's attitude, all other religions are in some way or other asking you not to drop desire, but to change the *object* of desire. That is the difference. They say, "Don't desire worldly things, desire heavenly things. Don't desire money, desire God." Now you can see the difference, the revolutionary change. Buddha says simply don't desire. It is not a question of what you desire; if you desire you will remain in misery. Don't desire, that's all. Be desireless, that's all. And when you are desireless you are calm and quiet and collected. When you are desireless the ego disappears; when you are desireless, misery disappears. And when you are desireless, you fall in tune with the law.

Your desire is always a conflict with the law. Your desire simply says that you are not satisfied with what is given to you. You ask for more, or you ask for something else. A desireless person simply says, "Whatsoever is, is. Whatsoever is happening is happening. I accept it and I go with it. I have no other idea in my mind. If this is what is happening, I will simply delight in it. I will enjoy it. I will be with it."

This is what I call surrender. Surrendering means non-desiring.

He is not hampered by the thought of the way.

If you are desiring God, paradise ... in fact, the very word "paradise" means a walled garden ... if you are desiring some beautiful palaces in the other world, then even the way – the path, the religion, the Bible, the Koran, the Gita – will hamper you. It will burden you, because a desiring mind is always disturbed, always wavering, always thinking whether it is going to happen or not, always doubting whether it has ever happened to anybody: "Am I foolish in desiring it? Does it really exist? Does it exist, the other world, the God, the happiness, the paradise? Or is it just a myth, a story for children, for people who need toys?" Then even the way becomes a tension, because you are using everything as a means to reach some end.

Buddha says the man of understanding is not even hampered by the thought of the way because he is not going anywhere, so there is no point in thinking of any "way". He is simply here! When you are going somewhere, you need a way. When you understand, you simply enjoy being here. This moment is enough. There is nowhere to go, so what is the point of a way, a path, a means? There is no end, no goal, nowhere to go.

That's my emphasis also. There is nowhere to go. Just be here. Just be here as totally as possible. Don't allow your mind to go anywhere. And in that moment when you are not going anywhere, everything falls into silence. Experience it. You can experience it right now, listening to me, if you are not going anywhere.

You can listen to me in two ways. One way is of the mind, of the desire. You can listen to me in order to find some clue so that you can become enlightened; to find some clue so that you can enter into the palace of God; to find some key. Then you will be uneasy, restless. Or you can listen to me without any idea of going anywhere. You can simply listen to me, you can just be here with me. In that silence when you are just here, delighting with me, listening to me as one listens to a waterfall, as one listens to birds chirping in the trees, as one listens to the wind blowing in the pines – just listening for no reason – then in that moment you are in tune with Tao, you are in tune with dhamma, you are in tune with the universe.

The universe is going somewhere; you fall in tune with it, you move with the river. Then you don't push the river. Then you don't have any other goal than the goal of the whole.

. . . nor is he entangled in karma.

A man who understands has nothing to do, he has just to be. His being is all his action. His action is his delight, he enjoys it. You ask a painter. If the painter is a real painter, then he enjoys painting, not that there is some result to it. There may not be, there may be; that is irrelevant.

Somebody asked van Gogh, "What is your best painting?" He was painting something, and he said, "This one – that which I am doing right now." People were wondering why van Gogh was painting at all because his paintings were not selling. Not a single painting was sold while he was alive. And he was dying, starving himself, because he had only just enough money to live. Each week his brother was giving him a certain amount of money, enough just to survive. So every week for three days he would eat and for four days he would fast to save money for colors, brushes, canvases – and his paintings were not selling at all. People used to think he was mad, but he was tremendously happy – starving and happy. What was his happiness? The very act of painting.

Remember, an action becomes a karma, a bondage, if you have some end, if you are "going somewhere" through it. If your action is just your delight – like children playing, making sand castles, enjoying, no goal to their activity, just playing, intrinsic play in the very activity – then there is no karma, then there is no bondage. Then each action brings more and more freedom.

. . . no prejudice, no compulsion, no discipline.

A man of understanding need not discipline himself. His understanding is his discipline. You need discipline because your understanding is not enough.

Someone wrote a letter to me saying that he knows what is right but he goes on doing what is wrong. He knows what is wrong, still he goes on doing it. "So how to change it, Osho?" he writes. Now if you really know what is right, how can you do wrong? Somewhere your knowledge must be borrowed, it cannot be yours. If you really know what is wrong, how can you do it? It is impossible. If you do, that simply shows you don't know.

Socrates used to say, "Knowledge is virtue." If you know something, it starts happening. But the knowledge must be real, and by real I mean it must be yours, it must have come through your own life, it must be an essence of your own experience. It should not be borrowed, it should not be academic, it should not be scriptural, it should not be just information. It should be your own experience, authentically lived. Then you cannot go against it, there is no way.

How can you pass through a wall knowing that it is a wall? You go through the door. You never come to me and say, "I know where the door is, but still I first try to go through the wall. It always hits my head. What to do now?" If you know where the door is you pass through it. If you say you know and still you try to go through the wall, that simply shows you don't know. You may have heard, somebody else may have told you, but you don't trust.

Your action shows what you know. Your action is the only proof of your knowledge, nothing else.

Buddha says no discipline is needed if understanding is there. Understanding brings its own discipline – intrinsic, inner. There are two sorts of discipline, as there are two sorts of knowledge. If knowledge comes from without, then you have to enforce discipline on yourself. If knowledge springs, wells up from within, then there is no need to enforce any discipline. Discipline comes as a shadow to it; it follows.

. . . no discipline, no enlightenment, and no going up through the grades.

And Buddha says there are no grades. People are there who come and say to me, "I am advanced but still not yet attained." They want from me a certificate also, so that I can give them an indication of how far they are advanced, on what grade they are.

Buddha says in fact there are no gradations. There are only two types of people – enlightened and unenlightened. There is no in-between. It is not that a few people are there who are just in the middle. Either you are alive or you are dead, there is no in-between. Either you know or you don't; there is no in-between. Grades don't exist.

All grades are tricks of the ego. The ego says, "Yes, I am not yet enlightened, but I am far advanced. Just ninety-nine degrees. One degree more and I will be enlightened. I am not far behind – I am far advanced." Drop all that nonsense. If you are not enlightened you are simply not enlightened.

All unenlightened people are the same and all enlightened people are also the same. The difference is just as if you are sleeping and somebody is sitting by your side fully alert and aware. This is the only difference. If you are awake, you are awake. You cannot say, "I am just in-between." There is no state like that. If you are asleep, you are asleep; if you are awake, you are awake.

The difference is small and yet tremendous. A person fully alert, sitting awake, and a person snoring by the side – both are the same human beings, same consciousnesses, but one is in deep darkness, lost, oblivious of itself; another luminous, alive, attained to its own inner flame. If something happens then they will react in different ways. The alert person is bound to react in a different way. His reaction will be a response; he will respond, knowing well what he is doing. If the sleepy person reacts, his reaction will be a mechanical reaction, not knowing what he is doing.

Buddha says:

> . . . *no discipline, no enlightenment, no going up through the grades, and yet in possession of all honors in itself – this is called the way.*

Buddha says if you surrender the ego, if you surrender your self, you come into a harmony with the law and everything starts happening on its own. You have only to surrender. If you are ready to disappear, you will be full of the law and the law will take care.

Have you watched it? If you trust the river you can float. The moment you lose the trust you start drowning. If you trust, the river takes you in her hands; if you become afraid you start drowning. That's why dead bodies start floating on the surface of the river, because dead bodies cannot doubt. Dead bodies cannot be afraid. Alive, the same persons went down into the river and drowned. When dead, they surface, they start floating on the surface. Now it is very difficult for the river to drown them – no river has been able to drown a dead body up to now. Alive, what happens? What happens? The dead man must know some secret. The secret is that he cannot doubt.

You must have heard the beautiful parable in Jesus' life – that his disciples are crossing the lake of Galilee and he is left behind and he says, "I will be coming soon. I have to say my prayers." And then the disciples were very much puzzled – he was coming, walking on the lake! They are afraid, frightened, scared. They think it must be some evil force. How can he walk on the water?

One disciple says, "Master, is it really you?" Jesus says, "Yes." Then the disciple says, "Then if you can walk, why can't I, your disciple?" Jesus says, "You can also walk – come!" And the disciple comes and he walks a few steps, and he's surprised that he is walking – but then doubt arises. He says, "What is happening? This is unbelievable."

The moment he thinks, "This is unbelievable. Am I in a dream, or some trick of the devil, what is happening?" he starts drowning. And Jesus says, "You, you of little faith! Why did you doubt? You have walked a few steps and you know that it has happened; then too you doubt?"

Whether this story happened in this way or not is not the point. But I also know; you can try. If you trust the river, just relax in the river, you will float. Then the doubt will arise, the same doubt that came to Jesus' disciple: "What is happening? How is it possible? I'm not drowning" – and immediately you will start drowning.

The difference between a swimmer and a non-swimmer is not much. The swimmer has learned how to trust; the non-swimmer has not yet learned how to trust. Both are the same. When the non-swimmer falls into the river, doubt arises. He starts feeling afraid – the river is going to drown him. And of course then the river drowns him. But he is drowning himself in his own doubt. The river is not doing anything. The swimmer knows the river, the ways of the river, and he has been with the river many times and he trusts; he simply floats, he is not afraid.

Life is exactly the same.

BUDDHA SAYS:

. . . and yet in possession of all honors in itself – this is called the way.

The man of understanding is in a total let-go. He allows the law to function. If you want old religious language, non-Buddhist language, you can call it surrender to God. Then the devotee says, "Now I am no more, only you are. I am just a flute on your lips, a hollow bamboo. You sing; the song will be yours,

I will be just a passage." This is old religious language. Buddha is not happy with the old language. Buddha is not happy with the poets' language; he likes the scientific language more. He talks the same way as Albert Einstein, or Newton, or Edison. He talks about the law – now it is for you to decide. The difference is only of language, but the basic thing is letting go, a total surrender.

The Buddha said:

> Those who, shaving their heads and faces, become shramanas and who receive instructions in the way, should surrender all worldly possessions and be contented with whatever they obtain by begging.
>
> One meal a day, and one lodging under a tree, and neither should be repeated, for what makes one stupid and irrational is attachments and the passions.

Buddha insisted for his sannyasins to shave their heads, their faces. These are just gestures, don't take them literally. They are just gestures, indications that you are ready to surrender. They don't have any other meaning. The only meaning is that you are ready to go with Buddha. When you take *sannyas*, when you are initiated, you are simply saying yes. You are saying, "Yes, I am coming with you. Even if you say to do something mad, I'm ready to do it." It is just a surrendering gesture.

Buddha used to say that a *shramana* should live in insecurity. That's why he said become beggars. Again, don't take it literally. Try to understand the spirit of it. He says you cannot possess anything, it is impossible to possess anything. Life is insecurity and there is no way to become secure. Death is coming and will destroy all your securities, so don't be bothered. Even if you are a beggar, be happy, be a beggar happily. There is no point in worrying too much about your security. Understand the insecurity of life, accept it – in that very acceptance you become secure.

And Buddha used to say:

> One meal a day and one lodging under a tree and neither should be repeated.

Because, Buddha says, if you repeat a certain thing again and again it becomes a habit, a mechanical habit. And when you become mechanical you lose awareness. So don't repeat. Go on changing the situation, so in every situation you have to be alert. Go on changing the town. Don't beg from the same door again and don't sleep under the same tree again. These are just devices so that you have to remain alert.

Have you watched it? If you move into a new house, for a few days you feel very uneasy. By and by you become accustomed to the new house and then you feel at home. It takes a little time: between three days and three weeks, a person begins to feel at home in the new house. Then the house has become a habit. Buddha says before that happens, move. Not even under the same tree should you sleep twice, otherwise there is a tendency in the mind to claim it.

Beggars also stake a claim. A beggar sits under a tree and begs; then he will not allow any other beggars to sit there. He will say, "Go somewhere else. This is my tree!" Beggars have their dominions. A beggar comes to beg in your neighborhood; he will not allow other beggars to go there, he will fight – this territory is his. You may not know it, but you belong to his territory. He will not allow other beggars to enter.

Buddha says don't allow the mind to become lazy, don't allow the mind to become mechanical. Remain alert, moving. Don't become stagnant, go on moving, because one becomes stupid and irrational if attachment and passions are allowed. If you become attached you become stupid, you lose intelligence.

The more secure you are, the more stupid you become. That's why it rarely happens that intelligent people come from rich families . . . very rarely. Because they are so secure, they have no challenges in life, they have all that they need – why bother? You cannot find many rich people whose money is inherited that are very sharp. They are almost always a little dull – they live in a sort of stupor, dragging. Comfortably dragging, conveniently dragging, dragging in Rolls Royces – but dragging, dull. Life seems to have no challenge because there is no insecurity.

Buddha used it as a device: become insecure so you become sharp. A beggar has to be very sharp and intelligent – he has nothing. He has to live moment to moment. That's why Buddha insisted for his sannyasins to become beggars. He called them *bhikkhus*. *Bhikkhu* means "a beggar". It was just a reversal. In India, sannyasins have always been known as swamis – swami means a master. Exactly, the word "swami" means "lord". Buddha changed the whole thing. He called his sannyasins *bhikkhus*, beggars. But he brought in a new dimension, a new meaning, a new challenge. He said, "Live moment to moment. Having nothing, you will never be secure – and you will never be stupid."

Have you watched? When you have money, you become lethargic. When you don't have money you become alert. If suddenly all is lost you will become very alert. If you have to keep yourself alive by begging, you cannot be certain about the tomorrow. Nobody knows what is going to happen, whether you will be able to get something or not, whether you will be able to find somebody to give you something or not; you don't know. Tomorrow is not settled, everything is uncertain. In uncertainty, in insecurity, your intelligence becomes more and more sharp. You become more brilliant.

The Buddha said:

There are ten things considered good by all beings, and ten things evil.

What are they?

Three of them depend upon the body, four upon the mouth, and three upon thought. Three evil deeds depending upon the body are: killing, stealing, and committing adultery. The four depending upon the mouth are: slandering, cursing, lying and flattery. The three depending upon thought are: envy, anger and infatuation. All these things are against the holy way, and therefore they are evil.

Look at the difference. Buddha says they are against the holy way. If you do these ten things you will be miserable, you will be continuously in pain, anxiety, anguish. It is difficult for a man to be violent and not be miserable. If you kill somebody you will remain in misery. Before you kill you will be in misery, when you kill you will be in misery, and after you have killed you will be in misery.

Destructiveness cannot bring happiness; destruction is against the law of creation. The law of creation is to be creative. So Buddha says if you are destructive you will be miserable. If you are envious, infatuated, competitive, ambitious, jealous, possessive, you will be in misery. The only criterion to know what is wrong is that it makes you miserable. Now this is a very different attitude. Not that God says, "Don't do this," not that there are ten commandments. Buddha also says there are ten things to be avoided, but not that there is a despot, somebody dictating, somebody like Adolf Hitler or Joseph Stalin sitting there on a golden throne in the heavens and dictating, "Do this and don't do that." There is nobody. It is for you to decide.

Buddha gives you just a criterion: whatsoever brings misery is wrong. He does not say it is a sin. Look at the emphasis. He says it is simply wrong – just as two plus two are not five. If you make two plus two five, nobody will say that you have committed a sin. It is simply wrong, a mistake.

In Buddhist terminology there is nothing like sin; only mistakes, errors. There is no condemnation. You can correct the error, you can correct the mistake. It is simple. You can put two plus two as four, the moment you understand.

All these things are against the holy way and therefore they are evil.

There is no other reason for them to be evil: simply because they create misery for you. In fact, you create it by following them. If you don't want to be miserable, then avoid these things.

When these evils are not done, there are ten good deeds.

And this is very significant. Listen to this sentence again:

When these evils are not done, there are ten good deeds.

Buddha does not talk about the good deeds. He says if you don't do these ten, you will be in harmony with the whole, with the law, and whatever happens will be good. Good is not that which one needs to do. Good is when you are not a doer; when you are in a let-go with the whole, moving with the law, with the river, good happens. Good is not an act.

Now there is no sin, only errors. And there is no virtue, only good deeds happening when you have surrendered yourself. So Buddha says avoid the bad deeds, the evil things. He is not saying practice the good ones, he is simply saying avoid the wrong and you will come in tune with the whole, you will become harmonious with the law, and then whatsoever happens is good. Good is like health. Don't be ill, then you are healthy. Just avoid illness, that's all, and you will be healthy. If you go to the doctor and you ask him what the definition of health is, he will not be able to define it. He will say, "I don't know. I can simply diagnose your illness. I can prescribe a medicine for the illness. When the illness has disappeared you will be healthy, and then you can know what health is."

The same is the Buddha's attitude. Buddha used to call himself a physician, a *vaidya*, a doctor. He used to say of himself, "I am just a doctor, a physician. You come to me, I diagnose your disease, I prescribe medicine. When diseases have disappeared, whatsoever is left, that presence is health."

When these evils are not done, there are ten good deeds.

So he is not giving you a positive discipline to be followed, just a negative understanding. Just try to understand, so that the error is not committed, so that you become harmonious with the whole. Harmony is happiness, and harmony is heaven. And harmony happens only when you are in tune with the whole. To be with the whole is to be holy.

Enough for today.

40

Chapter 3:

Be Therefore Mindful

THE BUDDHA SAID:

> If a man who has committed many a misdemeanor does not repent and cleanse his heart of the evil, retribution will come upon his person as sure as the streams run into the ocean which becomes ever deeper and wider.

> If a man who has committed a misdemeanor comes to the knowledge of it, reforms himself and practices goodness, the force of retribution will gradually exhaust itself as a disease gradually loses its baneful influence when the patient perspires.

THE BUDDHA SAID:

> When an evil-doer, seeing you practice goodness, comes and maliciously insults you, you should patiently endure it and not feel angry with him. For the evil-doer is insulting himself by trying to insult you.

THE BUDDHA SAID:

> Once a man came unto me and denounced me on account of my observing the way and practicing great loving kindness. But I kept silent and did not answer him. The denunciation ceased.

> I then asked him, "If you bring a present to your neighbor and he accepts it not, does the present come back to you?"

The man replied, "It will." I said, "You denounce me now, but as I accept it not, you must take the wrong deed back upon your own person. It is like an echo succeeding sound, it is like shadow following object. You never escape the effect of your own evil deeds. Be therefore mindful and cease from doing evil."

Man is a crowd, a crowd of many voices – relevant, irrelevant, consistent, inconsistent – each voice pulling in its own way, all the voices pulling people apart. Ordinarily people are a mess, virtually in a kind of madness. You somehow manage, you somehow manage to look sane but deep down, layers and layers of insanity are boiling within you. They can erupt any moment. Your control can be lost any moment, because your control is enforced from without. It is not a discipline that has come from your center of being.

For social reasons, economic reasons, political reasons, you have enforced a certain character upon yourself. But many vital forces exist against that character within you. They are continuously sabotaging your character. Hence every day you go on committing many mistakes, many errors. Even sometimes you feel that you never wanted to do it. In spite of yourself, you go on committing many mistakes – because you are not one, you are many.

Buddha does not call these mistakes "sins", because to call them sin will be condemning you. He simply calls them misdemeanors, mistakes, errors. To err is human, not to err is divine. And the way from the human to the divine goes through mindfulness. These many voices within you can stop torturing you, pulling you, pushing you. These many voices can disappear if you become mindful.

In a mindful state mistakes are not committed – not that you control them, but in a mindful state, in an alert, aware state, voices, many voices cease; you simply become one, and whatsoever you do comes from the very core of your being. It is never wrong. This has to be understood before we enter into these sutras.

In Humanistic Psychology there is a parallel to help you understand it. That's what Transactional Analysis calls the triangle of "PAC". P means parent, A means adult, C means child. These are your three layers, as if you are a three-storied building. The first floor is that of the child, the second floor is that of the parent, and the third floor is that of the adult. All three exist together. This is your inner triangle and conflict. Your child says one thing, your parent says something else, and your adult, rational mind says something else.

The child says "enjoy". For the child, this moment is the only moment; he has no other considerations. The child is spontaneous, but unaware of the consequences – unaware of past, unaware of future. He lives in the moment. He has no values and he has no mindfulness, no awareness. The child lives through feeling. His whole being is irrational.

Of course he comes into many conflicts with others. He comes into many contradictions within himself, because one feeling helps him to do one thing, then suddenly he starts feeling another feeling. A child never can complete anything; in the time he could have completed it, his feeling has changed. He starts many things but never comes to any conclusion. A child remains inconclusive. He enjoys but his enjoyment is not creative, cannot be. He delights – but life cannot be lived only through delight.

You cannot remain a child forever. You will have to learn many things, because you are not alone here. If you were alone then there would be no question – you could have remained a child forever. But the society is there, millions of people are there; you have to follow many rules, you have to follow many values. Otherwise there would be so much conflict that life would become impossible. The child has to be disciplined – and that's where the parent comes in.

The parental voice in you is the voice of the society, culture, civilization; the voice that makes you capable of living in a world where you are not alone, where there are many individuals with conflicting ambitions, where there is much struggle for survival, where there is much conflict. You have to pave your path, and you have to move very cautiously.

The parental voice is that of caution. It makes you civilized. The child is wild, the parental voice helps you to become civilized. The word "civil" is good. It means one who has become capable of living in a city; who has become capable of being a member of a group, of a society.

The child is very dictatorial. The child thinks he is the center of the world. The parent has to teach you that you are not the center of the world – everybody thinks that way. He has to make you more and more alert that there are many people in the world, you are not alone. You have to consider them if you want to be considered by them; otherwise you will be crushed. It is a sheer question of survival, of policy, of politics. The parental voice gives you commandments – what to do, what not to do. The feeling simply moves blind, the parent makes you cautious. It is needed.

And then there is the third voice within you, the third layer, when you have become adult and you are no longer controlled by your parents; your own reason has come of age, you can think on your own.

The child consists of felt concepts; the parent consists of taught concepts, and the adult consists of thought concepts. And these three layers are continuously in fight. The child says one thing, the parent says just the opposite, and the reason may say something totally different. You see beautiful food, and the child says to eat as much as you want. The parental voice says that many things have to be considered – whether you are really feeling hungry, or just the smell of the food, the taste of the food is the only appeal. "Is this food really nutritious? Is it going to nourish your body or can it become harmful to you? Wait, listen, don't rush."

And then there is the rational mind, the adult mind, which may say something else, totally different. There is no necessity that your adult mind should agree with your parents. Your parents were not omniscient, they were not all-knowing. They were as fallible, as human as you are, and many times you find loopholes in their thinking. Many times you find them very dogmatic, superstitious, believing in foolish things, irrational ideologies. Your adult says no, your parent says do it; your adult says it is not worth doing, and your child goes on pulling you somewhere else. This is the triangle within you.

If you listen to the child, your parent feels angry. So one part feels good – "You can go on eating as much ice cream as you want!" – but your parent inside feels angry. A part of you starts condemning, and then you start feeling guilty. The same guilt arises as it used to arise when you were really a child. You are no longer a child, but the child has not disappeared. It is there; it is just your ground floor, your very base, your foundation. If you follow the child, if you follow the feeling, the parent is angry and then you start feeling guilt.

If you follow the parent then your child feels that he is being forced into things he does not want to do. Then your child feels he is being unnecessarily interfered with, unnecessarily trespassed upon. Freedom is lost when you listen to the parent, and your child starts feeling rebellious.

If you listen to the parent, your adult mind says, "What nonsense! These people never knew anything. You know more, you are more in tune with the modern world, you are more contemporary. These ideologies are just dead ideologies, out of date – why are you bothering?" If you listen to your reason then also you feel as if you are betraying your parents. Again guilt arises. What to do? And it is almost impossible to find something on which all these three layers agree. This is human anxiety – never do all these three layers agree on any point. There is no agreement ever.

Now there are teachers who believe in the child, who emphasize the child more. For example, Lao Tzu. He says, "The agreement is not going to come. You drop this parental voice, these commandments, these Old Testaments. Drop all 'shoulds' and become a child again." That's what Jesus says. Lao Tzu and Jesus, their emphasis is to become a child again – because only with the child will you be able to gain your spontaneity, will you again become part of the natural flow, Tao. Their message is beautiful, but seems to be almost impractical. Sometimes, yes, it has happened – a person has become a child again. But it is so exceptional that it is not possible to think that humanity is ever going to become a child again. It is beautiful like a star . . . far distant, but out of reach.

Then there are other teachers – Mahavira, Moses, Mohammed, Manu – they say listen to the parental voice, listen to the moral, what the society says, what you have been taught. Listen and follow it. If you want to be at ease in the world, if you want to be peaceful in the world, listen to the parent. Never go against the parental voice. That's how the world has followed, more or less. But then one never feels spontaneous, one never feels natural. One always feels confined, caged. And when you don't feel free, you may feel peaceful but that peacefulness is worthless. Unless peace comes with freedom you cannot accept it. Unless peace comes with bliss you cannot accept it. It brings convenience, comfort, but your soul suffers. Yes, there have been a few people again who have achieved through the parental voice, who have really attained to the truth. But that too is very rare. And that world is gone. Maybe in the past, Moses and Manu and Mohammed were useful. They gave commandments to the world. "Do this. Don't do that." They made things simple, very simple. They have not left anything for you to decide; they don't trust that you will be able to decide. They simply give you a ready-made formula – "These are the ten command-ments to be followed. You simply do these and all that you hope, all that you desire will happen as a consequence. You just be obedient."

All the old religions emphasized obedience too much. Disobedience is the only sin – that's what Christianity says. Adam and Eve were expelled from the Garden of Eden because they disobeyed. God had said not to eat the fruit of the tree of knowledge and they disobeyed. That was their only sin. But every child is committing that sin! The father says, "Don't smoke", and the child tries it. The father says, "Don't go to the movie", and the child goes. The story of Adam and Eve is the story of every child. And then condemnation, expulsion . . . Obedience is religion for Manu, Mohammed, Moses. But that world has gone, and through it not many have attained. Many became peaceful, good citizens, respectable members of the society, but nothing much more.

Then there is the third emphasis on being adult. Confucius, Patanjali, or modern agnostics like Bertrand Russell – all humanists of the world emphasize: "Believe only in your own reason." That seems very arduous, so much so that one's whole life becomes just a conflict. Because you have been brought up by your parents, you have been conditioned by your parents. If you listen only to your reason, you have to deny many things in your being. In fact, your whole mind has to be denied. It is not easy to erase it. And you were born without any capacity to reason; that too is there. Basically you are a feeling being; reason comes to you very late. It comes when, in fact, all else that has to happen has happened. Psychologists say a child gains almost seventy-five percent of his whole knowledge by the time he is seven years old, fifty percent by the time he is four years old. This whole learning happens when you are a child, and reason is a very late arrival.

It is very difficult to live just with the reason. People have tried – a Bertrand Russell here and there – but nobody has achieved truth through it, because reason alone is not enough.

All these angles have been chosen and tried, and nothing has worked. Buddha's standpoint is totally different. That's his original contribution to human consciousness. He says not to choose any; he says move in the center of the triangle. Don't choose reason, don't choose parent, don't choose the child; just move in the very center of the triangle and remain silent and become mindful. His approach is tremendously meaningful. And then you will be able to have a clear perspective of your being. And out of that perspective and clarity let the response come.

We can say it in another way. If you function as a child, that is a childish reaction. Many times you function as a child. Somebody says something and you get hurt, and there is a tantrum and anger and temper . . . you lose everything. Later on you feel very bad about it – that you destroyed your image; everybody thinks you so sober and you were so childish, and nothing much was at stake. Or you follow your parental voice, but later on you think that still you are dominated by your parents. You have not yet become an adult, mature enough to take the reins of your life into your own hands.

Or sometimes you follow reason, but then you think that reason is not enough, feeling also is needed. And without feeling, a rational being becomes just the head. He loses contact with the body, he loses contact with life, he becomes disconnected. He functions only as a thinking mechanism. But thinking cannot make you alive, in thinking there is no juice of life. It is a very dry thing. Then you hanker, you hanker for something which can again allow your energies to stream, which can again allow you to be green and alive and young. This goes on, and you go on chasing your own tail.

Buddha says these are all reactions, and any reaction is bound to be partial – only response is total – and whatsoever is partial is a mistake. That's his definition of error: whatsoever is partial is a mistake, because your other parts will remain unfulfilled and they will take their revenge. Be total. Response is total, reaction is partial. When you listen to one voice and follow it you are getting into trouble. You will never be satisfied with it. Only one part will be satisfied, the other two parts will be very much dissatisfied. So two thirds of your being will be dissatisfied, one third of your being will be satisfied, and you will always remain in a turmoil.

Whatsoever you do, reaction can never satisfy you, because reaction is partial. Response – response is total. Then you don't function from any point in the triangle, you don't choose; you simply remain in a choiceless awareness. You remain centered. And out of that centering you act, whatsoever it is. It is neither child nor parent nor adult. You have gone beyond PAC. It is *you* now – neither the child nor the parent nor the adult. It is you, your being. That PAC is like a cyclone and your center is the center of the cyclone. (storm - 龍捲風)

So whenever there is a need to respond, the first thing, Buddha says, is to become mindful, become aware. Remember your center. Become grounded in your center. Be there for a few moments before you do anything. There is no need to think about it because thinking is partial. There is no need to feel about it because feeling is partial. There is no need to find clues from your parents, the Bible, Koran, Gita – these are all "P" – there is no need. You simply remain tranquil, silent, simply alert – watching the situation as if you are absolutely out of it, aloof, a watcher on the hills. aloof — distant, detached 疏離

This is the first requirement – to be centered whenever you want to act. Then out of this centering let the act arise – and whatsoever you do will be virtuous, whatsoever you do will be right.

Buddha says right mindfulness is the only virtue there is. Not to be mindful is to fall into error. To act unconsciously is to fall into error.

Now the sutras.

THE BUDDHA SAID: Chapter 5

If a man who has committed many a misdemeanor does not repent and cleanse his heart of the evil, retribution will come upon his person as sure as the streams run into the ocean which becomes ever deeper and wider.

Repentance means retrospective awareness, repentance means looking backwards. You have done something. If you were aware then no wrong could happen, but you were not aware at the time you did it. Somebody insulted you – you became angry, you hit him on the head. You were not aware what you were doing. Now things have cooled down, the situation has passed, you are no longer in anger; you can look backwards more easily. You missed awareness at that time. The best thing would have been to have awareness at that time, but you missed it, and now there is no point in crying and weeping over the spilt milk. But you can look, you can bring awareness to that which has already happened.

That is what Mahavira calls *pratyakraman*, looking back; what Patanjali calls *pratyahar*, looking in. That's what Jesus calls repentance. That's what Buddha calls *pashchattap*. It is not feeling sorry, it is not just feeling bad about it, because that is not going to help. It is becoming aware, it is reliving the experience as it should have been. You have to move into it again. You missed awareness in that moment; you were overflooded by unconsciousness. Now things have cooled and you'll take your awareness, the light of awareness, back. You move into that incident again, you look into it again as you should have really done; it is gone, but you can do it retrospectively in your mind. And Buddha says this cleanses the heart of the evil. This looking back, continuously looking back, will make you more and more aware.

There are three stages. You *have done* something, then you become aware – the first stage. The second stage: you *are doing* something and you become aware. And third stage, you *are going to do* something and you become aware. Only in the third stage will your life be transformed. But the first two are necessary for the third; they are necessary steps.

Whenever you can become aware, become aware. You have been angry – now sit down, meditate, become aware what has happened. Ordinarily we do it, but we do it for wrong reasons. We do it to put our image back together. You always think you are a very loving person, compassionate, and then you suddenly become angry. Now your image is distorted in your own eyes. You do a sort of repentance. You go to the person and you say, "I am sorry." What are you doing? You are repainting your image. Your ego is trying to repaint the image, because you have fallen in your own eyes and you have fallen in others' eyes. Now you are trying to rationalize. At least you can go and say, "I am sorry. I did it in spite of myself. I don't know how it happened, I don't know what evil force took possession of me, but I am sorry. Forgive me." You are trying to come back to the same level where you were before you became angry. This is a trick of the ego, this is not real repentance. Again you will do the same thing. *Repentance*

Buddha says real repentance is remembering it, going into the details fully aware of what happened; going backwards, reliving the experience. Reliving the experience is like unwinding; it erases. And not only that – it makes you capable

P – Parent
A – Adult
C – Child

of more awareness, because awareness is being practiced when you are remembering it, when you are becoming again aware about the past incident. You are getting a discipline in awareness, in mindfulness. Next time you will become aware a little earlier. This time you were angry; after two hours you could cool down. Next time after one hour you will cool down; next time after a few minutes; next time, just as it has happened you will cool down and you will be able to see. By and by, by slow progression, one day while you are angry you will catch yourself red-handed. And that is a beautiful experience – to catch yourself red-handed committing an error. Then suddenly the whole quality changes, because whenever awareness penetrates you, reactions stop.

This anger is a childish reaction, it is the child in you. It is coming from the "C". And later on, when you feel sorry, that is coming from the "P", from the parent. The parent forces you to feel sorry and go and ask forgiveness. You have not been good to your mother or to your uncle – go and put things right. Or it can come from "A", from your adult mind. You have been angry and later on you recognize that this is going to be too much; there is a financial loss in it. You have been angry with your boss, now you become afraid. Now you start thinking he may throw you out, or he may carry the anger within him. Your salary was going to be raised; he may not raise it now – a thousand and one things could happen, so you would like to put things right.

When Buddha says repent, he's not telling you to function from C or P or A. He is saying when you become aware, sit down, close your eyes, and meditate upon the whole thing – become a watcher. You missed the situation, but still something can be done about it: you can watch it. You can watch it as it should have been watched. You can practice, this will be a rehearsal, and by the time you have watched the whole situation you will feel completely okay. If then you feel like going and asking forgiveness, for no other reasons – neither the parent, nor the adult, nor the child – but out of sheer understanding, out of sheer meditation that it was wrong . . . It was not wrong for any other reason; it was wrong because you behaved in an unconscious way.

Let me repeat it. You go and you ask for forgiveness not for any other reason – financial, social, political, cultural; no – you simply go there because you meditated on it and you recognized and realized the fact that you acted in unawareness; you have hurt somebody in unawareness. You have to go and console the person at least. You have to go and help the person to understand your helplessness – that you are an unconscious person, that you are a human being with all the limitations, that you are sorry. It is not putting your ego back, it is simply doing something which your meditation has showed you. It is totally a different dimension.

If a man who has committed many a misdemeanor does not repent and
cleanse his heart of the evil, retribution will come upon his person as sure
as the streams run into the ocean which becomes ever deeper and wider.

Ordinarily what do we do? We become defensive. If you have been angry at
your wife or at your child, you become defensive; you say it had to be that
way, it was needed – it was needed for the child's own good. If you are not
angry, how are you going to discipline the child? If you are not angry with
somebody people will take advantage of you. You are not a coward, you are a
brave man. How can you just let people do things which should not be done to
you? You have to react. You become defensive, you rationalize.

If you go on rationalizing your errors . . . and all errors can be rationalized,
remember it. There exists not a single error which cannot be rationalized. You
can rationalize everything. But then, Buddha says, such a person is bound to
become more and more unconscious, more and more deeply unaware . . . *as*
sure as the streams run into the ocean which becomes ever deeper and wider.

If you go on defending yourself then you will not be able to transform
yourself. You have to recognize that there is something wrong. The very recog-
nition helps change. If you feel healthy and you are not ill, you are not going to
go to a physician. Even if the physician comes to you, you are not going to listen
to him. You are perfectly okay. You will say, "I'm perfectly well. Who says I am
ill?" If you don't think you are ill, you will go on protecting your illness. That is
dangerous; you are on a suicidal path.

If there has been anger, there has been greed, there has been something that
happens only when you are unconscious, recognize it – the sooner you do it the
better. Meditate upon it. Move to your center and respond from the center.

If a man who has committed a misdemeanor comes to the knowledge of
it, reforms himself and practices goodness, the force of retribution will
gradually exhaust itself as a disease gradually loses its baneful influence
when the patient perspires.

If you acknowledge it you have taken one very meaningful step towards
changing it. Now Buddha says one very important thing: "If you come to
acknowledge it, if you come to the knowledge of it, reform yourself." Ordinarily,
even if we sometimes recognize that "yes, something wrong has happened", we
don't try to reform ourselves, we only try to reform our image. We want
everybody to feel that they have forgiven us. We want everybody to recognize
that it was wrong on our part, but we have asked for their forgiveness and things
are put right again. We are again on our pedestal. The fallen image is placed
back on the throne. We don't reform ourselves.

You have many times asked forgiveness, but again and again you go on doing the same thing. That simply shows that it was a policy, politics, a trick to manipulate people – but you have remained the same, you have not changed at all. If you have really asked forgiveness for your anger or any offense against anybody, then it should not happen again. Only that can be a proof that you are really on the path of changing yourself.

BUDDHA SAYS:

> *If a man who has committed a misdemeanor comes to the*
> *knowledge of it, reforms himself and practices goodness . . .*

So, two things he is saying. First: the moment you feel that something goes wrong, something makes you unconscious and you behave in a mechanical way and you react, then you have to do something – and the doing has to become more aware. That is the only way to reform yourself.

Watch how many things you do unconsciously. Somebody says something and there is anger. There is not even a single moment's gap. It is as if you are just a mechanism – somebody pushes a button and you lose your temper. Just as if you push the button and the fan starts moving and the light goes on. There is not a single moment's hestitaion, the fan never thinks whether to move or not to move; it simply moves. Buddha says this is unconsciousness, this is mindlessness. Somebody insults you and you are simply controlled by his insult.

Gurdjieff used to say that a small thing transformed his life completely. His father was dying and he called the boy – and Gurdjieff was only nine years old – and he said to him, "I have nothing much to give you, but only one advice that was given by my father to me from his deathbed, and it has tremendously benefited me. Maybe it can be of some use to you. I don't feel that you will be able to understand it right now, you are too young. So just remember it. Whenever you can understand, it will be helpful." The father said, "Remember only one thing – if you feel angry, wait for twenty-four hours. Then do whatsoever you want to do, but first wait twenty-four hours. If somebody insults you, you tell him, 'I will come after twenty-four hours and do whatsoever is needed. Please give me a little time to think it over.'"

Of course the nine-year-old Gurdjieff could not understand what it was, but he remembered it. By and by, he became aware of the tremendous impact of it. He was completely transformed. Two things he had to remember – one, he had to be aware not to move into anger when somebody was insulting, not to allow himself to be manipulated by the other – he had to wait for twenty-four hours. So when somebody was insulting or saying something against him, he would simply remain alert not to be affected. For twenty-four hours, he had promised his dying father, he would remain cool and calm. By and by he became capable. And then he understood it – that after twenty-four hours, it is never needed. You cannot be angry after twenty-four hours. After twenty-four minutes you cannot be angry, after twenty-four seconds you cannot be angry. Either it is instant or it is not. Because anger functions only if you are unconscious; if you are this conscious – that you can wait for twenty-four seconds – finished! Then you cannot be angry. Then you have missed the moment, then you have missed the train; the train has left the platform. Even twenty-four seconds will do – you try it.

Buddha says one who acknowledges his errors . . . and he simply says *acknowledges*, he does not say "one who condemns", because there is nothing to condemn. It is human, it is natural; we are unconscious beings. Buddha used to say that existence is asleep in the mineral, totally oblivious; in the vegetable the sleep is not so deep, a few fragments of dreams have started moving around; in the animal, existence is dreaming; in man it has become a little aware – just a little. Those moments are few and far between. Sometimes months pass and you are not aware for a single moment, but in man there is the possibility of a few moments of awareness. In a Buddha, existence has become perfectly aware.

Watch existence all around. In these trees, Buddha says there are just a few fragments of dreams. In the rocks . . . fast, deep sleep, dreamless. In the animals – in the cat, in the dog, in the lion, in the tiger, in the birds – existence is dreaming, many dreams. In man it is surfacing just a little, a few moments of awareness.

So don't miss any opportunity, whenever you can become aware. And those are the best moments to become aware, when unconsciousness is pulling you deep down. If you can use those moments, if you can use those moments as challenges, existence will become more and more aware in you. One day your awareness becomes a continuous flame, an eternal flame. Then existence is perfectly awake, no sleep, no dream.

This is the meaning of the word "buddha". "Buddha" means one who has become absolutely aware. In no situation does he lose his mindfulness. His mindfulness has become just natural like breathing. Just as you breathe in and breathe out, in exactly the same way he inhales awareness, he exhales awareness. His centering has become permanent. He does not function from personalities – the personality of the child, the parent, the adult, no. He simply functions from a point which is beyond all personalities.

This is what Buddha calls "reform". The word "reform" is beautiful. It means "to make it again" – reform, to re-build, to re-create. Reform does not mean just reform, reform does not mean just modifying here and there. Reform does not mean that somewhere the plaster has fallen so you put it again, somewhere the color has disappeared, worn away, so you paint it again. Reform does not mean small modifications. Reform is a very revolutionary word. It simply means form it again, be reborn, be totally new, take a quantum jump, move from the old personality, be away from the old nucleus, attain to a new center.

He reforms himself, practices goodness . . .

Whatsoever you feel is your basic error, just don't get chronically attentive towards it, don't get obsessed by it. That too is a fault. There are many people, they come to me and they say, "We cannot control anger. We continuously are trying to control it, but we cannot control. What to do?" Buddha says don't become obsessive about anything. Recognize it, become aware, and do something just the opposite. If you feel anger is your problem, don't be too attentive towards anger; become more compassionate, become more loving. Because if you become too concerned about anger, where will you put the energy that will be released if you don't become angry? Create a path for the energy to move. It is the same energy. When you have compassion it is the same energy as it was in anger. Now it is positive, then it was negative. Then it was destructive, now it is creative. But it is the same energy – anger becomes compassion. So before you can change anger you will have to make new channels towards compassion.

Buddha says practice goodness, practice virtue. Find out your chief fault and create new pathways in your being. If you are a miser then just crying about it and talking about it is not going to help. Then start sharing. Whatsoever you can share, share. Do something that becomes a breakthrough, do something that goes against your past, do something you have never done before. It is possible that you are angry because you don't know how to have compassion. It is possible you are a miser because you don't know how to share. Buddha's emphasis is to be positive – do something so the energy starts moving and flowing. Then by and by it will be taken away from anger. Become conscious but don't be obsessed.

You will have to make a distinction between these two things because human mind is such that it goes on misinterpreting. When Buddha says become mindful, he is not saying become obsessed, he is not saying continuously think of anger. Because if you continuously think of anger you will create more and more angry situations for yourself. Be conscious, but there is no need to contemplate anger. Be conscious, but there is no need to be too much concerned. Take a note of it and then do something which changes your energy pattern. That's what he means when he says practice goodness.

. . . The force of retribution will gradually exhaust itself as a disease gradually loses its baneful influence when the patient perspires.

Somebody has taken too much alcohol. What do you do? You can give him a hot bath or you can put him in a sauna. If he can perspire, the alcohol will go with his perspiration. Buddha says to do virtue is like perspiration. Your unconscious habits evaporate through it. So not doing bad is actually doing good. Don't be negatively interested, be positive. If you just sit and think about all the wrongs that you have done, you will be giving them too much food. To give attention is to give food, to give attention means to play with the wound. Take note, be mindful, meditate, but don't play with the wound. Otherwise you will be making the wound again and again more alive. It will start bleeding. So don't become too concerned about your small things – they are small.

I have heard about a saint who used to beat himself every morning, and he would cry, "God, forgive me. I have committed a sin." This continued for forty years. Again and again he was asked about it. He had become a very respectable man, he was thought to be very holy, and nobody thought he had ever committed any sin because he was such a virtuous man. And for forty years people had watched him – he was always in the public eye, he was always surrounded by people. When he was asleep, then too people were surrounding him, and nobody had seen that he had ever done anything wrong; he was continuously praying. But every morning he would beat himself, blood would flow from his body. Continually he was asked, "What wrong have you done? What sin? Let us know." But he would not say. Only when he was dying, he said, "Now I will have to say, because last night God appeared in my dream and he said, 'You are creating too much fuss about it. Forty years is enough! And I have to tell you this, otherwise I won't allow you in heaven. You have not done anything wrong.'" Just when he was young he had seen a beautiful woman pass and desire arose in him, just an urge to have this woman. That was the only sin that he had committed – just a thought – and for forty years he had been beating himself. Even God had to appear to him in a dream: "Please, now . . . because tomorrow you are going to die. I will not allow you in heaven if you continue this. You have not done anything much, but you are creating too much fuss about it. Don't be fussy."

All errors are just ordinary. What extraordinary sin can you commit? All the sins have been committed already. You cannot find a new sin – it is very difficult, it is almost impossible to be original about sin. For millions of years people have committed everything that can be committed. Can you find anything new? It is impossible – and what can you commit? Bertrand Russell used to say that the Christian God seems to be almost absurd, because the Christian God says that if you commit a sin you will be thrown into hell for eternity. Now this is too much! You can throw a man into hell for five years, ten years, twenty years, fifty years. If a man has lived for seventy years you can throw him there for seventy years. That means he was continually sinning for seventy years – not even a gap, not even a holiday. Then too you can throw him into hell for seventy years at the most. And Christians believe in only one life. It is good that they believe in one life, otherwise what would they do? For one life's sins they throw you in hell for eternity! Just think of Hindus – with so many lives, one eternity will not be enough.

Russell used to say, "I count my sins – those which I have committed and also those which I have not committed, only thought about – and I cannot conceive how, for these small things, I am going to be thrown into hell and tortured for eternity. Even a very, very stern judge cannot send me to jail for more than four years." And he was right. What errors can you commit? What errors have you committed? Don't call them sin, because the very word has become contaminated, it has a condemnation in it. Buddha simply calls them "misdemeanors", ungraceful acts. Beautiful is his term – ungraceful acts, acts in which you behaved in an ungraceful way. You became angry or you said something that was not graceful, or you did something that was not graceful – just misdemeanors. *minor wrong doing 的行为 轻罪*

THE BUDDHA SAID: *Chapter 6*

When an evil-doer, seeing you practice goodness, comes and
maliciously insults you, you should patiently endure it and not feel
angry with him. For the evil-doer is insulting himself by trying to
insult you.

Try to understand this sutra. It always happens that if you become good, you will find many people becoming angry at you because your very goodness creates guilt in them. They are not so good; your being good creates a comparison. It is very difficult for people to forgive a good person. They can always forgive a bad person, but it is very difficult for them to forgive a good person. Hence for centuries they remain angry against a Jesus, against a Socrates, against a Buddha. Why does it happen? You can watch in life.

I was once in a university, I was a teacher there, and one clerk – who was the best on the whole staff and a very sincere worker – told me, "I am in trouble. The whole staff is against me. They say, 'Why do you work so much? When we

are not working you are also not supposed to work. Just two hours is enough –
just go on moving files from here to there; there is no need . . .'" His table was
always clean, with no files piling up, and everybody else's tables were full of files.
Of course they were angry, because this man's presence created a comparison. If
this man can do it, why can't they?

A good man is never loved, because he creates comparison. A Jesus has to be
crucified, because if such innocence is possible, then why are you not so
innocent? It becomes a deep wound in your ego. You have to crush this man;
only by killing him will you be satisfied. You have to poison Socrates because this
man is so truthful. Why can't you be so truthful? Your lies are revealed by this
man's truth. This man's reality, authenticity, makes you feel all pseudo. This man
is dangerous. It is as if in a valley of blind people one man comes who has eyes.

H. G. Wells has a story that there was a valley of blind people somewhere in
South America, and once a traveler came who had eyes. All the blind people
gathered together and they thought that something must be wrong with this
man; it had never happened. They decided to operate on the traveler. Of course,
in a valley of blind people, if you have eyes something is wrong with you.

> Mulla Nasruddin is a hypochondriac. Once he came to me and told
> me, "There must be something wrong with my wife."
> I said, "What is wrong with your wife? She looks perfectly
> healthy."
> He said, "There must be something wrong. She never goes to the
> doctor."

He goes every day, regularly, religiously, and every doctor of the town is
annoyed by him. Now he is worried about his wife. There must be something
wrong with her because she never goes to any doctor.

If you live with unhealthy people, to be healthy is dangerous. If you live with
insane people, then to be sane is dangerous. If you live in a madhouse, even if
you are not mad at least pretend that you are mad; otherwise those mad people
will kill you.

BUDDHA SAYS:

> When an evil-doer, seeing you practice goodness, comes and
> maliciously insults you . . .

They will come and insult you. They cannot tolerate the idea that you can be
better than them. It is impossible for them to believe that anybody can surpass

them. Then the surpasser must be a pretender, then he must be a deceiver, then he must be trying just to create an image about himself, about his ego. They become restless. They start taking revenge.

When an evil-doer, seeing you practice goodness, comes and maliciously insults you, you should patiently endure it . . .

You should remain at your center, you should patiently endure it, you should simply watch it, what is happening. You should not get disturbed about it. If you get disturbed then that malicious person has defeated you. If you get disturbed then you are conquered. If you get disturbed then you have cooperated with him. Buddha says just keep quiet, endure it, remain patient, and don't feel angry with him . . . *for the evil-doer is insulting himself by trying to insult you.* He is insulting his own potentiality.

When we crucified Jesus, we crucified our own innocence. When we crucified Jesus, we crucified our own future. When we crucified Jesus, we killed our own divinity. He was nothing but a symbol that this is possible to you also, that whatsoever has happened to him can happen to you also.

When we poisoned Socrates we poisoned our whole being, we poisoned our whole history. He was nothing but the coming star, the herald of the future. He was saying, "This is your potentiality. What I am is just a messenger to tell you that you can also become like me."

Buddha says: *for the evil-doer is insulting himself by trying to insult you.* You remain patient, you endure it, don't get angry.

THE BUDDHA SAID:

Once a man came unto me and denounced me on account of my observing the way and practicing great loving kindness.

It looks absurd. Why should people go to somebody, who has done nothing wrong to them, to denounce him? Why should they go and denounce Buddha? He has not done anything wrong to anybody. He is in nobody's way – he has renounced all competitiveness. He is almost a dead person as far as the world is concerned. Why should people go out of their way to denounce him?

His very presence is insulting to them. The very possibility that a man can be so good hurts them. Then why are they not so good? It creates guilt. That's why down the centuries people go on writing that a man like Buddha never existed, that Jesus is a myth, that these are just wish-fulfillments. These people never existed, these are human desires, fantasies; they never really existed. Or even if they existed they were not like they are depicted; they are just illusions, dreams. Why? Even today people go on writing against Buddha, against Jesus. Still today something hurts. Twenty-five centuries have passed since this man walked, but still there are people who don't feel at ease with the man. If he existed really, historically, then they are condemned. They have to prove that this man never existed, it is just a myth. Then they are at ease.

Once they have proved that there has never been a Buddha, never a Jesus, never a Krishna, then they can rest. Then they can be whatsoever they are. Then there is no comparison, they are the last word in existence. Then they can remain as they are without any transformation. Then they can keep on doing whatever they are doing, they can go on doing rubbish and talking garbage, and they can go on being unconscious drunkards as they are. But if ever a man like Buddha walked on the earth – with such flame, with such glow, with such glory – they feel hurt.

> *Once a man came unto me and denounced me on account of my observing the way and practicing great loving kindness. But I kept silent and did not answer him.*

That's what I mean when I say get out of the triangle of PAC. Because if you answer you will react. You remain quiet, you simply remain at your center; don't be distracted. You just remain silent, serene, collected, calm.

> *But I kept silent and didn't answer him.*

That has to be understood. Because what is the point in answering such a man? He will not understand in the first place. In the second place the possibility is he will misunderstand.

Pontius Pilate asked Jesus at the last moment when he was going to be crucified, "What is truth?" and Jesus remained silent, he didn't say a single word. His whole life he was talking about truth, his whole life was sacrificed in the service of truth – at the last moment, why is he quiet? Why is he not answering? He knows that the answer is futile, it won't reach home. There is every possibility that it will be misunderstood.

Silence is his answer – and silence is more penetrating. If some disciple had asked him he would have answered, because a disciple is one who is ready to understand, who is receptive, who will take care of whatsoever is said to him, who will feed on it, who will digest it. The word will become flesh in him. But Pontius Pilate is not a disciple. He is not asking it in a deep, humble attitude, he is not ready to learn. He is just asking – maybe out of curiosity, or just joking, or just trying to make a laughing stock of this man. Jesus remained quiet, silence was his answer.

futile– useless, 無的, vain

*unperturbed –
not worried
鎮定的*

AND BUDDHA SAYS: Chapter 7

I kept silent and did not answer him. The denunciation ceased.

Because that silence must have surprised the man. An answer would have been okay, he could have understood. But silence he couldn't understand at all. He must have been shocked. He is denouncing and Buddha is simply quiet, silent. He is insulting and Buddha is unperturbed. If he was perturbed, if he was disturbed and distracted, then the man could have understood the language. That language he knew, but he did not know this totally unknown language of silence, of grace, of peace, of love, of compassion.

He must have felt embarrassed, he must have felt puzzled. He could not figure it out. He was at a loss. The denunciation ceased. What is the point of going on now? This man seems to be almost like a statue. He has not answered, he has not reacted. Chapter 7

I then asked him, "If you bring a present to your neighbor and he accepts it not, does the present come back to you?"

Rather than answering him, when the denunciation ceased Buddha asked him: Chapter 7

"If you bring a present to your neighbor and he accepts it not, does the present come back to you?" The man replied, "It will." I said, "You denounce me now, but as I accept it not, you must take the wrong deed back on your own person. It is like echo succeeding sound, it is like shadow following object. You never escape the effect of your own evil deeds. Be therefore mindful and cease from doing evil."

He has shown something without saying it. He asked the man, "If you bring a present to a neighbor . . ." he calls it a present ". . . and he accepts it not, what will you do?" Of course the man must have said, "I will take it back." He was persuaded, now he cannot turn back. Buddha said, "And you have brought a present to me – maybe of insults, denunciation – and I don't accept it. You can bring it, that is your freedom, but whether I will accept it or not is my freedom, it is my choice."

This is something beautiful to be understood. Somebody insults you – the insult is not yet meaningful unless you accept it. Unless you immediately take it, it is meaningless, it is noise, it has nothing to do with you. So in fact nobody can insult you unless you take it, unless you cooperate with it.

So whenever you were insulted, *you* felt insulted. It was you – it was your responsibility. Don't say that somebody else insulted you. Why did you accept it?

Nobody can force you to accept it. It is the other person's freedom to insult, it is your freedom whether to accept or not. If you accept, then it is your responsibility; then don't say that he insulted you. Simply say, "I accepted the insult." Simply say, "I was not aware; in unawareness I simply accepted it and then I became disturbed."

Buddha says, "Accept only that which you need. Accept only nourishment." Why accept poison? Somebody brings a cup full of poison and he wants to present it to you. You say, "Thank you sir, but I don't need it. If sometime I want to commit suicide I will come and ask, but right now I want to live." There is no need; just because somebody has brought poison to you there is no necessity that you should drink it. You can simply say, "Thank you." That's what Buddha did.

He says, "But as I accept it not, what are you going to do with it? You will have to take it back. I feel sorry for you. You will have to take it on yourself, it will fall on you . . . just as a shadow follows the object, or the echo succeeds the sound. Now it will follow you forever and ever. Your insult will be like a thorn in your being. Now it will haunt you. You have not done something against me, you have done something against yourself."

To be a help to this poor man who has done something wrong against himself, Buddha feels sorry, Buddha feels compassion. He says, "Be therefore mindful. Do only that which you would like to follow you. Do only that which will follow you and you will feel happy. Sing a song, so if the echoes come they will shower more songs on you."

In Matheran, a hill station just near Pune, I used to have many meditation camps. During the first camp I went to see a place, an echo point. A few friends were there with me. One started barking like a dog and the whole valley echoed as if many dogs were barking. I told the man, "Take a lesson – this is the whole situation of life: life is an echo point. If you bark like a dog, then the whole valley will echo and it will follow and haunt you. Why not sing a song?" He understood the point and he sang a song, and the whole valley showered, echoed.

It depends on you. Whatsoever you do with others, in fact you are doing with yourself, because from everywhere things will come back a thousandfold. If you shower flowers on others, flowers will come and shower on you. If you sow thorns in others' paths, the path is going to be yours. We cannot do anything to anybody else without doing it to ourselves in the first place. We can do something to somebody else only if he accepts it, and that is not decidedly so. Maybe he is a Buddha, a Jesus, and he simply sits silently. Then the deed falls on our own being.

BUDDHA SAYS:

> *Be therefore mindful . . . He must have spoken in deep compassion . . .*
> *and cease from doing evil . . . because you will suffer unnecessarily.*

Let me repeat one thing so that you can remember it.

You have three layers: the child, the parent, the adult – and you are none. You are neither the child nor the parent nor the adult. You are something beyond, you are something eternal, you are something far away from all these struggling, conflicting parts. Don't choose. Just be mindful and act out of your mindfulness. Then you will be spontaneous like a child, and without being childish.

And remember the difference between being like a child and being childish. They are two different things. If you act out of mindfulness you will be like a child and yet you will not be childish. If you act out of your mindfulness you will be following all the commandments without following them at all. If you act out of your mindfulness whatever you do will be reasonable. And to be reasonable is to be really rational.

And remember, reasonableness is different from rationality. Reasonableness is a very different thing, because reasonableness accepts irrationality also as part of life. Reason is monotonous, rationality is monotonous. Reasonableness accepts the polarity of things. A reasonable person has as much feeling as reasoning.

So if you act out of your innermost core, you will become tremendously content; contented, because all layers will be fulfilled. Your child will be fulfilled because you will be spontaneous. Your parent will not feel angry and guilty because naturally all that is good will be done by you, not as an outer discipline but as an inner awareness. You will follow the ten commandments of Moses without ever having heard about them; you will naturally follow them. That's where Moses got them – not on the mountain but on the inner peak. You will be following Lao Tzu and Jesus – and you may not even have heard about Lao Tzu and Jesus. That's where they got their childhood again, that's where they were born. And you will be following Manu and Mahavira and Mohammed, very naturally, and still you will not be irrational. Your mind will be in total support, with it. It will not be against your adult rationality. Your adult rationality will be totally convinced by it, your Bertrand Russell will be convinced by it.

Then all your three conflicting parts fall into one whole. You become a unity, you are together. Then those many voices disappear. Then you are no longer many, you are one. This one is the goal.

So, be therefore mindful.

Polarity – difference

Enough for today.

61

Chapter 4:

Living the Dhamma

Chapter 8

THE BUDDHA SAID:

> Evil-doers who denounce the wise resemble a person who spits against the sky. The spittle will never reach the sky but comes down on himself.
>
> Evil-doers again resemble a man who stirs up the dust against the wind. The dust is never raised without doing him injury.
>
> Thus the wise will never be hurt but the curse is sure to destroy the evil-doers themselves.

THE BUDDHA SAID: *Chapter 9*

> If you endeavor to embrace the way through much learning, the way will not be understood. If you observe the way with simplicity of heart great indeed is this way.

THE BUDDHA SAID: *Chapter 10*

> Those who rejoice in seeing others observe the way will obtain great blessing.
>
> A shramana *asked the Buddha: "Would this blessing ever be destroyed?"*

THE BUDDHA SAID:

> *It is like a lighted torch whose flame can be distributed to*
> *ever so many other torches which people may bring along.*
> *And therewith they will cook food and dispel darkness,*
> *while the original torch itself remains burning ever the*
> *same. It is even so with bliss of the way.*

The first sutra:

THE BUDDHA SAID:

> *Evil-doers who denounce the wise resemble a person who spits*
> *against the sky.*

The first thing to be understood is why in the evil person the very desire arises to spit against the sky, why in the first place the evil person wants to denounce the wise. The evil person cannot allow himself to accept that somebody is wise – the very idea hurts him, hurts him very deeply. All evil arises out of egoistic attitudes, and this is very shattering to the ego – "I am not wise and somebody else is wise. I am not good and somebody else is good. I am still in darkness and somebody has attained to light." This is impossible to accept.

Two ways open: one is "I should try to become wise" – that is very difficult and arduous. The simpler and cheaper way is to denounce the wise, to say that he is not wise. Whenever you are faced with a challenge these two alternatives always present themselves before you, and if you choose the cheaper one you will remain in the evil.

Never go for the cheap, never go for the shortcut, because life is learned only the hard way. Arduous are its ways, long and uphill is the task, because learning cannot come easily – learning is not just collecting knowledge, it is not just collecting information. Learning has to change you. It is spiritual surgery, much has to be destroyed and thrown away. Much is rotten in you and has to be renounced. Much is just like a rock around your neck; it won't allow you to float, it will drown you. You have to cut off relationships with many things, with many attitudes, with many prejudices. You have to unburden yourself.

Learning – real learning, wisdom – comes only when you are transformed. It is not an additive process – you cannot just go on adding knowledge to yourself. You will have to go through a transmutation and that is hard. The easier way is to denounce. Whenever you face the challenge – somebody has become wise – immediately the shortcut is to say, "No, it is not possible. In the first place wisdom never exists, in the second place, even if wisdom exists, it cannot exist in this man. I know him well, I know his faults." And then you start magnifying his faults, and you start condemning him.

It is not just a coincidence that Socrates is poisoned, Jesus is crucified, Mansoor is murdered. It is not just a coincidence that all the buddhas are denounced. When they walk on the earth they walk continuously in danger, because there are so many who feel their egos hurting. Just to think that somebody has become enlightened is difficult. It is easy to denounce and to say, "No, in the first place enlightenment is impossible – it never happens, it is just an illusion, it does not exist. It is nothing but auto-hypnosis. This man is deluded, he has not become enlightened. We know him well, we have known him from his very childhood. How can he suddenly become an enlightened person? He is just like us, but pretending. He is a pretender, a deceiver."

This is the ego choosing the cheaper way. Beware of it. The desire arises in everybody to condemn, to deny. So whenever a person like Buddha is alive we condemn him, and when he dies, we worship in guilt. All worship arises because of guilt. First you denounce a person, knowing well that something has happened, but you can't accept it. Deep down in your own self you can see that the person is transfigured, he has a luminosity. You cannot really deny it; in your deepest core of being you feel that a ray of light has entered. But consciously, deliberately, you cannot accept it. It will be accepting your failure. You doubt yourself, you certainly doubt deep inside whatsoever you are doing. You doubt your condemnation, but still you go on.

Then one day the person is gone, Then only the fragrance remains, the memory. And when a person dies and you have been not accepting his reality, guilt arises. You feel, "I was not good, I missed the opportunity." Then you start feeling remorse. Now what to do? To balance the guilt, you worship the person.

That's why dead masters are worshipped. Very rare are the people who worship an alive master, because when you worship an alive master it is not out of guilt, it is out of understanding. When you worship a dead master it is out of guilt.

For example your father is alive and you have not respected him, you have not loved him. You have been in many ways against him. In many ways you have dishonored him, in many ways you have rejected him. And then one day he dies, and you start crying and weeping. And then every year you will do something to honor his memory. You will put a portrait of your father in your house, and you will put flowers. This is out of guilt. You never did it when he was alive. You never honored him with flowers. Now he is gone you feel guilty – you have not been good to the old man. You have not done that which needed to be done. You have not fulfilled your love and your duty. Now the opportunity is gone, and the man is no longer there to forgive you. The man is no longer there so that you can cry and weep and fall at his feet and say, "I have been bad to you, forgive me." Now you feel, in a certain way, deep guilt. Remorse arises – you put flowers on his grave, you respect the memory. You never respected the alive man and now you respect the memory.

Remember, if you had really loved the man, if you had really respected the man, there would be no remorse. Then there would be no guilt. Then you would have been able to remember him with no guilt, and that remembrance has a beauty. That remembrance is totally different, it has a totally different quality. The difference is tremendous. In fact you would have felt fulfilled.

It is not death that you weep for; it is always guilt. If you loved a woman, if you really loved a woman and you never betrayed her, and you never deceived her, when she dies of course you feel sad but in that sadness there is a beauty. You miss her, but there is no guilt. You remember her, you will always remember, it will always remain a cherished memory, but you don't go out of your way to cry and weep and to make much show of it. You don't exhibit it, there is no exhibitionism in it. You will cherish the memory deep in your heart. You will not carry a picture in your pocket, and you will not talk about the woman.

I used to know a couple – the husband had been very bad to his wife. He was a sort of Don Juan, and he had been betraying his wife in every way possible. Then she committed suicide – she committed suicide because of him. I was passing through their town so I went to see the husband, because somebody said that he was very unhappy. Since the wife had died his life had taken a change. I could not believe it. I thought he should have been happy. It was always a miserable relationship, a continuous conflict was there. I went to see him. He was sitting in his drawing room surrounded by many pictures of his wife – all around, as if the wife had become a goddess. And he started crying. I said, "Stop this nonsense! – because you were never happy with this woman and she was never happy with you, that's why she committed suicide. That's what you always wanted. In fact you have told me many times that if this woman dies you will be free. Now she has done that."

He said, "But now I feel guilty, as if I have been the cause of her death, as if I have killed her. Now I am not going to ever get married."

This is guilt, it is ugly.

When a Buddha dies many people worship him. They were there when he was alive, but they never came to him. When a Mahavira dies, for centuries and centuries people go on worshipping. These people were there when Mahavira was alive, but now they feel guilty.

Jesus was crucified. At the last moment even his own disciples deserted him; there was nobody to say, "I am his follower." Even the last disciple ... when Jesus was caught, he said to him, "Don't follow me because you will not be able to do it now." He said, "I will come, Master. I will go wherever they are taking you." Jesus said, "Before the sun rises you will have denied me at least thrice. Don't do it, leave me." But he insisted.

Jesus was caught, the enemies took him and the disciple followed in the crowd. The crowd became aware that he was somebody who looked like a stranger, and they asked him, "Who are you? Are you a disciple of Jesus?" He said, "Who is this Jesus? I have never heard the name." And thrice, actually thrice before the sun rose, he denied knowing Jesus. And when it happened the third time, Jesus looked back and he said, "The sun has not yet come over the horizon."

Nobody else must have understood, but the disciple must have cried deep down over the fact that he has denied Christ – he has said he does not know this man, and that he is a stranger in town and is simply there out of curiosity. At the last moment even the disciples of Jesus disappeared. Then he was crucified. Then disciples gathered, then more disciples gathered, then more and more. Now almost a third of humanity is Christian.

This seems to be a tremendous guilt. Just think, if Jesus were not crucified – not crucified – there would have been no Christianity at all. It is not Jesus that has created Christianity, it is the cross. That's why the cross became the symbol of Christianity. I call Christianity "Cross-ianity", not Christianity. In fact it is the cross, it is the death that created the guilt. It created so much guilt ... and what to do when guilt arises? You can compensate only by worshipping the man.

When a master is alive you love him; your worship has love in it and your worship has no exhibition in it. It is a natural flow of your heart. But when a master is dead and you have been always denying him, then you worship him. Your worship has a fanaticism in it, an exhibition in it. You want to prove something. Against whom? Against your own attitudes.

I have heard:

> "You sure looked depressed," a fellow said to Mulla Nasruddin.
> "What is the trouble?"
>
> "Well," said the Mulla, "you remember my aunt who just died? I was the one who had her confined to the mental hospital for the last five years of her life. When she died, she left me all her money. Now I have got to prove that she was of sound mind when she made her will six weeks ago."

That's what happens. First you deny a wise man – you deny that he is wise. You deny that he is enlightened, you deny that he is good. Then when he dies he leaves his whole legacy for you, he becomes your heritage. Now suddenly things change, take a 180-degree turn. You were denying this man because he was hurting your ego and now suddenly you start worshipping him because now he becomes ego-fulfilling. The cause remains the same, whether you condemn or you worship.

Hindus destroyed Buddhism completely in India, but they accepted Buddha as their tenth avatar. Why? Because now it is okay to deny Buddhism, but how can you deny the heritage of Buddha? He was the greatest Indian ever. If you deny him your ego will fall short. Now with Buddha your ego shines like a star, a pole star. You cannot deny Buddha. Now you go on claiming him – that he was the wisest man, the greatest man ever. Now your own ego feeds on the name of Buddha. Now you want it to be *your* Buddha – it was your Buddha, now you say, who transformed the whole face of Asia. He is the light of the world. Of course you killed Buddhists, you destroyed the Buddhist scriptures, you denied everything – but you carry on the name of Buddha.

Just think, when India became free and they had to choose a symbol for the flag, they chose a Buddhist symbol. Is Hinduism lacking for symbols in any way? There are millions of beautiful symbols in Hinduism. Why have they chosen the Buddhist wheel for the flag? Because now Buddha is part of their heritage. Now they would like to brag: "Buddha was born here in India, in this religious country. He is ours." When he was alive you were throwing stones at him. Now you claim he is yours. When Buddha was alive, in every town he was condemned; wherever he was passing he was condemned. Now every town claims that "he has been here", that "he was born here", that "he died here", that "he stayed here in this house", that "for forty years he was coming here, twenty times he came to this place". Every town in Bihar has some kind of claim like this. When he was alive, the whole of Bihar condemned him. Now the very name "Bihar" exists because of him, because he walked there. "Bihar" means "where Buddha walks". Now the whole place is called Bihar. Now they go on claiming Buddha. Nehru brought his bones back to India. Nehru was not a religious person at all, not at all – why did he do this? Now the Indian ego can feel very fulfilled; Buddha has to be brought home. The Indian ego was condemning him, now the same ego goes on worshipping him. Remember it. Your ego always denies – watch it.

These sutras are for you, remember. They are not airy-fairy things, they are not theories. They are very empirical, pragmatic: Buddha was a very pragmatic man.

Just the other day it happened, Mulla Nasruddin came to see me – after yesterday's morning talk. He shook hands with me and said, "Wonderful, wonderful sermon. Everything you said applies to somebody or other I know." These sutras apply to you, not to somebody or other you know. If somebody says that "X" has become enlightened, what is your first reaction? Watch it. You say, "X? That fool. He has become enlightened? Impossible!" Just watch your first impression. Be alert to what happens in your mind. Immediately you will start talking about all the defects and faults that you know. And watch that you are also exaggerating.

Sometimes it happens that if somebody says to you that some person has become enlightened, he has become very wise, you will say, "That man? I know him well from his very childhood. I have seen him, I have watched him. Enlightenment doesn't happen in a day. It is a process. It is not possible." Or you find something irrelevant. Buddha used to say that once in a town a man said to his friend, "Have you heard about our neighbor? He is such a virtuous man." The other said, "How come? It is not possible, it is impossible. I live by his side, we have lived together – how can it happen without me knowing it before you knew it? We are neighbors and I know everything, in and out. It is just a pretension. He is pretending, who does he think he can deceive?"

It is very difficult to accept that somebody is wise, because in accepting that somebody is wise you are accepting that you are ignorant – that is the problem. It is not the question of the other being wise, the question is in relation to you. When you accept somebody as beautiful, you accept very reluctantly. Talk to a woman about how beautiful some other woman is and she becomes reluctant, she starts immediately condemning. Because to accept that another woman is beautiful is to accept that you are not so beautiful. A comparison immediately arises – ego exists through comparison.

In Zen there is a story about one man who was a beautiful flute player. Somebody was praising him in the tea house, saying that he was a beautiful flute player. Immediately another person started condemning him. He said, "He is a liar and a thief – how can he play a flute beautifully?" Now there is nothing contradictory about it. You can lie and still be a beautiful flute player. You can be a thief, still you can play the flute beautifully. There is no contradiction. But the other man simply said, "He cannot play beautifully. He is a thief, he is a liar . . ." and this and that. "I know him – he cannot play." And when people so condemnatory, shouting, their very forcefulness carries weight. The person who had been talking about the flute player was silenced. Then he was talking to somebody else the next day and he said, "That man is a thief." The other man said, "How can he be a thief? He plays the flute so beautifully." Now again there is no relationship between the two, but this second man has a totally different vision. This second man is open to grow, who says, "How can he be a thief? I know him – he plays the flute so beautifully. Such an aesthetic person cannot be a thief. Impossible! I cannot believe it." Whether that person is a thief or not is not the question, but these two reactions will decide many things for these two persons.

When somebody says, "there is a good person", watch. Don't start condemning, because when you condemn goodness you condemn your own future. If you go on condemning goodness and wisdom you will never become good and never become wise, because whatsoever you condemn cannot happen to you. You will become closed. Even if that person is not good, even if that person is not wise, it is not good to deny. Accept it. What are you losing in accepting it? The very acceptance that the person can be good and wise will help *you* to become good and wise. Your doors open, you are no longer closed. If that person can become good and wise, why not you? If you think that the person is ordinary, don't condemn them. Simply be happy, accept it as good news – "That ordinary person has become wise, so I also can become wise because I am also ordinary." Why make it a negative point? That's why Buddha says:

Evil-doers who denounce the wise resemble a person who spits against the sky.

You are spitting on your own face. When you spit against the sky, the sky is not going to be corrupted by you. You will be corrupted by your own spitting. The spit is going to fall on you. Your whole effort is absurd. The sky will remain the sky.

The wise man is like the sky. That too is very symbolic. Sky means pure space. Why this proverb that spitting against the sky is foolish? Why? – because the sky is not there. If the sky were there, your spit might corrupt it. You spit against the wall – it will not come back to you. You spit against the roof – if you are expert it might not come back. You can practice it. There is no necessity that it will come back, because the roof is there; it can be corrupted. That which *is* can be corrupted; that which *is not* cannot be corrupted.

The wise man is not, his ego has disappeared. He is not a substance, he is just pure space. You can pass through him, you can spit through him, and there is no hindrance. The spit will pass through him, he will not catch hold of it.

If you insult a wise man, your insult is not taken by him. It is as if, in an empty room, you are shouting insults. Yes, you will create a sound, that's all. When the sound has disappeared the room is again the same. The room will not carry your insult, the room is empty.

The wise man is empty like the sky. The saying must be Buddhist, because Buddha says that the wise man means no self, no ego. The wise man means one who is non-existential. He is not there, he is a pure presence, no material in him. You can pass through him. There will be no obstruction found in him, no hindrance found in him.

> *Evil-doers who denounce the wise resemble a person who spits against the sky. The spittle will never reach the sky . . .*

Not that the sky is very far away. No, the sky is very close, you are in the sky. But it cannot reach the sky because sky is such pure existence. It is simply space and nothing else. Everything comes and goes and the sky remains innocent.

How many wars have happened on the earth? – but you cannot find any bloodstains in the sky. How many people have lived on the earth? How many misdeeds have been committed, murders, suicides? – but the sky carries no record, not even a trace. The past simply does not exist. Clouds come and go and the sky remains the same. Nothing corrupts it. A wise man becomes so spacious that nothing corrupts him. You can only believe that you are insulting him; your insult will come back to you. The wise man is like a valley; your insult will be re-echoed. It will fall upon you.

> *The spittle will never reach the sky but comes down on himself.*

That too has to be understood. The wise man is higher than you, the wise man is like a peak, a Himalayan peak. You are standing in the darkness, in the valley, in ignorance. If you spit against the higher, the spit will fall back on you. It is against nature, it is against gravity. So if somebody is insulted by your insult you can be certain that he is lower than you. If somebody is not insulted by your insult you can be certain that he is higher than you, that your insult cannot reach him. Because insults follow gravity. They go to lower depths.

So if you are angry you can only infuriate an inferior person. A higher person simply remains beyond you. You can infuriate only a weaker person, the stronger person remains unaffected by you. Through insults, you can manipulate only lower beings; higher beings are far beyond.

> *Evil-doers again resemble a man who stirs the dust against the wind. The dust is never raised without doing him injury. Thus the wise will never be hurt but the curse is sure to destroy the evil-doers themselves.*

Remember it. We go on doing things that are against us. We go on doing things that are suicidal. We go on doing things that will destroy our future.

Each act that you are doing is in some way defining your future. Beware –
don't do anything that is going to do harm to you. And whenever you try to
harm somebody, you are doing harm to yourself. Whenever you try to inflict
some wound, whenever you want to hurt, you are creating karma for yourself.
You will be hurt by it.

It happened, once a man came and spat on Buddha – actually. Buddha
wiped his face and asked the man, "Sir, have you anything else to say?" The man
was puzzled, embarrassed. He was not expecting such a reaction. He was
thinking Buddha would be angry. He could not believe his own eyes. He was
dumb, he was in a daze.

Buddha's own disciple, Ananda, was sitting by his side. He became very, very
angry. He said to Buddha, "What is this? If you allow people to treat you this
way, life will become impossible. You just tell me and I will put him right." He
was a strong man, this Ananda. He was a warrior, he was a cousin to Buddha
and he himself was a prince. He was very angry. He said, "What nonsense! Just
give me a hint and I will put him right."

Buddha laughed and he said, "He has not surprised me, but you surprise me.
Why are you jumping into it? He has not done anything to you. As far as his
spitting on me is concerned, I know I have insulted him in some past life. The
accounts are closed today. I am happy."

"Thank you sir," he said to the man. "I was waiting for you because the
account has to be closed. I have insulted you somewhere. You may not
remember, but I remember it. You may not know, but I know it. You may have
forgotten because you are not very aware, but I have not forgotten. Today I am
happy you came and you finished the whole thing. Now we are freed from each
other."

"This is my own doing," he said to Ananda, "that has come back to me."

Of course when you spit against the sky, it takes a little time to come back. It
does not come instantly, it depends on many things – but everything comes
back. Whatsoever you do is sowing a seed: one day or other you will have to
harvest, one day or other you will have to reap it. If you are miserable today,
these are seeds which have flowered. These seeds you may have sowed
somewhere in your past – this life, another life, somewhere. Whatsoever you are
today is nothing but your accumulated past. Your whole past is your present.
Whatsoever you are going to be tomorrow will grow from whatsoever you are
doing today.

Nothing can be done about the past, but much can be done about the future.
And to change the future is to change all. If you start changing your ways of life,

your ways of awareness, if you start understanding the laws of life . . . this is one of the fundamental laws, the law of karma: whatsoever you do you will have to reap. Never forget it for a single moment. Because forgetting it has created so much misery for you. Remember it. Again and again your old patterns, old tendencies, will force you just by habit to do the old things. Remember – and drop out of old habits, drop out of mechanical reactions; become more conscious. A small awareness, and great changes start happening.

I have heard:

> It happened in Japan. Once a mother visited her son at college and was pained to see suggestive pictures on the walls of his room. She said nothing, but hung a picture of Buddha among the others. When she came again to see the boy the other pictures were gone, only the one of Buddha was left. The boy said, "Somehow I could not keep him there and those pictures too – so they had to go."

Just a small thing, just a small picture of Buddha, and all those pornographic pictures had to go. What happened? The boy started feeling uneasy. How to put Buddha there with all those pictures? By and by Buddha's presence was felt; the more and more aware he became, the more pictures disappeared. Just a small ray of light is enough to dispel all darkness. Just allow the first ray! If you start becoming aware in a small way – nothing to be worried – by and by you will see all other pictures have gone and only awareness has remained. Buddha means awareness, the very word "buddha" means awareness.

If you really want to be happy and blissful, to be eternally blissful, if you are fed up with all the miseries that you have lived through, then bring awareness to your reactions. And start trusting the good.

In English you have an expression "too good to be true". This expression is very dangerous. Too good to be true? Just because something is good, you disbelieve it and think it can't be true? Change it, let it be this way: "Too good to be untrue." Believe in goodness, believe in light, believe in a higher reality – because whatsoever you believe becomes an opening to you. If you don't believe that a higher being than you is possible, then it is finished, all growth is stopped.

Trusting the reality of a Buddha or a Mahavira or a Jesus, a Zarathustra, is nothing but opening yourself to the possibility of the very idea that higher beings than you have existed, walked, lived – higher beings are possible. It is not impossible to be a buddha – the very notion, and a ray of light enters in your being. And that light starts transforming you; your very chemistry changes. It has nothing to do with superstitions, it has nothing to do with theological beliefs. It is just an opening of the heart. If you don't trust, if you insist that roses don't exist, then even if someday you come across a rose bush, you will not believe it. You will say, "There must be some illusion, somebody is playing a trick, or I am hallucinating, dreaming, because roses can't exist."

In the first place if you don't believe in the existence of roses the very possibility is that you may come across them and not even look at them, because we look only at things we believe are possible. We go on passing by, indifferent.

I have heard:

> It happened in a hospital. A nurse put a screen round a male
> patient's bed, gave him a specimen bottle and said, "I will be back in
> ten minutes for your specimen." Then another nurse came and gave
> the man a glass of orange juice. The man, who was something of a
> wit, poured the orange juice into the specimen bottle. When the first
> nurse came back, she took a look and said, "This specimen is a little
> too cloudy."
>
> "So it is," agreed the patient. "I will run it through again and see if
> I can clean it up." And as he put the bottle to his lips – the nurse
> fainted.

Just your belief, just the very idea – what is this man doing? He was simply drinking orange juice. But once you believe a certain thing it becomes effective. Now the nurse thinks he is drinking his urine. It is only in her idea – but ideas are great realities, they change your outlook.

If you are looking for beauty you will find beauty. If you believe beauty does not exist, you may come across it but you will not look for it. You see only that which you are looking for.

Faith, trust, simply means this much – that we are not the ultimate, we are not the crescendo of existence; a higher reality is possible. To believe in a Jesus or a Buddha is simply to believe in your own future, that you can grow. To believe in Buddha is to believe in growth, that there is still something that can happen to you.

That's why in the past centuries people were never as bored as they are today – because now nothing more is possible. You are just in a rut. The more people become materialistic, the more they are bored. You cannot find more bored people than Americans. They have everything that man has been hankering for down the centuries and they are bored to death, because they have no future. And when there is no future there is no meaning.

You have a beautiful car, you have a beautiful house, you have a beautiful job – so what? The question arises: "So what? Where are you going? In a rut, moving in the same wheel again and again and again. The same morning, the same evening, the same work, the same money pouring in – what to do now?" Then people play small games just to pass the time, but they know that nothing is going to happen. That creates boredom.

Never in the history of human beings has man been so bored, because before there was always a possibility, there was an opening into the sky – you could have become a Buddha, you could have become a Jesus or a Krishna. You were always growing. You were not stuck on in a wheel; there was growth.

Suddenly, you are trapped in a wheel in this century. There is no God. Nietzsche says, "God is dead and man is free." Free for what? – to be bored! Free not to grow, free to rot, free just somehow to vegetate and die.

Freedom is meaningful only when it brings growth. Freedom means only that there is a possibility to grow – better flowers are possible in you. Your potentiality has yet a destiny – that brings meaning, that brings enthusiasm, that brings a thrill. Your life starts throbbing with meaning.

Remember more and more that you are the cause of your misery, and you can become the cause of your bliss. You are the cause of the hell you are living in, and you can create the heaven also. You alone are responsible and nobody else.

Never try to do harm to anybody because all will fall back on you. If you can do something good, do. If you can help somebody, help. If you can have some compassion, love, let it flow, because it will be coming back. In moments of need you will have something to depend upon, to fall upon. Love as much as you can, help, and don't be bothered whether the help is paying off right now or not. It pays, it pays tremendously. Don't be bothered about the time and the place – it pays. Someday, whenever you are in need, it rushes toward you. It goes on accumulating.

Mulla Nasruddin kept begging the tuba player to play. "Well, all right, since you insist," he said. "What shall I play?"

"Anything you like," said Nasruddin. "It is only to annoy the neighbors."

People go on doing things like that. They may not be enjoying it at all, but if it annoys the neighbors it is enough enjoyment for them. This is morbid, but this is how people are. People enjoy torturing, and then when they are tortured they cry and they say that life is very unjust and God is not just. Buddha says there is no God. He simply drops the possibility of God. So that you cannot throw the responsibility on anyone else he says there is a law, no God, and the law follows its own course. If you follow the law you will be happy, if you don't follow the law you will be unhappy. He drops the idea of God just to help you, because with a God the possibility remains that we can do something wrong and then we can cry and weep and pray and say, "I was a fool, but now God can save me." You cannot pray to a law, you cannot say to the law, "I was a fool." If you were a fool you have to suffer, because the law is not a person. It is absolutely indifferent, it simply follows its own course.

If you fall on the ground and your bones are broken and you have many fractures, you don't go and complain to the law of gravity, "Don't be so much against me. You could have at least given me a warning. Why did you get so angry?" No, you never complain about the law of gravity because you know if you follow rightly it is protective. Without the law of gravity you will not be here on the earth, you will be floating in the sky. The law of gravitation keeps you on the earth, it is your very root. Without it you will not be here. It allows you to walk, it allows you to be. If you do something wrong then you will suffer, but the law does not punish you and it does not reward you. It has nothing to do with you personally. You punish yourself, you reward yourself. Follow the law and you reward yourself. Don't follow the law, disobey the law and you are a victim, you suffer.

Buddha calls the law dhamma – that is his God. He takes personality out of it, because with personality man has created too much trouble. Then Jews think that they are the chosen people of God, so he is going to be a little lenient with them. This is nonsense. Christians think they are the chosen people of God because he sent "his only begotten son" to save them, so whoever follows Jesus will be saved. But that seems like nepotism – because you are related to Jesus and he is the son of God . . . You are related, therefore you are saved. This is nonsense.

Buddha takes all personality out of God. Then there is no need for anybody to understand Japanese, English, Hebrew, Sanskrit. Hindus say that Sanskrit is God's bona fide language – *devavani*, God's own language. All other languages are just human, Sanskrit is divine. And this same kind of foolishness exists all over the world. Buddha takes the very base out from under it. He says God is not a person, it is a law. Follow it, obey it, and you reward yourself. Don't follow it and you suffer.

Thus the wise will never be hurt but the curse is sure to destroy the evil-doers themselves.

So remember it as a fundamental rule that whatsoever you do to others you are really doing to yourself – whatsoever, I say, you do to others you are doing it to yourself. So watch out.

THE BUDDHA SAID:

If you endeavor to embrace the way through much learning, the way will not be understood. If you observe the way with simplicity of heart, great indeed is this way.

This way, this dhamma, this law, this ultimate law of life, cannot be understood by learning, by knowledge, by reading scriptures and memorizing philosophies. You have to live it to know it. The only way to know is to live it. The only way to know is existential, it is not intellectual.

I have heard a very famous anecdote:

> Years ago word spread through academic communities about a young scholar at a Talmudic college in Poland. He was hailed for his great learning and his concentration on his studies. Visitors came away deeply impressed by the young man. One day an outstanding Talmudic authority called and asked the head of the college about the young man. "Does this young man really know so much?"
>
> "Truly," answered the old rabbi with a smile, "I don't know. The young man studies so much that I cannot understand how he could find time to know."

If you are too engaged with your intellect, you will not find time to be engaged with your total being. If you are too much in your head you will miss much that is available. The way can be known only if you deeply participate with existence. It cannot be understood from the outside, you have to become a participant.

Just recently, a professor of psychology was here. He teaches in Chicago. He is an Indian, but lives in America. He had come for a visit – he has been writing for almost two years: "I am coming, I am coming." Then he came, and he wanted to know about meditation. For ten, twelve days he was here and he watched others meditating, and he said, "I am watching." But how can you watch meditation? You can meditate, that is the only way to know about it. You can see a meditator from the outside – you can see that he is dancing, or that he is standing silent, or that yes, he is sitting – but what are you going to know about it?

Meditation is not sitting, meditation is not dancing, meditation is not standing still. Meditation is something happening is the person's very being, deep inside. You cannot observe it, there cannot be any objective knowledge about it.

I told him, "If you really want to see – dance."

He said, "First I have to see, first I have to convince myself that it is something, only then will I do it."

I said, "If you stick to your condition you will never do it. Because the only way to know is to do it. And you say you will do it only when you have known it – then it is impossible. You are putting such an impossible condition that it will never happen."

It is as if somebody says, "I will love only when I have known what love is."

But how can you know love without loving? You can watch two lovers holding each other's hands, but that is not love. Even two enemies can hold hands. Even while two persons are holding hands they may not be in love, they may be just pretending. Even if you see two persons making love to each other, there may be no love. It may be something else; it may be just sex, no love. There is no way to know about love from the outside. There are things which are only allowed to be revealed to you when you become an insider.

BUDDHA SAYS:

> *If you endeavor to embrace the way through much learning, the way will not be understood.*

There are things that can be understood by learning – they are outside things, objective things. That is the difference between science and religion. Science needs no subjective experience. You can remain outside and watch; it is an objective approach towards truth. Religion is a subjective approach. You have to go in, withinwards; it is introspective. You have to dive deep within your own being. Only then can you know. Only from your own center will you be able to understand what the way is, what the dhamma is – or, call it what godliness is – but you will have to participate. You can know godliness only by becoming a god, there is no other way. You can know love only by becoming a lover. And if you think that it is too risky without knowing it first – and going into love *is* risky – then you will remain without love, you will remain a desert.

Yes, life is risk, and one should be courageous enough to take risks. One should not always be calculating. If you go on just calculating your whole life, you will miss all.

Take risks, be courageous. There is only one way to live and that is to live dangerously. And this is the danger – that one has to move without knowing, one has to move in the unknown. Hence, trust is needed.

BUDDHA SAYS:

> *If you endeavor to embrace the way through much learning, the way will not be understood.*

You can see it. You can look at scholars, great scholars, and somehow you will find they are missing. They may know much about the Veda, the Bible, the Koran; they can recite, but you can see there is no radiance in their eyes. Yes, there is much dust that they have gathered from scriptures, much smoke that they have gathered through knowledge. They are well informed – but almost dead. They have missed life somehow, they could not find time to know what life is.

I have heard:

> A great scholar and a clergyman stopped in a pet shop and asked the price of a parrot. The shopkeeper said he would not sell him that parrot because all it did was utter profanity. "But," said the shopkeeper, "I have another parrot coming in from South America. When I get it trained I will phone you to pick it up."
>
> Several months later the clergyman was told to stop by and see the parrot the storekeeper had for him. The shopkeeper ushered him into a back room where the parrot was perched with a string on each foot. The proprietor pulled the string on the right foot and the bird recited "The Lord's Prayer" from beginning to end.
>
> "This is wonderful and edifying!" exclaimed the scholarly preacher – that's what he himself had been doing his whole life. Then he pulled the string on the left foot and the parrot burst into "Nearer My God to Thee". "This is tremendous!" cried the preacher. "Now tell me, what would happen if I pulled both strings at the same time?" Before the shopkeeper could reply the parrot said, "You damned fool! I would fall on my ass!"

It is simple, even a parrot knows it, but a pundit, a preacher? He is worse than a parrot. He simply lives in ideas, he lives in logic, he lives a verbal life. He has forgotten real roses, he is only acquainted with the word "rose". He has forgotten real life, he only knows the word "life". Remember, the word "life" is not life, the word "love" is not love, the word "God" is not God. The real life is an existence, is an experience.

It happened:

> A recent graduate from agriculture school was making a governmental inspection of a farmer's land and stock. He told them he was making an appraisal so that the government could help the farmer get out of the red. So he inspected everything, making careful notes in his neat little notebook. When he thought he had everything listed he saw an animal stick its head around the side of a barn. "What is that thing? And what is it for?" asked the young man. It was an old goat, but the farmer was not going to help the all-wise young inspector. "You are the expert," said the farmer. "You tell me."
>
> Now it was very difficult. He had never seen such a thing. He had been learning in the university, he knew everything about

agriculture, but he had never done anything. He had no experience. He had never come across such an animal as a goat.

Consequently the young man sent off a wire to the capitol asking them to identify for him "a long, lean object with a bald head, chin whiskers, an empty lean stomach, a long sad face, and cadaverous eyes." The next day he got a reply from the secretary of agriculture: "You blithering idiot! That is the farmer!"

Remember, the head can be very disconnective; it can disconnect you from life. Use the head but don't be confined to it. Use your intellect to approach existence, don't make a barrier out of it.

If you endeavor to embrace the way through much learning, the way will not be understood. If you observe the way with simplicity of heart, great indeed is this way.

With simplicity of heart . . . Life can be known only with a simple heart. The head is very complex and life is very simple. It is difficult from a complex head to understand the simple life. Life is simply simple. You have also to be simple.

A child understands more. He has a rapport with life. A poet understands more. He has a rapport. A mystic understands more – tremendously deep and profound is his understanding because he puts his head completely away. He looks through the eyes of a child, he approaches with wonder, awe. He is surprised at every step. He has no ideas, no fixed ideas to project. He has no prejudices: he is neither a Hindu, nor a Mohammedan, nor a Christian. He simply is. He has a throbbing heart, a loving heart. That is enough requirement to know what life is.

Great then indeed is this way . . . known – known through the heart. Better to call it felt – felt through the heart. Life is very simple. Just sometimes put your head away, sometimes behead yourself, sometimes look with no clouds in the eyes – just look. Sometimes sit by the side of a tree – just feel. By the side of a waterfall – listen. Lie down on the beach and listen to the roar of the ocean, feel the sand, the coolness of it, or look at the stars and let that silence penetrate you. Or look at the dark night and let that velvety darkness surround you, envelop you, dissolve you. This is the way of the simple heart.

If you approach life through this simplicity you will become wise. You may not know the Veda, you may not know the Bible, you may not know the Gita, but you will come to know the real song of life – and that is where the real Gita is, the real song is. You may not know the Veda, but you will come to know the real Veda – that which is written by existence itself.

This life is a book, this life is a Bible, this life is a Koran. Recite it! Recite this life. Sing it, dance it, be in love with it – and by and by you will know what the way is, because by and by you will become more and more happy. The more happy you become, the more you are acquainted with the way, the right way. And whenever a step goes out of line, immediately you feel pain. Pain is an indication that you have missed the law, and happiness is an indication that you have been in harmony. Happiness is a by-product. If you go in accordance with the law you are happy. Unhappiness is an accident. It simply shows you have gone far away from the law.

Make happiness and unhappiness your criterion. That's why I go on saying that I am a hedonist. In fact Buddha is a hedonist, Mahavira is a hedonist, Krishna is a hedonist, Mohammed is a hedonist, because they all want you to become tremendously happy. And they show you the path.

The path is: become simple, trust more, doubt a little less. If you really want to doubt, doubt doubt, that's all. Doubt doubt; trust trust – and you will never miss.

Those who rejoice in seeing others observe the way will obtain great blessing.

And Buddha says not only those who follow the way are benefited, but even those who rejoice in seeing others following the way, they are tremendously blessed.

Yes, it is so. Because by rejoicing that so many people are moving towards meditation . . ."Good – I have not been moving yet, I have not yet gathered courage, but so many people are moving – good" . . . even this will make you happy because this will open your doors. You are not condemning them, you are not saying that meditation is impossible. You say, "It is possible – I am not yet courageous enough, but you are going on the way – go happily! My congratulations for you, my greetings! One day I hope also to come and follow you."

Buddha says if you greet a sannyasin you have greeted your future. If you see somebody moving on the path and you feel happy, tremendously happy – knowing well that you are not following on the path, you are not yet ready for it, but you don't condemn the man, in fact you rejoice, you help him to go on the path – then you have started following the path. That's what I said in the beginning: in life whenever you hear somebody has become a sannyasin, don't start condemning him – rejoice. When somebody has started meditating, don't condemn him that he has gone mad or something – rejoice. By your rejoicing you are bringing your own meditative possibilities closer to you. By rejoicing you have set foot on the path in a deeper way. Inside it has happened, outside it will come. That is not so important either.

THE BUDDHA SAID:

> Those who rejoice in seeing others observe the way will obtain great
> blessing.

That's why in India a sannyasin has always been respected tremendously. Even sometimes one who is just wearing an orange robe and is not a sannyasin at all – even he is respected, because who are we to decide whether he is a true sannyasin or not? Buddha says, "Rejoice!"

I have heard an old story:

> A man who was a great robber robbed the palace of the king, and by the time he was escaping it was known, so guards followed him. He was in tremendous danger. He came to the bank of a river and the horses of the soldiers were following and he could hear the noise that was approaching close, and the river was big and there was no bridge. He was afraid, and it was a cold night – so what to do?
>
> Seeing nothing, no possibility, he saw a sannyasin sitting under a tree. He threw off his clothes, became naked, closed his eyes, started meditating – of course, pretending, because he had never known what meditation is. But you can pretend, you can close your eyes, you can sit in the lotus posture. He closed his eyes. The guards came, the police arrived. There was nobody, just these two sannyasins. They touched their feet. The man inside started feeling very, very guilty. "This is not good," he thought. "I am a thief, a robber, and these people are touching my feet. And I am just a pseudo-sannyasin. And if so much respect is given to a pseudo-sannyasin, what will happen if I really become a sannyasin?" A ray of light entered into his life. He dropped his old ways, he became a sannyasin.
>
> His fame spread. One day even the king came to touch his feet. And the king asked him, "How did it happen to you? How did you renounce the world? I also hope, dream, that one day that great blessing will shower on me, God will give me courage to renounce everything. How did you renounce, sir? Tell me your story. That will give me courage."
>
> The ex-robber started laughing. He said, "I will tell you. You helped me much – your soldiers following me."

The king said, "What do you mean?" Then he told the whole story. He said, "And when I saw that a pseudo-sannyasin like me – a robber, a murderer – can be respected, suddenly it became impossible for me to go back to my old ways. And I felt so beautiful when they touched my feet. I had never felt that before. It was such a beautiful moment. And since then I have been meditating, and since then I have really renounced the world, and I am tremendously happy. I have arrived home."

Buddha says even those who rejoice seeing others observe the law . . . Never condemn, even if sometimes it is possible . . . and it is always possible. When there are real coins, there are bound to be counterfeit coins also. When so much respect is given to sannyasins, there are bound to be people who will be deceiving. But that is not the point. What can they deceive? What can they cheat? What have you got? But rejoice.

A shramana *asked the Buddha: "Will this blessing ever be destroyed?"*

Will it be just a temporary thing if we rejoice in others being in meditation? The *shramana* has heard, he knows that if you meditate you attain to eternal bliss. But just by rejoicing because others are reaching . . . *Will this blessing ever be destroyed?*

THE BUDDHA SAID:

It is like a lighted torch whose flame can be distributed to ever so
   many other torches which people may bring along. And therewith
   they will cook food and dispel darkness, while the original torch
   itself remains burning ever the same. It is even so with the bliss of
   the way.

Buddha is saying those who follow the way, they become blissful, but even those who simply rejoice seeing so many people following the way, they also become blissful. And not only temporarily, not only momentarily – their bliss is also eternal. In fact, by their very rejoicing they have become fellow travelers. Deep inside they have gone on the journey; the outside will follow – that is not the basic point.

But when you condemn those who are following the path, when you condemn those who are meditating, when you condemn those who are somehow trying to feel and grope in the dark for the way, you are condemning yourself. You are cursing yourself. Your doors will be closed, your potentiality will remain a potentiality, will never be actualized.

You are like a seed, and if somebody has flowered and bloomed, rejoice! In that very rejoicing you will start sprouting. Don't say that there are no flowers because they have not happened to you. If you say there are no flowers because they have not happened to you so how can they happen to anybody else . . .

Friedrich Nietzsche says the same thing. He says, "How can there be any God? If there is any God then I am God. If I am not a God, there cannot be any God. How can I tolerate the idea that somebody else is a God? Impossible, I cannot allow this idea." He says, "God is dead, God does not exist." But then man is left in limbo. Then there is no way to go up. Then you can go on growing old, but you never grow up, you never become a grown-up. Remember it! Growing old is not growing up. Growing up means exactly what it says – growing up, growing upwards. Growing old is horizontal, growing up is vertical. Growing up means growing up like a tree. Growing old is like a river – it remains horizontal, it does not change its level, it doesn't change its plane.

If somebody else is growing up, rejoice, celebrate. At least one human being has become a buddha. Good – he has shown the path. In fact, in him all human beings have become buddhas in essence, because whatsoever can happen to one human being can happen to every other human being. We may not become buddhas for lives together, but that doesn't matter. One man has become a buddha – he has shown the possibility. Maybe we have to wait long, but we can wait because the morning is coming closer. It has to come; it has come to one person, it will come to us also. It is dark and the night is very long, but now there is hope.

Rejoicing with a buddha is creating hope for yourself. Then your life is no longer hopeless. A hopeless life is a bored life, and a hopeful life, the very possibility . . . maybe it will happen after many, many lives; that doesn't matter, one can wait – but one can wait with hope.

It is like a lighted torch whose flame can be distributed to ever so many other torches which people may bring along. And therewith they will cook food and dispel darkness while the original torch itself remains burning ever the same. It is even so with bliss of the way.

Enough for today.

The Truth Beyond Magic

Chapter 11

THE BUDDHA SAID:

It is better to feed one good man than to feed one hundred bad men.

It is better to feed one who observes the five precepts of Buddha than to feed one thousand good men.

It is better to feed one srotapanna *than to feed ten thousand of those who observe the five precepts of buddha.*

It is better to feed one skridagamin *than to feed one million of* srotapannas.

It is better to feed one anagamin *than to feed ten millions of* skridagamins.

It is better to feed one arhat than to feed one hundred millions of anagamins.

It is better to feed one pratyak buddha *than to feed one billion of arhats.*

It is better to feed one of the buddhas either of the present or of the past or of the future than to feed ten billions of pratyak *buddhas.*

It is better to feed one who is above knowledge, one-sidedness, discipline, and enlightenment than to feed one hundred billions of buddhas of past, present or future.

Let us first talk a little about the disease called man. Man is a disease because deep down the very being of man is split, it is not one. Hence continuous disease, uneasiness, anxiety, angst, anguish. Schizophrenia is just a normal state of affairs. It is not that a few people become schizophrenic, man is born schizophrenic. It has to be understood.

Man is born in dis-ease, born as dis-ease. When you entered your mother's womb, the first moment of your life was based on two parents, the mother and the father. Your very beginning was dual, divided – male/female, yin/yang, positive/negative. The first unity of your being was already based on division. Half of you came from one parent, the other half from another parent. From the very beginning you have been two.

So schizophrenia is not something that happens to a few unfortunate people, it is just the normal state of affairs. Man is born split, hence continuously there is a duality, an indecisiveness, a wavering. You cannot decide who you really want to be, you cannot decide where to go, you cannot choose between two alternatives, you remain ambiguous. Whatsoever you do, a part of you remains against it. Your doing is never total. And a doing that is not total cannot be fulfilling; a doing that is chosen only by one part of your being against the other part, will create a greater and greater rift in your being. This has to be understood.

Unity is in the end, not in the beginning. You can become a unitary being, you can become non-dual, you can come to yoga – yoga means unity, unison, integration, individuation – but that is in the end, not in the beginning. In the beginning is the dual, in the beginning is the division, in the beginning is disease.

So unless you understand it and make an effort to transform it . . . The merger has not yet happened; it has happened on one level only – on the level of the body. On the level of the body you have become one, your mother and your father have melted – on the plane of the body. You have become one body. Out of two bodies a new unity has arisen, but it is only of the body, in the body, not deeper than the body. Deep in your mind you are split. And if you are split in your mind there is no way to go beyond the mind. Only a mind that has become a unity, integrated, one, becomes capable of going beyond.

This sutra of Buddha is tremendously significant. A very simple sutra, but don't take it literally. Of course literally also it is true, but it is the whole progression – how to become one, how to dissolve the twoness on all levels of your being, from the most gross to the most subtle, from the circumference to the center . . . how to drop all duality and come to a point where suddenly you are one. That point is the goal of all seekers, because once you have become one, your misery disappears.

Chaos — Disorder
混乱 混乱

（handwritten annotation）

Misery is because of the conflict. Misery is because your house is divided, misery is because you are not one, you are a crowd – a thousand and one voices inside you pulling you and pushing you in all sorts of ways and all directions. You are a mess, a chaos. It is a miracle how you manage not to go mad, because you are boiling with madness. It is a miracle how somehow you go on remaining sane, how you are not lost in this crowd. But whether lost or not, you are sitting on a volcano which can erupt any moment.

Remember this: madness is not something that happens to a few unfortunate people, madness is something everybody is prone to. Madness is something you are carrying within you like a seed – it can sprout any moment; it is only waiting for the right season, the right climate, the right opportunity. Any small thing can trigger it and you will simply go berserk. You are berserk because your foundation is split. It is possible to become one, but then one has to be very aware about this whole situation.

I have heard:

> Mulla Nasruddin went to his psychiatrist and asked if the good doctor could not split his personality.
> "Split your personality?" asked the doctor. "Why in heaven's name do you want me to do a thing like that?"
> "Because," said Mulla Nasruddin, "I feel so lonesome!"

Don't just laugh at it. Maybe that's why you never work hard to become a unity, because this duality gives you a certain company. You can talk with yourself, you can have a dialogue – everybody is having a dialogue, continuously. Sitting in your chair, what are you doing when you close your eyes? The continuous dialogue is there. You question and you answer, from this side, from that side. Watch this dialogue. If this dialogue stops will you not feel lonesome? Will you not feel very alone, will you not feel very empty if this dialogue stops? Will you not suddenly feel that all noise has disappeared? Will you not become frightened that there is only silence?

No, you go on feeding this dialogue. You go on helping this dialogue to be there. Either you are talking with others, or if it is not possible, because others are not always available, then you are talking with yourself. While you are awake you are talking with others, while you are asleep you are talking with yourself.

What is your dream? A drama that you enact inside your being to create a society, because you are so lonesome. In the dream you are the director, you are the story writer, you are the actor, you are the screen and you are the audience – you alone, but you create a beautiful drama. The whole day and the whole night what are you doing? Talking with yourself! This constant talking, this constant dialogue with yourself – is it not boring?

Yes, you are bored, you are bored with yourself, but still you have chosen the lesser evil – you think that if this dialogue stops you will be even more bored. At least there is something to say, something to do inside. Left alone with no dialogue you will be simply lost. This dialogue keeps you a little alive, throbbing with life. Mulla is right. He says, "I am feeling so lonesome."

Remember, the whole effort of the spiritual path is to help you to become alone, because only when you are ready to become alone, when you are ready to fall into inner silence, when you are no longer clinging to this constant inner talk, then only can you become a unity. Because this constant inner talk helps you to remain dual, divided.

Just the other night a friend came to me and he said that in the night sometimes he falls from his bed and only in the morning he becomes aware of it. And one day it happened that he found himself ten feet away from his bed. So what is happening? Now he must be getting into deep dreams, nightmares, and the dreams must be so deep that even if he falls from his bed...he found himself ten feet away from the bed – that means the slumber must be like a coma. I asked him one thing: "Do you talk too much in the day?" He said, "No." Then that explains it. There are two types of people: talkers and listeners, T-people and L-people. Talkers talk the whole day, then in the night they have to listen; then they go to listen to a religious discourse or something – they go to the church in the dream, to the priest. The whole day they have been talking – one has to compensate – they listen in their dreams. People who have to listen during their day, who have become listeners, talk in the night. They shout, they say the things they always wanted to say but could not manage in the day – nobody was ready to listen to them.

It happens to people that when they go to a psychoanalyst and the psychoanalyst listens to them, patiently, attentively – of course he has to listen because he is paid for it – their dreams start changing. Their talking in their dreams by and by subsides, the quality of the dream changes, because now they have found somebody who listens to them – they have become the talker and they have found a party who listens attentively. Their dreams become more silent, they are not talking and shouting in the night. Their nights are more silent, more at ease.

Remember, whatsoever you miss in the day you will do in your dreams. The dream is complementary, it compensates and completes whatsoever has remained incomplete in the day. If you are a beggar in the day, in the night you will dream that you are an emperor. If you are an emperor during the day, in the night you will dream that you have become a buddha, a beggar.

That's how it happened. Buddha was born in an emperor's palace but he started dreaming about becoming a beggar. When after twelve years he came back home, enlightened, his father said, "Stop all this nonsense! You are my only son. Come back, I'm waiting for you. This whole kingdom is yours. And in our family there has never been a beggar."

Buddha laughed and he said, "Maybe, sir, in your family there has never been a beggar, but as far as I am concerned, I have been dreaming for many lives of becoming a beggar." When you become very rich you start thinking that poor people must be living in tremendous beauty, relaxedness. When you live in a city, a megalopolis like Bombay or Tokyo or New York, you think villages are beautiful. Ask the villagers – they are hankering to move to Bombay, to Tokyo, to New York. They dream. When you are poor you dream about the rich, when you are rich you dream about the poor.

Watch your dreams: they will show you that something that is lacking in the day is being fulfilled. In the day you are one part of your polarity, in the night you become another part of your polarity. You are two. So not only does a dialogue continue within you in your dreaming, but in your moments of being awake there is also a dialogue. If you are a bad man while awake, you will become a saint while you are asleep. If you are a saint while awake, you will become a sinner while you are asleep. That's why your so-called saints are so much afraid of sleep, they go on reducing their sleep – because the whole day somehow they manage to remain saints, but what to do about the night? The whole day they have been celibate, they have not looked at any woman's face, they have avoided life – but what to do in the night? All those faces they have avoided, but could not avoid, surface in their being. Beautiful women, more beautiful than they have ever seen in the daytime, erupt. They think that it is Indra, the God of heaven, who is sending *apsaras,* divine temptresses to destroy them. Nobody is sending any *apsaras*, nobody is interested in these poor fellows. Why should Indra be interested? For what?

No, this is compensatory. In the day they control their saintliness. In the night when they relax – and they have to relax, they have to rest – and when they rest, everything is relaxed; their control is also relaxed. Suddenly all that they have been repressing comes up.

Your day and your night are in constant dialogue. Psychoanalysts say that watching your day life is not as significant as watching your dream life, because in the day life you are pretenders, hypocrites. You go on showing faces which are not true. In the dream you are more real; you are no longer hypocrites, no longer pretenders, you don't have any mask. That's why all the psychoanalysts try to analyze your dreams. This is ironic but it is true that your dream life is truer than

hypocrites – 偽君子

your daytime life, that while you are asleep you are more authentic than when you are awake. This is unfortunate but this is so. Man has become so deceptive.

What I'm saying to you is this: unless you become a unity this will continue. In the day you can control, you can become a good person. In the night you will become a bad person, you will become a criminal in your dreams. You will do the same things that you have been controlling the whole day, exactly the same things. If you have fasted in the day, you will feast in your dream. Your denied part will take its revenge. And you cannot go both ways together. That's the disease called man, that's the angst, the anguish of man – you cannot go both ways. You cannot be good and bad together, you cannot be saint and sinner together, that is the difficulty. You have to choose. And once you choose, you are torn apart, you are in a dilemma, you are on the horns of a dilemma. The moment you choose, difficulty arises.

That's why many people choose not to choose; they live a life of drifting – whatsoever happens, happens. They don't choose, because the moment they choose, this creates anxiety.

Have you watched, observed, that whenever you have to make a decision you become very, very anxious? Maybe it is a very ordinary decision. You are purchasing a pair of shoes and you cannot decide which pair, and anxiety arises. Now it is rubbish – but still anxiety arises.

Anxiety has nothing to do with great decisions, anxiety has something to do with decision as such. Because you are two, whenever you decide, both parts try to dominate. Your mother tries to dominate, your father tries to dominate. And of course you know well they never agreed about anything, and they don't agree within you either. Your mother says this pair is good. Your father says don't listen to her, she is foolish; this pair is right. Your male energy says one thing, your female energy says another thing. Your female energy has different attitudes; it looks at the beauty of the pair of shoes, the shape, the form, the color, aesthetics. The male energy has a different attitude. It looks at the durability of the shoe, the price, the power – whether the shoe has a powerful shape so when you go walking on the streets your male ego is exhibited through it.

Each thing that the male ego chooses has to be somehow a phallic symbol. The male ego chooses a car with great speed – a phallic symbol, forceful. You will always find impotent people sitting in great phallic cars – impotent people. The more impotent they become, the more powerful a car they choose. They have to compensate.

The male ego always chooses that which will fulfill the male ego: "I am powerful" – that is the basic consideration. The feminine ego chooses something that gives another sort of power – "I am beautiful." Hence they never agree. If your mother purchases something, your father is bound to disagree with it. They are not made to agree, their visions are different.

It happened:

> Mulla Nasruddin tried many girls, but his mother would reject them all. So he came to me. He said, "Sir, help me. Whomsoever I choose, my mother is so dominating and so aggressive and she immediately rejects. I am tired. Am I going to remain a bachelor my whole life?"
>
> I told him, "You do one thing. You choose a woman considering your mother's likes and dislikes. Only then will she approve."
>
> Finally he found one woman. He was very happy, he said, "She walks like my mother, she wears clothes like my mother, chooses the same colors, cooks the food the same way. I hope she will like her."
>
> I said, "You go." And the mother liked the girl, she liked her tremendously and Mulla came to see me but he was very sad. I said, "Why are you sad?"
>
> He said, "It seems I am going to remain a bachelor for my whole life."
>
> I said, "What happened? Your mother didn't like her?"
>
> He said, "She liked her, she liked her tremendously – but my father? He rejects her. Now it is impossible! My father says, 'She is just like your mother. One is enough! And I'm fed up. Don't you get into the same trouble! What are you doing? Again the same mistake?'"

These two polarities in you are the basis of your anxiety, and the whole effort of a buddha, of a master, is to help you to go beyond this duality.

It is said about Chuang Tzu that he dreamed one night that he had become a butterfly, moving from one flower to another in the garden. In the morning when he awoke he was very puzzled. He was a great teacher, a great master, one of the greatest buddhas ever born on the earth. His disciples gathered and they looked at him, and he was very sad. They said, "Master, you have never been sad. What has happened?"

He said, "There is a problem to be solved by you, and the problem is that I, Chuang Tzu, dreamed in the night that I had become a butterfly."

They laughed, they said, "Now the dream is gone, you are awake, why bother about it?"

Chuang Tzu said, "Listen to the whole thing. Now, a problem has arisen: if Chuang Tzu can dream, and in dream can become a butterfly, why can't it happen the other way round? A butterfly can go to sleep and dream that she has become a Chuang Tzu. Now, who is who? Whether Chuang Tzu dreamed that he had become a butterfly, or the butterfly is dreaming that she has become a Chuang Tzu – this is the problem that is making me very sad."

It is said that no one from his disciples could solve this conundrum, this koan. How to solve it? How to decide who is who? But if there had been somebody deeply meditative, he would have answered. In fact, Chuang Tzu has posed the question just to know whether somebody has really become meditative among his disciples. Because then neither the butterfly is true, nor Chuang Tzu is true, but the one who is puzzled – the one who watched Chuang Tzu becoming a butterfly and who watched the butterfly becoming Chuang Tzu – that watchfulness, that awareness, that witness is the only reality. This is the meaning of the concept of maya – that all that you see is unreal; only the seer is real. Go on moving towards the seer, otherwise you live in a magical world. You can change from one magic world to another . . .

Man lives in lies; people call their lies their philosophies. Freud has said somewhere, a very penetrating insight, that man cannot live without lies. As humankind is, Freud seems to be right. We cannot live without lies. Without lies it is difficult, because then you will need courage. Your lies make life smooth, they function like lubrication, they help you move more easily. Somebody believes in a God, that makes life a little smoother. You can throw your responsibility on somebody. Somebody believes that there is a world beyond. Maybe here we are miserable but there, paradise is waiting for us, ready to welcome us. It helps.

Marx has said that religion is the opium of the people. Yes, he is also right in a way. All hopes are lies, all expectations of the future are lies. Yes, religion can be an opium, but so can communism – anything that gives hope for the future, in this world or in another world; anything that helps you to sacrifice your present for something that may happen, may not happen; anything that gives you a feeling of meaning; anything that gives you a feeling that you are a hero, anything that helps to feed your ego.

Once the Maharani of Gwalior invited me to Gwalior for a series of talks. After she heard the first talk she was very much disturbed; she had a very Hinduistic mind, a very dogmatic mind – orthodox, old-fashioned. She was very much disturbed. She came to see me in the afternoon and she said, "Sir, what you say is appealing but it is dangerous. And I have come with one request: please don't destroy people's faith."

I told her, "If a faith can be destroyed, it is not worth much. If a faith can be destroyed, it must be a faith in lies. A faith that is really a faith in truth is never afraid of being destroyed; it cannot be destroyed because truth cannot be destroyed."

Hindus are afraid, Christians are afraid, Mohammedans are afraid, Jainas are afraid, everybody is afraid – don't destroy our faith! In their faith they are just hiding their lies, their magic worlds, their dreams, their expectations. They are very touchy. If you just poke into their ribs their faith is skin-deep, not even that. They immediately become irritated because their faith is not anything deep in their heart, it is just a belief in the mind.

The Maharani of Gwalior said to me, "My son is very interested. Listening to you, he became fascinated – but I prevented him from coming with me to see you. I have not brought him to you – you are dangerous and he is young, and he can become too impressed by you. So I have not brought him at all."

What is this fear? Are you clinging to lies? Only lies are afraid of being broken, only lies need protection. Truth in itself is self-evident. So if you have some faith which is just a lie, it makes you secure, I know. It helps to adjust with the world, I know – but it is not going to help you ultimately. Sooner or later you will be awakened out of your dreaming and you will see your whole life has been a wastage.

There is no need to cling to anything outside, because it is not yet in any way possible for you to decide what is true and what is false outside. Right now it will be better that you just move inwards to it and forget all about the outside. Don't be bothered about Hinduism, Christianity, Mohammedanism; don't be bothered about Vedas and Gitas and Korans. Just go in and let one thing be your goal: to know who is this consciousness, what is this consciousness, who I am.

This sutra is a gradual indication of the inner journey. Listen to it.

THE BUDDHA SAID:

It is better to feed one good man than to feed one hundred bad men.

Who is a bad man and who is a good man? What is the definition? The bad man is one who is inconsiderate of others. The bad man is one who uses others and has no respect for others. The bad man is one who thinks he is the center of the world and everybody is just to be used. Everything exists for him. The bad man is one who thinks that other persons are just means for his gratification. Keep this definition in mind, because you ordinarily think the bad man is the criminal. The bad man may not be the criminal; all bad men are not criminals. All criminals are bad, but not all bad men are criminals. A few of them are judges, a few of them are very respectable people, a few of them are politicians, presidents and prime ministers. A few of them are even parading as saints.

So when we are talking about this sutra, remember the definition of a bad man – Buddha says a bad man is one who has no consideration for others. He simply thinks only about himself – he thinks he is the center of existence and feels the whole existence is made for him. He feels authorized to sacrifice everybody for his own self. He may not be bad ordinarily, but if this is the attitude then he is a bad man.

Who is a good man? Just the opposite of the bad man: one who is considerate of others, who gives as much respect to others as he gives to himself. One who does not pretend in any way that he is the center of the world, but who has come to feel that everybody is the center of the world. The world is one, but millions of centers exist. He is very respectful. He never uses the other as a means; the other is an end in himself or herself. The good person's reverence is tremendous.

Watch, watch your own life. Are you using your wife just for your sexuality? You may not go to a prostitute. Ordinarily you think that a person who goes to a prostitute is bad, but that is a very gross definition. If you are using your wife just as a sexual object, you are as bad as anybody else. The only difference between you and the person who goes to a prostitute is that you have a permanent prostitute, your marriage is a permanent arrangement and the other man makes arrangements day by day. You have a car in your garage and he uses a taxi.

If you don't respect your wife, then your wife is a prostitute – if you don't respect her as a person in her own right. What does it mean? It means if she is not feeling in the mood to make love, you will not force her; you will not say, "I am your husband and I have the right, legal right. . . " No, you will respect her. You will respect her intention. Good if you both agree – if the other is not agreeing, you will not coerce the other in any way. You will not quote scriptures saying that a wife has to sacrifice to the husband, you will not say that a wife has to treat the husband as if he is a god. All this is nonsense, all this is a male-oriented trip.

If a wife is using her husband only as an economic support, as financial security, then it is prostitution. Why do you condemn a prostitute? Because she sells her body for money. But if a wife just thinks to make love to the husband because he has money, and with him there is security and the future is not uncertain, if she goes on staying with him and sleeps with him with no love in her heart, then she is prostituting herself. Then, in her mind, the husband is nothing but his money, his bank balance.

When Buddha talks about who a good man is, he defines the good man as one who respects the other as much as he respects himself. Jesus says, "Love the other as you love yourself" – that is the definition of a good man. His respect is tremendous, his reverence is tremendous. Even if a child is born in your house, you don't enforce your ideology on the child. You may be a Mohammedan, you may be a Hindu, a Christian. A child is born in your home but you don't force the child to become a Hindu or Christian or Mohammedan. If you force the child, you are not respectful towards the child. You are just using an opportunity – the child is helpless, and has to depend on you. He has to follow you. If you take him to the temple or to the church he has to come, because it is necessary for his survival to say yes to you no matter what you say. If you are using this opportunity then you are exploiting a helpless child. Maybe it is your child, but you are exploiting.

If the world consists of good people, children will be totally free, not forced into any religion. There will not be Christians and Hindus and Mohammedans in the world; there will be only good people, growing people, and they will choose wherever they feel their heart fits. Maybe it is a temple, or it is a church or a mosque or a gurdwara. They will choose their religion, that is their freedom. They will choose their life, that is their freedom. You don't enforce anything. You love your child but you don't give your knowledge to him. You love your child but you don't poison his being with your ambitions. You love the child but you don't possess him. You help the child not to grow according to you, but to grow according to his being, to be himself. Then you are a good person.

It is better to feed one good man than to feed one hundred bad men . . . because if you feed bad men you feed badness; if you feed good men you feed goodness. Help the world to become better. Don't leave the world just the same as you have found it – make it a little better, make it a little more beautiful. Let there be a few more songs, a few more celebrations. Let there be a few less wars, a few less politicians. Let there be more love, less hatred. That is the meaning when Buddha says feed one good man – that is better, far better, than feeding one hundred bad men.

It is better to feed one who observes the five precepts of Buddha than to feed one thousand good men.

Now who is this whom Buddha calls "one who follows the five precepts of Buddha"? The five precepts are: no possessiveness, no theft, no violence, no untruth, no sexuality. One who follows these five precepts of the Buddha, he is not just good – he is not just good to others, he is not just moral – he is starting to be religious. That is the difference between the good man and the religious man. The good man lives through intellect. He thinks, contemplates, he tries to find ways through thinking, and he comes to feel, "As I have the right to exist, others also have the right to exist; as I would like to be free, and others also like freedom." This is his considered opinion. He thinks about it. He is not religious; he is a very intelligent man. A Bertrand Russell is a good man, a moral man, but he is not religious. Whatever he comes to think is good, he will do. But goodness comes out of logic, as a syllogism – it is a conclusion of thinking.

The religious person is not only good through thinking, but starts being good by *being*. He starts to grow into meditativeness. The religious person follows these five precepts.

They are all negative: no theft, no untruth, no sexuality, no violence, no possessiveness. The religious man is negative because he himself has not yet experienced what truth is. He has come to feel the truth through somebody else: he follows the Buddha, he lives close to a master, he has seen somebody becoming a flame, he has watched it happen somewhere but it has not happened in himself. He is attracted, he is convinced of the truth of it, but still it is from the outside – he is a follower.

THAT'S WHY BUDDHA SAYS:

> *It is better to feed one who observes the five precepts of Buddha than to feed one thousand good men.*

His approach is still negative, because the positive truth can be attained only by you. Somebody else may have attained, and watching that person, being in deep rapport, you may feel that yes, there is truth – but that remains outside of it, it is not your experience. You are thirsty and you see somebody who is coming from the river, his thirst is gone. You can see from his face, from the glow in his eyes, that his thirst is quenched. You can feel that he must have found a source of water, and you can follow him towards the river, but still you have not quenched your thirst. But this is better than to be just good. Then you are not moving just with your intellect, now you have started moving with your intuition. Now you are not just a head; you are moving, leaning towards the heart.

How to believe something which you have never tasted? How to believe something which you have never experienced? How to believe in something which you have never seen happen even to somebody else? When a buddha passes through the world, many people are thrilled, their enthusiasm surges high, they start feeling that yes, the world does not end with worldly things, there is something more to it. The very presence of a buddha – his coolness, his silence, his overflowing bliss and compassion – his enlightened luminous being, just his vibe – pulsates you toward a new life, opens doors of the unknown. But still, Buddha says, you are following; you are not yet capable of your own light. Your eyes are dazzled but you have not attained to your own flame.

> *It is better to feed one* srotapanna *than to feed ten thousand of those who observe the five precepts of Buddha.*

Then, Buddha says, it is better to feed a sannyasin – *srotapanna* means a sannyasin, one who has entered into the river; one who is not just standing on the bank and watching others swimming in the river, thrashing around, enjoying, celebrating in the coolness of the river. The religious man is standing on the bank. He can see that there are people in the river, tremendously happy, but he has not been yet able to gather courage to take a jump. He has still much involvement with the riverbank, in the world. He has much involvement in ordinary, mundane things – money, power, prestige, family, body, health, a thousand and one things. He is not yet courageous enough to let go. *Srotapanna* means one who has surrendered, who has entered the stream. *Srotapanna* exactly means what I mean by *sannyas*: the courageous person who has taken the jump. It is almost an insane jump, because those who are standing on the bank will laugh, and they will say, "What are you doing? Where are you going? You don't know swimming. First learn swimming, then enter." But how can one learn swimming without entering the river?

Their logic is impeccable. They say, "First learn, first know, then go. But first learn on the bank, otherwise you are taking a risk. The river may be too deep for you and you may not be able to come back. And who knows where it is going? And these people who are in the river, maybe they are all deluded, maybe they are all mad. Just look, the majority is standing on the bank; only a few people are in the river. The majority cannot be wrong. The few can be wrong, the mass cannot be wrong. There are only a few sannyasins in the world, very rare are buddhas in the world – maybe they are deluded. Don't be in a hurry. Maybe they are deceiving others – who knows? Maybe they have some other hidden motives. Wait and watch. Don't do such a thing in a hurry."

But such things are done only in a hurry. If you wait and watch, waiting and watching becomes your mechanical habit. Then you simply go on waiting and watching. That's what many are doing for many lives.

BUDDHA SAYS:

It is better to feed one srotapanna *than to feed ten thousand of those who observe the five precepts of Buddha.*

Because the *srotapanna* will have some experience of the stream. He will have his own experience to depend upon, he will have some taste of the stream, he will have the cool experience of the stream – that it relaxes, that worldly cares and anxieties disappear, that one stops struggling. Anguish by and by moves distant and distant and goes far away; ordinary cares and anxieties disappear.

One becomes more collected and calm. But this can be known only by a *srotapanna*, a sannyasin.

A sannyasin has taken an existential step. He has moved into the abyss. He has risked his life. Buddha says respect a man, feed a man who has risked his life. Maybe you are not yet courageous, but be close to people who are courageous. Courage is also infectious like everything else. Find people who have entered the stream. Be with them, feed them, at least that will give you an idea what is happening to somebody. You may start dreaming, desiring it. Your hidden energies may start surfacing. You may start feeling the challenge of the unknown.

The religious person is negative, the *srotapanna* is positive. The religious person follows somebody else, the *srotapanna* has entered into the stream of life, into the stream of consciousness. He has dropped his ego. Now he is no longer a follower of a buddha.

This has to be understood. Ordinarily if you are my sannyasins, my disciples, people will say that you are my followers. By becoming a sannyasin, in fact you have become part of me; you are no longer a follower. Before you became a sannyasin you may have been a follower. Then you decided that following is not enough, that you are ready to go with me headlong, that you are ready to go with me wherever I am going. Once you are a sannyasin you are not a follower, you are part of the energy I am, you are just one with me. People ask me, "If we don't take *sannyas*, will you not help me, will you not help us?" I say, "I will help, that is not the problem, but you will not be able to take the help because you will stay separate, you will stay on the bank."

The river is ready to take you to the ocean, the invitation is already given to you – it is a standing invitation – but you are on the bank. What can the river do? It cannot snatch you away from the bank. And it wouldn't be good, even if it were possible, because you have to drop into the river on your own. Only then is it freedom. If you are snatched by the river, if I take you away forcibly, it cannot help you. It can destroy you, it cannot give you freedom. How can it give you ultimate freedom, moksha? From the very beginning it will be a bondage. So I will not take you like a flooded river takes people; I will have to wait. You will have to come to me, you will have to enter into the stream, you will have to become part of the stream.

The *srotapanna*, or the sannyasin, is positive. Now, instead of non-truth, truth arises in him. Non-truth was just a preparation so that truth can enter. Instead of non-violence or no-violence, love and compassion arises. Nonviolence was just a preparation for it. No-violence, no-untruth and other negatives are just medicinal. You are ill; the physician gives you a medicine to destroy the illness. When the illness is destroyed then health arises in you. Medicine never brings health, it only destroys the disease. Health cannot be brought by any medicine, there is no health-giving medicine. Health is your inner being – once the hindrances are removed your waters of life start flowing; once rocks are removed your fountain bursts forth.

Health is something natural, no medicine can give it to you. Disease is something unnatural. Disease enters you from the outside; an outside medicine can take it away. Health is your innermost core, it is you. When you are naturally yourself you are healthy.

The religious man is under treatment, he is hospitalized. The *srotapanna* has come back home – he is no longer hospitalized, he is not under treatment, his health has started sprouting. His spring of life is flowing well. He is positive. His goal is not non-violence, his goal is not to get rid of what is untrue. His goal is not to delete something, to eliminate something, his goal is not to destroy something; his goal is to help that which is already bubbling up, radiating in his being.

It is better to feed one skridagamin *than to feed one million of* srotapannas.

Buddha goes deeper and deeper. A *skridagamin* is one who will die and will come once again in life. His samadhi is just coming closer. The *srotapanna* is one who has jumped into the stream from the bank; a *skridagamin* is one whose river is coming very close to the ocean. He is getting ready to take the ultimate, the final jump. But he will come back once more. Just that much difference. A *srotapanna* will be born seven times – that is the distance from the riverbank to the ocean. A sannyasin will be born seven more times; a *skridagamin* once more, only once more. Then his accounts will be closed, then he will have passed through the final graduation from life, then this world is no more for him. But once more he will come, maybe for his post-graduation.

It is better to feed one anagamin *than to feed ten millions of* skridagamins.

The *anagamin* is one who will not come again. *Anagamin* means one who has passed beyond the point of coming back, who has crossed the shore of this world. Once he has died he will not be coming again to the world. He is just on the verge of disappearing into the ocean. The river is just there – just there on the threshold, ready to jump. He will not even look back.

The *skridagamin* is looking back, hesitating a little, would like to come back once more. This world is beautiful, it attracts. It has many celebrations, many flowers bloom here. The *skridagamin* is one for whom subtle desires are still lurking somewhere in the deep unconscious. Yes, he knows that one has to go, but a little more he would like to linger on this shore. Before he takes the final jump and disappears forever, he would like to taste this life once more, just as a farewell, to say goodbye.

The *anagamin* is one who will not look back, he will not even say goodbye. He is totally finished. The *skridagamin* is perfectly certain that a better world is waiting, but still a little longing for the past.

You always feel that – a little nostalgia. When you are leaving a house where you have lived for twenty years, have you watched? – you look back. Or you leave a town you have lived in for twenty years, where you were born – you look back. Even when the train leaves you go on looking out of the window, your eyes a little wet with memories, nostalgia, the past, the whole past. You have been here for so long. You loved here, you hated here, you had friends, you had enemies, you had many sorts of experiences here; you owe so much to this life. Yes, you are ready to go, you are already in the train, but still the eyes of longing look backwards.

The *skridagamin* will come once again, the *anagamin* will not. His departure is total, perfect. He will not look back, he has no nostalgia. The future that is about to happen is far more beautiful; this world simply has disappeared from his consciousness. The golden peaks of waiting for him, the oceanic infinity is waiting for him. He does not hanker any more for the bounded existence of a river. Yes, there were many flowers on the bank and beautiful trees and shadows and many dreams, but that is gone. Gone is gone.

BUDDHA SAYS:

> It is better to feed one anagamin *than to feed ten millions of*
> skridagamins. *It is better to feed one arhat than to feed one*
> *hundred millions of* anagamins.

The arhat is one who has dropped into the ocean, disappeared. The *anagamin* is one who is just on the verge of disappearing, just on the boundary line – one step more and he will become an arhat. Just a little distance and he will become an arhat – one drop more, just the last straw is needed on the back of the camel and the camel will collapse.

The *anagamin* is boiling at ninety-nine degrees; one degree more . . . The arhat is one who has crossed one hundred degrees and evaporated. Arhat is one who has evaporated.

BUDDHA SAYS:

> *It is better to feed one arhat than to feed one hundred millions of*
> anagamins.

Arhat

The arhat is one whose ego is lost, who has become part of the whole. He no longer exists as himself, now he exists as the universe, as the whole. In fact that is the meaning of the word "holy" – one who has become whole. The arhat is holy – not holy in the sense Christians use the word "saint", no, not in that sense. The Christian word "saint" is ugly. It comes from a root "sanctus" meaning sanctioned by the church. That is ugly – how can you sanction someone? Who is there to sanction? No government can issue certificates for saints – even the government that exists in the Vatican, even the Pope has no authority. A saint cannot be certified, but the Christian word "saint" means one who is certified by the Pope. Arhat does not mean a saint in that way. Arhat means one who has lost himself in the whole and has become holy.

> *It is better to feed one* pratyak *buddha than to feed one billion of arhats.*

Who is this *pratyak* buddha? *pratyak Buddha*

The arhat is one who has followed buddhas and arrived home. The *pratyak* buddha is one who has never been a disciple to anybody, who has come searching alone – his journey has been absolutely alone, his path has been absolutely alone. A *pratyak* buddha is a rare phenomenon. There are millions of arhats down the centuries, but very far and few in between are *pratyak* buddhas, who have struggled absolutely alone. And of course, they are needed, otherwise arhats will not be possible. *Pratyak* buddhas are needed so that others can follow them; they are the pioneers, they are the breakthroughs, they create the path.

Remember it: the *pratyak* buddha is one who moves in the jungle of life for the first time and creates a path by his very movement. Then others can follow. Those others will reach to the same point, to the same goal, but they will be arhats. They have not created the path, they are not the pathfinders, they are not the path builders. More respect is to be given to a *pratyak* buddha because no path was there: he created the path.

> *It is better to feed one of the buddhas, either of the present or of the past*
> *or of the future, than to feed ten billions of* pratyak *buddhas.*

Then what is the difference between a *pratyak* buddha and a buddha?

A *pratyak* buddha is one who creates the path and never bothers if anyone is following him or not. He has no compassion. He is a lonely traveler and he has found alone, so he thinks everybody can find. What is the point of going and telling people? He is not a master. A *pratyak* buddha makes the path – not for others, remember. He is just moving and the path is created by his movement . . . a small footpath in the jungle. Because he has moved, others follow him; that is for them to worry about – he never cares. He is a lonely traveler, and he thinks what can happen to him can happen to others.

When Buddha himself became enlightened these two alternatives were before him: whether to become a buddha or a *pratyak* buddha. For seven days he remained quiet: there was every possibility he may have chosen to be a *pratyak* buddha. Then the whole humanity would have missed something of tremendous value. It is said that Brahma came with all his gods from heaven – it is a beautiful parable. They bowed down at the feet of Buddha and they prayed to him: "Open your eyes and teach us whatsoever you have found." But Buddha said, "What is the point? If I can find, others can also find." He was leaning towards becoming a *pratyak* buddha. His logic was perfect: if I can find, then why not others? "And," he said, "even if I teach, those who want to listen, only they will listen to me. Those who are ready to go, only they will go with me. They can go without me. And those who are not ready to go, they won't listen and they will not go even if I shout from the house tops. So why bother?"

The gods discussed between themselves what to do, how to convince this man. A great opportunity has happened in the universe and if he becomes a *pratyak* buddha, then again the message will be lost. Of course, a few people will again find the way, but there is a possibility to make a superhighway. A footpath can disappear very soon; the trees can overrun it again. It has to be prepared in such a way that for centuries to come people can follow the path and the trees and the jungle will not destroy it, will not cover it over again. They discussed, they argued amongst themselves, then they found an argument. They came to Buddha again and they said, "You have to teach, because we watched, we looked all around the world. Yes, you are right, there are a few people who will immediately follow you. And we know that those are the people, even if you don't say anything they will find – a little later, maybe a few more steps, but they will find; we are certain about it, they are already on their search. So maybe your teaching will bring the understanding sooner, but nothing much more is going to happen – you are right.

"And there are people – millions we know, we have seen, we have looked into the hearts of humanity – who will not listen, who are deaf to any person like you. So, talking to them is not of any meaning. But we have seen a few people who are just in between the two, just lurking on the boundary. They will not go if you don't speak. And if you speak they will listen and they will gather courage. So just please, for those few people..." And Buddha could not argue, he had to concede, and he became a buddha and dropped the idea of becoming a *pratyak* buddha.

Buddha is one who has found his path; not only that – he created that path in such a way that many more can follow it. He has tremendous compassion for others, for all those struggling human beings who are groping in the dark.

It is better to feed one of the buddhas then to feed ten billions of pratyak *buddhas.*

It is better to feed one who is above knowledge, one-sidedness, discipline, and enlightenment than to feed one hundred billions of buddhas of past, present or future.

And then he comes to the last point, the zero point – even beyond a buddha. As far as human intellect can go, Buddha seems to be the last point. That's why we call Gautama Siddhartha "the Buddha", because that is as far as language can go. But there is a point beyond language, there is a point which is not express-ible – beyond symbols, ineffable: that Buddha calls going beyond even being a buddha. Then one is not even in any way thinking that he is enlightened, then one has no discipline, then one has no character. Then one is not – one is simply empty space.

In a buddha at least a little desire exists to help others, a compassion exists for others. But that too will be a bondage. That means the Buddha still thinks, "Others are and I am, and I can help others." Still the last subtle boundary of "I" and "you", of "me" and "thou" exists. The last point, Buddha says, is a zero point where all knowledge disappears, all experience disappears – even the experience of nirvana – because there is nobody to experience it. It is difficult to say anything about it, only negative descriptions are possible.

You can find this point in all the religions. They have different words for it. Jews, Christians, Mohammedans, Hindus, call this point God. That is their way of saying "the beyond". But the Buddhist way seems to be far superior. Jainas, Sankhyas, Yogins, call this state moksha, absolute freedom. Or others call it *kaivalya*, absolute aloneness. But still, all these words confine it. Buddha has not used any word, he simply says:

It is better to feed one who is above knowledge, above one-sidedness, above discipline, above enlightenment, than to feed one hundred billions of buddhas of the past, present, or future.

These are the possibilities within you. Ordinarily you exist as a bad man, so you are existing on the minimum, on the lowest rung. Try to become a good man. It is better than to be bad, but don't think it is the goal – it is all comparative, it is all relative.

I have heard:

> Mulla Nasruddin was in love with a woman. He went to the girl's father and requested that he should be allowed to have his daughter's hand. The father was completely willing, he said, "I'm absolutely happy, I have nothing to say against it, but my wife will not agree. She thinks with your long, hippie-like hair, with your poetic style of life, with your unisex dress, she thinks you look effeminate."
>
> Mulla brooded over it and he said, "She is right – in comparison to her."

Everything is comparative. The good man is good in comparison to the bad, but in comparison to the religious man, he is just like the bad man. The sannyasin is good in comparison to the religious man, but how to compare him with the *skridagamin*? – and so on and so forth. The more you travel on the inner path, the more higher peaks become available to you. Never rest content unless you have reached the very last, the uttermost. And the uttermost is beyondness – where nothing exists, or only pure existence remains. That purity is the goal and in that purity you become one. Until that purity is achieved, somehow duality persists – first in a gross way, then in a subtle way, then in a very, very subtle way. First in the conscious, then in the unconscious, but it goes on; then even in the superconscious it persists – it goes on creating shadows. So remember it: the goal is to disappear completely. The goal is to transcend all duality, all definition. The goal is to become one with the whole.

Enough for today.

Chapter 6:

The Twenty Difficult Things

THE BUDDHA SAID:

There are twenty difficult things to attain or accomplish in this world:

1. *It is difficult for the poor to practice charity.*
2. *It is difficult for the strong and rich to observe the way.*
3. *It is difficult to disregard life and go to certain death.*
4. *It is only a favored few that get acquainted with a Buddhist sutra.*
5. *It is by rare opportunity that a person is born in the age of a buddha.*
6. *It is difficult to conquer the passions, to suppress selfish desires.*
7. *It is difficult not to hanker after that which is agreeable.*
8. *It is difficult not to get into a passion when slighted.*
9. *It is difficult not to abuse one's authority.*
10. *It is difficult to be even-minded and simple-hearted in all one's dealings with others.*
11. *It is difficult to be thorough in learning and exhaustive in investigation.*
12. *It is difficult to subdue selfish pride.*

13. *It is difficult not to feel contempt toward the unlearned.*
14. *It is difficult to be one in knowledge and practice.*
15. *It is difficult not to express an opinion about others.*
16. *It is by rare opportunity that one is introduced to a true spiritual teacher.*
17. *It is difficult to gain an insight into the nature of being, and to practice the way.*
18. *It is difficult to follow the steps of a savior.*
19. *It is difficult to be always the master of oneself.*
20. *It is difficult to understand thoroughly the ways of Buddha.*

Life is not a bed of roses. It is difficult, it is complex. It is very rare to be alive in the true sense of the word. To be born is one thing; to be alive quite another. To be born is to be just biologically here; to be alive is a totally different dimension – the dimension of spirituality.

Unless you are spiritual you are not yet alive. But to move from the biological realm to the spiritual realm is very difficult, arduous. It is the greatest challenge there is. It is the greatest quantum leap – from the body to the soul, from the material to the immaterial, from the visible to the invisible, from time to timelessness, from out to in. It is arduous.

Buddha, in this sutra, says there are twenty difficult things. These twenty difficult things can become twenty steps of the challenge. Buddha is talking about these twenty difficult things not to make you beware of them, to avoid them – it is an invitation, it is a challenge. These twenty Himalayan peaks are just a challenge for you, a great invitation. Don't remain in the valley. The valley is very secure, convenient, comfortable. You will live comfortably, you will die comfortably, but you will not grow. You will only grow old, but you will not grow. Growth happens only when you are accepting a challenge. Growth happens only when you start living dangerously. These twenty things are indicative of how one should live.

There is only one way to live and that is to live dangerously, courageously. You become rightly a human being only when you have accepted this challenge of the Buddha.

We will go into these twenty things. They look small on the surface, but Buddha cannot talk about small things. You will have to go into the depth of these small things, and then you will see – they are really difficult.

Before we enter this sutra, one thing I would like to tell you – that the search for truth is the search for the impossible. Religion itself is nothing but a passion for the impossible. The beauty is that that "impossible" happens; that impossible also becomes possible. But you have to pay for it, and you have to pay tremendously. You have to sacrifice yourself utterly. You have to stake your whole life. If you stake your so-called life, you will attain to what Buddha calls to be alive, to what Jesus calls to be reborn, to what Hindus call to be twice born, *dwij*. Then a totally new dimension and a totally new quality of being arises in you . . . uncorrupted by time and space, uncontaminated by anything, absolutely and eternally virgin.

Long for the impossible. Desire the impossible.

THE BUDDHA SAID:

There are twenty difficult things to attain or accomplish in this world.

First: it is difficult for the poor to practice charity.

Because unless you have it, how can you share it? To share something with somebody else you must have it first. In the first place you must have it; only that can be shared which you have. This is something that we go on forgetting continually. I see so many people trying to share their love and they don't have any love. Of course, their sharing brings misery to them and to others – because you can share only that which you have. You may think you are sharing your love, but you share only your misery in fact, because that is what you have. You go with hope, you move with dreams, but what is the actual result of it? In fantasy love is good; in reality it becomes a misery, a hell.

You don't have love in your being; that energy does not exist there. First you have to become radiant with love, only then can you share it. Before you can become a lover, you have to become love. People think that they will become love only by becoming a lover. Stupid is their logic, illogical is their way of thinking. You cannot become a lover unless you have love – and love you don't have. Everybody goes on believing that one has the capacity to love; one has just to find somebody to receive it. One is full of love energy; one needs only just a receiving end. That's how people go on moving, searching. Many times they find beautiful people, but the total result is miserable. They think they are sharing love – they share only their loneliness. They think they are sharing something divine – they share only their ugliness. They think they are sharing their innermost being but they share only their dirty surface. They themselves are not aware of their innermost core.

That is the meaning of a poor man.

When Buddha talks about a poor man, he does not mean a man without money. When Buddha talks about a poor man, he means a man who is not rich inside . . . a loveless man. How can he share? How can he become a tremendous sharing? No, charity is not possible. Charity is possible only when you are over-flowing. Overflowing is charity.

It is difficult for the poor to practice charity.

And remember it the other way around also. Whenever you are unable to share, whenever you are unable to practice charity, note it– you must be poor. You may have much in the eyes of others, but deep down you must be poor if you cannot share.

You possess only that which you can give. Only by giving do you become the possessor. If you cannot give, then you are not in possession, you are not the master. Then the thing that you think you possess, is possessing you. Then you are possessed by your possession.

Charity is a beautiful flowering of one who has, one who is in possession of his being; one who is not poor, one who is rich. You may be a beggar on the streets. It has nothing to do with your bank balance. The rich person may be a beggar but if he has his being, authentic being – if he can love, if he can sing, if he can dance, if he can see poetry in the world – he is rich. You may not have anything at all. As far as material things go, you may not have anything. But you have something of the spiritual . . . something which cannot be taken away from you.

Observe this fact: that which you really possess cannot be taken away from you. You can only give it – if you want – but nobody can take it away. That which you don't possess, and by which you are possessed, you can never give – it can only be stolen or taken away, robbed.

Your love cannot be robbed. There is no way to rob it. You can give it vol-untarily, you can give it freely, but nobody can rob it. You can be killed, but your love cannot be killed. There exists no way to murder love. Love seems to be more eternal than your so-called life. Your life can be destroyed very easily . . . just a hit on the head, just a bullet through the heart; very simple! But nothing can destroy love. Love seems to be the only eternal thing; something not belonging to the world of time. You can give it, but nobody can take it. Your money, your respectability, your power, your prestige – they all can be taken away from you.

That which can be taken away from you creates a clinging in the mind. You become poorer and poorer, because you have to cling more and more, you have to protect more and more, and you are always afraid and trembling. The so-called rich people are continuously trembling. Deep down they are always afraid because they know that that which they have can be taken away. They can never be certain about it. The very uncertainty goes on eating at their heart like a worm.

You possess only that which grows out of you, which belongs to you, which is rooted in you. A rich man is one who has poetry in life, dance in life, celebration in life, silence in life, centeredness in life, rootedness in life . . . who blooms into his inner sky. The rich man is one who is so full, like clouds in the rainy season . . . ready to shower on anybody who becomes available. Or like an opening bud . . . ready to share its fragrance with any wind that passes by, or any traveler that comes by. Sharing is overflowing.

Buddha says this is one of the most difficult things, to try to share that which you don't have – and that's what people are doing. They go on trying to love without ever considering the fact that love has not yet grown in their heart. In fact, you don't love yourself – how can you love others? The very basic is missing. You are not happy alone – how can you be happy together with somebody else? If you are unhappy alone, when you come together with somebody you will bring your unhappiness to be shared. That's all you have – your poverty, your rottenness, your misery, your depression, your sadness, your angst, anxiety, anguish . . . your disease.

Try to possess something – that which cannot be taken away by anybody, not even by death. Difficult, but possible. It looks impossible. How to be loving without finding a lover? Our whole mind has been conditioned in a wrong way. You can dance without an audience, why can't you love without there being somebody else? You can sing without a listener, why can't you love without a lover? Your mind has been conditioned wrongly. You think you can love only when there is somebody to love.

Practice love. Sitting alone in your room, be loving. Radiate love. Fill the whole room with your love energy. Feel yourself vibrating with a new frequency, swaying as if you are in the ocean of love. Create vibrations of love energy around you and you will start feeling immediately that something is happening – something in your aura is changing, something around your body is changing; a warmth is arising around your body, a warmth like a deep orgasm. You are becoming more alive. Something like sleep is disappearing. Something like awareness is arising. Sway into this ocean. Dance, sing, and let your whole room be filled with love.

In the beginning it feels very weird. When for the first time you can fill your room with love energy, your own energy, which goes on falling and rebounding on you and makes you so happy, one starts wondering, "Am I hypnotizing myself? Am I deluded? What is happening?" Because you have always thought love comes from somebody else. A mother is needed to love you, a father, a brother, a husband, a wife, a child – but somebody.

Love that depends on somebody is a poor love. Love that is created within you, love that you create out of your own being, is real energy. Then move anywhere with that ocean surrounding you and you will feel that everybody who comes close to you is suddenly under the influence of a different kind of energy. People will look at you with more open eyes. You will be passing them and they will feel that a breeze of some unknown energy has passed them; they will feel fresher. Hold somebody's hand and his whole body will start throbbing. Just be close to somebody and that person will start feeling very happy for no reason at all, you can see it. Then you are becoming ready to share. Then find a lover, then find a right receptivity for you.

I have heard a small anecdote:

> The greatest surprise of Mary's life was receiving a half dollar on her fourth birthday. She carried the coin about the house and was seen sitting on the steps admiring it.
>
> "What are you going to do with your half dollar?" her mother asked.
>
> "Take it to Sunday school," said Mary promptly.
>
> "To show to your teacher?"
>
> Mary shook her head. "No," she said, "I'm going to give it to God. He will be as surprised as I am to get something besides pennies."

Whatever you are giving to people is just pennies, not even that. And then one day when your love fails . . . in fact it has never been there even to fail; it has been missing from the very beginning . . . but your belief that you were a loving person fails one day. Then you start thinking of God, and prayer. Godliness and prayerfulness are possible only when your love has succeeded. When you have become a great lover, then only prayerfulness can arise. But almost always it happens that people who have failed in their life start going to the temple and to the church. Of course, they bring their empty hearts . . . completely dry, not even tears in their hearts. Then they pray and nothing happens. In fact you are missing love energy, and without love energy, prayerfulness cannot arise. Prayerfulness is a refined phenomenon of the same energy as love. It is out of love that the subtle fragrance of prayerfulness arises.

Existence is also tired of your pennies, is also tired of your poverty. Existence is also tired of your misery. Bring celebration to existence, bring something alive. Don't bring deserts – bring gardens. Don't bring corpses – bring somebody dancing, alive.

Buddha's first sutra says: Try to become rich so that you can share.
Second:

(2) *It is difficult for the strong and rich to observe the way.*

Yes, it is very difficult for the strong and the rich to observe the way. They are too much in their pride, they are too egoistic; they are not ready to surrender. People surrender only when they have become absolute failures. People surrender only when they have nothing to surrender. When life has completely crushed them, when they are bankrupt, then they surrender. But what is the point of surrendering when you are a bankrupt? People remember the spiritual path only when nothing else seems to help. In deep hopelessness they remember. But it is only when you are full of hope, radiant, vibrating; when there is meaning in your life, when you feel the hands of destiny in your life, when you are riding on waves, when you feel at the top of the world – those are the moments to remember, to move towards the way.

BUT, BUDDHA SAYS:

It is difficult for the strong and rich to observe the way.

Why is it difficult for the strong? Because the strong thinks, "I am enough unto myself. What is the need to ask for help?" The weak thinks, "I am not enough unto myself so I have to need, I have to ask for help." But only when you are strong do you have energy to ask. Only when you are strong is there a possibility that you can touch higher realms. Out of impotence you cannot reach higher realms. You need an inner strength. It is difficult for the strong to move towards the way, but that is the only possibility. So if you are feeling strong, move towards the way, because these are the right, positive moments; this is the opportunity. When you are feeling successful, this is the time to remember. When everything is going well, don't miss this opportunity – this is the time. Looks absurd, because our logic is this – that when we are happy, we never remember the higher realms. We completely become oblivious. This childish attitude seems to be the common attitude. When you are ill, suddenly you start feeling very religious. When death is close by and you are getting older and older and you start stumbling in life and your feet are no longer strong enough to hold you and you are trembling, you start remembering the divine. People go on postponing their religiousness for their old age.

In India they say *sannyas* is for old people. When you are almost dead, when you are ready to be thrown on the junkyard, when one foot is already in the grave, then turn your eyes towards your inner world. People go on postponing for the very end. The inner search seems to be the last item on their list. They have a shopping list and the inner exploration is the last. When they have purchased everything – consistent, inconsistent, relevant, irrelevant – when they have wasted all their energy, when nothing is left, when they are just exhausted, then they remember the inner.

But in fact, the spiritual search is for the young, it is for the strong. Buddha initiated a new trend in *sannyas*. He dropped the old Hindu concept that one should become a sannyasin in old age.

Hindus have four stages – they are very calculating, mathematical. Manu seems to be the greatest mathematician of life, very clever. He has divided life into stages: twenty-five years for education, then twenty-five years for living the life of a householder in the world, the life of a householder, then twenty-five years for getting ready to leave the world. Looking after children who have become grown-ups now, who are getting married, who are coming from their universities; and then the last is *sannyas*, the fourth stage of life. That means after seventy-five years. The last – when everything else has happened, when there is nothing else, then the search into your inner world. This seems to be very insulting! It seems you somehow relate spirituality with death, not with life.

Godliness, meditativeness, should be in the very center of life. And Buddha says it is difficult when you are young but that is the challenge. It is difficult to observe the way when you are strong, but that is the challenge. It is difficult to become meditative when you are rich – but that is the only way.

When you are rich and strong and young, when energy is streaming, when you are ready to do something – when you are ready to go into an adventure, when you have courage, when you can take risks, when danger has an appeal for you – when death has not weakened you, when you are full of zest and life, that is the point to take the challenge and move into the unknown.

The third:

It is difficult to disregard life and go to certain death.

It is very difficult to disregard life. Life is enchanting, hypnotizing. It is beautiful, it is a miracle, a magic world – but made of the stuff dreams are made of. It is difficult to awake in this beautiful dream. When you are having a nice dream . . . maybe you are on a trip with Marilyn Monroe or something like that. Or you have become the president of the United States. When you are having a beautiful dream, nice, everything is happening as you always wanted it, and then somebody shakes you awake, you become aware – but the dream is lost. You feel annoyed: "Is this the right moment? Could you not wait a little longer? I was having such a beautiful dream."

But a dream is a dream, beautiful or not. A beautiful dream is also a dream; so futile, a wastage.

Buddha says, *It is difficult to disregard life* . . . Yes, when life has deserted you then it is very simple. When life itself has deserted you, when you are left behind and life has gone out of you, or is going out of you; when life has oozed out of you and you are left just like a dead dry thing, then it is very easy to disregard life. Even then it seems difficult. Even in old age people go on behaving childishly.

I have heard:

An ancient man described his recent visit to a bordello.

"How old are you anyway?" the madam asked him.

"I am ninety-three," he said.

"Well, you have had it, sir," she told him.

"I have? Ah – then how much do I owe you?"

Now his memory is gone, but still he has come in search of a prostitute. He cannot remember anything, but the passion persists. He must be just on his deathbed. He may have been carried by others to the bordello. To the very end . . . This is my observation – that out of a hundred persons, almost ninety-nine die thinking of sex. In fact when death comes, the idea of sex becomes very strong because death and sex are opposite each other; they are polar opposites. Sex brings birth, and death is the end of the same energy that was realeased by birth. So, while dying, a person becomes obsessively interested in sex. And that becomes the beginning of another birth.

To die without thinking about sex is a great experience. Then something of tremendous import has happened to you. If you can die without thinking of sex at all, no lurking shadows of sex in your mind, of lust for life, you are dying as one should die. Only one percent of people die that way. These are the people Buddha calls *srotapanna* – those who have entered into the stream, those who have become sannyasins, those who have taken a step towards understanding what is real and what is unreal, those who have become discriminative of what is dream and what is true.

It is difficult to disregard life and go to certain death.

Even when death is coming, then too it is difficult to disregard life – even when death has become certain. In fact, death is the only certainty. Everything else is uncertain. Everything else may happen, may not happen, everything else is accidental. Death is absolutely certain – the day you were born, death became certain. With the very birth, only one thing has become absolutely certain, that you will die.

Death is certain. You may know it or you may not know it; you may look at it, you may not look at it – but death is certain. Death seems to be more real than whatsoever you call your life. Still, even with so much certainty, one is afraid to go into it; one clings with uncertain life, with dreamlike life. Buddha says it is difficult to accept death and move into death, and it is difficult to disregard so-called life. But a man of understanding starts disregarding life and regarding death. He respects death more because death is more certain, must be more part of reality than so-called life – because the so-called life is just like dreaming.

You have lived for thirty or forty or fifty years. Now look back, think retrospectively. What has happened in these fifty years? Was it real or just a long dream? Can you make any distinction whether it was real or a dream? How will you distinguish? Maybe you have dreamed it all. Maybe it was just an idea in your mind. What proof have you got that it was real? What is left in your hand? Nothing . . . emptiness. And you call it life? Only emptiness results out of it. Buddha says, better to call it death. Now look into death – maybe there is where you will find real life.

It is difficult, but a person who becomes interested in death, intrigued by the phenomenon of death, becomes a different type of person. He is a *srotapanna*. The people who cling to the bank are the people who think this life is all. The people who try to understand, penetrate deeply into life, become aware that this is not the real thing. Then they take a jump into the river that is going somewhere else – towards death.

Meditation is an effort to die voluntarily. And in deep meditation one dies. In deep meditation, the so-called life disappears and for the first time you encounter death. That experience of encountering death makes you deathless. Suddenly you transcend death. Suddenly you know – that which is going to die is not you. All that can die, you are not. You are neither your body nor your mind nor your self. You are simply pure space – which is never born and never dies.

People talk about death very rarely. Even if they talk about it, they talk very reluctantly. If they are forced to talk about it, they feel embarrassed – even people who believe that the soul never dies, even people who believe that after death a person goes to the eternal, to paradise.

In his *Unpopular Essays*, Bertrand Russell has an anecdote:

> F. W. H. Myers, whom spiritualism had converted to belief in a future life, questioned a woman who had lately lost her daughter as to what she supposed has become of her soul.
>
> The mother replied, "Ah, well, I suppose she is enjoying eternal bliss, but I wish you would not talk about such unpleasant subjects."

Now if really she is enjoying eternal bliss, why is this subject unpleasant? One should be happy to talk about it. In fact it is unpleasant to talk about it, and just to hide the unpleasantness we have invented so many theories, beliefs, that after death one goes to eternal heaven. Everybody has to somehow convince himself that he will not die.

Buddha's teaching is that you have to accept the fact that you will die. Not only that – that all that you think you are, absolutely, in toto, is going to die. Buddha is very stern about it.

If you ask Mahavira, he will say that body will die, mind will die, but your soul? – no, your soul will remain. Now there is some protection. We can think, "Okay, the body will die. We would like it not to die, but we can accept. The body is not me." In India you can find many monks, sadhus, just contemplating: "I am not the body, I am not the body. I am the soul eternal." Now, what are they doing? If they really know that they are the soul eternal, then why this constant repetition? Whom are they trying to fool? Why this constant repetition that "I am not the body"? If you are not, you are not – finished! No, they don't believe it really; they are trying to hypnotize themselves. "I am not the body" – repeating it continuously for many years, they may persuade themselves that "I am not the body", but that is not going to be their experience. It will remain just an auto-suggestion. They have befooled themselves, they have fallen into a delusion. And then they are saying, "I am the eternal soul – infinite, *sat-chit-ananda* – true, existential, blissful." They are fighting with death and they are trying to find some place where they can hide from death.

Buddha's approach is totally different. He says there is no place to hide. You have to go headlong into it. And Buddha says your body will die, your mind will die, your so-called soul will die – everything, in toto. You are going to die. Nothing is going to remain.

This is very, very difficult to even conceive. But, Buddha says, if you can conceive of this, if you are ready for this, only then you will be able to know that innermost space which is beyond time and space. But remember – *you* don't know that space at all, so it has nothing to do with you. Whatever is your identity is going to die completely, and that which is going to remain has nothing to do with you. So Buddha says don't ask about that. Because you are such rationalizing animals, such tricky fellows, that if he says, "Yes, there is an inner space that will remain," you will say, "Okay, that's what I call my soul." Again you are back in the old trap. 'So, I am going to survive. Nothing to be afraid of." You will find some identity with that inner space.

Buddha keeps completely quiet. He must have been tempted many times to talk about it. It is very difficult to keep secrets when you know – but Buddha has kept the secret.

It is really almost superhuman to keep secrets. You may have observed the fact. Whenever somebody says to you, "Don't tell it to anybody, keep it a secret," then you are in a difficulty. The whole mind tends to tell it to somebody. There seems to be a natural thing in it. It is as if you eat something; then how can you hold it forever and ever inside your stomach? It has to be defecated, it has to be thrown out. Otherwise you will have permanent constipation and it will be very disturbing. The same happens with the mind. Somebody says something to you: "Keep it a secret." Your husband comes home and he says, "Listen, keep it a secret." Now the wife is in trouble, because something has gone into the mind. It has to come out, otherwise there will be a mental constipation. She feels very heavy unless she can find somebody. She is going to talk to the servant. And of course she will say, "Don't tell it to anybody." And the servant will rush faster to his home, to his wife, because – what to do? Within minutes the whole town will know.

It is very difficult to keep a secret. You can keep a secret only if it has not come from the outside, remember it. If it has come from the outside, it has to go outside; it cannot be kept. If it has arisen in your own being, if it has flowered within you, if it has existential roots in your own being, you can keep it a secret – because it has not come from the outside; there is no need for it to go back outside.

Buddha could keep this secret because it was his own experience. Nobody had told it to him, he had not found it in the Vedas, he had not heard it from the traditional sources, he had not read about it. It had not entered into him from the outside; it had bloomed within his own being – it was his own flower. When something blooms in you, it is yours; it is for you to keep or to share.

Buddha is continually tempted. A thousand times, I think almost every day, people must have been coming to him and asking him, "Yes, we can understand that the body will die, the mind will die – but the soul? the self? the atman?" And Buddha goes on saying flatly, "*Everything* will die. Everything that you know as your identity will die. You will die completely and that which will be saved, you don't know anything about."

When you disappear, then you will know that which remains. That has nothing to do with you. That existed before you existed. That exists just now, just parallel to you. You never meet with it. You are two parallel lines; you never meet. You are hiding it – when *you* are not, it is revealed. Buddha says, go into death as deeply as possible. And that is possible only if you start disregarding your so-called life. To disregard it means to know it – it is a dream.

The swain and his girl had just encountered a bulldog that looked mean and hungry.

"Why, Percy," she exclaimed as he started a strategic retreat. "You always swore you would face death for me."

"I would," he flung back, "but that damned dog ain't dead yet!"

People say they can face death, but when it comes to facing it suddenly their whole courage disappears. People say that they can surrender their life very easily. It is not so easy. Lust for life is very deep. You have watered it for many lives; its roots have gone deep into your being. Even if you cut a few branches, it makes no difference; even if you cut the whole tree, it makes no difference – new shoots will be coming out.

It is only a favored few that get acquainted with a Buddhist sutra.

Buddha says it is very few, a very favored few, a fortunate few, a chosen few, a blessed few, who become acquainted with the wisdom of a buddha. Because to be in contact with a buddha, you have to pass through a few experiences that life is illusory, that death is certain. Unless your illusion about life is shattered completely, you will not listen to a Buddha; he is irrelevant, he does not exist for you.

Buddha exists for you only if you have become alert that this life is fleeting, slipping by; that this life is just a shadow, not a reality . . . a reflection in the mirror. When all your dreams about life are shattered, then you become interested in a buddha. And when you become interested, only then is there a possibility to understand Buddhist wisdom, the wisdom of an awakened man.

Who is an awakened man? One who has come to know what is dream, one who has come to know what is not dream. When you are asleep, dream looks real. In the morning when you awake, then you know that it was unreal. A Buddha is one who has awakened – awakened out of this so-called life and has come to realize that it is a dream.

If you are also feeling the pain, the frustration, the misery of this dream life, this futile life, only then you start moving towards a source of light; otherwise not. Buddha says those are the few favored ones.

Fifth:

It is by rare opportunity that a person is born in the age of a buddha.

Yes, it is so, because a buddha is rarely there. Thousands of years pass, then a person becomes a buddha. And even then it is not necessary that he will start teaching. He may not teach at all. He may simply disappear into the unknown. There is no necessity that he should become a master. So, buddhas are few, and then buddhas who become masters and help people on the way are even fewer.

It is by rare opportunity that a person is born in the age of a buddha. So if you can find a person who is awakened, if you can find a person who is a little different from you, if you can find a person in whose eyes you don't see the clouds of sleep and around whom you can feel the aura of awakening, then don't miss the opportunity, because it may not be for many lives that you will come across such a man again.

It is difficult to conquer the passions, to suppress selfish desires.

It is difficult to conquer passions. That's why Buddha says a courageous man will not bother to go to the top of the Himalayas. Yes, that is difficult, but nothing compared to conquering your own passions. A real man of courage will not try to go to the moon – it is difficult, but nothing compared to conquering your own passions and lust for life. The greatest adventure in life is to become passionless, to become free of lust. To just be, without any hankering to be something else; to just be here now; with no desire for the future, no desire for any repetition of the past . . . with no projection.

It is difficult not to hanker after that which is agreeable.

Why do we live in dreams? – because dreams many times are agreeable. That is the trick of the dreams, that's how they persuade you; that is their bait.
I have heard:

> Mulla Nasruddin stood quietly at the bedside of his dying father.
> "Please, my boy," whispered the old man, "always remember that wealth does not bring happiness."
> "Yes, father," said Nasruddin, "I realize that, but at least it will allow me to choose the kind of misery I find most agreeable."

That's what we are doing – trying to find a misery which appears agreeable. That's your whole search.
Buddha says:

It is difficult not to hanker after that which is agreeable.

Agreeable or disagreeable is not the point. A dream can be agreeable, a lie can be agreeable; sometimes poison can be agreeable, sometimes suicide can be agreeable – that is not the point. The point is what is real. The real person endeavors to know the real, and the unreal person tries only to find things that are agreeable, comfortable, convenient. Look, watch out. Don't go after the agreeable, otherwise dreams will go on pulling you and pushing you here and there, and you will remain like a driftwood. Let your emphasis be on what is real. Even if it is not agreeable, choose the real.

Let me repeat it: even if the real is not agreeable to you, choose the real, become agreeable to it. Then only you can come to truth; there is no other way.

It is difficult not to get into a passion when slighted.

Anger is so easy; so mechanical. You need not have any awareness for it, it is robotlike. Somebody insults you; you become angry. Buddha says, try: When somebody insults you, remain calm and quiet. Don't miss this opportunity. This is an opportunity to get out of your mechanical world, this is an opportunity to become more conscious. The person is giving you a beautiful chance to grow. Don't miss it.

Whenever you find an opportunity where it is natural to be mechanical, try to be non-mechanical, become more conscious of the situation. And that will become your growth ladder. Somebody insults you – it is very easy to be hurt. It is mechanical; you are not needed for it, no intelligence is needed for it. It is very easy to get into a rage, anger, fire. No intelligence is needed for it. Even animals do it, so nothing is special in it.

Do something special. Remain calm and quiet and collected. Relax, watch inside that the mechanical thing does not possess you. Become a little loosened from your mechanical habits and your benefit will be tremendous. You will start becoming more and more aware.

It is difficult not to abuse one's authority.

Very difficult – because in the first place people seek authority just to abuse it.

You have heard Lord Acton's famous dictum that power corrupts. It is not true. His observation is right in a way, but not true. Power never corrupts anybody, but still Lord Acton is right because we always see people being corrupted by power. How can power corrupt people? In fact, corrupted people seek power. Of course, when they don't have power, they cannot express their corruption. When they have power, then they are free. Then they can move with the power, then they are not worried. Then they come into their true light, then they show their real face. Power never corrupts anybody; only corrupted people are attracted towards power and when they have power, then of course they use it for all their desires and passions.

It happens. A person may be very humble. When he is seeking a political post he may be very humble, and you may know him – you may have known that for his whole life he was a simple and humble person – and you vote for him. The moment he is in power, there is a metamorphosis; he is no longer the same person. People are surprised – how has power corrupted him? In fact, that humbleness was false, bogus. He was humble because he was weak. He was humble because he had no power. He was afraid he would have been crushed by powerful people. His humbleness was his politics, his policy. Now he need not be afraid, now nobody can crush him. Now he can express his true reality. Now he looks corrupted.

BUDDHA SAYS:

It is difficult not to abuse one's authority.

Difficult, because in the first place only people who want to abuse their authority become interested in authority. If you have some authority, watch. Even small authorities corrupt people. You may be just a constable standing on the crossroads, but if you have the opportunity, you will abuse it; you will show yourself who you are.

> Mulla Nasruddin used to serve as a constable. He caught hold of a woman who was driving a car and of course, a woman and a car driver never go together, so she was going wrong. Mulla took his notebook and started writing.
> The woman said, "Wait! I know the chief minister, so don't be worried."
> But Mulla continued writing; he didn't pay any attention.
> The woman said, "Do you know, I also know the governor!"
> But the Mulla continued writing.
> The woman said, "Listen, what are you doing? I even know the Prime Minister!"
> Mulla said, "Listen lady, do you know Mulla Nasruddin?"
> She said, "No, never heard of him."
> He said, "Unless you know Mulla Nasruddin, nothing is going to help you."

When you have authority, it is so easy, hmm? You can see it all around. You are just standing at the ticket window of a railway station and the booking clerk goes on doing something – and you can see that he has nothing to do. He goes on turning pages here and there. He wants to delay, he wants to show you that he has the authority. He says, "Wait." He cannot miss this chance to say no to you.

Watch it in yourself also. Your son comes and says, "Daddy, can I go out to play?" You say, "No!" You know well and the son knows well that you will allow him in the end. So the son starts shrieking and jumping and screaming and he says, "I want to go!" Then you say, "Okay, go." And you know it; it has happened before the same way, and there was nothing wrong in allowing him to go outside and play. Why did you say no? If you have authority, you want to show it. But then the son also has some authority. He starts jumping, he creates a tantrum, and he knows that he can create trouble and the neighbors will hear, and people will think badly about you, so you say, "Okay, go." In every human encounter you will see it happening – people are throwing their authority all around; either bullying people or being bullied by others.

And if somebody bullies you, you will immediately find some weaker person somewhere to take revenge. If your boss bullies you in the office, you will come home and bully your wife. And if she is not a liberated woman who will fight with you, then she will wait for the child to come home from school and she will bully the child. And if the child is old-fashioned, not American, then the child will go to his room and crush his toys, because that is the only thing he can bully. He can show his power over the toy. But this goes on and on. This seems to be the whole game. This is what real politics is.

To get out of the political mind is the meaning of this sutra:

It is difficult not to abuse one's authority.

So whenever you have some authority . . . and everybody has some authority or other. You cannot find a person, you cannot find the last person in the chain who has no authority; even he has some authority, even he has a dog he can kick. Everybody has some authority somewhere, so everybody lives in politics. You may not be a member of any political party; that doesn't mean that you are not political. If you abuse your authority, you are political. If you don't abuse your authority, then you are non-political.

Become more aware not to abuse your authority. It will give you a new light in how you function, and it will make you so calm and centered. It will give you tranquility and serenity.

It is difficult to be even-minded and simple-hearted in all one's dealings with others.

It is very difficult, because people are cunning. If you are simple-hearted, you will be cheated. Buddha says, be cheated. It is better to be cheated than to cheat. If these are the only alternatives – to be cheated or to cheat – then Buddha says choose the first, be cheated. At least your inner being will remain uncorrupted.

That is the meaning when Jesus says, "If somebody slaps your face, then give him the other cheek also. If somebody forces you to carry his load for one mile, go two miles. And if somebody tries to steal your coat, give him your shirt also."

The whole meaning is that it is better to be cheated, because when somebody is cheating you, he can cheat you only of meaningless things. When you cheat somebody, you are losing something of your inner being . . . something which is tremendously valuable.

It is very difficult to be even-minded and simple-hearted in one's dealings with others.

It is very simple to be simple-minded when you are alone. That's why many people go to the Himalayas or to the monasteries, where they drop out of the world. It is very simple not to cheat when you are alone. It is very simple to be simple when you are alone – but what is the point? Of course, when you are alone you cannot be dishonest. Of course, when you are alone you cannot lie. Of course, when you are alone you cannot be egoistic, you cannot be competitive, you cannot deceive, you cannot hurt. But that doesn't mean that you have changed and transformed. The real test is in the world.

So, never leave the world – change yourself. It is very easy to change the circumstances, but that is not the real thing – change your consciousness.

It is difficult to be thorough in learning and exhaustive in investigation.

Mind tends to be lazy – all laziness is in the mind. Mind wants to avoid any effort; that's why it does not want to move in new dimensions. It keeps clinging to the old, to the familiar, because it knows that it is very efficient there. It has a certain proficiency and skill and now, once you have settled, you don't want to change it. Many people go on living with a woman or with a man, not because they love the woman or man but just because it is familiar. Now it will be a trouble to move with another person and start from ABC. They are simply lazy. People go on living the way they are living – even if it is miserable, even if nothing exists out of it except anguish, but they continue, because at least it is familiar, known; they have become skillful about it. And they can go on sleeping.

Mind is lazy. This laziness is one of the barriers.

BUDDHA SAYS:

It is very difficult to be thorough in learning and exhaustive in investigation.

You have not even been thoroughly aware of your life, which is the most important thing. You have not even investigated what it is. You have taken it for granted, on the surface. All your knowledge about your life is borrowed. Whatsoever you know is not what you know – it is from somebody else.

I have heard:

> A student nurse was faced with the following question on an
> examination paper: "Name five reasons why mothers' milk is better
> for babies than cows' milk."
>
> She answered. First: because it is fresher. Second: because it is
> cleaner. Third: because the cats can't reach it. Fourth: because it is
> easier to take with you on journeys.
>
> Try as she would, she could not think of a fifth reason. You try . . .
> even these four are not reasons. In desperation, she glanced at the
> paper of a male student sitting next to her, and then wrote, Fifth:
> because it comes in such cute little containers.

This is the way you borrow knowledge, looking here and there. This is all that
you know. You have not looked directly. And unless you look directly, you will
remain stupid, you will remain mediocre.

It is difficult to subdue selfish pride.

One of the most arduous things in life is not to think of oneself as extraordinary. Of course, this is the most ordinary thing in the world to think, because
everybody thinks he is extraordinary. Everybody thinks he is extraordinary, so
the feeling of being extraordinary is the most ordinary thing. Look around –
still you go on thinking that you are extraordinary.

Buddha says it is very difficult, but if you really want to move on the path,
just be ordinary. Don't claim any extraordinariness. And this is the beauty of
the whole thing – the moment you become ordinary, you become extraordinary. The moment you don't claim that you are exceptional, you are exceptional
. . . because the claim to be exceptional is so ordinary. Everybody is claiming he
is unique, exceptional. People may say it, may not say it, but deep down they
know who they are.

Become alert. How can you be extraordinary? Either everybody is extraordinary – then you are also extraordinary – but what is the point? If
extraordinariness is just a common quality of everybody, then what is the point
of claiming it? Either everybody is extraordinary, because everybody comes
from the same source of existence, or everybody is ordinary, because everybody
comes from the same source of existence.

Whatever you think about you, think about others also. And whatever you
think about others, think about yourself also. Then pride will disappear. Pride is
always vain, pride is always for wrong reasons. Pride is like a fever and you can
never be healthy with it.

It is difficult not to feel contempt towards the unlearned.

Buddha specifically mentions it. When you see somebody who is more ignorant than you, you suddenly feel a contempt. It is very difficult not to feel that contempt. Because when you see somebody more learned than you, you feel jealous. Both these things go together – contempt for those who are behind you and jealousy for those who are ahead of you. Contempt and jealousy simply show that you are continuously comparing yourself with others.

Never compare, because all comparison is foolish. Everybody is just himself, just herself. What is the point of comparing? Who are you to compare? And who are you to fix a criterion to decide who is learned and who is not learned? Who are you to follow a criterion for who is beautiful and who is not beautiful? Who are you? Why should you judge? Jesus says, "Judge ye not."

It is difficult to be one in knowledge and practice.

Unless the knowledge is your own, there will always be a rift between what you know and what you do. Because whatsoever you do cannot be transformed by knowledge gathered from others; it cannot be changed by borrowed knowledge. It changes only when your insight flowers. It is difficult to have a synthesis, a harmony in life between what you know and what you do.

Watch what you do – in fact, that is indicative. That and only that is what you know. Whatsoever you know and you don't do, you don't know at all. Drop it, throw it! It is rubbish! Watch your doing, because that is your real knowledge.

You say anger is bad and you don't want to do it, but then somebody insults and you become angry and you say, "What to do? In spite of myself I became angry. I know very well that anger is bad, poisonous, destructive. I know it, but what to do? – I became angry."

If you come to me, I will say, "You don't know that anger is poisonous. You have heard about it. Deep down you know that anger is necessary; deep down you know that without anger you will lose your standing, everybody will be bullying you. Without anger, you will not have any spine; your pride will be shattered. Without anger, how can you exist in this world of continuous struggle for survival?" This is what you know, but you say, "I know anger is poisonous."

Buddha knows anger is poisonous. You have heard Buddha, you have listened to Buddha, you have learned something from him – but that is *his* knowledge.

Whatsoever is your doing, remember – it is your knowing. Go deep into your doing to find out exactly what you know. And if you want to transform your doing, then borrowed knowledge won't do. If you really want to know what anger is, go into it, meditate over it, taste it in many ways. Allow it to happen inside you, be surrounded by it, be clouded by it, feel all the pang and the pain and the hurt of it, and the poison, and how it brings you low, how it creates a dark valley for your being, how you fall into hell through it, how it is a downward flow. Feel it, know it. And that understanding will start a transformation in you.

To know truth is to be transformed. Truth liberates – but it must be your own.

It is difficult not to express an opinion about others.

Very difficult. We go on unconsciously expressing our opinion about others. Do you know others? You don't know even yourself – how foolish it is to express opinions about others! You may have known somebody for a few days. You know his name, you know how he walks; you have known him in a few situations, how he acts, but do you know him ? He is a vast continent. You have known only a fragment of it. It is as if a page torn from the Bible has come into your hands . . . the winds have brought it to you, torn loose, and you read a few sentences. They are also not complete – somewhere a word is missing, somewhere the ink has been washed away by the rain, somewhere mud has settled on it . . . and then you decide about Jesus, or you decide about Christianity. It will be foolish. It is as if you are brought into a movie that is being shown, and you enter from one door, you look at the movie, and you go out through the other door. Just for a few seconds you are inside, and you decide about the whole story? It will be foolish. It will be sheer stupidity on your part. In fact, you will not decide about a movie in this way. You will say, "I have not seen the whole movie. I don't know what went before, what was coming afterwards, and I have only been here in the movie hall for a few seconds. Just a few images were there, and they are almost incomprehensible to me – I don't know the context." But that's how we know persons.

A life is a tremendously rich phenomenon. One never knows, because only a part of it is expressed in the actions, only the tip of the iceberg – the real thing remains inside. What you do is a very small tiny part of what you are. What you do is a very small part of what you think, of what you feel, of what you dream, of what you fantasize, of what goes on inside your being . . . just fragments.

Buddha says, *It is difficult not to express an opinion about others* – but take the challenge. Resist the temptation. Don't express your opinions about others and you will grow in understanding. Because your opinion becomes a barrier to understanding; it becomes a prejudice.

It is by rare opportunity that one is introduced to a true spiritual teacher.

In fact, to be introduced to a true spiritual teacher is a very unique phenomenon. First, nobody is searching truth. Even if a master passes by, you will remain completely oblivious of his existence. That's how it happened when Buddha passed. Millions of people remained oblivious. When Jesus passed, people had not even heard his name. He was an unknown figure. When Mahavira was here, very rare souls came in contact with him. You can come in contact with a master only when you are really seeking truth intensely, passionately; when you have a fiery desire to know, and you are ready to stake everything for it. When you are ready to know, when you are ready to become a disciple, only then can you come into contact with a master, only then can you be introduced to the world of a master. Your readiness to become a disciple will be your introduction.

It is very difficult to become a disciple. It is easy to become a student, because a student has no personal relationship. He comes in order to know things. You go to the university, you are a student. If you come to me as a student, you will miss me, because then you hear only what I say and you will collect it as information; you will become more knowledgeable. A disciple means one who is ready to trust somebody . . . very difficult . . . ready to go with somebody into the unknown, uncharted world. Only a very courageous soul becomes a disciple. To learn, one needs to be humble. To learn, one needs to be totally empty, receptive, sensitive, meditative.

A student needs concentration, a disciple needs meditation. Concentration means he has to listen correctly to what is being said. Meditation means you have to be present rightly; not only listen rightly – that is only a small part of it. You have to be present, in tune, in harmony, in deep rapport, so your heart can beat with the master's heart, so you can vibrate with his frequency. A moment comes between the master and the disciple when they both start vibrating in the same rhythm. Then something is transferred, then something transpires between them. That which cannot be said can be transferred in those moments. That which cannot be expressed can be handed over in those moments. A transmission beyond scripture . . . that's how Zen Buddhists express it . . . a transmission beyond scripture, a transmission that is immediate, direct.

It is difficult to gain an insight into the nature of being, and to practice the way.

. . . Because one has to go inwards. We go outward so easily. To go outward is to go downward; it is easy. To go inward is to go upward. It is an uphill task, it is difficult. To go to others is simple – the way of the world. To go to oneself is difficult – it is not the way of the world, not the way of the crowd. Only very few people, rare souls, try to move inwards.

It is difficult to gain an insight into the nature of being and to practice the way.

First, it is difficult to have an insight into your own being, and then it is even more difficult to practice it, because then you will be practicing nothingness. Then you will be walking as an emptiness. Then you will not be there. Because if you go into the deepest core of your being, you will find that the human being is like an onion – you go on peeling it, layer upon layer . . . go on peeling it . . . and in the end only emptiness is left in the hand. Then you have come to the very core of the onion – that is from where it has developed. Out of nothingness it has become something. Out of the immaterial, matter has arisen. Out of no-being, being has gathered.

It is difficult to know it, first, because who wants to know that one is not? Who desires to disappear? Who longs for total, ultimate death? It is difficult first to know it and then it is even more difficult to practice it – because when you are nobody, nothing is left to practice.

To walk like a buddha is really the impossible. It *happens*. It is incredible, it cannot be believed. How does Buddha walk? Have you ever pondered over it? He has no desire to go anywhere, still he walks. He has no desire to do anything, still he lives. He has no desire to achieve anything, still every morning he gets up, starts helping people. He has nothing to achieve now, nowhere to go – then why does he go on breathing? He is practicing nothingness. It is one of the most incredible phenomena – to come to know that you are not and then still to exist.

Many disappear. Those who disappear, Buddha calls them *arhatas*. When they come to know their inner emptiness, they simply dissolve into it. Then what is the point of even breathing? Why breathe? why eat? why drink? why be? They simply disappear.

Those who try hard – knowing well that they are not, but who still try hard – to help others, knowing well that others are just in dream, knowing well that others also don't exist in reality . . . To have compassion on phantoms, to have compassion on shadows and still make an effort to help them, is the most impossible thing. But it happens.

You exist because of passion, desire. Buddha has to exist for compassion. He has no desire. There is nothing – no future for him. All that has to happen has happened. Still he practices the way. He moves as alert as he wants you to move. He behaves in the way he wants you to behave.

Jesus was leaving his disciples on the last night and he washed their feet. They were very embarrassed and they said, "What are you doing, master?"

And Jesus said, "There is no need for me to touch your feet, but I am doing it so that you will remember – don't become too egoistic. Remember that your master touched your feet, so when people come to you as disciples, don't become too egoistic that you know and they don't know, that they are ignorant. Touch their feet." Jesus says that he's touching their feet just to help them to remember.

Buddha says, "I behave the way you should behave. Not that there is any more discipline for me, but I go on behaving the way I would like you to behave. For you, still there is much to be done."

A Buddha is absolute freedom. He can be in any way, there is no problem. But still he goes on following a discipline. Every morning he sits in meditation. What compassion!

Somebody, his great disciple Sariputta, asked Buddha, "Why do you sit in meditation? Because you are twenty-four hours in meditation."

Buddha said, "That's right, but if I don't sit, others will take advantage of it. They will think, If Buddha is not meditating, why should we bother?"

Now he has no need to meditate, but he sits under the tree every morning so that others can sit under the tree.

It is difficult to gain insight into the nature of being, and to practice the way.

It is difficult to follow the steps of a savior.

Because to follow the steps of a savior is to commit suicide. You have to dissolve yourself by and by. The closer you come to a savior, the more you disappear, the more and more you disappear. When you come the closest, you are not there. One who is ready to dissolve is ready to become a disciple.

It is difficult to be always the master of oneself.

Small things prove that you are a slave. Somebody insults you and anger arises – you are simply proving that he is the master. He can insult you any day and can create anger in you, you are not the master of your anger. Somebody comes and flatters you and you smile. He has brought the smile in you; he is the master. You are not the master.

Buddha says it is very difficult, but try – try in every way to remain a master. Don't allow anybody to manipulate you. Don't allow anybody to reduce you to just a mechanism. Remain a master in every situation and if you make effort, sooner or later you will start feeling a new power, a new surge of energy in you.

And the last, the twentieth:

It is difficult to understand thoroughly the ways of Buddha.

It is difficult because you are not a buddha yet. Only the similar can understand, only the equal can understand. A Jesus can be understood only by a Jesus. A Buddha can be understood only by a buddha. How can you understand? If you live in the valley, if you have the language of the valley and somebody comes from the top of the hill where you have never been, and he talks about the sunlight and the clouds, and the beautiful colors of the clouds, and the flowers that bloom on the top of the hill, how will you understand? You know only the valley, the darkness, and your crawling life. You will misinterpret, you will translate whatsoever he is saying into the language of your valley. That's why buddhas say, "Come, come with us. Come to the reality we exist in. Come to the top. There only will you be able to understand it." It is not a question of logical discourse, it is a question of changing and transforming your plane of being.

What I am saying to you, you can listen to it; in a certain intellectual way you can understand it also, but you will always feel puzzled. You will always feel that this man is talking in contradictions. Sometimes he says this, sometimes he says that. You will always remain in a confusion.

Just the other night some one came to me and said, "I was never so confused as I have become listening to you."

I said, "That's right! You were thinking that you know. Now you know that you don't know. You were thinking that everything is okay. Now you know nothing is okay. You were thinking that this valley is all that exists. Now you know there are unknown peaks. Now the challenge has penetrated your heart. Now the desire has arisen and much has been stirred by the desire. You don't know what those peaks are, but you have started longing for those peaks."

Confusion is bound to happen, because the language of the valley and the language of the peak are two different languages. There has been a meeting between the two; chaos has arisen.

"But don't be bothered by it," I told her. 'Start moving towards the direction I am indicating, and as you move higher your confusion will start changing into a fusion. Confusion will be left behind in the valley. By the time you reach the peak, everything will be crystal clear."

It is difficult to understand thoroughly the ways of Buddha.

It is enough if you can even understand a bit of it. Try hard. Don't leave any stones unturned. Try hard to understand. Knowing well it is almost impossible – but try hard; by your very effort, you will become integrated. A center will be born in you, and that center will become a transforming point.

One day you are all destined to be buddhas. The whole thing will be understood only on that day, not before it. You will have to grope in the dark, but don't be lazy – grope. The door is there, certainly. If you go on groping, you are bound to find it. The hill exists. If you take courage and start moving beyond the valley, you are bound to reach. Yes, arduous is the path, dangerous is the path, but that is the only way one matures, grows and attains to life abundant.

Enough for today.

Chapter 7:

In Accord with the Way

A MONK ASKED THE BUDDHA:
*Under what conditions is it possible to come to the
knowledge of the past and to understand the most
supreme way?*

THE BUDDHA SAID:
*Those who are pure in heart and single in purpose are
able to understand the most supreme way. It is like
polishing a mirror which becomes bright when the dust is
removed. Remove your passions and have no hankering
and the past will be revealed unto you.*

A MONK ASKED THE BUDDHA:
What is good and what is great?

THE BUDDHA ANSWERED:
*Good is to practice the way and to follow the truth. Great
is the heart that is in accord with the way.*

Life in itself is not the goal. The goal surpasses life; the life is just an opportunity
to realize the goal. The goal is hidden deep in life. You cannot find it on the
surface, you will have to penetrate to the very center. The life is like a seed. In
itself it is not enough. You will have to work hard so the seed sprouts, becomes
a tree and comes to bloom.

This is one of the most fundamental things to remember – that man has to
surpass himself, that life has to transcend itself. If you don't understand this,
then you will be lost in the means and you will forget the end. That's what

happens ordinarily. We become too attached with life and we forget that life was just an opportunity to understand something deeper than life, higher than life, something superior, far superior.

If you get too obsessed with life itself, it is as if somebody is sent to the university and he becomes too attached to the university and he cannot leave, even conceive of leaving it. The university is there just to educate you for something greater. For the universe, the university is to prepare you; that's why we call it the "university", It itself is not the universe but just a preparation. In the East, life is considered to be just like a university, a discipline, a training for something far beyond it. If you become too attached with life, then you will be coming back again and again every year to the university. Then it is futile, pointless. A university is to get ready, and it has to be left behind one day. It is just a preparation. If the preparation becomes endless, then it becomes a burden.

That is what has happened to many people. They take life as the goal. Then they go on preparing, they go on preparing endlessly. They never go on the journey, they simply prepare for the journey. If their life turns out to be just an impotent gesture, no wonder! It is natural, it has to be so.

Just think about yourself – always consulting timetables, always getting ready to leave, always making inquiries at the tourist office and never leaving, never going anywhere? You will go mad!

Nothing is wrong with life itself, but if your attitude is this – that life is an end unto itself – then you will be in trouble. Then your whole life will become meaningless. The meaning is there, but the meaning is transcendental to it. The meaning is there, but you will have to penetrate to that core where it is revealed.

To think of life as the goal is to remain on the periphery. That periphery Buddha calls the "wheel". The symbol of the wheel is very significant and has to be understood. The periphery, Buddha calls the wheel . . . it goes on moving. You can watch a bullock cart – the wheels move. They move on something that is unmoving – the center remains unmoving; the hub remains unmoving. On an unmoving hub, the wheel goes on moving.

If you only look at the wheel, you will be looking at the temporal. If you become capable of looking at the hub, you will be able to penetrate the eternal. If you only look at the periphery, you will be watching the accidental. If you become capable of reaching the center, the hub, you will be able to know the essential. And unless you come to know the essential, you will be repeating the same thing again and again and again. The world is called the wheel because things go on repeating themselves again and again, and you by and by become repetitive. And the more you repeat yourself, the more you are bored. The more you are bored, the more dull and stupid you become. You lose intelligence, you lose freshness, you lose awareness. You become a robot, a mechanical thing.

Watch people around you. They have become robots. They just go on doing the same thing again and again. Every morning, every evening, they go on moving in the same rut, and of course they look dead. There is no spark in their eyes; you cannot find any ray of light.

Buddha calls this continuous repetition of the wheel "samsara", To get out of it, to get out of this rut, is nirvana.

Before we enter the sutra, a few things have to be understood.

Life is the game of games, the ultimate game. It has tremendous meaning in it if you take it as a game and you don't become serious about it. If you remain simple, innocent, the game is going to impart many things to you.

Sometimes you were a tiger, and sometimes you were a rock, and sometimes you became a tree. Sometimes you become a man; sometimes you were an ant, and sometimes an elephant. Buddha says all these are games. You have been playing a thousand and one games, to know life in every possible way. By playing game after game, the player may experience all the permutations of matter in evolution. That is the goal of life.

When you exist like a tree, you know life in one way. Nobody else can know it except the tree. The tree has its own vision. When clouds come in the sky and the sun shines and there is a rainbow, only the tree knows how to feel it. It has a perceptivity of its own. When the breeze passes by, the tree knows how to be showered in it. When a bird starts singing, only the tree knows, only the tree has ears for it . . . for its music, its melody. The tree has a way to know life – its own way. Only a tree knows that way.

A tiger has another way of knowing life. He is playing another game. An ant is playing a totally different game. Millions of games . . . All these games are like classes of a university. You pass through each class; you learn something. Then you move into another class.

Man is the last point. If you have learned all the lessons of life, and the lesson of being a human being, then only will you become capable of moving into the very center of life. Then you will be able to know what godliness is, or what nirvana is. All through these games you have been trying to approach the ultimate – through many directions, in many ways, in many perceptivities. But the goal is the same – everybody is trying to know what the truth is. What is the mystery of this life? Why are we here and who am I? What is this that goes on existing? There is only one way to learn it, and that is the way of existence. But if you just move from one class to another like a sleepwalker, a somnambulist, unconscious, dragged from one class to another, not moving deliberately and consciously, you will miss.

That's how many people arrive at the point of being human beings, and they cannot see anything of the beyond. That simply shows they have missed the lessons. They avoided the lessons. They were in the classes but they have not got the point. Otherwise every person who has arrived at the stage of being human must be religious. Being human and being religious must become synonymous. They are not synonymous. Very rarely a few people are religious. And by religious I don't mean a person who goes to the church every Sunday. By religious I don't mean a person who is Christian, Mohammedan, Hindu, Jaina, Buddhist. By religious I don't mean that you belong to a religious organization.

When I say religious, I mean a person who is aware that life is so full of transcendence . . . that from everywhere life is overflowing into something bigger than life . . . that every step is leading you towards godliness, truth, nirvana, freedom . . . that whether you know it or not, you are moving towards the ultimate temple. When a person starts feeling it in his very guts, then a person is religious. He may go to the church, he may not go to the church; that is irrelevant. He may call himself a Christian or a Mohammedan or a Hindu; that is irrelevant. He may not call himself anything. He may belong to some organization, he may not belong – but he belongs to existence, to the ultimate.

And when I say godliness, existence, the ultimate, or God, remember that I mean that which transcends. That which is always ahead of you. You are always coming closer to it, approaching closer and closer and closer, but it always remains ahead of you. It is that omega point which always remains the goal. You come close to it but you can never possess it. It cannot be ever in your hands. You can drop yourself completely in it, you can merge yourself in it, but still you will know that much remains to be known. In fact the more you know, the more you feel that much remains to be known. The more you know, the more you become humble. The mystery, infinite, ineffable, cannot be exhausted. That inexhaustible source, that transcendental source is what I mean by the divine, the ultimate, godliness. And by calling a person religious, I mean one who has become alert about the transcendental.

When you are alert about the transcendental your life has a beautiful charm, a grace. Then your life has energy, intelligence. Then your life has a sharpness, a creativity. Then your life has a holy aura to it. By becoming aware of the transcendental, you become part of the transcendental. It has penetrated in your awareness. A ray of light has entered into the dark night of your soul. You are no longer alone, and you are no longer a stranger in existence. You are deeply rooted in it. This is your home.

A religious person is one who feels existence as his home. A religious person is one who feels existence constantly evolving and evolving, going higher and higher, towards that ultimate omega point where you disappear, where all limitations disappear and only infinity is left, only eternity is left.

So this game of life has to be played very skillfully. Buddha's word for skill is *upaya*. It is one of his most beautiful words. He says, "Be skillful." If you are not skillful, you will miss much that is valuable. Being skillful means being aware. Don't just go on dragging yourself half asleep, half awake. Shake yourself into awareness. Bring more awareness into each act of your life, into each step of your being. Then only, with open eyes, you start seeing something that cannot ordinarily be seen when you are asleep, when you are unconscious. Shake all the dust from the eyes. Be skillful and live life consciously; otherwise life becomes boring.

You feel it. You know how it feels. Sooner or later everything feels boring; one is bored to death. One goes on living because one is not courageous enough to commit suicide. One goes on living just in the hope that sooner or later one will die – death is coming.

> Mulla Nasruddin was going on a world tour and he was traveling in a ship for the first time, and he was very seasick. The captain came to him and said, "Don't be worried, Nasruddin. I have been working as a captain for twenty years and I have never seen any man die from seasickness. Don't be worried."
>
> Mulla said, "My God! That was my only hope – that I might die. You have taken away even that hope!"

People are living just in the hope that some day or other they are going to die. So they go on saying to themselves, "Don't lose heart – death is coming."

If you are waiting for death, if you are so bored, then there is no possibility for any encounter with the beyond. The encounter can only happen in radiance, in sharpness, in awareness.

But why do we get bored? The Buddhist explanation is of tremendous import. Buddha says you have done the same things – not only in this life; you have been doing them for millions of lives, hence boredom. You may not consciously remember them, but deep down the memory is there. Nothing is lost as far as memory is concerned. There is a reservoir of memory. Buddha calls it *alaya vigyan*, reservoir of memory. It is exactly what Jung calls the collective unconscious. You carry it. The body changes, the identity changes, but the bundle of memories goes on jumping from one life to another. And it goes on accumulating, gathering. It goes on becoming bigger and bigger. Nothing is lost as far as the memory record is concerned.

If you look into yourself, you have the whole record of the existence in you.

Because you have been here from the very beginning – if there was any beginning. You have been always here. You are an intrinsic part of this existence. All that has happened to existence has happened to you also, and you carry the record. You may not know it, but you have loved millions of times. Again falling in love – it is nothing new, it is a very old story. You have done all the things that you are doing. You have been ambitious, you have been greedy, you accumulated wealth, you became very famous, you had prestige and power – this has happened many, many times, millions of times and you carry deep down in the unconscious the reservoir of memories. And whatsoever you are doing now looks futile, pointless, meaningless.

I have heard:

> A newspaper reporter was interviewing Mulla Nasruddin on his hundredth birthday. "If you had your life to live over," he asked, "do you think you would make the same mistakes again?"
>
> "Certainly," said the old Mulla, "but I would start a lot sooner. I would start a lot sooner . . ."

This is what is happening. Out of your mistakes you only learn how to start them sooner, you don't learn how to drop them. You only learn how to start them sooner and how to do them more efficiently next time.

Buddha says if you can penetrate this reservoir of memories then you will be really fed up. Then you will see – "I have been doing the same thing again and again." And then in that state of awareness, you will start doing something new for the first time. And that will bring a thrill, fresh air into your being.

There are two time concepts in the world. In the West, the linear time concept has been prevalent. Christians, Jews, Mohammedans – they are all offshoots of the Judaic concept of life. They have believed in the linear concept of time; that time is moving in a line. The Eastern concept – the Hindu, the Buddhist, the Jain concept – is different. It is circular. Time is moving in a circle.

If time is moving in a line, then things are not repeated again. The line goes on moving; it never comes back to meet and move on the same old track again. If time is thought to be circular, then everything is being repeated. And the Eastern time concept seems to be more true – because every movement is circular.

Just watch all the movements. The seasons moving around the year are circular – again comes the summer . . . again, again. In the same way it moves. The earth moves in a circle, the sun moves in a circle, the stars move in a circle. And now Albert Einstein has suggested that the whole universe is also moving in a circle. Not only that – Einstein introduced a very strange concept to physics, and that is the concept of circular space. The whole of space is circular.

The East has always thought that the circle is the natural way of things. Things move in a circle and by and by they become circular. All movement is circular. Then time has also to be circular, because time is nothing but pure movement. If you think about time as circular then your whole world view changes.

Your whole life is also circular according to the Eastern way of seeing. A child is born. Birth is the beginning of a circle, death is the end of the circle. The old man in his last moments again becomes as helpless as a child. And if things have gone rightly, he will become as innocent as a child; then the circle is complete. Then his life was a round-shaped life. Then his life will have grace. If the circle is not complete, then life will have something missing in it. Then there will be holes in his life, and his life will be tense. It will not be round, graceful.

Buddha says that in each life the wheel moves once. The circle becomes complete. Another life – the wheel moves again. The spokes are the same – again childhood, again youth, again old age; the same desires, the same passions, the same lust, the same rushing, the same ambition, the same struggle, conflict, the same aggression, the same ego, and again the same frustration, the same misery. This goes on and on and on. If you can penetrate into your deepest memories, then you will be able to see that you are not doing anything new here. That's why in the East they say there is nothing new under the sun. Everything has been done millions of times.

So it became a very methodological thing in Buddhism and Jainism for every seeker to penetrate into his past memories; it became a necessary thing. Because Buddha says unless you can see the whole nonsense of repetition, you will continue to repeat.

Just think about it. If you come across the whole record and you see that millions of times you fallen in love, and every time you were miserable . . . Now it is time enough to understand. Now don't be foolish again. If you see that millions of times you were born and you died again, and every birth brings death, now what is the point in clinging to life? Then renounce it. If you see that every time you expected something you were frustrated, your expectations were never fulfilled, then what is the point now? Now drop expecting. This became a basic meditation – to go into one's past memories.

If you look, in even one life you will see constant repetition. Even in your old age you go on being the same way. It simply shows that you have not learned anything in life. Everybody passes through experiences, but that is not necessarily a learning. There is a difference between passing through life and learning. Learning means you go on looking at your experiences. You keep a record of the experiences, you observe your experiences, and you gather certain wisdom through them. You were angry and you did something foolish. Again you are angry and you do something foolish. Again you are angry – but you never take account of all your angers, and you never look at the mechanicalness of it. You don't learn a lesson out of it. Then you have experienced, but you have not learned anything.

If you simply experience, you become old. If you learn, you become wise.

Not all old people are wise. Wisdom has nothing to do with old age. A real man of understanding can become wise any time. Even as a child he can become wise. If you have a penetrating understanding, even a single experience of anger and you will be finished with it; it is so ugly. A single experience of greed and you will be finished with it; it is so poisonous.

I have heard:

"I am leaving home!" shouted Mahmud to his father, Mulla Nasruddin. "I want wine, women, adventures!" His old man got up out of his chair.

"Don't try to stop me!" shouted Mahamud at him.

"Who is trying to stop you?" exclaimed old Mulla. "I am coming with you."

The same foolishness continues. Young and old, educated, uneducated, poor, rich – all seem to be in the same boat. They don't seem to learn. If you learn, a totally different vision arises in your life.

I have heard:

It was in the early barnstorming days of aviation, and the old fellow had finally worked up enough nerve to take a flight on a plane. When the rickety plane landed, the old fellow crawled out and said "Sir, I want to thank you for both of those rides."

"What are you talking about?" asked the pilot. "You had only one ride."

"No," replied the passenger, "I had two rides – my first and my last."

If you understand a thing, then it is your first and last. Then you have had enough of it. Then it is not one ride, it is two rides.

This sutra today consists of a question from a monk.

A monk asked the Buddha: Under what conditions is it possible to come to the knowledge of the past and to understand the most supreme way?

Buddha insisted on it very much. He said, first move towards the past, first

137

go backwards – because that is where you have lived for millennia. Just look what you have been doing there. What has been your experience up to now? Go into it. Gather some lessons out of it. Otherwise you will tend to commit the same mistakes again and again.

And there is a natural mechanism which does not allow you to remember it ordinarily. When a person dies and is reborn again, there comes a gap between his past life and the new life – a layer of oblivion, forgetfulness. It is natural, because it will be very difficult for you to live if you keep remembering all that has happened before.

Not only at the end of life; every day it is happening. Millions of things happen in the day. You don't remember all. Not that they are not recorded – they are all recorded. It is unbelievable how the mind goes on recording minute, small things. Whatsoever happens around you . . . you may not be even aware that it is happening, but the mind goes on recording. For example, you are listening to me, you are focused on me and you are deeply in concentration – but the train is passing by. You may not have heard it at all as far as your consciousness is concerned. If somebody asks you later on, "Was there a train going by? Did you hear the noise?" you may say, "I don't remember because I was so concentrated." But your mind has recorded it. Even without your knowing it, mind goes on recording. If you are hypnotized and then asked, the mind will play back everything.

If I ask you suddenly, "What happened on the first of January five years ago? What happened? Can you remember?" You will be simply blank. That does not mean that nothing happened on that day. Something must have happened – a quarrel with your wife, or a headache. In twenty-four hours, the first of January, five years ago – something must have happened. Twenty-four hours cannot be vacant, otherwise you would have become a buddha. If you had remained empty for twenty-four hours, nothing happening, then nirvana would have happened! But you don't remember at all. You will shrug your shoulders that you don't remember.

Unless something very special happened on that day – if there was a car accident and you were almost killed, maybe you will remember it. Or some other type of accident – you got married; you will remember it because there is no way to forget it now. You cannot forget and you cannot forgive yourself for it. It remains like a wound. But otherwise you are completely forgetful. But if you are hypnotized and you go into a deep trance and the hypnotist asks you, "Now go backwards. Remember the first of January, five years back, and start relating what happened from the morning," you will relate such minute things –the tea was cold and you didn't like it at all. The night was not good and you had a nightmare. Things like this you will remember, minute details – that a dog was barking when you were taking your morning tea, that the cup had fallen from your hand and broken. Small things – that you were passing by the side of a tree and the tree had bloomed, and you will remember the smell. Or that it had rained and there was a beautiful smell coming out of the earth. You may not only remember, you will relive it. It will be so clear.

Everything is recorded. But you have to forget it; otherwise your mind will be so cluttered with unnecessary information that you will not be able to manage your life. So there is a natural mechanism that goes on sorting things out inside you. Much work continues for twenty-four hours a day; a great sorting out goes on. Whatever is inessential is thrown into the basement; you may never need it. Then the secondary things, which are not so absolutely irrelevant, which you may need sometime but for which there is no urgency; they are put into the subconscious, within reach. If sometimes you need them, you can bring them back to consciousness. And very few things, which you will need every day, are left in the conscious.

For example, two plus two is four – this remains in the conscious; you will need it every day, every moment. The fact that this is your wife and this is your husband remains in the conscious. If you go on forgetting every day, it will create difficulties in life. Your name and your address and your phone number . . . Everything else, almost ninety-nine point nine percent, falls into the basement and disappears forever. But it remains there underground. It can be recalled by specific methods. That's what they are doing in primal therapy – they are trying to recall all that has disappeared into the tunnels of the unconscious, to relive it. Once it is relived, you are freed from it.

What primal therapists are doing now, Buddha has done twenty-five centuries ago and in a greater way, in a deeper way. Not only with this life – he has done it with the whole past. You have to pass through the womb again in your memory. Then you have to go back to the death that happened in the last life. Then go on moving, back to the birth in the last life. In this way one goes on moving back and back and back. And the more you practice it, the more you become efficient in revealing all the mysteries that you have been carrying.

You are carrying a great record, and if you can relive it, you will be able to find out a few lessons from it. Those lessons will be of tremendous value. They will be liberating. They will liberate you from your past.

Once you are liberated from the past, you are liberated from the future also because then there is nothing left to project. Once you are liberated from your past lives, you are liberated from life itself. Then all desires to cling to life disappear. Then you don't want to be born again. Then you don't want to cling. Then you are not afraid of death. Then you don't want to be confined in any womb, in any body. You don't want to be embodied again. You would like absolute freedom.

This learning can be done in two ways – either while you are living, learn it . . . If you do that, you will become a buddha, slowly. If you have not done that, then go backwards and relive your past experiences, your past lives.

The monk asked Buddha:

Under what conditions is it possible to come to the knowledge of the past and to understand the most supreme way?

Because first you have to understand your past lives, then only can you ask in a meaningful way how to get out of it . . . where is the exit? the way? When Buddha talks about the way, he means the way out. You have entered into life, now where is the way out?

I have heard:

> Mike was going to Dublin for the last time and his friend Pat was giving him a few hints on what to do and where to go in the big city.
> "What do I do when I go to the zoo?" asked Mike.
> "You be careful about the zoo," advised Pat. "You will see fine animals if you follow the words 'To the Lions', or 'To the Elephants', but take no notice of 'To the Exit'. It is a fraud. It is outside I found myself when I went to look at it."

That we have been doing – we have been avoiding the door that takes us out of life. We have avoided it for so long that it has almost become invisible to us. We have ignored it so long that it almost does not exist for us. Even if we come across it, we will not be able to recognize it. "To the Exit" . . . those words have become very faint; they have almost disappeared. We know only the entrance into life, we don't know the exit.

The entrance of course we know, because we have entered many times. Again and again we enter in the womb. Here you die and there you enter; almost within minutes, at the most within days. Here you die . . . even while dying, your mind starts planning where to enter. You have not yet died and you are planning already for the future – where to enter, how to enter. The fantasy has started working again.

Remember, it is your decision to enter the womb; that's why you enter. You are not thrown into it, you choose it. As the entrance exists, so does the exit.

THE MONK IS ASKING:

Under what conditions is it possible to come to the knowledge of the past and to understand the most supreme way?

The Buddha said:

> *Those who are pure in heart and single in purpose are able to understand the most supreme way.*

Those who are pure in heart and single in purpose . . . People who live in their heads will find it very difficult to move into the past, because the head is always in the future. The head is really a mechanism to plan for the future. It always moves ahead of you. It is like radar – in a plane, you must have seen a radar screen; the radar scans ahead of the plane. That is its whole purpose . . . a hundred miles ahead, two hundred miles ahead. On the radar screen, the clouds that are a hundred miles ahead start appearing. Within minutes the plane will be reaching that spot, so the pilot has to know beforehand. If he comes to know only when he has reached, then it will be too late; the speed is so great.

Mind is a radar screen, your head is a radar system. It goes on groping into the future, planning for the future. It is never here in the present. With the past, mind has nothing to do; the past has already disappeared. The whole interest of the head is in the future. Even if sometimes it looks at the past, it looks only to find a few clues for the future. Even if it wants to look into the past, it is just as a help to prepare for the future. The interest, the center of interest is the future.

Buddha says . . . *pure in heart and single in purpose.* People who are not in the head but in the heart, only they can enter into past lives. The heart is very close to the unconscious basement, the head is farthest away. The heart is closer to your navel center. Just somewhere near the navel is the corresponding point in the body with your unconscious. You have to come to the heart. The heart is midway between the head and the navel.

If you become more and more full of feeling, full of heart, you will become capable of knowing, of entering into that great story of your past lives. It is not only your biography, it is the biography of the whole universe. Because sometimes you were a tree, and in your mind, deep down in the unconscious, you are still carrying all those memories of being a tree. Someday you were a tiger, and someday you were a cat, and someday you were an elephant. Someday you were a woman, and someday you were a man . . . millions of memories are there. The whole drama of life is there, in a very condensed form. If you go into it, it starts playing. You can again listen to those sounds. That's why in hypnosis it is possible that if you hypnotize a person and tell him that now he has become a tiger, he becomes a tiger.

You may have seen hypnotists doing it on the stage. They tell a man, "You have become a woman. Now walk!" And the man walks like a woman. It is very difficult, but he manages. He may have never walked like a woman. Now, how does he suddenly start walking like a woman? It is very difficult, because the woman has a totally different structure of the body. Because of the womb existing in her body, she has a different type of skeleton. She moves in a different way. Her movement is more round and more shapely. A man moves differently. But under the influence of hypnosis, the man can walk like a woman, the woman can walk like a man. Not only that. A person who has never heard a single word of Arabic or Latin or Chinese can be provoked under hypnosis to speak Chinese. If the hypnosis is really deep, he may start speaking Chinese. It is a miracle, and the hypnotist has not been yet able to explain it.

How to explain it? What happens?

The explanation is simple if you understand Buddha's hypothesis. Buddha says – and all the Eastern masters agree – that an individual has been everything in his past life. You have been Chinese, you have been Japanese, you have been a German, or Tibetan. So if somewhere deep in your memories the life that you lived as a Chinese person is still there, it can be provoked under hypnosis. It can be revealed. You can start speaking Chinese. You have never heard a single word of it, you don't know anything about it.

A human being is vast. It is not so confined as you think. You think you are a Hindu, or a Mohammedan, or a Christian, or an Indian, or Japanese, or Chinese. These are just boundaries on your conscious mind. In the unconscious, you are an infinite territory. You are all. Not only Hindu and Mohammedan and Christian, but even a tiger, a cat, a mouse, a lion, a tree, a rock, a cloud. You are vast. You are as vast as this universe. Once you start entering, you will become tremendously aware that no limitation exists. All limitations are a sort of belief. You believe, that's why they are there. If you drop them, they start disappearing.

Those who are pure in heart and single in purpose . . .

People who are more heart-oriented are single in purpose. They are not crooked, they are not cunning. The head is very cunning. The head is like a fox – very calculating and subtle in its ways. If it wants something, it will never go direct. If it wants something, it will go zigzag. It will say something else, it will do something else. It would like to get something else. The head is very political, diplomatic. You can watch it in yourself – how the head goes on deceiving, how the head goes on being political. It is never authentic. It cannot be.

The heart is authentic. It knows no deception. It goes direct. The heart moves in straight lines, the head goes zigzag. Buddha says a person who wants to move into his past lives will need singleness of purpose. Crookedness won't do. One will have to follow straight, simple, direct . . . *to understand the most supreme way.* These people who are simple, heart-oriented, single, straight, direct, immediate – these people enter easily.

It has become more and more difficult since the days of Buddha to enter into past lives. It was so simple in Buddha's time. People were simple. Almost every sannyasin that was initiated by Buddha had to pass through past experiences. And the same was true with Mahavira.

There is a famous story. A prince was initiated by Mahavira, but he had lived almost always in comfort, in richness. And now with Mahavira, life was very hard. He had to move on the road naked, to sleep on hard floors with no clothes. It was difficult. The first night he started thinking of dropping out; this was not for him. There were so many mosquitoes – as there have always been in India; they seem to be the constant enemies of meditators. He could not meditate . . . so many mosquitoes . . . and he was naked and it was cold, and the place where he was sleeping was just in the middle of the whole crowd, and hundreds of sannyasins were staying there. The whole night he could not sleep; people were coming and going. It was very crowded and he had never lived that way; that was not his way of life.

So in the night he started feeling that the next morning he would leave. It is said that in the middle of the night Mahavira came to him. The prince was surprised. He said, "Why have you come?"

Mahavira told him, "I have been watching you. I know your difficulty. But this has happened before. This is in fact the third time. You have been initiated twice before in your other lives and each time you have left."

He said, "What do you mean?" And Mahavira told him to do a certain technique of meditation that he calls *jati smaran* – the method to remember one's past life. And he told him, "You just do this the whole night. Sit in meditation and by the morning, whatsoever you decide . . ."

The man went into his past life. It seems very simple in the story, it must have been. People must have been simple. He went into his past life so easily. And by the morning he came back and he was full of new light. He touched Mahavira's feet and he said, "I have decided to stay. Enough is enough. I looked into it . . . Yes, you were right. How long can I go on repeating it again and again? It is insulting to take *sannyas* and leave it; it is below dignity.

"No, it is not good for a warrior like me to be afraid of mosquitoes, to be afraid of small inconveniences. But you were right. Twice also it has happened the same way. I was initiated and the first night I became disturbed, and the next morning I left. I was going to do it again! I am so grateful to you that you reminded me; otherwise I would have committed the same thing again, thinking that I am doing it for the first time."

All the sannyasins of Buddha and Mahavira had to pass through *jati smaran*, through the memory of all the past lives. Today it has become very difficult – difficult because the head has become very heavy. The head is so heavy and energy is so much monopolized by the head that it is not flowing in the heart at all. And the path towards past lives goes through the heart.

So if you want to remember past lives – and it is a great experience, very revealing and very liberating – you will have to live a very simple-hearted life for a few months and years . . . the life of feelings. Don't allow your thinking to dominate you; let feeling balance it. Don't allow logic to be dictatorial; let love decide. By and by you will see – the ways of the heart are very simple, and they are always single in purpose.

When the heart falls in love with somebody, then there is no problem; then your love object is the only love object for you. The moment the heart has fallen in love with a woman, then that is the only woman in the world. Then all other women have disappeared for you. The heart is single in purpose. But if the head had fallen in love – in fact it has not fallen in love, it simply pretends – then it is difficult. Then any woman that passes on the street attracts you, provokes you. Then any passing influence distracts you. Love knows single purpose because love is really of the heart. If you are here with me through the heart, then it is a totally different relationship Then it is going to be eternal. Then I can die, you can die, but the relationship cannot die. But if it is only of the head, if you are simply convinced by what I am saying, not convinced by what I am . . . if you are only convinced by what I am saying – my logic, my argument – then this relationship is temporary. Tomorrow you will be convinced by somebody else. Tomorrow somebody else can give you a better argument; then it disappears.

. . . the pure in heart and single in purpose are able to understand the most supreme way.

Once you have seen your past lives, suddenly you see the way out. Because so many times you have come in again and again. The way to come in is really the way to go out also. You just have to move in the opposite direction. The way is the same. The entrance and the exit are not two. The direction is different. When you enter into the house, you enter through the door. You go out of the house and you get out through the same door. Just your direction is different. So, Buddha says, if you look into your past lives and you see that again and again you are clinging with life, clinging with lust, ambition, ego, greed, jealousy, possessiveness – those are the ways you have been coming in again and again. And those are the ways to go out.

If greed is the way to come in, no-greed is the way to go out. If ego is the way to come in, no-ego is the way to go out. If lust, desire, passion, is the way to come in, then no-passion, no-desire, or desirelessness is the way to go out.

It is like polishing a mirror which becomes bright when the dust is removed. Remove your passions and have no hankering, and the past will be revealed unto you.

So Buddha says three things. First, pure in heart, then single of purpose, and third, he says that your consciousness is so cluttered that your mirror is not reflecting. Otherwise, you have such a beautiful mirror with such a penetrating clarity that wherever you move your mirror of consciousness, you will be able to see everything that exists in that dimension. If you move your mirror towards the past, the whole past, *in toto*, will be revealed to you. If you move your mirror towards the future, the whole future will be revealed to you. If you move your mirror to the present, the whole present will be revealed to you. Your consciousness is your key.

It is like polishing a mirror which becomes bright when the dust is removed.

Too much dust of thinking, too much dust of impressions, is covering your mirror. You have completely forgotten – the mirror looks like a brick. Clean it, wash it – that's what we are doing in meditations. It is just an effort to clean the mirror so it mirrors whatsoever is.

Remove your passions and have no hankering and the past will be revealed unto you.

A monk asked the Buddha: What is good and what is great? The Buddha answered: Good is to practice the way and to follow the truth. Great is the heart that is in accord with the way.

Tremendously beautiful is his definition of the great. Understand it as deeply as possible. *Good is to practice the way . . .* First one has to know the way – no greed, no violence, no desire. In a way, all are negatives. Because whatsoever you know as positive has been the door to come in. Eliminate the positive and you will find the door to go out.

Good is to practice the way . . . Buddha says, knowing the way, recognizing the way in a clear, mirrorlike consciousness, the first thing that one has to do is to practice it. Just by recognizing, it won't help. Just by recognizing, it is not going to transform you. You have to walk, you have to have discipline.

Good is to practice the way and to follow the truth.

You have had a vision of truth. It is very far away like a distant star. Clear vision . . . but the distance is great. You have to follow, you have to move towards it slowly, gradually. You have to prepare for the journey. This Buddha calls good. This is what virtue is.

And great is the heart that is in accord with the way.

When you are practicing, there is bound to be a little struggle. When you are disciplining yourself, there is bound to be a little conflict, because the old habits will come in the way. You have always been greedy, now suddenly you decide not to be greedy. The whole past will come in the way, will distract you. Old habits will again and again possess you; again and again you will forget and waver. There is bound to be struggle.

So Buddha says it is good but not great. Great is the man whose struggle is gone, whose discipline also is gone. One who is simply moving spontaneously in accord with the way is great. That's what Buddha calls great – being in accord; the person is so surrendered that following the way is now natural. Not to desire has become as natural to the person as it is ordinarily natural to desire. Not to be ambitious has become as natural as it is natural for people to be ambitious. People are habitually in discord with the way, and the great person becomes naturally in accord.

Pythagoras calls this state *harmonia*. That is the right word – in accord. *Harmonia*, in harmony . . . Lao Tzu calls this Tao. Buddha calls it dhamma. To be in accord . . . as if you are not swimming, not struggling; you are completely relaxed and floating with the river. You are so one with the river that there is not even a slight distance between you and the river. You don't have any of your desires, you don't have any private goals. You go with the river to the ocean.

A man of harmonia, accord, Tao, dhamma, is the most beautiful flowering in this world. He is the lotus flower of consciousness.

Great is the heart that is in accord with the way.

But it cannot happen immediately. First you will have to discipline yourself, and then you will have to drop discipline also. First you will have to make it a point to relax, and then you will have to forget relaxation also. First you will have to fight with your old, ingrained habits, and once you have got over them, you have to drop new habits that you must have created in fighting with the old. First you have to meditate, then one day you have to drop meditation also.

Meditation is good. Dropping of meditation is great. Being a saint is good, being holy is great. Being a good person is good, but not great. Because a good person still carries a subtle fight with the bad. He is constantly conflicting with the devil, with the evil inside himself. He is not at ease, he cannot relax. He knows that if he relaxes, the old, the past, is big and powerful and he will be possessed and he will be thrown off balance. He has to continuously balance himself. A good man, a saint, is still not in absolute accord. He is trying hard, he is trying his best, and it should be appreciated that he is trying – that's why Buddha calls him good.

So never be satisfied by good. Remember, to be great is the goal . . . to be so deeply in accord that you simply disappear and only the dhamma remains, only the Tao remains, only nature remains. You are just a wave in the ocean and you don't exist separately. Your separate existence, your self, has to be dropped.

The bad man has a self. The self is created by fighting against the law, against nature. The bad man has a self; he creates the self by fighting against the dhamma. Whatsoever is good, he fights against it and creates a self. The good man also has a self. He fights against his bad habits that he has created in the past. Because of the fight, he has also a self. The bad man has an ego, the good man has an ego. The bad man's ego is based on his mischief, the good man's ego is based on his virtue, but both have egos.

The great is one whose ego has disappeared, who is completely immersed, merged into the whole. To be so merged into the whole, to be in such a harmony, is to be great. That is what is required. That is what has to be remembered continuously. Never lose sight of it.

Life is just a training. One has to become so transcendental that not even good satisfies. One has to be continuously in a divine discontent to attain to this excellent transcendence where you are lost and only the whole is . . . when you have completely surrendered, when you have given way to the whole . . . you have become just a space.

If you want to use non-Buddhist terms, you can call it surrender to God. You are so empty that God can descend in you. If you want to use Buddhist terms, then he says, you are not there – now only the law functions, now only the dhamma, the Tao goes on functioning. To function in such accord is bliss.

Enough for today.

Chapter 8:

A Light unto Yourself

A MONK ASKED THE BUDDHA:
What is most powerful and what is most illuminating?

THE BUDDHA SAID:

Meekness is most powerful for it harbors no evil thoughts, and moreover it is restful and full of strength. As it is free from evils it is sure to be honored by all.

The most illuminating is a mind which is thoroughly cleansed of dirt, and which, remaining pure, retains no blemishes. From the time when there was yet no heaven and earth till the present day, there is nothing in the ten quarters which is not seen or heard by such a mind. For it has gained all knowledge and for that reason it is called illuminating.

Life can be lived in two ways. One is that of the soldier, and the other that of the sannyasin. Either you can fight with life or you can relax with life. Either you can try to conquer life or you can live in a deep let-go.

The path of the soldier is the wrong path because it is impossible to conquer life – the part cannot conquer the whole. Frustration and failure are absolutely certain. You can play around with the idea but it is not going to succeed; it is doomed to failure. The soldier tries to conquer the life, and in the end finds he has been crushed, defeated, destroyed. Life destroys nobody, but if you fight with it you will be destroyed by your own violence.

Life is not against you. How can it be? Life is your mother. It is life that has brought you here; you are born out of it. You are a ray of its light, a wave of its ocean. You are intrinsic and organic to it, you are not separate. But if you start fighting your own source of energy, you will be destroyed. Your very concept of fight will poison you. And of course, the more you feel that you are losing the battle, the harder you will fight. The harder you fight, the more frustrated you become.

The soldier's way is the ordinary way. Almost ninety-nine point nine percent of people follow it – hence there is so much misery, hence there is so much hell. It is created by you, by your wrong approach to life. Once you understand it you start getting in with the whole, you start getting into a dance with the whole. You lose fighting, you start cooperating. And the moment you decide to cooperate, you have become a sannyasin.

The religious person is one who has no idea of separation from the whole . . . who never thinks, never dreams that he is separate . . . who has no private goal of his own . . . who simply moves with life in total trust. If you cannot trust life, who are you going to trust? If you cannot allow life to flow through you, you will be missing – you will be missing this tremendous opportunity to be alive. Then you will get worried, then you will be caught in your own mind. And then misery is the natural outcome.

To understand that conflict is not the way to be happy is the greatest understanding. Understand that cooperation is the way to be blissful, and your dark night of the soul is over and the morning has come. The sun is rising on the horizon . . . you will be transformed. This very understanding that cooperation is the key, not conflict, is a transforming force. Trust is the key, not doubt. Violence is not the way, but love. This is the basic framework.

Now the sutra:

A monk asked the Buddha: What is most powerful and what is most illuminating?

We are all asking only these two questions. First, what is most powerful? Because we are all on a power trip. We want to be powerful because we feel we are impotent, we feel we are weaklings, we feel we are limited. A thousand and one limitations surround you; everywhere you come against a wall and you feel powerless. Each moment of life brings you the feeling of helplessness. So the question is very pertinent, a very human question. What is the most powerful thing in the world? The monk must have been a seeker of power.

Now, you have to understand it – the very effort, the very desire to be powerful, is one of the obstacles to attaining power. People who try to become powerful never become powerful. They are destroyed by their own search, because the effort to become powerful means you are in conflict. You want to fight – that's why you want to be powerful. Otherwise, why do you need power in the first place? You must have some aggression, some violence, some grudge. You want to prove and perform; you want to prove to others that you are powerful and they are not. Deep down somewhere, like a shadow in the unconscious, an Adolf Hitler is seeking its way towards your conscious mind – or a Nadir Shah, or a Napoleon, or an Alexander. Everybody is carrying an Alexander within himself.

This desire for power has created many things in the world. Science has come out of a desire for power, and it has created power, but that power is destroying humanity. It has come to such a state that people like Albert Einstein feel that they have committed a crime against humanity. In the last days of his life, somebody asked Einstein, "If you were born again, what would you like to become?"

He said, "Never a physicist again, never a scientist. Rather, I would like to become a plumber."

He was a very sensitive man, very understanding. And only in the end could he understand that he had released so much energy, that he had made humanity aware of such a destructive force – atomic energy – that if humanity destroys itself he is bound to be one of the persons most responsible for it.

The very framework of science is to conquer nature. That is the very terminology of science – "conquest of nature". We have to overpower nature and we have to destroy all its mysteries. We have to find all the keys of power, wherever it is. But the very idea takes you away from nature, makes you antagonistic to it and becomes destructive. The ecology of the earth has been destroyed by this power seeking. On the outside and in the inside both, the natural rhythm of life is disturbed.

I have heard:

> A very unusual idea occurred one day to Frederick of Prussia. He was in the country when he saw some sparrows eating some grains of wheat. He started to think about it, and reached the conclusion that these small birds consumed a million pecks of wheat a year in his kingdom. This could not be allowed. They would have to be either conquered or destroyed. Since it was difficult to exterminate them, he offered a price for each dead sparrow. All Prussians became hunters and soon there were no more sparrows in the country. What a great victory . . .

Frederick of Prussia was very happy. He celebrated the event as a great conquest over nature. He was very happy until the following year when he was told that caterpillars and locusts had eaten the crops, because without sparrows the whole rhythm of life was destroyed. Sparrows go on eating caterpillars and locusts. There being no sparrows, the whole crop was destroyed by caterpillars. Then it was necessary to bring in sparrows from abroad. And Frederick said, "I certainly have made a mistake. God knows what he is doing."

The great scientific minds nowadays are coming to recognize, by and by – slowly, reluctantly – that a great mistake has been made.

The very desire to be powerful is against nature, because the desire to be powerful is antagonistic. Why do you need to be powerful? You must be thinking in terms of destroying somebody. Power is needed to destroy, power is needed to dominate, power is needed to conquer.

When the monk asked, "What is the most powerful thing in the world?" in fact the actual word must have been siddhi. The monk must have asked, "What is siddhi, what is psychic power?" Science tries to penetrate nature to get more power, and there are many systems that penetrate your innermost being – but again the goal is to get more power. Whether you become powerful in a scientific way or you become powerful in a psychic way, it makes no difference. Now the West is becoming interested in the psychic sciences, but the urge is the same – to be more powerful.

So first try to understand why a person seeks power in the first place. The very desire is that of a soldier. You want power because without power you cannot be a great ego. For ego, power functions as food, nourishment. You seek power because only with power will you be able to say "I am". The more money you have the more power you have, the more you can feel at ease with your "I am". The more you can destroy people the more you can feel that nobody can destroy you.

Now psychologists say that people are interested in murdering, killing, in war, because when they kill others they feel powerful. They feel power over death, they think they can create death. They can kill others; now they feel in a deep way that they have become immortal. Even death is under their control. It is foolish, but the idea arises. People who love killing are people who are afraid of death.

Adolf Hitler was very much afraid of death – so much so that he never allowed anybody to stay with him in his room in the night. Not even a girlfriend was ever allowed, he was so afraid of death. Who knows? – the girlfriend may turn out to be a spy, may be an agent in the hands of the enemy. He never trusted even love. He was one of the most lonely men who has ever existed on earth . . . and so afraid, continuously trembling. But he went on killing people – that was just to balance the fear. The more he killed, the more he felt that he had power. The more he felt that he had power, the more he felt that death could not destroy him. He started feeling as if he was immortal.

Have you watched? – in wartime people look radiant. In wartime people look very fresh. Ordinarily they look bored. When war starts, you can see – their step has changed, their eyes now have a glimmer, a radiance . . . their faces look more alive, as if the dust of the boredom is gone. Something sensational is happening. It should not be so, but whenever there is war people feel a power over death – they can kill. Immediately, in the shadow of their unconscious they feel, "Even death is within our domain. We can bring it or we can prevent it." People love destruction just as a measure of providing security against death. The search for power is the search not to be surrendered, not to feel helpless, not to be in a state where you are not in control.

The religious person is doing just the opposite. He is seeking a state where he is not in control but the whole is in control – call it the divine, call it the transcendental, call it existence or whatsoever you like to call it. The religious person is one who wants to be in such a deep harmony that there is no question of conflict. He is seeking love, he is seeking a love affair with the universe. He never asks about power. He asks how to lose separation, how to merge. He asks, "How to be in such a total surrender that I don't move in any way against the whole or separate from the whole, so that I can move with the river of life. And wherever the river of life goes, I can go with it."

What is most powerful? asked the monk.

The Buddha said: *Meekness is most powerful.*

Jesus says, "Blessed are the meek, for they shall inherit the earth." The statement looks absurd, because . . . the meek? They have never been powerful enough to inherit the earth. And we cannot conceive that they will ever be able to inherit the earth. But Jesus is saying something very true: Blessed are the meek. And when he says they shall inherit the earth, he is giving you the same message that Buddha is. *Meekness is most powerful* – that is his meaning when he says they shall inherit the earth.

Meekness is powerful, but the power has a totally different connotation now. Meekness is powerful because now there is nobody against you. Meekness is powerful because you are no longer separate from the whole – and the whole is powerful. Meekness is powerful because you are no longer fighting, and there is no way of your being defeated. Meekness is powerful because with the whole, you have already conquered. All victory is with the whole. Meekness is powerful because you are riding on the wave of the whole. Now there is no possibility of your ever being defeated.

It looks paradoxical, because the meek person is one who does not want to conquer. The meek person is one who is ready to be defeated. Lao Tzu says, "Nobody can defeat me because I have accepted defeat already." Now how can you defeat a defeated person? Lao Tzu says, "Nobody can defeat me because I am standing as the last person in the world. You cannot push me any further back – there is no 'further back'. I am the last person." Jesus also says, "Those who are last in this world will be first in my kingdom of God." Those who are the last will be the first? It does not seem possible in this world. In this world, aggressive people, violent people tend to power, tend to be victorious. You will find the most mad people in the most powerful places, because to reach to that point one has almost to be crazy for power, the competition is such. The competition is so violent that how can a meek person reach to a state of power? No . . . but that is not the meaning.

When Buddha says *Meekness is most powerful*, he is saying you cannot defeat a meek person because he has no desire to conquer. You cannot force a meek person to be a failure because he never wanted to succeed. You cannot enforce a meek person to be poor, because he has no desire for riches. Poverty is his richness; not to be anybody in particular is his way of life. To be a nobody is his very style. What can you take away from him? He has nothing. He cannot be cheated, he cannot be robbed. In fact, he cannot be destroyed because he has already surrendered that which can be destroyed. He has no self, no ego of his own.

It happened when Alexander was going back to Greece from India, he wanted to take a sannyasin with him. When he was setting out to conquer India his teacher, the great philosopher Aristotle, had told him, "When you come back, bring a gift to me. I would like to see a sannyasin from India." That is something original to the East; that contribution of *sannyas* belongs to the East. The West has given great warriors, the East has given great sannyasins. Aristotle was intrigued with the very idea of *sannyas*, what it is.

Alexander, on his way back, remembered and he inquired. The people of that village where he was staying told him, "Yes, there is a sannyasin, but we don't think you will be able to take him back." He laughed at the foolishness of the villagers, because who can prevent Alexander? He said, "If I want to take the Himalayas, even they will follow me. So you don't be worried, just tell me where he is." They told him.

He was a naked fakir, a naked man standing just by the side of the river outside the village . . . a beautiful person. Dandamis was his name – that's how Alexander's historians have remembered him. Two soldiers were sent. They told the sannyasin, "Alexander the Great wants you to follow him. You will be a royal guest. Whatsoever you need will be provided, every comfort will be made possible. Accept the invitation."

The naked man started laughing. He said, "I have dropped all wandering. I don't go anywhere anymore. I have come home."

They said, "Don't be stupid. The great Alexander can force you to go. If you don't go as a guest, you will go as a prisoner; the choice is yours. Either way you will have to go."

He started laughing again. He said, "I have dropped the very thing that can be imprisoned. Nobody can make me a prisoner. I am freedom."

Alexander himself came. He took his sword out and he told the sannyasin, "If you don't come with me, this sword is here and I will cut your head."

The sannyasin said, "You can do it. In fact I have done it already. I have cut my head myself. And if you cut my head, you will see it falling down on the ground and I will also see it falling on the ground, because I have become a witness." It is said that Alexander could not gather courage to kill this man. He was so happy, he was so fearless, he was so blissful.

When Buddha says meekness is most powerful, he means that one who does not exist as an ego is meek. One who does not exist as an ego cannot be conquered, cannot be defeated, cannot be destroyed. He has gone beyond.

By going beyond the ego, you go beyond death. By going beyond the ego, you go beyond defeat. By going beyond the ego, you go beyond powerlessness. This is a totally different concept of power – the power of a sannyasin.

This power is no more out of conflict. This power is not created out of friction. You say electricity is created out of friction. You can create electricity out of friction, you can create fire out of friction. If you rub both your hands, they will become hot. There is a power that comes out of friction – by conflict. And there is a power that comes by cooperation – not by friction but by harmony. That's what Buddha says – "One who is in accord with the way is great." One who is in accord with the way is powerful. But to be in accord with the way, one has to be meek.

Blessed are the meek. Certainly they shall inherit the earth. History will never know about them, because history has nothing to do with them. History knows only friction, history knows only mischief. History knows only mischief-mongers. History knows only mad people – because history records only when something goes wrong. When everything goes absolutely in tune, it is out of time and out of history also.

History does not report much about Jesus – in fact, nothing. If the Bible were not in existence, there would have been no record about Jesus. And I would like to tell you that many people like Jesus have existed, but we don't have any record of them. History never took any note. They were so meek, they were so silent, they were so in tune, so deep in harmony that not even a ripple was created around them. They came and they left, and they have not left even a footprint.

History has not been recording buddhas. That's why when you hear about a Buddha or a Mahavira or a Zarathustra, they look like mythological figures, not historical. It appears that they never existed, or they only existed in the dreams of man, or they existed only in the poetries of a few imaginative, romantic people. They look like wish-fulfillments. They look like how we would like man to be, but not realities.

They were real. They were so real that no trace has been left behind them. Unless you create some mischief, you will not be leaving your signature on history. That's why history records only politics, because politics is the mechanism of mischief. The politician is in conflict. The religious person lives in harmony. He lives like trees. Who creates records about trees? He lives like rivers. Who records anything about rivers? He moves like clouds. Who bothers about clouds?

The meek person is one who is in harmony – and Buddha says he is the most powerful. But this concept of power is totally different. To understand it, a few things will be good to remember.

In Japan they have a beautiful science – aikido. The word "aikido" comes from a word "ki". "Ki" means power. The same word in Chinese is "chi". From "chi" comes t'ai chi – that too means power. Just equivalent to ki and chi is the Indian word "prana". It is a totally different concept of power. In aikido they teach that when somebody attacks you, don't be in conflict with that person – even when somebody attacks you, cooperate with him. This looks impossible, but one can learn the art. And when you have learned the art, you will be tremendously surprised that it happens – you can cooperate even with your enemy. When somebody attacks you, aikido says go with him.

Ordinarily when somebody attacks you, you become stiff, you become hard. You are in conflict. Aikido says even take an attack in a very loving way. Receive it, it is a gift from the enemy. He is bringing great energy to you. Receive it, absorb it, don't conflict. In the beginning it looks impossible. How? Because for centuries we have been taught about one idea of power, and that is of conflict, friction. We know only one power and that is of fight. We know only one power, and that is of no, saying no. You can watch it even in small children. The moment the child starts becoming a little independent, he starts saying no. The mother says, "Don't go out." He says, "No, I will go." The mother says, "Keep quiet." He says, "No. I want to sing and dance." Why does he say no? He is learning the ways of power. "No" gives power.

Aikido says, "Say yes. When the enemy attacks you, accept it as a gift." Receive it, become porous. Don't become stiff, become as liquid as possible. Receive this gift, absorb it, and the energy from the enemy will be lost and you will become the possessor of it. There will be a jump of energy from the enemy to you.

A master of aikido conquers without fighting. He conquers by non-fighting. He is tremendously meek, humble. The enemy is destroyed by his own attitude; he is creating enough poison for himself. There is no need for you to help him. He is suicidal, he is committing suicide by attacking. There is no need for you to fight with him.

You just try it sometimes. You have watched it – the same phenomenon happening in many ways. You see a drunkard walking on the road, and then he falls in the gutter. But he is not hurt. By the morning you will see him again going to the office, perfectly healthy and okay. The whole night he was in the gutter. He fell, but he has not broken his ribs or his bones, he has no fracture. You fall and you will immediately have a fracture. What is happening when a drunkard falls? He falls so totally, he goes with it. He is drunk, he cannot resist.

It is said about Chuang Tzu . . . He came across an accident. A bullock cart had gone upside down, had fallen in a ditch. The driver was hurt very much, the owner was hurt; he had fractures. But a drunkard was traveling in the bullock cart with the owner and he was not hurt at all. He was not even aware of what had happened, he was still snoring. He had fallen on the ground, the others were crying and weeping, and he was fast asleep. Chuang Tzu said, "Seeing this, I understood what Lao Tzu means when he says 'let go.'"

Children are doing this every day. Watch children – the whole day they fall here and there, but they are not hurt. You try to do the same and it will be impossible for you – you will have to be hospitalized! Within twenty-four hours you will be hospitalized. The children fall in accord. When they fall they are not resisting, they are not going against the fall, they are not trying to protect themselves. They don't go stiff. In fact, they fall in a very relaxed way.

Aikido, t'ai chi – or what Jesus calls meekness, what Buddha calls meekness – depend on the same principle, the principle of harmony.

Try it in your life; just try in small experiments. Somebody slaps your face. Try to absorb it, receive it, feel happy that he has released energy to your face and see how it feels. You will have a totally different feeling. And that has happened many times unawares – a friend comes and slaps you on your back, you don't know who it is and then you look. He is a friend, so you feel happy. It was a friendly slap. If you look back and he is an enemy, you feel hurt. The quality of the slap immediately changes with your attitude. If it is a friend you accept it, it is beautiful, it is a loving thing. If he is an enemy then it is not loving, it is full of hate. The slap is the same, the force of the impact is the same, but your attitude changes.

You can watch it many times. It is raining, and you will be walking home. You can take it in an aikido way or you can take it in the ordinary way. The ordinary way is that you will see that your clothes will become wet, or you may get cold, or this may happen, or that may happen. And you will be against the rains. You will be running towards home in a bad mood, antagonistic. This has happened many times.

Try aikido – relax, enjoy the falling drops of water on your face. It is tremendously beautiful. It is so soothing, so cleansing, so refreshing. What is wrong in your clothes getting wet? Why be so worried about it? They can be dried. But why miss this opportunity? The heaven is meeting with the earth. Why miss this opportunity? Why not dance with it? Don't rush and don't run. Slow down, enjoy. Close your eyes and feel the drops falling on your eyelids, moving across your face. Feel the touch of it, accept it . . . a gift from heaven. And suddenly you will see – it is beautiful, and you have never looked at it that way.

Try it in ordinary life experiences. Conflict you have always been in; now try accord. And suddenly you will see that the whole meaning changes. Then you are no longer in antagonism with nature.

Suddenly the sun comes out, the clouds have disappeared and a great light falls on your face. Take it easily, take it as a love gift from the sun. Close your eyes, absorb it. Drink the light. Feel happy, blessed. And you will see – it is a totally different energy. Otherwise you start perspiring . . . you may perspire still, because heat is heat, but deep down the meaning has changed. Now you perspire but you feel good. Nothing is wrong in perspiring. It cleanses you, it takes toxins outside, it releases poison from the body. It is a purifying fire. Just the attitude . . .

Meekness is most powerful.

And meekness means the attitude of no-friction, no-conflict . . . the attitude of harmony. "I am not; existence is", is what meekness is. "I am not, the whole is" – that is the meaning of meekness.

Ordinarily we live through the ego and we suffer. And the ego goes on misinterpreting.

Last night I was reading a beautiful anecdote:

> Some years back a senator from the Interior Committee visited an Indian Reservation in Arizona, where he made a fine speech full of promises of better things, as politicians always do. "We shall see," he said, "a new era of Indian opportunity." To this the Indians gave a ringing cry of "Hoya! Hoya!"
>
> Encouraged, the senator continued, "We promise better schools and technical training." "Hoya! Hoya!" exclaimed the audience with much enthusiasm. "We pledge better hospitals and medical

assistance," said the senator. "Hoya! Hoya!" cried the Indians.

With a tear running down his cheek, the senator ended, "We come to you as equals, as brothers, so trust us." The air shook with one long mighty "Hoya!"

Greatly pleased by his reception, the senator then began a tour of the reservation. "I see you have fine breeds of beef cattle here," he said. "May I inspect them?"

"Certainly, come this way," said the chief, "but be careful not to step in the hoya."

The ego is just "hoya", a misunderstanding. It is non-existential, yet the dirtiest thing possible. The very idea that "I am separate from existence", is dirty. The very idea that "I have to fight with my own energy source", is foolish and absurd.

But sometimes, what happens? You seem to conquer. That is a misinterpretation. When your ego sees that it is conquering, it is not the case that the ego is conquering. In fact, it is just a coincidence – sometimes you are going to the left and the whole of existence is also going to the left, and you coincide. But you think you are succeeding, you think, "I am gaining power." Sooner or later you will be in trouble, because it cannot always be so. It can always be so only if you are meek.

A meek person becomes so sensitive that he is never against the whole. He is always sensitive to feeling where the whole is going. He rides on the horse and goes with the horse. He does not try to give a direction, he trusts the horse.

It happened:

> With a grinding of brakes, the officer pulled up his motorcar and shouted to a little boy playing in the field, "I say, sonny, have you seen an airplane come down anywhere near here?"
>
> "No, sir," replied the boy, trying to hide his slingshot. "I have only been shooting at that bottle on the fence."

A small child can be forgiven. He is afraid that maybe because of his slingshot the airplane has fallen. He can be forgiven if he is hiding his slingshot. But this is what your so-called great personalities are doing. That's what all egoists are doing. They go on thinking that things are happening because of them.

It happened:

> Drought struck the countryside, and the parson of the church prayed for rain. Rain came in such torrents that a flood followed. A rescue party in a boat spied the parson sitting on the roof of his house watching the current swirl by. "Your prayers were sure

answered," shouted one.

"Yes," said the careful, stranded one. "I figure it ain't bad for a little church like ours."

Sometimes your prayers are fulfilled – not because of your prayers, but just because by coincidence the whole was also going in that way, in that direction. Your prayers coincided. Sometimes your efforts are fulfilled because they coincide. Ego is coincidental. You go on collecting your ego just out of coincidences. But this cannot happen always, that's why one feels miserable. One day you are succeeding, another day you are failing, and you cannot figure it out – what is happening? Such a great intellectual, such a great man of understanding, power, strength, logic, reason – failing? What is happening? You cannot believe it, because just now it had been succeeding. Ego is always in trouble because there cannot always be a coincidence. Sometimes you are with the whole, unknowingly; sometimes you are not with the whole. When you are with the whole, you succeed. The whole succeeds always, you never.

The meek person is one who says, "I am not, only the whole is." He drops himself completely. He does not become a barrier. He allows the whole to have its way.

Buddha says this is real power.

Meekness is most powerful, for it harbors no evil thoughts and moreover it is restful and full of strength.

When you fight, you dissipate energy. When you fight, you lose energy. Buddha says, don't fight, preserve your energy, and you will be powerful. One who goes on preserving his energy becomes such a tremendous pool of energy that his very being is powerful. Just his presence is powerful, his presence is magical, miraculous. Coming close to him, you will start feeling that you are being changed and transformed. Coming close to him, you will feel your darkness disappearing. Coming close to him, you will feel a silence descending. Just coming close to him, you will feel you are being lifted to another plane of being, to another altitude of being, to another dimension. People come to me and they ask how to find the right master. The only way to find is just to be close, and be silent, be in harmony. And if in that harmony and silence you start feeling that you are soaring higher and higher, then this person is your master. Then this person is going to become your door for the ultimate. Then your energy fits with his energy, then something between you and him falls in tune. Then something between you and him transpires, becomes a solid force.

You cannot decide by your intellect who is a master. You cannot decide by argumentation, and you cannot decide by your prejudice. You have heard many definitions – that the master should be like this or like that. Those definitions won't help, because a person may be fulfilling all the definitions and still he may not fit you; your and his energies may not be complementary. And unless your energies are complementary, compensatory, completing each other, making a circle, then you cannot go high with that person. Going high has to be felt.

Meekness is powerful for it harbors no evil thoughts.

When you have evil thoughts – "evil thoughts" means thoughts of violence, of destruction, thoughts of aggression, egoistic thoughts, ego-oriented thoughts – then you dissipate energy. Then these thoughts take too much energy out of you. They are never going to be fulfilled. You are sowing stones; they are not going to sprout. Your whole energy will be wasted.

. . . And moreover it is restful and full of strength.

Rest should be the criterion of power. A man of power is absolutely at rest, he has no restlessness in him – because restlessness is nothing but dissipation of energy. When you are feeling restless, you are dissipating energy. Hence in the East, the meditator became the symbol of power. When a person meditates, he loses all restlessness. His thinking stops, his body movements stop; he becomes like a marble statue . . . totally still, unmoving. In that moment he is a pool of energy. He is tremendously powerful.

If you see somebody meditating, sit by his side, and you will be benefited. Sitting by the side of someone who is in a meditative mood, you will move into meditation also. His energy will pull you out of your mess. Meditation is nothing but absolute rest. How you bring that absolute rest depends on many things. There are a thousand and one methods to create that rest. My own methods are such that first I would like you to become as restless as possible, so nothing is left hanging inside you, restlessness has been thrown out – then move into rest. And there will be no disturbance, it will be easier.

In Buddha's time, such dynamic methods were not needed. People were more simple, more authentic. They lived a more real life. Now people are living a very repressed life, very unreal life. When they don't want to smile, they smile. When they want to be angry, they show compassion. People are false, the whole life pattern is false. The whole culture is like a great falsity; people are just acting, not living. There is much hangover; many incomplete experiences go on being collected, piled up inside people's minds. So just sitting directly in silence won't help. The moment you try to sit silently, you will see all sorts of things moving inside you. You will feel it almost impossible to be silent.

First throw those things out so you come to a natural state of rest. Real meditation starts only when you are in rest. All the dynamic meditations are preparatory to real meditation – they are just basic requirements to be fulfilled so that the meditation can happen. Don't treat them as meditations; they are just introductory, just a preface. The real meditation starts only when all activity has ceased – activity of the body and activity of the mind.

It is restful and full of strength.

Remember, this definition of power is different from the ordinary definition of power. The ordinary definition of power depends on comparison. You are more powerful than your neighbor, you are more powerful than this man or that woman. You are powerful in comparison with somebody else. The power that Buddha is talking about is non-comparative; it has nothing to do with anybody else. Power is your own state. When you are full of energy, you are powerful. When you are leaking energy, you are powerless.

"Evil thoughts" are like holes through which energy leaks. Restlessness is like leaking, continuous leaking. You create energy every day, a tremendous amount of it, but you waste it – sometimes in anger, sometimes in sexuality, sometimes in greed, sometimes in competition, sometimes for no reason at all . . . just because you have it, what to do with it?

There is a famous Sufi story about Jesus. Jesus comes to a town and he sees a man drunk, shouting, lying down on the street. He comes close to him, shakes the man and says, "What are you doing? Why are you wasting your life in such a way?"

The man opens his eyes and says, "My Lord, I was ill. You cured me. Now what else can I do? Now I am healthy. I was always ill and confined to my bed. You cured me, now what am I supposed to do? Now I have energy and I don't know what to do with it." Jesus feels as if he has committed a crime by helping this man. He becomes very sad. He goes into the marketplace of the town, but he is sad. There he sees a young man following a prostitute with lustful eyes, almost oblivious of the whole world. Jesus stops that young man and says, "What are you doing? The eyes are not given for this. The eyes have been given to see God. What are you doing? Why are you wasting this gift?"

The man looks at Jesus, touches his feet, and says, "My Lord, I was blind. You cured me. Now what to do with these eyes? I don't know anything else." Jesus becomes very sad, he leaves the town. He comes out of the town and there he finds a man trying to commit suicide by hanging himself from a tree. His preparation is complete; he is just going to take the final step when Jesus comes. He says, "Wait! What are you doing? Such a precious gift of God – life! And you are going to destroy it! Are you mad?"

The man looks at Jesus and says, "My Lord, I had died. You resurrected me.

Why did you resurrect me? Now I am in trouble. I don't want this life at all! What to do with it?"

You have energy and you don't know what to do with it, so you go on wasting it. There are people who say they are "killing time". Killing time means killing life! Killing time means killing opportunity to grow, to mature, to come home.

The power that Buddha is talking about is the power that comes when you don't do anything with your energy and you simply delight in its presence . . . a sheer delight in being full of energy . . . the sheer delight of a young, green tree . . . the sheer delight of a cloud, a white cloud wandering in the sky . . . the sheer delight of a lotus flower . . . the sheer delight of the sun coming out of the clouds . . . the sheer delight of being so full of energy, vibrant, alive, throbbing. When you don't put your energy to any purpose whatsoever, then energy itself starts moving in a vertical line. If you put it to work, to some action, it moves in a horizontal line. Then you can make a big house, you can have more money, you can have more prestige, this and that. When you put energy to work, it moves in the horizontal line. When you don't put energy to work, you simply delight in its presence, you are happy that it is there, then it moves in a vertical line.

I am not saying to stop all work. I am saying, find a few moments for the vertical movement also. Horizontal movement is okay, but not enough. It is necessary for life – but man cannot live by bread alone. You can get bread through horizontal work – but love, meditation, godliness, nirvana, they exist on the vertical line. So sometimes just sit and do nothing. Sitting silently, doing nothing, and something goes on growing within you. You become a reservoir, and you start throbbing with an unknown delight. When you are full of energy, you are in contact with the whole. And when you are in contact with the whole, you are full of energy.

As it is free from evils it is sure to be honored by all.

The monk had asked:

What is most powerful and what is most illuminating?

The most illuminating is a mind, says Buddha, which is thoroughly cleansed of dirt, and which, remaining pure, retains no blemishes. Thoughts are like dirt, clinging to the mirror of the mind. Thoughts, desires, imaginations, memories – all are forms of dirt. Because of them, the purity of the mind is lost. Because of them, the capacity to reflect, the mirrorlike quality of the mind is lost. A continuous cleaning is needed.

So, meditation is not something that you do once and forget about, because each moment of life you go on gathering dust. It is just like a traveler who is traveling. Each day he goes on gathering dust on his clothes, on his body. Every day he has to take a bath to cleanse his body. Again the next day he will be gathering dust. Meditation is like a daily bath. It is not something that once you have done it, you are finished. It should become like a natural thing, matter of fact. As you eat, as you go to sleep, as you take a bath, meditation should become a natural part of your life. At least twice a day you should cleanse your mind.

The best times are the morning, when you are getting ready for the day and the workaday world . . . Cleanse your mind so you have clarity, so you have transparency, so you don't commit errors, mistakes, so you don't have any evil thoughts, so you don't have any egoistic thoughts . . . you go in a purer way to the world. You don't go with corrupting seeds. And the next best time is before you go to sleep, again meditate. The whole day the dust collects. Clean the mind again . . . fall asleep. If you really start cleaning it, you will see tremendous changes happening. If you clean it rightly before you go to sleep, dreams will disappear. Because dreams are nothing but the dust gathered the whole day – it goes on moving inside you, goes on creating fantasies, illusions.

If your meditation is going right, your dreams will by and by disappear. Your night will become a peaceful sleep with no dreams. And if the night is without dreams, in the morning you will be able to come up very fresh, young, virgin. Then meditate again, because even if there have been no dreams, with the very passage of time, dust collects. Even if you have not been traveling on dusty roads, just sitting in your house, dust collects. Even if your windows and doors are closed, in the morning you will find that your room has gathered a little dust. Dust collects. The very passage of time is dust-collecting. So in the morning, again meditate. And if you meditate rightly and you become a silent pool of energy, you will move in the world in a totally different way – non-conflicting, non-aggressive, in harmony. Even if somebody hates you, you will transform that energy into love.

Then you will move in the world deeply, skillfully, with the attitude of aikido. Whatsoever is happening you will take it, receive it in deep love and gratitude. Even if somebody insults you, you will accept it in deep love. Then the insult will be no longer an insult, and instead you will be nourished by it. With the insult, the person has thrown a certain amount of energy in your direction. He is losing it, you can gain it. You can simply receive it, welcome it. And if this becomes your natural way of life – the way of the sannyasin, not the way of the soldier – every moment you will feel things are growing into a new light and your mind is becoming more and more illuminating.

*The most illuminating is a mind which is thoroughly cleansed of dirt
and which, remaining pure, retains no blemishes. From the time when
there was yet no heaven and earth till the present day, there is nothing in
the ten quarters which is not seen, or known, or heard by such a mind.*

When your mind is pure, uncontaminated, unpolluted, when not even a
thought flickers in your mind, and there is no smoke around your mind – your
mind is like a clear sky without clouds – Buddha says you will be able to see
everything that is. You will be able to know everything that is. Your sensitivity
will be infinite, and whatsoever has existed from the very beginning of time will
become available to you. Your knowing will become perfect.

*For it has gained all knowledge and for that reason it is called
illuminating.*

And this illumination, this luminosity, does not come from anything outside
you. It explodes from your innermost core.

You are like a lamp which is covered by many curtains, dark curtains, and
no light comes out of it. Then by and by you remove one curtain, then another
curtain, then another curtain. Slowly, rays of light start coming – not clear, but
a glow. More curtains are removed – the glow becomes more penetrating, more
clear. More curtains are removed . . . one day, when all curtains are dropped,
you suddenly see that you are a lamp unto yourself.

When Buddha was dying, this was his last message to the world. Ananda, his
chief disciple, was crying and weeping. And Buddha said, "Stop! What are you
doing? Why are you crying and weeping?"

Ananda said, "You are leaving us. I was with you for forty years. I walked
with you, I slept with you, I ate with you, I listened to you – I was just like a
shadow to you, and yet. . . . You were available and I could not become enlightened. Now I am crying that you are going, you are leaving. Without you it
seems impossible for me to become enlightened. Even with you I could not
become – I have missed such a great opportunity. Without you . . . now there is
no hope. That's why I am crying. I am not crying because you are dying,
because I know you cannot die. I am crying because now for me there is no
hope. Now, with your death, starts my dark night of the soul. For eons of time,
millions of years, I will be stumbling in the darkness. Hence I am crying – not
for you, for myself."

Buddha smiled and said, "Don't be worried about that, because your light is
in your own being. I am not taking your light away. I was not your light.
Otherwise you could have become enlightened – if it were in my power to make
you enlightened, you would be already. It is your innermost capacity to become

enlightened. So be courageous, Ananda, and be a light unto yourself . . . *appa deepo bhava* . . . be a light unto yourself."

Buddha died and after only twenty-four hours, Ananda became enlightened. What happened? This is one of the mysteries. For forty years he lived with Buddha, and just twenty-four hours after Buddha died, he became enlightened. The very death worked like a great shock. And the last message penetrated very deep.

When Buddha was alive, Ananda was listening so-so – as you listen to me. You listen and yet you don't listen. You say, "Okay. If I miss today, tomorrow I will be listening again, so what is the hurry? If this morning is missed, nothing is missed; other mornings will be following."

So he had listened half-asleep, half-awake. Maybe he was tired, maybe the night was not good and he had not slept. Maybe the journey was too long and too exhausting. And Buddha was saying the same thing again and again and again, so how long can you listen? One starts feeling that one already knows. One starts feeling, "Yes, I have heard this before, so what is the point? Why not take a little sleep? A little nap will be good."

But when Buddha was dying, Ananda must have been alert, utterly alert. He was really trembling – the very idea of millions of years again stumbling in darkness. And Buddha says, "Don't be worried, your light is within you." That struck home. Maybe that was the first time Ananda had heard. Those forty years he must have been missing; that may have been the first time he was not deaf. He had clarity. The very situation was such that he was trembling to his roots, he was shaking to his very foundations. Buddha was leaving . . . and when you have lived with a man like Buddha for forty years, it is difficult. The very idea to be without him is difficult. It is impossible to imagine. Ananda must have thought of committing suicide. It is not reported in the Buddhist scriptures, but I say he must have thought about committing suicide. That idea must have happened to him; it is so human. Living forty years with Buddha, and then Buddha is dying and nothing has happened to him. He has remained desertlike, not even an oasis. He has missed the opportunity.

His eyes must have become clear. This death must have penetrated him like a sword. Sharp must have been this moment. And Buddha said, "Be a light unto yourself," and died. He died immediately. This was his last utterance on this earth: Be a light unto yourself.

This struck home, this penetrated Ananda's heart, and within twenty-four hours he became enlightened.

That source of luminosity is within you. It is not outside you. If you seek it outside, you seek in vain. Close your eyes and go within yourself. It is there . . .

waiting since eternity. It is your innermost nature. You are luminosity, your being is luminous. This luminosity is not borrowed, it is your innermost core. It is you.

You are light – a light unto yourself.

From the time when there was yet no heaven and earth till the present day, there is nothing in the ten quarters which is not seen or known or heard by such a mind. For it has gained all knowledge and for that reason it is called illuminating.

Meekness is power and meditation is illumination. Both are two aspects of the same coin. On one side it is meekness, egolessness; on another side it is purity of mind, illumination. They go together; you will have to work on both these things simultaneously, together. Become more and more egoless and become more and more meditative. And the greatest power will be yours, and the greatest knowing will be yours, and the greatest light will be yours.

Enough for today.

Chapter 9:

Reflections of Emptiness

THE BUDDHA SAID:

Those who have passions are never able to perceive the way, for it is like stirring up clear water with hands. People may come there wishing to find a reflection of their faces, which, however, they will never see. A mind troubled and vexed with passions is impure, and on that account it never sees the way.

O monks, do away with passions. When the dirt of passion is removed the way will manifest itself.

THE BUDDHA SAID:

Seeing the way is like going into a dark room with a torch. The darkness instantly departs while the light alone remains. When the way is attained and the truth is seen, ignorance vanishes and enlightenment abides forever.

Who is a buddha? Or what is buddhahood? Unless you have a clear concept about it, it will be difficult to understand the sayings of Buddha. To understand those sayings, you will have to understand the source from where they arise. To understand the flower you will have to understand the roots. Unless you understand the roots, you can appreciate the flower but you will not be able to understand it.

Who is a buddha? Or what is buddhahood? The word "buddha" means pure awareness, a state of absolute awareness. A buddha is not a person but a state – the ultimate state, the ultimate flowering. The word "buddha" has nothing to do with Gautama the Buddha. Before Gautama the Buddha there have been many buddhas, and after Gautama the Buddha there have been many buddhas. Gautama the Buddha is only one among many who have attained to that ultimate consciousness.

The word "buddha" is just like the word "christ". Jesus is only one of the christs, only one of those who have attained to the ultimate flowering. There have been many christs and there will be many more. Remember it – buddhahood is not in any way confined to Gautama the Buddha; he is just one example of what buddhahood is. You see one rose flower. It is not *the* rose flower, it is only one of the rose flowers. Millions have existed before, millions exist right now, millions will exist in the future. It is simply a representative; this rose flower is simply a representative of all the rose flowers that have been, are, and will be.

A buddha is not defined by his personality. He is defined by the ultimate state of his being, which is beyond personality. And when a buddha speaks, he does not speak like a person. He speaks through his ultimate awareness. In fact to say that he speaks is not accurate, not right. There is nobody to speak, there is no "self" in him to speak. And in fact, he has nothing to say. He simply responds. Just as if you go and start singing in a valley, the valley responds – the valley simply echoes you. When you come to a buddha, he simply mirrors you. Whatever he speaks is just a reflection. It is an answer to you, but he himself has nothing to say. If another buddha comes to him, both will remain absolutely silent, two mirrors facing each other . . . nothing will be reflected. The mirrors will reflect each other but nothing will be reflected. Two mirrors – just think of two mirrors facing each other. If Christ comes to see Buddha, or if Buddha somewhere on the roads of life comes across Lao Tzu, they will be absolutely silent – there will be no echo.

So when Buddha is speaking, remember it. He is not saying anything in particular. He is simply reflecting the people. That's why a buddha can never be very consistent. A philosopher can be very consistent; he has something to say. He remembers it, he clings to it, he never says anything that goes against it . . . he manages it. A buddha is bound to be contradictory because each time somebody faces him, something else will arise. It will depend on the person who faces him. It is just like a mirror. If you come before the mirror, it is your face that is reflected. Somebody else comes, then it is his face. The face will go on changing. You cannot say to the mirror, "You are very inconsistent. Sometimes you show a woman's face and sometimes a man's face, and sometimes a beautiful face and sometimes an ugly face." The mirror will simply keep quiet. What can he do? He simply reflects; he reflects whatsoever is the case.

Buddha's sayings are very contradictory. Jesus is contradictory, Buddha is contradictory, Krishna is contradictory. Lao Tzu is tremendously contradictory. Hegel is not contradictory, Kant is not contradictory, Bertrand Russell is not contradictory. Confucius is not contradictory, Manu is not contradictory. They each have a certain dogma. They don't reflect you, they have something to say and they go on saying it. They are not like mirrors, they are like a photograph. The photograph doesn't bother about who you are; it remains the same. It is dead. It has a clear-cut definition and form.

Buddhahood is a formless awareness. Remember it, otherwise many times you will come across contradictions and you will not be able to figure out what is happening.

When Buddha died, immediately there was much controversy and the followers divided into many sects . . . because somebody had heard Buddha saying one thing, and somebody else had heard something absolutely contradicting it. There was no possibility – how could one man say all those things? Somebody must be lying!

People started sorting themselves out. They sorted out into many different schools; Buddha was cut in pieces. Somebody carried his hand, somebody his head, somebody his legs – but he was no longer an alive phenomenon. Now, each of these philosophies are very consistent – very consistent, very logical – but dead. Buddha is not a philosopher, he is not a systematizer. Buddha is not logical in any way. He is simply alive, and he reflects everything that is.

So when you come to a buddha, he answers *you*. He has no fixed answer to give to you, he answers *you*. He has no public face – all his faces are private, and they depend on you. If you bring a beautiful face to him, you will see your own face reflected. And if you come without any face, pure, mirrorlike, nothing will be reflected. Then Buddha disappears, he has nothing to say.

Those who lived with Buddha, they knew. When they had their own minds, those minds were reflected in him. When their minds dropped they really became meditators, and when they looked at Buddha there was nobody . . . just emptiness, a valley, pure silence . . . primal innocence, but nobody there.

These sayings have been collected, compiled, by a certain school. They are very consistent. Many sayings have been dropped that were apparently contradictory. Many that were ambiguous have not been included. These sayings were collected by a particular school. At some point I will be discussing other sources, and many times you will come across contradictions. Remember it. And those who are gathered around me have to understand this absolutely clearly, because I will be contradicting myself every day. It depends on the climate. If the weather is cloudy, I am cloudy. If the sun is shining bright and clear, I am that way.

You not only come to me with questions, you also come with the answers. Maybe the answer is not known to you, maybe the answer is hidden in your unconsciousness, lurking somewhere in the darkness of your soul. The question is conscious, and the answer you are carrying is unconscious. My function is to make your answer clearly obvious to you, to bring it to light.

I am bound to be contradictory. I am not a public man, I am not interested in crowds. I am interested in you, and whatever I say to you is said to you and is irrelevant for others. When I talk personally, then I am talking to a particular person. To others it may not be relevant. Even to the same person it may not be relevant tomorrow, because he will be changing. Life is continuous change, and I am only consistent with life and nothing else. So I am bound to be contradictory. If sometimes you come across contradictions, don't be in a hurry, and don't try to figure it out somehow, and don't try to fix them. Let them be as they are.

A man like Buddha has to be contradictory. He has to contain all contradictions because he contains all the possibilities of humanity. He contains all possible questions and all possible answers. He contains all the possible faces and all the possible phases. He contains the whole past of humanity, the present and the future. That is the meaning when Buddha says, "When you have come home, when your innermost being is luminous, all will be known – all that was past, present and future. Nothing remains unknown. In that knowing light everything is revealed." But *everything* . . . and things are not consistent. That's the beauty of the world, that things are not consistent. Things have different qualities, different personalities. All things are beings in their own way, and Buddha is simply reflecting . . . a reflection, a mirror.

These sayings start always with "the Buddha said". Remember it. When it is said, "The Buddha said", it simply means he has nothing to say. He reflected, he reflected you back. He simply showed you who you are. He revealed you to yourself. He brought you to your own center.

> *Those who have passions are never able to perceive the way, for it is*
> *like stirring up clear water with hands. People may come there wishing*
> *to find a reflection of their faces, which, however, they will never see.*
> *A mind troubled and vexed with the passions is impure, and on that*
> *account it never sees the way.*

> *O monks, do away with passions. When the dirt of passion is removed*
> *the way will manifest itself.*

Many things of tremendous import are said in this sutra. First, Buddha says,

Those who have passions are never able to perceive the way.

What is passion? Passion is a sort of fever, a sort of trembling of your being, a sort of inner wavering. Passions means you are not content as you are. You would like something else, you would like something more, you would like a different pattern of life, a different style. Then you think you will be happy and contented.

A mind full of passion is a mind full of discontent with the present. A mind with passion desires, hopes, but never lives. It postpones. It says "tomorrow", always tomorrow; it is never here and now. A mind full of passion always goes on missing the present – and the present is the only reality there is, so a mind full of passion goes on missing reality. It cannot reflect that which is, it cannot reflect the truth, it cannot reflect the dhamma, the way. It cannot reflect the real that surrounds you because you are never here.

Watch your mind. Whenever there is a desire, you have gone astray. You cannot be in the future, remember. You cannot be in the past, remember. That is impossible; that doesn't happen in the way things are; that simply doesn't happen. You cannot be in the past – the past is no more, how can you be in the past? But more or less you are always in the past. You are in the memory of the past. That is a way of *not* being, not a way of being. That is a way of not being. Or, you are in the future – which is impossible, because the future is not yet. How can you live in a house that does not yet exist? But you live there. Man goes on doing miracles! These are the real miracles: man goes on living in the past, which is no more, and he starts living in the future, which is not yet. You love the woman you have not found yet, or you go on loving the woman who is dead. The mind clings either to the past or to the future.

This is a way of not being. This is how we miss existence. This is how, by and by, we become phantoms, shadows, ghosts. Watch yourself. As I see people, millions remain in a ghost's life.

Living in memories, or living in imagination – that is the way of passion. Passion is a wavering – either to the left or to the right, but never in the middle. And the middle is the truth, the present is the truth, the door to reality.

BUDDHA SAYS:

Those who have passions are never able to perceive the way.

We are always on the way – there is no other way to be – but we never perceive that which we are always a part of. How can the unreal meet the real? A mind full of passion cannot meet with the real. And this continues.

Children are full of passion. One can understand – they are childish, they don't know life yet. Young people are full of passion. One can forgive them too;

they are still so young, that means they are still foolish – they will have to learn. But even old people, dying, on their deathbeds, are still full of passion? Then it is too much; an old man cannot be forgiven. A child is okay, a young man can still be forgiven, but an old man? – impossible to forgive. He has lived his whole life and he has not come to understand a simple fact – that you cannot be in the future and you cannot be in the past. He has lived his whole life and he has been frustrated each moment of it, and yet he goes on expecting. He has lived his whole life, desiring and desiring and desiring, and nothing has come out of it. Death has come, and life has not yet arrived. He has been only waiting, preparing for life – life has not happened. Yet he goes on hankering for more life.

I have watched people dying – it is very rarely that a person dies without passion. When a person dies without passion, the death is beautiful. It has tremendous significance, it has intrinsic value. But people die ugly deaths. Even death cannot shake them out of their dreams and passions and fevers. Even death cannot make them realize what is happening.

I have heard a very beautiful anecdote:

> The doorbell rings at the whorehouse, and the madam answers it but she sees no one. Then, looking down, she sees a man with no arms or legs sitting on a platform with wheels. She says to the guy, "What could you possibly want here?"
>
> The guy looks up at her, smiles and says, "I rang the doorbell didn't I?"
>
> Now that's enough!

To the very end, even dying, people think of sex. There is some interconnection because sex brings birth, so death and sex are really very deeply connected. If you have not been able to sort it out while you were fully alive, it will be very difficult to sort it out while you are dying. Because when death comes, it also brings its polarity, its shadow. Life starts with sex, life ends with death, and when death comes the sex energy has a last bout; it flares up. That very flare leads you into another life and the wheel starts moving again. Dying with a sexual, passionate mind, you are again creating a new life, a new birth. You have started seeking a womb. Sex means the search for a womb has started. You are not even dead yet but the search has started. Your soul is already preparing to take a jump into another womb.

Buddha says if you can die without passion, you have broken the desire. You may never be born again. Or even if you are born it is going to be only once. Maybe a little karma is left, accounts have to be closed, things finished – but basically you are free.

When the mind is free of passion, the mind is free. Freedom means freedom from passion, and only a free mind can see what is real. Only a free mind – free from passions – can see what is here.

Those who have passions are never able to perceive the way, for it is like stirring up clear water with hands.

Have you watched sometimes? In a full moon night you go to the lake – everything is silent . . . not even a ripple on the surface of the lake . . . and the moon is reflected so beautifully. Shake up the water, create a few ripples in the water with your hands, and the moon is divided into fragments; the reflection disappears. You may see silver all over the lake, but you cannot see the moon. Fragments and fragments – the totality is broken, the integration gone.

Human consciousness also can be in two states. One state is the state of passion – when there are many ripples and waves hankering for some shore somewhere in the future, or still clinging to some shore in the past. But the lake is disturbed. The surface is not calm, quiet and tranquil. The surface cannot reflect the reality; it distorts. A mind full of passion is a mechanism for distortion. Whatsoever you see, you see through a distorted lens.

Go to a lake on a full moon night and watch these two things in the lake: first, see everything quiet, calm, the moon reflected, a tremendous beauty, and everything so still – as if time has stopped. And everything so *present* – as if only the present is. Then create ripples, or wait for a wind to come and distort the reflection. Then the whole reflection is gone or distorted; then you go on looking and you cannot find the moon, you cannot figure out what the moon looks like. You cannot make it out from the reflection.

These are the two states of the mind also. A mind without any thought, desire, passion, is quiet . . . quiet like a lake. Then everything, as it is, is reflected. And to know that which is, is to know truth. It is all around you; it is just that you are not in a state to reflect it.

When your passions drop, by and by things start falling in line, they become integrated. And when the reflection is perfectly clear, you are liberated. Truth liberates. Nothing else liberates. To know that which is, is to be free, is to be absolute freedom.

Dogmas cannot liberate you, creeds cannot liberate you, churches cannot liberate you. Only truth liberates. And there is no way to find the truth unless you have come to create a situation in yourself where that which is, is mirrored.

Those who have passions are never able to perceive the way.

Consciousness has to become without content. That is the meaning of being passionless. When you are – simply, you are – I call it primal innocence. You are not hankering, desiring for anything; you are just in this moment, absolutely here and now. A great contentment arises in your being, a tremendous satisfaction arises in your being. You feel blessed.

In fact, that is what you are seeking. In all your desires you are seeking a state of contentment. But desires cannot bring it. Desires create more ripples on your lake; desires create more restlessness in you.

You are desiring only one thing – how to come to a state where everything is just contentment . . . nowhere to go . . . one is simply delighted. Just by being, one is blissful. Just by being, one can dance and sing. That is what you are seeking. Even in your desires, in your greed, in your sexuality, in your ambition, that's exactly what you are seeking – but you are seeking in a wrong direction. It cannot happen that way – it has never happened that way. It can happen in only one way, the way of the Buddha, the way of Krishna or Christ. The way is the same; it belongs to nobody. That way is right now, here, available to you . . . you just have to come *here* to meet it. You are escaping somewhere else, you are never found at home. Whatever address you give, you are never found there; you are always somewhere else. Life comes and seeks you. Of course it trusts you, and it comes to your so-called address but you are never there. Life knocks at the door and the room is empty, the house is empty. It goes into the house, looks everywhere, but you are not there. You are somewhere else. You are always somewhere else – somewhere else is your house. Ordinarily people think that they have to seek the ultimate, to seek the divine. The truth is just the opposite – it is seeking you, but you are never found.

What Buddha is saying is, if you are passionless you will be found. You will be immediately found because you will be sitting in the present moment. Your mind will not be wavering, your flame will be absolutely unwavering. In that very moment of meditation you meet existence, you meet truth. You become free.

Those who have passions are never able to perceive the way.

But one thing has to be remembered. You can drop worldly passions – many people do, they become sadhus, monks, they move to the monasteries. But they don't drop the passion as such. Now they start thinking of God, now they start thinking how to achieve in the other world. Their achiever's mind continues, only their language has changed. Now they no longer desire money, they no longer desire a bank balance, but still they desire security – security in the hands of God.

When you are seeking a bank balance, or when you are going to an insurance company to be insured, these are just different languages for your deep search for security. You leave them behind, then you become a Christian or you become a Hindu. By becoming a Christian, what are you seeking? You are again seeking security. You are thinking, "This man Jesus is the begotten son of God. I will be more secure with him." Or you are seeking to become a Hindu. You think, "These Hindus, they have been longest in the profession of religion. They must know, they must know all the secrets of the trade. They must have keys. Many civilizations have come and gone, but these Hindus have some trick – they continue. Babylon is no more, Assyria is just ruins, the old civilization of Egypt exists only in the museums. Many civilizations have existed on this earth and gone; only a few treasures are left here and there. But these Hindus are something; they have persisted. They have not been destroyed by time, they have a certain quality of eternity. They must know some secret. Become a Hindu."

But you are seeking security. If you are seeking security, your mind still carries the same passion, desire, fear. You may not be interested in this world. There are many people who come to me and they say, "This is impermanent, momentary; this world is not worthwhile. We are seeking something like permanent bliss." So, nothing has changed. In fact, they seem to be greedier than ordinary people. Ordinary people are satisfied with momentary things. These people seem to be very dissatisfied. They are not satisfied with momentary things – a beautiful house and garden, a beautiful car, a beautiful woman or a husband, a wife and children, they are not satisfied. They say, "These are all momentary, sooner or later they will be taken away. We are seeking something that cannot be taken away." These people are more greedy . . . their passion knows no bounds! They think they are religious; they are not. A religious person is one who has dropped all passion – passion as such. Just by changing the language, nothing is changed.

I have heard:

> Mulla Nasruddin was saying to his friend, "I have never called you a son of a bitch."
>
> "Yes you did!" The friend was very angry. He insisted, "Yes you did!"
>
> "No I didn't!" Mulla repeated. "All I said was, 'When you get home throw your mother a bone.'"

But it is the same! Just by changing your language, nothing is changed. The so-called religious person is as worldly as worldly people, sometimes even more so. I have come across many religious people, many Jaina monks – they seem to me more worldly than their followers. Because "the world" does not mean the world. The world simply means passion, desire, greed. They are hankering for moksha, hankering for the other world, heaven, paradise. Their dreams are full of future.

Your dreams are also full of future, but your future is not so big. Hmm? You think only a few days ahead, or at the most a few months. If you are very, very imaginative, at the most a few years, that's all. Your passion is not so strong. Their passion seems to be mad: they are not only thinking a few years ahead, they are thinking a few lives ahead – the other world. Their desires have gone berserk, they are mad! They can leave and renounce the world, but that renunciation is false because they are renouncing this world for better worlds. When you renounce one thing for something better, it is a bargain not a renunciation. You go to the film, to the movie. Of course, you have to renounce five dollars. You have to sacrifice five dollars immediately. But nobody calls it renunciation.

It is a bargain: if you want to live in heaven, in paradise, you have to pay for it. Remember this – that whenever you are paying something for something, it is not renunciation. The very idea of paying makes it immediately clear that it belongs to the world of desire, because life is free and nobody needs to pay for it.

Let me repeat it: life is absolutely free, nobody needs to pay for it. The moment you start paying for it, it is not life. It must be something like a commodity in the market – maybe in the religious market, but it must be some commodity.

If somebody asks you to renounce because that is the way to gain, then he is asking you to pay for it, sacrifice for it. He is talking economics not religion. He is talking finance. He is telling you, "This much you have to pay. If you want to be in God's paradise, you will have to pay these things. You will have to sacrifice." And of course it appeals to you, because you know the logic. How can you get anything free? You have to pay for it. And when you want to see God, you have to pay tremendously. You have to pay with all your pleasures; you have to become frozen, dead. You have to renounce life. So you become a "good boy", a "nice boy" and now God feels very happy: "Look, this man has renounced everything for me. Now he should be allowed into heaven."

Paradise is not to be earned, you are not to pay for it. You have only to learn to enjoy it, that's all. If you know how to enjoy it, it is available right now. You have not to pay for it.

But our whole mind has been trained by economists and politicians. They say you will have to pay. Sacrifice your childhood for education so that when you are young you can have a beautiful house, a family, respect, a respectable job. You will have to pay for it – sacrifice your childhood so that when you are a young adult you have all the pleasures of the world. Then when you are a young adult your wife says, "Build up some insurance, because the children are growing and they will need support. We will be growing old – and in our old age, what are you going to do?" Sacrifice your youth for old age so that in old age you can retire comfortably. So you sacrifice your youth for your old age.

And then what do you do when you retire? Now your whole life is gone in always preparing for something else. And the more you prepare, the more you become skillful in preparing – that's all. You can prepare more. A man who becomes skillful in preparing is never ready to live. He becomes more ready to prepare, that's all. That's how the whole of life is missed. And then in your old age they say, "Now prepare for the other world. What are you doing? Pray, meditate, go to the church. Now become religious. What are you doing? Death is coming. Prepare for the afterlife."

Now this whole logic is foolish! The childhood sacrificed for youth, the youth sacrificed for old age, the old age sacrificed for the afterlife. Everything is just a sacrifice. When does the time come to enjoy?

Let me say to you – if you want to enjoy, never prepare. If you want to enjoy, enjoy! Do it right now, because there is no other way to do it. If you become a great preparer, skillful, efficient in preparations, you will always prepare but you will never go on any journey. You will become so skillful in preparing, packing and unpacking, that you will not know how to go on the journey. You will only know how to pack and unpack again. That's what people are doing in life.

Life is free, it is a gift . . . a gift of existence. Enjoy it. Let this go as deep as possible in your heart; let this secret be no longer a secret. Life is a gift! Let there be dancing in the streets.

There is no need to prepare. Preparation is always a shadow of passion. When you desire for the future, of course you have to prepare for it. In the present, no preparation is needed. The present has already arrived. The trees are already green, and the roses have flowered, and the birds are calling you. Where is the point in preparing?

This craziness of preparing is absolutely human. You will never find it anywhere else. Have you ever seen any animal preparing for anything? any tree preparing for anything? any star preparing for anything? They must be all laughing: "Man is so ridiculous an animal!" They must be all laughing: "What has gone wrong?" They are enjoying, just now they are enjoying.

Reality must be more clearly reflected in animals, in birds, in rocks, than in man. Man's mind is full of ripples. These ripples have to be dropped.

Man is in a very strange situation. Below man is nature – absolutely unconscious and blissful. Above man are the buddhas – absolutely conscious and blissful. Man is just in-between – a passage, a bridge, a rope stretched between two eternities. Man is neither as happy as the cuckoo in the garden nor as happy as the Buddha. He is just in-between – stretched, tense, wants to move both ways at once, becoming more and more split. That's why I say schizophrenia is not a special disease, it is a very common phenomenon. It is not unusual. Everybody is schizophrenic, has to be. The very situation of humanity is schizophrenic. Man is not unconscious so he cannot be like trees, enjoying without preparation. And he is not yet buddhalike, so he cannot enjoy without preparation. He is not in the present. He is just in the middle.

But it is nothing to be worried about. You can never be as happy as the tree now. There is no way of going back – that world is lost. That is the meaning of Adam's expulsion from the Garden of Eden – he is no longer part of the unconscious bliss. He has become conscious by eating the fruit of the tree of knowledge. He has become man. Adam is human, and every human being is Adamlike. Every childhood is in the Garden of Eden; every child is as happy as the animals, as happy as the primitive, as happy as the trees. Have you watched a child running in the forest, on the beach? – he is not yet human. His eyes are still clear, but unconscious. He will have to come out of the Garden of Eden.

It is not that Adam was once expelled – every Adam has to be expelled again and again. Every child has to be thrown out of the garden; it is part of growth. The pain is that of growth. One has to lose it to gain it again, to gain it consciously. That is man's burden and his destiny, his anguish and his freedom, man's problem and man's grandeur both.

Buddha is nothing but Adam coming back, re-entering the Garden of Eden. But now he comes with full awareness. Now the circle is complete. He comes dancing, he comes absolutely blissful. He is as blissful as any tree, but not unconscious. He has gained consciousness, he has risen towards consciousness. Now he is not only blissful – he is aware that he is blissful. A new quality has entered.

That's what is trying to enter in you – knocking your head from everywhere. That's what I mean when I say God is searching for you – I mean that consciousness wants to happen to you. Allow it to happen. Recognize that existence, nature, is searching for you. Let go, fall into accord with it. That's what Buddha calls dhamma – being in accord with nature . . . fully in accord, but aware. And don't wait. Don't wait for some age when the whole of humanity will become aware and passionless. That will be a futile waiting; you will be waiting in vain.

I have heard:

> A drunkard was walking home when he came upon a group of men digging a big hole in the middle of the street. "Watcha doing?" he asked.
>
> "We are building a subway," came the answer.
>
> "When you gonna finish it?" he asked.
>
> "Ah, in about eight years."
>
> The drunk thought for a while and then shouted back, "Ah, the heck with it. I'll take a taxi."

Humanity will someday become collectively conscious – that possibility exists – but nobody knows when. Millions of years will pass, and millions of individuals will have to become buddhas before it can happen. Then one day it is possible that buddhahood may become a natural phenomenon. But before it happens you have to strive individually; you cannot wait for it. That waiting will be suicidal. And if everybody waits for it, it will never happen because for it to happen a certain amount of individual souls are needed to become buddhas.

Now a few experiments are being done with meditation. It has been found that if in a village, a small village of four hundred people, the number of meditators rises at least one percent . . . for example, if in a village of five hundred people, five persons start meditating, the crime rate in the village falls immediately. People commit fewer crimes, just because one percent of the village is meditating. It affects the whole consciousness – just one percent. And they are just meditating, they are not buddhas. If one percent of humanity becomes buddhas, the whole quality will change. Consciousness will become easier, may become almost natural and spontaneous.

So if you are waiting, you are waiting in vain. And if you are waiting and everybody goes on waiting, it is never going to happen. Do something about it, because by doing something about it you will be creating a situation in which it will become easier and easier for it to happen to others.

Those who have passions are never able to see the way, for it is like stirring up clear water with hands. People may come there wishing to find a reflection of their faces which however they will never see.

That's why you don't know who you are. You have not been able to see your own face in your mind. What to say of other things? What to say about the face of truth, existence? You have not been able to look at your own face in your mind, even that much reflection is not possible. The face does not become a reality, you see only fragments because the mind is continuously shaking, wavering.

The flame is never in a state of tremendous rest, so everything is flickering. Sometimes you see one of your eyes, sometimes you see your nose, sometimes you see one of your hands, sometimes you see a part of your face, but everything is muddled. And if you want to figure it out, it becomes a Picasso painting. You don't know what is what. Everything is muddled, in a mess. You don't know your identity, who you are, so you cling to outer supports – your name, your father's name, your family name, your certificates from the university, your degree. These are outer supports; they help you somehow to have some idea who you are. But really you don't know who you are. How can you know yourself if you only know that you are a doctor or an engineer or a plumber? What has that to do with your being? You can be a plumber, you can be a doctor, you can be an engineer – that has nothing to do with your essential being. These are all accidents. You can be white or you can be black, but that has nothing to do with your essential being. These are just accidents, nothing essential. The difference between a white man and a black man is just of a small amount of pigment. If you go to the market, the pigment will not cost more than four pennies. That is the only difference between a black man and a white man. Very non-essential, but has become so tremendously important.

What is the difference between a rich man and a poor man? . . . just accidents. Between a successful man and a failure? . . . just accidents. These accidents don't really define you. But we don't know how to define ourselves in any other way, so we go on clinging to this fragment or that, and making something out of it.

The reality of your being is within you. You just need a silent mind and it will be reflected. You will know who you are, and that will become your first step to knowing what this reality is. What is this whole game? What is this magical world? By knowing yourself, you will have taken the first step of knowing existence, knowing the whole. By knowing yourself absolutely, you have taken the last step of knowing the whole. By knowing yourself, you know what godliness is. There is no other way – because you are gods, but you have not been able to see your face.

A mind troubled and vexed with passions is impure, and on that account it never sees the way.

O monks, do away with passions. When the dirt of passion is removed the way will manifest itself.

The way will manifest itself. There is no need to discover it. All that is needed is that you have an innocent, pure mind. And when Buddha says pure, he does not mean a mind that is moral, he does not mean a mind that is religious. His definition of purity is more scientific; he says purity is a mind that is without thought. A moral man is moral, but he has moral thoughts; an immoral man is immoral, but he has immoral thoughts. As far as the mind is concerned, both are full of thoughts. A worldly man has worldly thoughts, a religious man has religious thoughts. Whether you are singing a song from the latest movie or you are chanting a religious prayer, it makes no difference – your mind is wavering, your mind is not silent.

So by "pure", Buddha does not mean moral, no – he simply means a mind that has no content. All content brings impurity; whatever the content it is impure. He is not using the word "impurity" in any condemnatory sense, he is using it only in a very scientific sense – anything foreign, anything alien, makes the mind impure.

Mind is just pure reflection, the capacity to reflect. If the mind has some ideas in it, the ideas will not allow its reflection to be pure. Then projection starts, and the reflection is destroyed. So whether you have religious ideas or non-religious ideas, whether you are a communist or a democrat, it makes no difference. Christian, Mohammedan, Hindu, Sikh – it makes no difference. If you have ideas, your mind is impure.

A mind full of consciousness will be empty of all contents. It will be neither a Christian nor a Hindu nor a Jew. You will not be a moral person nor an immoral person. You will simply be. That being, that be-ness, is purity. That's what I call primal innocence. Then all dust is washed away and you are just a reflective force.

O monks, do away with passions. When the dirt of passions is removed the way will manifest itself.

And then suddenly you will see – the way has always been here now, only you were missing it. It is impossible to lose the way. You can try – that's what you have been doing – you can try, and for moments you can also believe you have succeeded. But in fact it never happens. You cannot lose the way; there is no way to lose the way. There is no way to go astray. You can believe in your dreams that you can go astray, but in reality you cannot go astray. Any time, when you become awake, you will simply laugh that you have been thinking that you have gone far away. You have never even gone out of your home, you have always lived here. Just with closed eyes you go on dreaming and dreaming and dreaming.

In a dream you can go as far away as you like, but in reality there is no way to go anywhere except here. Because wherever you are, reality is. You are part of reality and you exist only as an organic part to reality. You cannot go away, you cannot separate yourself. You are intermingled with existence, you are interwoven with existence. We are not dependent, we are not independent – we are interdependent, we are members of each other. There is no way to go anywhere.

So when the mind is pure, when the dirt of passion is removed, the way will manifest itself. Suddenly you will see – the way is standing before you. Suddenly you will recognize that you have been always standing in the doorway, on he threshold. You will start laughing. The whole game has been so ridiculous.

A really religious person never loses the sense of humor. And if you see a religious person who has no sense of humor, you can be certain he has not come home yet. Because a religious person . . . the more he understands, the more he sees the ridiculousness of the game, the more he starts laughing. How did it all become possible? How did I dream, how long have I been in dreams? – and those dreams looked so real.

THE BUDDHA SAID:

Seeing the way is like going into a dark room with a torch. The darkness instantly departs while the light alone remains. When the way is attained, and the truth is seen, ignorance vanishes and enlightenment abides forever.

A beautiful maxim to be remembered. Seeing the way is like going into a dark room with a torch. If you go into a dark room with a torch, with a lamp, the darkness immediately disappears – immediately! Buddha says "instantly". It does not take time; it is not that you bring light in, then the darkness lingers a little while, decides whether to leave or not, takes a little time and then goes. No, no time is needed because darkness is not real. If it were real, it would take a little time – maybe a split second, but it would take a little time to go out. It would have to travel, and traveling takes time. Sometimes it may be a lazy darkness, it may take a little longer time. Sometimes it may be a fast runner; then it will go fast. But anyway it will take time if it is real.

When you bring light, the very bringing of the light is the disappearance of the darkness. Darkness is not, only light is. When darkness is, in fact there is nothing. It is only the absence of light, that's all. Darkness has no positive existence, it is just absence of light. So when you bring presence, the absence is no longer there.

Buddha says this world is just like darkness. Once you bring light to it, once you become aware, once you drop your passions and become meditative, once the mind attains to the purity of meditation, suddenly the light is there. Darkness dissipates, disappears instantly, immediately, within no time.

> Seeing the way is like going into a dark room with a torch. The darkness instantly departs while the light alone remains. When the way is attained and the truth is seen, ignorance vanishes and enlightenment abides forever.

Enlightenment is that which has always been the case. Enlightenment is that which has always been there. You were not aware, you were fast asleep. It was just sitting by your side waiting for you to awaken. Enlightenment is your nature, is your very being. From the very beginning it has been there. It is there right now. If you can flare up in awareness, you can attain it immediately. It is a sudden illumination. But if you want, you can take your time, you can move slowly, gradually. You can turn over and go to sleep again and wait a little more. But whenever you open your eyes, you will find it. It has been always there. Just for the asking it could have been achieved any time; it was never difficult. It seems difficult because you are asleep. Once you are awakened, you will laugh. How was it difficult? Why was it difficult? It was something that was present, only you had to claim it.

The way *is*.

Waves come and go . . . the ocean is. Minds come and go . . . no-mind is. Roles come and go . . . Buddha is. Buddha is your original face, your originality, your very being.

O monks, do away with passions.

Drop desiring. Our desiring culminates everything. Our desiring becomes our interpretation of everything. The more you desire the more miserable you will be, because the more you desire the more will be your expectation. The more you desire the less grateful you will be, because the more you desire the more you will feel that "man proposes and God disposes". The less you desire the more grateful you be, because the less you desire the more you will see how much is given without desiring, without asking. If you don't desire at all, you will be in tremendous gratitude, because so much is given already. Life is such a gift . . . but we go on with our mind.

I have heard:

> A man was reckoned to be the laziest man in the country and
> naturally spent most of his time sleeping. He was so inactive and so
> useless that at one time the townspeople thought it would be a good
> idea to bury him whether he was dead or alive.

They made a crude coffin, came around with it to his house, put him in it without any protest from his family, and started off with the live old critter for the cemetery. Of course there was no resistance from him; he was so lazy. He said, "Okay." Or he may not have even said that. He may have just watched what was going on. But before they got to the cemetery, they were stopped by a stranger who had heard of the grim proceedings. They told the stranger the man would not work and had not a grain of corn on his place, and the town was sick of providing him with food. "Enough is enough," they said, "and we are fed up."

"If you boys will hold off, I will gladly give that man a wagonload of corn," said the stranger. Before the townspeople could reply, a head was raised out of the coffin, and the almost-deceased asked, "Is that corn shucked?"

The lazy man is worrying about the corn, whether it is shucked or not. He is ready to die, but if he has to shuck the corn, then it is too much effort. A man who is surrounded by laziness looks at everything through his laziness. His laziness becomes his interpretation of things. If you are sleepy, you will look at life with sleepy eyes, naturally. And if you miss life, it is natural – because life is possible only if your eyes are fully alive, if your eyes are radiant with life. If you look at life with alive eyes, there is a meeting, a communion.

We live surrounded by clouds of desire. Then those desires become our interpretation. Then we go on thinking according to those desires.

It happened:

Applicants for a job on a dam had to take a written examination, the first question of which was: "What does hydro-dynamics mean?" Mulla Nasruddin, one of the applicants for the job, looked at this, then wrote underneath it: "It means I don't get the job."

Whatever meaning we give to life, *we* give it to life. Buddha is saying if you want to know the real meaning of life, then you have to drop giving all meanings to it. Then the way reveals itself. Then life opens its mysterious doors. You stop giving meaning to it – your desires are giving meaning to it; they are defining the undefinable. And if you remain clouded with your desires, whatsoever you know is nothing but your own dreaming. That's why we say in India that this life, this so-called life lived through desires, is maya, it is a magical thing. You create it, you are the magician. It is your maya, your magic.

We don't live in the same world, remember. We live in separate worlds because we don't live in the same desires. You project your desires, your neighbor is projecting his desires. That's why when you meet a person and you want to live with them, with a woman or with a man or with a friend, difficulties arise. That is a clash of two worlds. Everybody is good alone. Together, something goes wrong. I have never come across a wrong person, but every day I have to watch and see and observe wrong relationships. I never come across a wrong person, but every day I come across wrong relationships. It seems that almost all relationships are wrong. Because two persons live in two worlds of desire, they have their own magical worlds. When they come together those worlds clash.

It happened:

> One night Mulla Nasruddin was sitting on one side of the fire and his wife on the other. Between them lay the cat and the dog, lazily blinking at the fire. The wife ventured this remark, "Now dear, just you look at that cat and dog. See how peacefully and quietly they get along together. Why can't we do that?"
>
> "That's all right," said Nasruddin, "but just tie them together and see what will happen."

Tie two persons together – that's what a marriage is – and see what happens. Suddenly the two worlds . . . It seems almost impossible to understand the woman you love. It should not be so – you love her – but it seems impossible to understand. It is impossible to understand the man you love. It should not be so – you love him – but it seems impossible to understand. It is very easy to understand strangers; it is very difficult to understand people who are very close. To understand your mother, father, brother, sister, friend, is very difficult. The closer you are the more difficult – because the worlds are clashing.

These worlds surround you like a subtle aura. Unless you drop this magical creation that you go on feeding, you will remain in conflict. You will remain in conflict with persons, you will remain in conflict with existence – because the other has his world, and you have your own private world. They never go together.

You have to drop your private mentation. Dropping mentation is what meditation is all about. You have to drop your thinking, desiring. You have just to be, and suddenly everything falls into an organic whole, becomes a harmony.

And these desires are the root of the darkness that is surrounding you. These desires are the support, the foundation of the darkness that surrounds you. These desires are the hindrances that don't allow you to become alert.

Beware of these desires. And remember – the word "beware" means "be aware". That is the only way. If you really want to get rid of these desires, don't start fighting them. Otherwise you will miss again. Because if you start fighting with your desires, that means you have created a new desire – to be desireless. Now this desire will clash against other desires. This is just changing the language; you remain the same. Don't start fighting with the desires. When Buddha says, "Do away with passions, o monks," he does not mean to fight with the passions. Because you can fight only if there is a prize, if you are going to attain something. Then again a desire has arisen – in a new shape, a new form, but it is the same old desire.

Don't fight, just be aware.

Beware of desires. Become more watchful, more alert, and you will see – the more alert you are the less desires are there. Ripples start subsiding, waves start disappearing. And one day, suddenly . . . any moment it can happen, because all moments are as potential as any other. There is no auspicious moment for it to happen. It can happen in any ordinary moment, because all ordinary moments are auspicious. There is no need for it to happen under a bodhi tree. It can happen under any tree, or even without a tree. It can happen under the roof of your house. It can happen anywhere . . . because godliness is everywhere.

But by and by become aware. Create more and more awareness, collect more and more awareness. One day the awareness comes to such a point, the energy is so much that it simply explodes. And in that explosion, darkness disappears and light is. Immediately darkness disappears, instantly darkness disappears – and light is. And that light is your own luminosity, so you cannot lose it. Once known, it becomes your eternal treasure.

Enough for today.

Chapter 10:

The Discipline Beyond Discipline

THE BUDDHA SAID:

> *My doctrine is to think the thought that is unthinkable; to
> practice the deed that is not doing; to speak the speech that
> is inexpressible; and to be trained in the discipline which is
> beyond discipline. Those who understand this are near;
> those who are confused are far. The way is beyond words
> and expressions, is bound by nothing earthly. Lose sight of
> it to an inch or miss it for a moment, and we are away
> from it forever more.*

This sutra is one of the most important, one of the very central to Buddha's
message. The very essence of his message is there like a seed. Go patiently with
me into it, try to understand it. Because if you understand this sutra, you would
have understood all that Buddha wants you to understand. If you miss this
sutra, you miss all.

THE BUDDHA SAID:

> *My doctrine is to think the thought that is unthinkable;
> to practice the deed that is not doing; to speak the speech that is
> inexpressible; and to be trained in the discipline that is beyond
> discipline.*

The choice of the word "doctrine" is unfortunate, but there are difficulties in
translating. Buddha must have used the word *siddhanta*. It has a totally different
meaning. Ordinarily it is translated as doctrine; it should not be translated so.

But the problem is that in the English language there is no equivalent to *siddhanta*, so I will have to explain it to you.

A doctrine is a consistent, logical theory. A *siddhanta* has nothing to do with logic, theory, consistency. A *siddhanta* is a realization, it is an experience. A doctrine is intellectual, *siddhanta* is existential. You can make a doctrine without being transformed by it. You can make a great doctrine without even being touched by it. But if you want to achieve a *siddhanta* you will have to be totally transformed, because it will be a vision of a totally different person.

The word *siddhanta* means the assertion of one who has become a siddha, one who has achieved, one who has arrived – it is his statement. You can be a great philosopher, you can figure out intellectually many things, you can systematize your inferences and you can create a very consistent, logical syllogism which almost appears like truth, but is not truth. It has been manufactured by your mind. A doctrine is man-made; a *siddhanta* has nothing to do with man and his effort. A *siddhanta* is a vision – you come upon it.

For example, a blind man can think about light and can try to figure out what it is all about. He can even listen to great treatises on light and he can create a certain idea about it, what it is. But he will be as far away from light as he was before. He can even expound a doctrine about light, he can explain its physics, he can explain its structure. He can go deep into the constituents of light, he can talk about it, he can write a Ph.D on it, a thesis. He can be given a doctorate by a university because he has propounded a doctrine – but still he does not know what light is. He has no eyes to see.

A *siddhanta* is that which you have seen, which has been revealed to you, which has become your own experience, which you have encountered. A doctrine is almost imaginary, it is not real. A doctrine is almost always borrowed. You can hide your borrowing in many ways – subtle, cunning ways. You can reformulate, you can take from many sources and you can rearrange everything, but a doctrine is a borrowed thing – nothing original in it. A *siddhanta* is absolutely original, new. It is your authentic experience. You have come to see what reality is. It is an immediate perception, it is a benediction, it is a blessing, it is a grace, a gift. You have arrived and you have seen what truth is. The statement of a realization is *siddhanta*. Propounding a doctrine is one thing; giving expression to a *siddhanta* is totally different.

I have heard:

> Once Mulla Nasruddin was talking to a few of his friends. He was telling his pals about the wonderful vacation he and his family had just had in the United States. "It is a wonderful country," he

exclaimed. "Nowhere in the world is a stranger treated so well. You walk along the street and you meet a well-dressed fellow with lots of dollars. He tips his hat and smiles at you, and you talk together. He invites you into his big car, and shows you the town. He buys you a fine dinner, then takes you to the theater. You have more fine food and plenty of drinks, and he invites you to his house and you sleep nice all night. Next morning . . . "

"Wait, Nasruddin," a listener said, "did all this really happen to you?"

"No, not exactly, but it all happened to my wife", said Nasruddin.

A doctrine is that which has happened to somebody else. You have heard about it. It has not happened to you – it is borrowed, dirty, ugly. A *siddhanta* is virgin.

A doctrine is a prostitute. It has been moving through many minds, through many hands. It is like dirty currency; it goes on changing its owner. A *siddhanta* is something absolutely fresh. It has never happened before, it will never happen again. It has happened to you. A *siddhanta* is deeply individual, it is a personal vision of reality.

What happened to Buddha is a *siddhanta* – what Buddhists propound is a doctrine. What happened to Christ is a *siddhanta* – what Christians talk about is a doctrine. What happened to Krishna is a *siddhanta* – what Hindus go on bragging about is a doctrine. What I am saying to you is a *siddhanta* – if you go and repeat it, it will be a doctrine. That's why I say it is a very unfortunate choice of words to put into Buddha's mouth. *My doctrine is to think. . . .* No, let it be: "My *siddhanta* is to think," my realization is to think, my own understanding is to think . . . He is not proposing a theory, he is simply expressing an experience.

A few more things before we enter into the sutra.

A *siddhanta* is by its very nature paradoxical – it has to be so, because life is paradoxical. If you really have experienced it, then whatsoever you see and say is going to be paradoxical. Life consists of contradictions. We call them contradictions; life does not call them contradictions. They are complementaries. Day and night dance together, life and death dance together, love and hate move hand in hand. We call them contradictions – in life they are not so. Life is big and vast, immense. It comprehends all the contradictions into it; they are complementaries.

When a person has realized, whatsoever he says is going to have the taste of paradox. That's why all great religious assertions are paradoxical. They may be in the Vedas, in the Upanishads, in the Koran, in the Bible, in the Tao Te Ching – wherever and whenever you find truth, you will find it paradoxical – because the truth has to be total and totality is paradoxical.

A doctrine is never paradoxical, a doctrine is tremendously consistent –

because a doctrine is not worried about reality. A doctrine is worried about being consistent. It knows no reality. It is a mind game, and the mind is very, very logical. The mind says don't allow any contradiction in it. The mind says if you talk about light then don't talk about darkness because that will be inconsistent. Forget about darkness. The mind tries to prove that life is non-contradictory, because that is the mind's choice. Mind is afraid of contradictions, becomes very shaky when it comes across a contradiction. It insists on its own pattern. Mind is logical, life is not. So if you find something very logical, beware – something must be wrong in it. It must not be part of life, it must be man-made.

Everything existential is contradictory. That's why people go on arguing about God. Why, if God loves man so much, did he create death? The mind finds it very difficult to accept the idea that existence contains life and also death. If it was up to you, if you were the creator of the world, if your mind was the creator, then you would have never done that. But think of a life where no death exists. It will be sheer boredom, tedium. Think – if death is impossible, then you will be continuously in hell. If mind had created the world, then there would be only love and no hate. But think of a world where only love exists. Then it will be too sweet – sweet to the point of being nauseating. It will lose all taste, it will lose all color, it will be flat. Love is beautiful because of the possibility of hate.

If mind were to create the world, or Aristotle were asked to create the world, then there would have been only day, no night; only work, no play. Then think what would have happened! Maybe that's the reason God created man in the very end – first he created other things; otherwise man would start giving advice! According to the Bible, first God created trees and the earth and the sky and the stars and the animals and the birds and the whole thing – then he waited and waited. Then he created humans. And first he created the man, then he created woman – because the man, just out of politeness, might have kept quiet, but a woman cannot keep quiet. God must have been afraid. Don't create a human being, otherwise he will start giving advice – "do this, don't do that". And for the woman he waited till the last, and since he created woman he has disappeared! Otherwise the woman would have nagged him to death.

If Aristotle had been asked to create the world, or to help it to be created, then the world would have been absolutely consistent – absolutely consistent. But then it would have been a world of misery and hell. Life is beautiful because there are contradictions. Work is beautiful because there is play. Work means you are doing something to get something out of it. Play means you are simply doing it for its own sake. No, Aristotle wouldn't allow it, Plato wouldn't allow it.

In his *Republic*, Plato says there will be no possibility for any poets: "We won't allow them. They are dangerous people, they bring contradiction in the world – poets are dreamers and they talk in ways that are vague, ambiguous. You cannot make anything out of what they are saying, what they mean." In Plato's world, in his *Republic*, logicians and philosophers will be the kings; they will decide.

It has not yet happened, only a few things like that have happened. For example, Soviet Russia was more Platonic, China is more Platonic. These two countries have been run by logic, and you cannot find more miserable people anywhere. Well-fed, well-sheltered – because logic is a great arranger of things; everything has been arranged – only life is missing. Somehow the people are not happy, because man cannot live by bread alone. You need the opposite also. The whole day you work, in the night you rest. You need darkness also.

A doctrine is a logical statement of a theory – and logic is like a chameleon, it goes on changing its color. It is not reliable because it is not based in reality. It is not responsible because it is not based in reality. It is untrue because it is a partial truth.

Remember, a partial truth is more untrue than a total untruth, because a partial truth gives a feeling of being true. It is only half true, and nothing can be half true. Either it is true or it is not true. A half-truth is absolutely untrue, but its logic gives it a feeling of being true; at least it appears to be on the way to truth.

It is not even on the way to truth. And logicians go on doing somersaults, they go on changing their standpoints, because in fact they have not come to anything that is really real, just their mind games. One day one game, another day another game; they go on changing. They remain consistent – consistent with their own train of thought, but inconsistent with reality.

I have heard:

> "It is difficult to explain what a course of logic will do for a person's thinking, but let me illustrate," said Mulla Nasruddin to his son. "Suppose two men came out of a chimney. One is clean, one dirty. Which one will take a bath?"
>
> "The dirty one, naturally," answered the boy.
>
> "Remember," chided Nasruddin, "that the clean man sees the dirty one and sees how dirty he is, and vice versa."
>
> "Now I get it, Dad," answered the boy. "The clean one, seeing his dirty companion, concludes he is dirty too. So he takes the bath. Am I right now?"
>
> "Wrong," said Nasruddin nonchalantly. "Logic teaches us this – how could two men come out of a chimney, one clean and one dirty?"

Once you start playing the game of logic there is no end to it, and you will never win. The logician will always win. The logician will always win because logic can always find a way and you have nothing to compare with, you have no reality. That's why so many philosophies exist, and all opposing each other, and not a single conclusion has been arrived at yet. Down the centuries, for almost five thousand years man has argued; man has not been doing much but just arguing. Thousands of philosophies have been created, very neat and clean logic. If you read one philosopher you will be convinced. If you read his opponent you will be convinced. Read the third one, you will be convinced – and you will be getting into a mess. By and by you will be convinced by all and you will be mad, because you will not know now what is true.

They are all wrong because the logical approach is wrong.

There are two ways to know reality. One is just to close your eyes and think about it. I call it "about-ism". It is always about and about, it never goes directly. You go on beating around the bush. You never beat the bush exactly – just around. You never penetrate the center of a problem, you simply go round and round. It is a merry-go-round. You can enjoy it – logicians enjoy very much, it is so beautiful to come with a new theory that explains everything – but it is just in the mind. You close your eyes, sit on your easy chair and think "about". This is not going to give you reality.

Reality is already there, you have not to think about it. You have to allow it. You have to drop all thinking so that you can see what is the truth, so that you can see that which is. If you go on thinking you cannot see that which is. It is impossible. Your thoughts will create smoke around you. Your consciousness will be covered by the smoke, your eyes will not have clarity, you will not have sensitivity and continuously you will be searching and seeking your own ideas, imposing them, projecting them on reality. You will not give reality a chance to reveal itself.

A doctrine is arrived at through logical thinking. A doctrine comes through the process of "about-ism". A *siddhanta* is arrived at not by closing your eyes, not by thinking too much but by dropping thinking as such, in toto – by opening your eyes with no prejudice, with no a priori conceptions, and looking direct into reality, facing reality directly. It is already there, it only needs you to be there.

And when you are absolutely without any thought – your mind is still, your memory is still, your thinking has completely ceased to be – then reality erupts, explodes. Then you become a receiver. Then *siddhanta* arises.

My siddhanta is to think the thought that is unthinkable . . .

The first thing, Buddha says, is to think the thought that is unthinkable. It is a contradiction, a paradox. Now, no logician will ever utter such nonsense. It is from the very beginning nonsensical. That's why logicians go on saying that Buddha, Jesus, Bodhidharma, Lao Tzu, Zarathustra – these people are all nonsense. Their propositions are meaningless because they say one thing and in the next breath they contradict it. Now look at this sentence: *My siddhanta is to think the thought that is unthinkable . . .* Now just in a small sentence, absolute contradiction – to think the unthinkable. How can you think the unthinkable? If it is really unthinkable you cannot think. If you can think, then how can it be unthinkable? Simple, illogical – but what Buddha means has to be understood. Don't be in a hurry; that's why I say go patiently. When he wants to say something, he means it. He is saying there is a way to know things without thinking. There is a way to know things without mind. There is a way to see into reality directly, immediately, without the vehicle of thought. You can be connected with reality without any agent of thinking – that is what he is saying. He is saying that the mind can completely cease its activity, completely drop its activity and yet be – still, a reservoir – and see into reality. But you will have to experience it, only then you will be able to understand.

Sometimes try just to see. Sitting by the side of a rosebush, just look at the rose flower; don't think, don't even give names. Don't even classify. Don't even say that this is a rose – because a rose is a rose is a rose; whether you call it "rose" or something else makes no difference. Don't label it, don't give it a name, don't bring language in. Don't bring any symbol in, because a symbol is a method of falsifying reality.

If you say "this is a rose", you have already missed. Then you have brought in some past experience of other roses, which are not. Now your eyes are full of roses – rows of roses. In your life you must have come across many types of roses – white and yellow and red, all those roses are there floating in your eyes. Now you are crowded by your past memories and then, on the other side of all those memories is this rose which is real. Now the crowd of the unreal is so great that you will not be able to reach and touch the real.

When Buddha says drop thinking he means don't bring the past in. What is the point of bringing it in? This rose is here, you are here. Let it be a deep meeting, a communion, a connection. Melt a little with this rose, let this rose melt a little in you. The rose is ready to share its fragrance; you also share your being, your consciousness, with it.

Let there be a handshake with reality. Let there be a little dance with this rose, dancing in the wind. You also move, be, look, feel – close your eyes, smell, touch, drink. This beautiful phenomenon that is facing you . . . don't go here and there, just be with it. No more right and left, just be direct like an arrow moving towards the target. If you in bring words, language, you bring in society, you bring the past, you bring other people. Tennyson has said something about the rose. Shelley has said something about the rose. Shakespeare has said something about the rose, or Kalidas. Once you bring language, Shakespeare and Kalidas and Bhavabhuti and Shelley and Keats are all standing there. Now you are too full of your own ideas, now you are in a crowd, lost. You will not be able to see the simple truth.

The truth is so simple. Yes, it is just like a rose flower in front of you. It is utterly there. Why go somewhere else? Why not move into *this* reality? Why go and find the past and future? Don't say this rose is beautiful, because the rose needs no compliments from you. Let it be a feeling. This rose does not understand human language, so why puzzle this rose? Why say it is beautiful? The rose knows nothing of beauty and nothing of ugliness. For this rose, life is not divided and split; this rose is not schizophrenic. This rose is simply there, with no idea of what beauty is and what ugliness is. Don't call it beautiful – when you call it beautiful you have brought in a concept. The mind has started functioning. Now you may have a little experience of the rose, but it will not be true – your mind will be a distortion. You will think of this rose just as a representative of all other roses.

Plato says that every real thing is just a representative of something ideal. He says that it is the idea of rose that is real, and the rose is just a reflection of that idea. This is nonsense, this is really absurd. This rose exists here now. But for Plato, the reality is unreal and ideas are real. For Buddha it is just the opposite: the reality is the real and ideas are unreal. If you follow Plato you will become a philosopher. If you follow Buddha you will become religious. Religiousness is not a philosophy, it is an experience. So try it. Sometimes allow your no-mind to function. Sometimes push aside all your thinking and let reality penetrate you. Sometimes let there be a blessing from reality; allow it to deliver its message to you.

But we go on living in words, and we pay too much attention to the words.

I had a teacher in the university and we used to go for a walk together. After few days I said, "I will not come with you. Better I should go alone."

He said, "Why?" It was because he was so much obsessed with names. Every tree that he would see, he had to say to which species it belonged. Every flower – what it contains, its history. If he would see a rose, he would not see the rose, he would see the whole history of roses: how they came from Iran, in what century, who brought them to India – because it is not an Indian flower. He would never look at the flower – again and again I would pull him back: "This flower is enough. What is the point? Flowers don't have histories, only human beings have. This flower does not bother whether it is in Iran or in India. This flower has no idea of any past, it lives just here now. It is neither Hindu nor Mohammedan, nor Indian nor Iranian. It is simply there. It is not even a rose!"

But it was difficult for him. Any bird he would see, he would say, "Wait, let me listen. What species of bird is this? From where has it come? Has it come from Siberia, or from Middle Asia? Or is it a Himalayan bird?" After a few days I said, "You excuse me and go alone, because I am not interested from where this bird has come. This bird is here, it is enough. I am not interested in the scientific, historical explanation."

Explaining things, for a few people, is almost a disease. Through their explanations they try to explain away everything. They are obsessed with explanation. They think that if they can name a thing, label a thing, they know it. They are very uneasy unless they can label a thing, know a thing by name, categorize it, pigeonhole it – unless they do, they are very uncomfortable. It seems as if a certain thing is just offending them – why are you there without any classification? Once they have categorized it, pigeonholed it, put a label on it, then they are at ease. They have known it; they are finished with the thing.

I have heard:

> After the Second World War a German soldier raped a French
> woman and told her, "In nine months you will have a son – you may
> call him Adolf Hitler." To which the French woman replied, "In nine
> days you will have a rash – you may call it measles."

But by calling names, it changes nothing. What you call something is absolutely irrelevant. Whatever is, is! By your giving it a name it never changes, but for you it changes. Just by giving it a name, reality becomes different to you.

It happened:

> A lion and an ass made an agreement to go out hunting together. By
> and by they came to a cave where many wild goats abode. The lion
> took up his station at the mouth of the cave and the ass, going within,
> kicked and brayed and made a mighty fuss to frighten them out.
> When the lion had caught many of them, the ass came out and asked
> him if he had not made a noble fight and routed the goats properly.
>
> "Yes indeed," said the lion. "And I assure you, you would have
> frightened me too if I had not known you to be an ass."

It may make a difference to you by calling names, but it does not make any difference to reality. It may make a difference to you because you live surrounded by your language, concept, verbalization. You immediately go on translating everything into language.

De-language yourself – that's what Buddha means. Un-mind yourself, un-wind yourself – that's what Buddha means. Otherwise you will never know what is true.

My siddhanta *is to think the thought that is unthinkable.*

You cannot think about reality. There is no way to think about it. All thinking is borrowed. No thinking is ever original. All thinking is repetitive, all thinking is mechanical. You can go on chewing and re-chewing the same things again and again and again, but nothing new ever arises out of thinking. Thinking is old, rotten. It is a junkyard.

You cannot think about reality because reality is every moment original. It is every moment so new that it has never been like that before. It is so absolutely fresh that you will have to know it. There is no other way to know it than knowing it. The only way to know love is to love. The only way to know swimming is to swim. The only way to know reality is to be real. Mind makes you unreal. Mind makes you too much like thoughts – mindstuff, words, concepts, theories, philosophies, doctrines, scriptures, isms. Mind does not give you the real thing, it gives you only reflections – and those reflections are also distorted.

Buddha says, attain to a clarity. Just see, just be. And then you will be able to think that thought which is unthinkable. You will be able to have a meeting with reality.

The thought that is unthinkable – only that is worth thinking. All else is just wasting life energy.

To practice the deed that is non-doing.

This is what Lao Tzu calls *wu-wei*. Action in inaction – again another paradox. But a *siddhanta* has to be paradoxical.

To practice the deed that is not doing . . .

Ordinarily we know only deeds which we can do. We are surrounded by our doing. We don't know that there are things which are beyond our doing and still are happening. You are born. You have not given birth to yourself, it has simply happened, and it could not happen in a better way. You are breathing –

but you are not breathing as an act; it is happening. You can try to stop it and then you will see you cannot stop it. Even for a few seconds you cannot stop it; you will have to relax, you will have to allow it. Breathing is life. It is *happening*.

All that is essential is *happening*, and all that is non-essential, non-existential, is to be done. Of course your shop will not be run if you don't run it. Of course you will not become a prime minister or a president if you don't struggle for it. Nobody has ever become a prime minister without struggling for it; without violence you cannot become a prime minister. You will have to compete – a cut-throat competition. You will have to be cruel, you will have to be aggressive. You will have to *do* it, only then it can happen. All that depends on your doing is accidental and all that goes on without you is essential.

Religion's whole concern is the essential, the world of the essential. You are there; not that you have done it yourself, you are simply there for no reason. You have not earned it, it is nothing of your doing. It is a benediction, it is a gift. You are there: existence has willed you to be there, it is not your own will.

Watch it, understand it – when such a thing like life, so precious, can happen without your doing, then why bother? Then allow more and more the dimension of happening. Drop more and more doing. Do only that which seems needful. Don't be bothered too much with the doing. That is the meaning of a sannyasin. The householder, the *grihastha*, is one who is simply possessed by the dimension of doing. He thinks that if he is not going to *do*, nothing is going to happen. He is a doer. A sannyasin is one who knows that whether he is going to do it or not, all that is essential is going to continue to happen. The non-essential may disappear, but that is irrelevant – the essential will continue.

Love is essential; money is non-essential. To be alive is essential; to live in a big house is non-essential. To be fulfilled, contented, is essential; rushing, being ambitious, always trying to reach somewhere, trying to perform, trying to prove that you are somebody, is non-essential. People live only in two dimensions: the dimension of the doer and the dimension of the non-doer.

BUDDHA SAYS:

To practice the deed that is not doing . . .

He says practice that. He says "practice", because there is no other way to say it. The word "practice" looks like doing, that's the paradox. He says, "Do that which cannot be done." Do that which only happens. Allow, he means – allow that which happens, allow life to be there, allow love to be there. Allow existence to penetrate you, to infiltrate you. Don't continue to be a doer.

And he does not mean don't do anything at all – he says don't emphasize it. Maybe it is needful. You have to clean your room; without your doing it, it is not going to happen. So do it! – but don't get obsessed with it. It is just a minor part. The major part of life, the central part of life, should be like a happening. As the lightning happens in the clouds, so life happens. As rivers go on rushing towards the ocean and dissolve, so love happens.

So happens meditation – it has nothing to do with your doing. Your doing is not essential for it to happen. It can happen when you are sitting and not doing anything. In fact it happens only then, when you are not doing anything and you are sitting. I insist for you to do many things as methods, but the insistence is only this – that you have to be tired, otherwise you won't sit. It is as if you tell a child, "Sit silently in the corner of the room." He cannot sit; he is so restless, he is so full of energy! He wants to do this and that and run around. The best way is to tell him to go and run around the house seven times, or around the block – then come back. Then, without your telling him, he will sit silently.

That's the whole point of my insistence to do Dynamic Meditation, do Kundalini Meditation, do Nataraj Meditation – be spent, so that for a few moments you can allow happening. You will not reach meditation by doing, you will reach meditation only by non-doing. And in non-doing will happen the real thing.

The real thing cannot be produced; it always happens. One has to be just sensitive and open and vulnerable. It is very delicate. You cannot grab it. It is very fragile . . . fragile like a flower. You cannot grab it; if you grab it you will destroy it. You have to be very soft. It is not hardware, it is software. You have to be really soft, you have to be feminine.

BUDDHA SAYS:

Practice the deed that is not doing . . .

That is the message of all the great ones, the really great ones. The greatest realization on this earth has been this: that we are unnecessarily creating too much fuss. That which is to happen is going to happen if we wait. In the right season, the harvest; in the right season, the fruition. In the right season everything happens. If a man can learn only one thing – how to wait prayerfully – nothing else is needed. Ecstasy is a *prasad*, a gift of existence.

You just try. Practice what Buddha says. At least for one hour become a non-doer. At least for one hour, deep in the night, sit alone. Don't do anything – not even chanting a mantra, not even transcendental meditation. Don't do anything. Just sit, lie down, look at the stars. That too should not be hard. Look very softly. Don't focus; remain unfocussed, like an unfocussed photograph – hazy, blurred, not knowing where the boundaries are. Just remain silent in the darkness. If thoughts come let them come; don't fight with them either. They will come and they will go – you just be a watcher. It is none of your business whether they come or they go. Who are you? They come without invitation, they go without pushing. They come and go, it is a constant traffic. You just sit by the side of the road and watch.

When I say watch, don't misinterpret me. Don't make watching an effort. Otherwise people become very stiff and they start watching in a very stiff and tense way. Again they have started doing. What I am saying, or what Buddha is saying, is – be in an attitude of not doing. Be lazy! Just be lazy and see what happens. You will be amazed. Some day – just sitting, just sitting, not doing anything – some day, from some unknown source a lightning, a benediction. Some day, in some moment, suddenly you are transfigured. Suddenly you see a quiet descending upon you. It is almost physical.

If a real meditator, a person who can relax, sits silently and allows, even somebody who is not a meditator will feel the presence – will feel that something is happening. You may not be able to figure it out what it is; you may feel strange or a little scared, but if you sit by the side of a meditator . . . Now, it is difficult to use the right word, because the word "meditator" again gives the impression as if he is doing something – "doing meditation". Remember again and again – language has been developed by non-meditators, so the whole language is, in a subtle way, wrong. It cannot express. When somebody is sitting there – just sitting there like a tree, like a rock, not doing anything – it happens. Something from the above descends, penetrates his very core of being. A subtle light surrounds him, a glow, a blessing can be felt around him – even by those people who don't know what meditation is. Even passing by, they will also feel the impact of it.

This benediction has been called godliness. God is not a person, it is a deep experience when you are not doing anything and existence simply flows in you . . . the immensity of it, the beatitude of it, the grace of it. You are not doing anything, you are not even expecting anything, you are not waiting for anything. You have no motive. You are just there like a tree standing in the winds, or like a rock just silently sitting by the side of a river. Or like a cloud perched on the hilltop – just there, no movement of your own. In that moment you are not a self, in that moment you are a no-self. In that moment you are not a mind, you are a no-mind. In that moment you don't have a center. In that moment you are immense . . . vastness with no boundaries – suddenly the contact. Suddenly it is there! Suddenly you are fulfilled, suddenly you are surrounded by some unknown presence. It is tremendous.

THAT'S WHAT BUDDHA SAYS:

Practice the deed that is not doing; to speak the speech that is inexpressible.

And if you want to say something, say that which cannot be said. Express the inexpressible. What is the point of saying things which can be said? – anybody knows them, everybody knows them. If you really want to express something, express the inexpressible.

What is the way to express the inexpressible? It can be expressed only through being. Words are too narrow. It can be expressed only by your existence, by your presence – in your walking, in your sitting, in your eyes, in your gestures, in your touch, in your compassion, in your love. The way you are – it can be expressed through it.

Buddha talks, but that is not very essential. More essential is his being, that he is there. Through his talking he allows you to be with him. The talking is just persuading you. Because it will be difficult for you to be in silence with a Buddha. He has to talk, because if he is talking you feel that everything is okay, you can listen. If he is not talking how will you listen? You don't know how to listen when nobody is talking. You don't know how to listen to that which cannot be expressed.

But by and by, living around a master, a Buddha, a Jesus, by and by you will start imbibing his spirit. By and by, in spite of you, there will be moments when you will relax, and not only that which he is saying will be reaching into your heart, but that which he is also will penetrate. And with him the whole dimension of happening opens. That's the meaning of *satsang*, being in the presence of a master.

. . . And to be trained in the discipline beyond discipline.

And Buddha says there is a discipline which is not a discipline.

Ordinarily we think about discipline as if somebody else is trying to discipline you. Discipline carries a very ugly connotation – as if you are being disciplined, as if you are just to obey. The center that is disciplining you is outside you. Buddha says that is not discipline, that is surrendering to slavery.

Be free – no need to be disciplined from any outside source. Become alert, so that inner discipline arises in you. Become responsible, so that whatsoever you do, you do with a certain order, a certain cosmos to it; so that your being is not a chaos, so that your being is not in a mess.

So there are two types of discipline. One can be forced from the outside – that's what politicians go on doing, priests, parents go on doing. And there is a discipline that can be provoked in you – that can be done only by masters. They don't enforce any discipline on you, they make you simply more aware so you can find your own discipline.

People come to me and they ask, "Why don't you give a certain discipline? What to eat, what not to eat. When to get up in the morning and when to go to bed." I don't give you any such discipline, because any discipline that comes from outside is destructive. I give you only one discipline – what Buddha calls the discipline of the beyond, the discipline of transcendence.

I give you only one discipline and that is of being aware. If you are aware you will get up in the right time. When the body is rested, you will get up. When you are aware you will eat only that which is needed, you will eat only that which is least harmful to you and to others. You will eat only that which is not based on violence. But awareness will be the decisive factor. Otherwise you can be forced to become obedient, but deep down you go on being rebellious.

I have heard a Second World War story:

A sergeant and a private were up on a charge of kicking the colonel. When asked for an explanation, the sergeant replied, "Well, sir, the colonel came round the corner as I was coming from the gym. I only had my plimsolls on, he was in riding boots, and he trod on my toe. I am afraid the pain was so great, sir, that I lashed out – and before I realized who it was, sir."

"I see," said the orderly officer. "And what about you, soldier?"

To which the private replied, "I saw the sergeant kick the colonel, sir. So I thought to myself the war must be over, so I can also kick!"

Whenever somebody enforces a discipline on you, deep down you resent it, deep down you are against it. You may surrender to it but you surrender always reluctantly. And that's how it should be – because the deepest urge in a human being is for freedom. To be free is the search. Down the centuries, for millennia, in many lives, we have been searching how to be free. So whenever somebody comes – even for your own sake, for your own good – and enforces something upon you, you resist. It is against human nature, it is against human destiny.

Buddha says there is no need to be obedient to somebody else; you should find your own awareness – be obedient to it. Be aware, that is the only scripture. Be aware, that is the only master. Be aware and nothing can ever go wrong.

Awareness brings its own discipline like a shadow, and then the discipline is beautiful. Then it is not a slavery, then it is a harmony. Then it is not as if enforced, then it is a flowering out of your own being, a blooming.

. . . And to be trained in the discipline that is beyond discipline.

People ordinarily seek somebody to tell them what to do – because they are afraid of their freedom, because they don't know that they can rely on their own sources, because they are not self-confident, because they have always been told what to do by somebody else, so they have become addicted to it. They are searching for father figures their whole lives. Their God is also a father, nothing else – and the search for a father figure is anti-life. You should learn how to be free from all father figures. You should learn how to be yourself. You should learn how to be aware and responsible. Then only you start growing. Maturity is always growing towards freedom. Immaturity is always a sort of dependence and a fear of freedom.

A child is dependent – it's okay, it can be understood, he is helpless. But why remain a child your whole life? That is the revolution Buddha brought into the world. He is one of the most rebellious thinkers of the world. He throws you to yourself. It is dangerous, but he takes that risk. And he says everybody has to take that risk. There is every possibility you may go astray – but life is risk. It is better to go astray on your own accord than to reach heaven following somebody else. It is better to be lost forever and be yourself, than to reach paradise as a carbon copy, as an imitator. Then your paradise will be nothing but a prison. And if you have chosen hell on your own accord, out of your own freedom, your hell will also be heaven – because freedom is heaven.

Now here you will see the difference between Christianity and Buddhism. Christianity says Adam was expelled because he disobeyed God. Buddha says obey only yourself, there is no other God to be obeyed. Christianity calls disobedience the original sin, and Buddha calls obedience the original sin. Tremendous is the difference. Buddha is a liberator, and Christianity created an imprisonment for the whole of humanity.

Buddha's liberation is pure. He teaches you rebellion, but his rebellion is not a political rebellion. He teaches you rebellion with responsibility, with awareness. His rebellion is not a reaction – you can be obedient, you can be disobedient. What is Buddha saying? Buddha is saying neither be obedient nor be disobedient – because disobedience is again being conditioned by somebody else. You go on doing something because your father says don't do it, but again your father is manipulating you – in a negative way. You go on doing something because the society says don't do it, but again the society is determining what you do.

Buddha says rebellion is not reaction. It is neither slavery nor reaction, neither obedience nor disobedience. It is an inner discipline. It is a discipline, it has a tremendous order, but it comes from your inner core. You decide it.

We go on throwing our responsibility on others. It is easier. You can always say that your father said to do it, so you have done it – you are not responsible. You can always say the leader said to do it, so you have done it – you are not responsible. The whole country was going to do it, was going to war and was killing people in other countries – you have done it because you simply obeyed orders, you simply obeyed.

When Adolf Hitler's colleagues were caught after the Second World War, they all insisted before the court that they were not responsible, they were simply obeying orders. Whatever order was given they were obeying. If the order was given, "Kill a million Jews!" they killed. They were simply following orders, they were simply obedient. They were not responsible.

Now look and watch: you may be simply trying to find someone who says "do this" so you can throw the responsibility on him. But this is not the way – to throw the responsibility on anybody else? Life is yours and responsibility is yours! If you understand Buddha, the world will be totally different. Then there cannot be any more Hitlers, then there cannot be any more wars – because there cannot be any obedience from the outside, and everybody responsible will think on his own. Not that "Hindus are killing Mohammedans, so I have to kill" . . . not "Mohammedans are burning temples, so I have to burn temples because I am a Mohammedan." Each individual should become a light unto himself, and he should decide – not as a Mohammedan, not as a Christian, not as an Indian, not as a Pakistani; he should decide according to his own consciousness, not according to anything else. This is what Buddha calls the discipline that is beyond discipline.

This is the definition of a religious person: he thinks the thought that is unthinkable; he practices the deed that is not doing; he speaks that which is inexpressible, ineffable; and he practices the discipline that is beyond discipline.

Those who understand this are near; those who are confused are far.

If these four things are understood, you are close to truth. If you don't understand then you are far away from the truth.

The way is beyond words and expressions, is bound by nothing earthly.
Lose sight of it to an inch or miss it for a moment, and we are away from
it forever more.

Those who understand it are close . . . Now let this be a criterion for you – you can judge. Let this be a touchstone for your growth. If you feel these four things are happening in your life – how ever, in whatever quantity, maybe a very small quantity but if they are happening – then you are on the right track. If you are going away from these four things, you are going away from the way, the dhamma, the Tao.

The way is beyond words and expressions, is bound by nothing earthly.

The ultimate truth is not bound by anything that you can see, that you can touch. It is not dependent on your senses. The ultimate truth is not material, it is immaterial. It is not earthly. It cannot be caused by anything. That's why it can never become part of science. You can mix hydrogen and oxygen and you can cause water to be there. There is no way to create ecstasy that way. There is no way to cause godliness that way, there is no way to cause truth that way. You can destroy water by separating hydrogen and oxygen, you can create water by mixing hydrogen and oxygen, but there is no way to destroy truth or to cause it. It is uncaused.

It is not a chain of cause and effect. You cannot create it; it is already there. You cannot destroy it, because you *are* it. It is the very life. You can only do one thing – either you can close your eyes to it, you can forget about it, you can become absolutely oblivious of it, or you can remember, see, realize.

If you are lost in too much doing, ambition, riches, money, prestige, power, then you will lose track of the truth which is always beside you – just at the corner, just within reach but you are keeping your back to it. Or you can allow it. If you become a little more meditative and less ambitious, if you become a little more religious and less political, if you become a little more unworldly than worldly, if you start moving more withinwards than without, if you start becoming a little more alert than sleepy, if you come out of your drunk state, if you bring a little light into your being, then . . . then you will be close, close to home. You have never been away. Then your whole life will be transformed, transfigured. Then you will live in a totally different way; a new quality will be there in your life which has nothing to do with your doing, which is a gift, a benediction.

Lose sight of it to an inch, says Buddha,

Or miss it for a moment, and we are away from it forever more.

Look into it for a single moment, come close to it even a single inch, and it is yours – and it has always been yours. This is the paradox of a *siddhanta*. This is not a doctrine, this is Buddha's realization. He is simply trying to share his realization with you. He is not propounding a philosophy or a system of thought. He is simply pointing towards the moon, the reality. Don't look at his pointing fingers, otherwise you will miss; you will become a Buddhist. Look at the moon the finger is pointing to. Forget the finger completely and look at the moon and you will become a buddha.

This is the problem that humanity has to settle. It is very much easier to become a Christian than to become a Christ, very much easier to become a Buddhist than to become a buddha, but the reality is known only by becoming a Christ or a buddha. By becoming a Christian or a Buddhist you are again becoming carbon copies. Don't insult yourself that way. Have a little respect for yourself. Never be a Christian and never be a Buddhist and never be a Hindu. Just be consciousness undefined, unbound, unmotivated. If you can do that much, all else will follow of its own accord.

Enough for today.

Chapter 11:

Spiritual Enlightenment

THE BUDDHA SAID:

> *Look up to heaven and down on earth and they will remind you of their impermanency.*
>
> *Look about the world and it will remind you of its impermanency. But when you gain spiritual enlightenment you shall then find wisdom.*
>
> *The knowledge thus attained leads you anon to the way.*

THE BUDDHA SAID:

> *You should think of the four elements of which the body is composed. Each of them has its own name and there is no such thing there known as ego. As there is really no ego, it is like unto a mirage.*

I am reminded of the fateful day of 21 March 1953. For many lives I had been working – working upon myself, struggling, doing whatsoever can be done – and nothing was happening. Now I understand why nothing was happening. The very effort was the barrier, the very ladder was preventing, the very urge to seek was the obstacle. Not that one can reach without seeking – seeking is needed, but then comes a point when seeking has to be dropped. The boat is needed to cross the river but then comes a moment when you have to get out of the boat and forget all about it and leave it behind. Effort is needed, without effort nothing is possible – and also only with effort, nothing is possible.

Just before 21 March 1953, seven days before, I stopped working on myself. A moment comes when you see the whole futility of effort. You have done all that you can do and nothing is happening. You have done all that is humanly possible. Then what else can you do? In sheer helplessness one drops all search. And the day the search stopped, the day I was not seeking for something, the day I was not expecting something to happen, it started happening. A new energy arose – out of nowhere. It was not coming from any source. It was coming from nowhere and everywhere. It was in the trees and in the rocks and the sky and the sun and the air – it was everywhere. And I had been seeking so hard, and I was thinking it was very far away, and it was so near and so close. Just because I was seeking I had become incapable of seeing the near. Seeking is always for the far, seeking is always for the distant – and it was not distant. I had become far-sighted, I had lost the near-sightedness. The eyes had become focused on the far away, the horizon, and they had lost the ability to see that which is just close, surrounding you.

The day effort ceased, I also ceased. Because you cannot exist without effort, and you cannot exist without desire, and you cannot exist without striving.

The phenomenon of the ego, of the self, is not a thing, it is a process. It is not a substance sitting there inside you; you have to create it each moment. It is like pedaling bicycle. If you pedal it goes on and on; if you don't pedal it stops. It may go on a little because of the past momentum, but the moment you stop pedaling, in fact the bicycle starts stopping. It has no more energy, no more power to go anywhere. It is going to fall and collapse.

The ego exists because we go on pedaling desire, because we go on striving to get something, because we go on jumping ahead of ourselves. That is the very phenomenon of the ego – the jump ahead of yourself, the jump into the future, the jump into the tomorrow. The jump into the non-existential creates the ego. Because it comes out of the non-existential, it is like a mirage. It consists only of desire and nothing else; it consists only of thirst and nothing else.

The ego is not in the present, it is in the future. If you are in the future, then ego seems to be very substantial. If you are in the present, the ego is a mirage; it starts disappearing.

The day I stopped seeking . . . and it is not right to say that I stopped seeking, better will be to say the day seeking stopped. Let me repeat it: the better way to say it is "the day the seeking stopped" – because if I stop it, then I am there again. Now stopping becomes my effort, now stopping becomes my desire, and desire goes on existing in a very subtle way. You cannot stop desire; you can only understand it. In the very understanding is the stopping of it. Remember, nobody can stop desiring, and the reality happens only when desire stops.

So this is the dilemma. What to do? Desire is there and buddhas go on saying desire has to be stopped, and they go on saying in the next breath that you cannot stop desire. So what to do? You put people in a dilemma. They are in desire, certainly. You say it has to be stopped – okay. And then you say it cannot be stopped. Then what is to be done?

The desire has to be understood. You can understand it, you can just see the futility of it. A direct perception is needed, an immediate penetration is needed. Look into desire, just see what it is, and you will see the falsity of it and you will see it is non-existential. And desire drops and something drops simultaneously within you.

Desire and the ego exist in cooperation, they coordinate. The ego cannot exist without desire, the desire cannot exist without the ego. Desire is projected ego, ego is introjected desire. They are together, two aspects of one phenomenon.

The day desiring stopped, I felt very hopeless and helpless. No hope because no future – nothing to hope because all hoping has proved futile, it leads nowhere, you go in circles. It goes on dangling in front of you, it goes on creating new mirages, it goes on calling you, "Come on, run fast, you will reach." But however fast you run you never reach.

That's why Buddha calls it a mirage. It is like the horizon that you see around the earth. It appears but it is not there. If you go it goes on running from you. The faster you run, the faster it moves away, the slower you go, the slower it moves away, but one thing is certain – the distance between you and the horizon remains absolutely the same. Not even a single inch can you reduce the distance between you and the horizon.

You cannot reduce the distance between you and your hope. Hope is horizon. You try to bridge yourself with the horizon, with the hope, with a projected desire. The desire is a bridge, a dream bridge – because the horizon exists not, so you cannot make a bridge towards it, you can only dream about the bridge. You cannot be joined with the non-existential.

The day the desire stopped, the day I looked and realized into it . . . it simply was futile; I was helpless and hopeless. But that very moment something started happening. The same started happening for which for many lives I had been working and it was not happening.

In your hopelessness is the only hope, and in your desirelessness is your only fulfillment, and in your tremendous helplessness suddenly the whole existence starts helping you. It is waiting. When it sees that you are working on your own, it does not interfere. It waits. It can wait infinitely because there is no hurry for it. It *is* eternity. The moment you are not, on your own – the moment you drop, the moment you disappear – the whole existence rushes towards you, enters you. And for the first time things start happening.

Seven days I lived in a very hopeless and helpless state, but at the same time something was arising. When I say hopeless I don't mean what you mean by the word hopeless. I simply mean there was no hope in me. Hope was absent. I am not saying that I was hopeless and sad. I was happy in fact, I was very tranquil, calm and collected and centered. Hopeless, but in a totally new meaning. There was no hope, so how could there be hopelessness? Both had disappeared. The hopelessness was absolute and total. Hope had disappeared and with it, its counterpart hopelessness had also disappeared. It was a totally new experience – of being without hope. It was not a negative state. I have to use words, but it was not a negative state. It was absolutely positive. It was not just absence, a presence was felt. Something was overflowing in me, overflooding me.

And when I say I was helpless, I don't mean the word in the dictionary sense. I simply say I was selfless. That's what I mean when I say helpless. I have recognized the fact that I am not, so I cannot depend on myself, so I cannot stand on my own ground – there was no ground underneath. I was in an abyss, a bottomless abyss. But there was no fear because there was nothing to protect. There was no fear because there was nobody to be afraid.

Those seven days were of tremendous transformation, total transformation. And the last day the presence of a totally new energy, a new light and new delight, became so intense that it was almost unbearable – as if I was exploding, as if I was going mad with blissfulness. The new generation in the West has the right word for it – I was blissed out, stoned. It was impossible to make any sense out of it, what was happening. It was a non-sense world, difficult to figure it out, difficult to manage into categories, difficult to use words, language, explanations. All scriptures appeared dead and all the words that have been used for this experience looked pale, anemic. This was so alive. It was like a tidal wave of bliss.

The whole day was strange, stunning, and it was a shattering experience. The past was disappearing, as if it had never belonged to me, as if I had read about it somewhere, as if I had dreamed about it, as if it was somebody else's story I have heard, and somebody told it to me. I was becoming loose from my past, I was being uprooted from my history, I was losing my autobiography. I was becoming a non-being, what Buddha calls *anatta*. Boundaries were disappearing, distinctions were disappearing. Mind was disappearing; it was millions of miles away. It was difficult to catch hold of it, it was rushing farther and farther away and there was no urge to keep it close. I was simply indifferent about it all. It was okay. There was no urge to remain continuous with the past.

By the evening it became so difficult to bear it – it was hurting, it was painful. It was like when a woman goes into labor when a child is to be born, and the woman suffers tremendous pain – the birth pangs.

I used to go to sleep in those days near about twelve or one in the night, but that day it was impossible to remain awake. My eyes were closing, it was difficult to keep them open. Something was imminent, something was going to happen. It was difficult to say what it was – maybe it was going to be my death – but there was no fear. I was ready for it. Those seven days had been so beautiful that I was ready to die, nothing more was needed. They had been so tremendously blissful, I was so contented that if death were coming, it was welcome. But something was going to happen – something like death, something drastic, something that would be either a death or a new birth, a crucifixion or a resurrection – but something of tremendous import was just around the corner. And it was impossible to keep my eyes open. I was as if drugged.

I went to sleep around eight. It was not like sleep. Now I can understand what Patanjali means when he says that sleep and samadhi are similar. Only with one difference – that in samadhi you are fully awake and asleep also. Asleep and awake together, the whole body relaxed, every cell of the body totally relaxed, all functioning relaxed, and yet a light of awareness burns within you . . . clear, smokeless. You remain alert and yet relaxed, loose but fully awake. The body is in the deepest sleep possible and your consciousness is at its peak. The peak of consciousness and the valley of the body meet. I went to sleep. It was a very strange sleep. The body was asleep, I was awake. It was so strange – as if one was torn apart into two directions, two dimensions; as if the polarity had become completely focused, as if I was both the polarities together . . . the positive and negative were meeting, sleep and awareness were meeting, death and life were meeting. That is the moment when you can say the creator and the creation meet. It was weird. The first time, it shocks you to the very roots, it shakes your foundations. You can never be the same after that experience; it brings a new vision to your life, a new quality.

Around twelve my eyes suddenly opened – I had not opened them. The sleep was broken by something else. I felt a great presence around me in the room. It was a very small room. I felt a throbbing life all around me, a great vibration – almost like a hurricane, a great storm of light, joy, ecstasy. I was drowning in it. It was so tremendously real that everything else became unreal. The walls of the room became unreal, the house became unreal, my own body became unreal. Everything was unreal because now there was for the first time reality.

That's why when Buddha and Shankara say the world is maya, a mirage, it is difficult for us to understand. Because we know only this world, we don't have any comparison. This is the only reality we know. What are these people talking about – this is maya, illusion? This is the only reality. Unless you come to know the really real, their words cannot be understood, their words remain theoretical. They look like hypotheses. Maybe this man is propounding a philosophy –

"The world is unreal." When Berkeley in the West said that the world is unreal, he was walking with one of his friends, a very logical man; the friend was a skeptic. He took a stone from the road and hit Berkeley's feet hard. Berkeley screamed, blood rushed out, and the skeptic said, "Now, the world is unreal? You say the world is unreal – then why did you scream? This stone is unreal – then why did you scream? Why are you holding your leg and showing so much pain and anguish on your face? Stop this! It is all unreal?"

Now this type of man cannot understand what Buddha means when he says the world is a mirage. He does not mean that you can pass through the wall, he is not saying that you can eat stones, and it will make no difference whether you eat bread or stones. He is not saying that. He is saying that there is a reality, and once you come to know it, this so-called reality simply fades away, simply becomes unreal. With a higher reality in your vision the distinction arises, not otherwise.

In a dream, the dream is real. You dream every night. Dreaming is one of the activities that you go on doing most. If you live sixty years, for twenty years you will sleep and almost ten years you will dream. Ten years in a life of sixty years – nothing else do you do so much. Ten years of continuous dreaming – just think about it! Every night . . . and every morning you say the dreams were unreal, and again in the night when you dream, the dreams become real.

In a dream it is so difficult to remember that it is a dream. But in the morning it is so easy. You are the same person, dreaming and awake, so what happens? In the dream there is only one reality, so how to compare – how to say it is unreal? Compared to what? It is the only reality. Everything is as unreal as everything else, so there is no comparison. In the morning when you open your eyes another reality is there. Now you can say it was all unreal. Compared to this reality, the dream becomes unreal.

There is another kind of awakening – and compared to the reality of that awakening, this whole reality becomes unreal.

That night for the first time I understood the meaning of the word maya. Not that I had not known the word before, not that I was not aware of the meaning of the word. As you are aware, I was also aware of the meaning but I had never understood it before. How can you understand without experience? That night another reality opened its door, another dimension became available. Suddenly it was there, the other reality, the separate reality, the really real, or whatsoever you want to call it – call it the divine, call it truth, call it dhamma, call it Tao, or whatsoever you will. It was nameless. But it was there – so opaque, so transparent, and yet so solid one could have touched it. It was almost suffocating me in that room. It was too much and I was not yet capable of absorbing it.

A deep urge arose in me to rush out of the room, to go under the sky – it was suffocating me. It was too much! It would kill me! If I had remained a few moments more, it would have suffocated me – it looked like that. I rushed out of the room, came out in the street. A great urge was there just to be under the sky with the stars, with the trees, with the earth . . . to be with nature. And immediately as I came out, the feeling of being suffocated disappeared. It was too small a place for such a big phenomenon. Even the sky is a small place for that big a phenomenon. It is bigger than the sky, even the sky is not the limit for it. But then I felt more at ease.

I walked towards the nearest garden. It was a totally new walk, as if the force of gravity had disappeared. I was walking, or I was running, or I was simply flying, it was difficult to decide. There was no gravitation, I was feeling weightless – as if some energy was taking me. I was in the hands of some other energy. For the first time I was not alone, for the first time I was no longer an individual, for the first time the drop had come and fallen into the ocean. Now the whole ocean was mine, I was the ocean. There was no limitation. A tremendous power arose as if I could do anything whatsoever. I was not there, only the power was there.

I reached to the garden where I used to go every day. The garden was closed, closed for the night. It was too late, it was almost one o'clock in the night. The gardeners were fast asleep. I had to enter the garden like a thief, I had to climb the gate. But something was pulling me towards the garden. It was not within my capacity to prevent myself. I was just floating.

That's what I mean when I say again and again "float with the river, don't push the river". I was relaxed, I was in a let-go. I was not there. It was there, call it God – God was there. I would like to call it "it", because God is too human a word and has become too dirty by too much use; it has been polluted by so many people. Christians, Hindus, Mohammedans, priests and politicians – they all have corrupted the beauty of the word. So let me call it "it". It was there and I was just carried away . . . carried by a tidal wave.

The moment I entered the garden everything became luminous, it was all over the place – the benediction, the blessedness. I could see the trees for the first time – their green, their life, their very sap running. The whole garden was asleep, the trees were asleep. But I could see the whole garden alive, even the small grass leaves were so beautiful.

I looked around. One tree was tremendously luminous – the maulshree tree. It attracted me, it pulled me towards itself. I had not chosen it, existence itself had chosen it. I went to the tree, I sat under the tree. As I sat there things started settling. The whole universe became a benediction.

It is difficult to say how long I was in that state. When I went back home it was four o'clock in the morning, so I must have been there by clock time at least three hours – but it was an infinity. It had nothing to do with clock time. It was timeless. Those three hours became the whole eternity, endless eternity. There was no time, there was no passage of time; it was the virgin reality – uncorrupted, untouchable, unmeasurable.

And that day something happened that has continued – not as a continuity, but it has continued as an undercurrent. Not as a permanency – each moment it has been happening again and again. It has been a miracle each moment.

Since that night I have never been in the body. I am hovering around it. I became tremendously powerful and at the same time very fragile. I became very strong, but that strength is not the strength of a Mohammed Ali. That strength is not the strength of a rock, that strength is the strength of a rose flower – so fragile in its strength, so fragile, so sensitive, so delicate. The rock will be there, the flower can go any moment, but still the flower is stronger than the rock because it is more alive. Or, the strength of a dewdrop on a leaf of grass just shining in the morning sun – so beautiful, so precious, and yet can slip away any moment. So incomparable in its grace, but a small breeze can come and the dewdrop can slip and be lost forever.

Buddhas have a strength which is not of this world. Their strength is totally of love. Like a rose flower or a dewdrop, their strength is very fragile, vulnerable. Their strength is the strength of life not of death. Their power is not of that which kills; their power is of that which creates. Their power is not of violence, aggression; their power is that of compassion.

But I have never been in the body again, I am just hovering around the body. And that's why I say it has been a tremendous miracle. Each moment I am surprised I am still here, I should not be. I should have left any moment, still I am here. Every morning I open my eyes and I say, 'So, again I am still here?' Because it seems almost impossible. The miracle has been a continuity.

Just the other day somebody asked a question – "Osho, you are getting so fragile and delicate and so sensitive to the smells of hair oils and shampoos that it seems we will not be able to see you unless we all go bald." By the way, nothing is wrong with being bald – bald is beautiful! Just as black is beautiful, so bald is beautiful. But that is true, and you have to be careful about it. I am fragile, delicate and sensitive. That is my strength. If you throw a rock at a flower nothing will happen to the rock – the flower will be gone. But still you cannot say that the rock is more powerful than the flower. The flower will be gone because the flower was alive. And the rock – nothing will happen to it because it is dead. The flower will be gone because the flower has no strength to destroy. The flower will simply disappear and give way to the rock. The rock has a power to destroy because the rock is dead.

Remember, since that day I have never been in the body really; just a delicate thread joins me with the body. And I am continuously surprised that somehow the whole must be willing me to be here, because I am no longer here with my own strength, I am no longer here on my own. It must be the will of the whole to keep me here, to allow me to linger a little more on this shore. Maybe the whole wants to share something with you through me.

Since that day the world is unreal. Another world has been revealed. When I say the world is unreal I don't mean that these trees are unreal. These trees are absolutely real – but the way you see these trees is unreal. These trees are not unreal in themselves – they exist in truth, they exist in absolute reality – but the way you see them you never see them; you are seeing something else, a mirage. You create your own dream around you, and unless you become awake you will continue to dream. The world is unreal because the world that you know is the world of your dreams. When dreams drop and you simply encounter the world that is there, then the real world appears.

There are not two things, godliness and the world. Godliness *is* the world if you have eyes, clear eyes without any dreams, without any dust of dreams, without any haze of sleep; if you have clear eyes, clarity, perceptiveness, there is only godliness. Then somewhere it is a green tree, and somewhere else it is a shining star, and somewhere else it is a cuckoo, and somewhere else it is a flower, and somewhere else a child and somewhere else a river – then only godliness is. The moment you start seeing, only godliness is.

But right now whatsoever you see is not the truth, it is a projected lie. That is the meaning of a mirage. And once you see, even for a single split moment, if you can see, if you can allow yourself to see, you will find immense benediction present all over, everywhere – in the clouds, in the sun, on the earth.

This is a beautiful world. But I am not talking about your world, I am talking about my world. Your world is ugly, your world is a world created by a self, your world is a projected world. You are using the real world as a screen and projecting your own ideas on it.

When I say the world is real, the world is tremendously beautiful, the world is luminous with infinity, the world is light and delight, it is a celebration, I mean my world – or your world if you drop your dreams.

When you drop your dreams you see the same world as any buddha has ever seen. When you dream you dream privately. Have you watched it? Dreams are private, you cannot share them even with your beloved. You cannot invite your wife into your dream – or your husband, or your friend. You cannot say, "Now, please come tonight into my dream; I would like to watch the dream together." It is not possible. Dreaming is a private thing, hence it is illusory; it has no objective reality. Godliness is a universal thing. Once you come out of your private dreams, it is there. It has been always there. Once your eyes are clear, a sudden illumination – suddenly you are overflooded with beauty, grandeur and grace. That is the goal, that is the destiny.

Let me repeat. Without effort you will never reach it, with effort nobody has ever reached it. You will need great effort, and only then there comes a moment when effort becomes futile. But it becomes futile only when you have come to the very peak of it, never before it. When you have come to the very pinnacle of your effort – all that you can do you have done – then suddenly there is no need to do anything any more. You drop the effort.

But nobody can drop it in the middle, it can be dropped only at the extreme end. So go to the extreme end if you want to drop it. Hence I go on insisting: make as much effort as you can, put your whole energy and total heart in it, so that one day you can see: "Now effort is not going to lead me anywhere." And that day it will not be you who will drop the effort, it drops of its own accord. And when it drops of its own accord, meditation happens.

Meditation is not a result of your efforts, meditation is a happening. When your efforts drop, suddenly meditation is there . . . the benediction of it, the blessedness of it, the glory of it. It is there like a presence, luminous, surrounding you and surrounding everything. It fills the whole earth and the whole sky. That meditation cannot be created by human effort. Human effort is too limited. That blessedness is so infinite . . . You cannot manipulate it; it can happen only when you are in a tremendous surrender. When you are not there, only then it can happen. When you are a no-self – no desire, not going anywhere – when you are just here now, not doing anything in particular, just being, it happens. And it comes in waves and the waves become tidal. It comes like a storm and takes you away into a totally new reality.

But first you have to do all that you can do, and then you have to learn non-doing. The doing of non-doing is the greatest doing, and the effort of effortlessness is the greatest effort.

Your meditation that you create by chanting a mantra, or by sitting quiet and still and forcing yourself, is a very mediocre meditation. It is created by you, it cannot be bigger than you. It is homemade, and the maker is always bigger than the made. You have made it by sitting, forcing yourself into a yoga posture, chanting "Rama, Rama, Rama" or anything – "blah, blah, blah" – anything. You have forced the mind to become still. It is a forced stillness, it is not that quiet that comes when you are not there. It is not that silence which comes when you are almost non-existential. It is not that beatitude which descends on you like a dove.

It is said when Jesus was baptized by John the Baptist in the Jordan River, God descended in him, or the holy ghost descended in him like a dove. Yes, that is exactly so. When you are not there, peace descends in you, fluttering like a dove, reaches your heart and abides there and abides there forever.

You are your undoing, you are the barrier. Meditation is when the meditator is not. When the mind ceases, with all its activities – seeing that they are futile – then the unknown penetrates you, overwhelms you. The mind must cease for godliness to be. Knowledge must cease for knowing to be. You must disappear, you must give way. You must become empty, then only you can be full.

That night I became empty and became full. I became non-existential and became existence. That night I died and was reborn. But the one that was reborn has nothing to do with that which died, it is a discontinuous thing. On the surface it looks continuous but it is discontinuous. The one who died, died totally; nothing of him has remained.

Believe me, nothing of him has remained, not even a shadow. It died totally, utterly. It is not that I am just modified – transformed, a modified form, a transformed form of the old. No, there has been no continuity. That day of 21 March, the person who had lived for many, many lives, for millennia, simply died. Another being, absolutely new, not connected at all with the old, started to exist.

Religiousness just gives you a total death. Maybe that's why the whole day previous to that happening I was feeling some urgency like death, as if I was going to die – and I really died. I have known many other deaths but they were nothing compared to it, they were partial deaths. Sometimes the body died, sometimes a part of the mind died, sometimes a part of the ego died, but as far as the person was concerned, it remained. Renovated many times, decorated many times, changed a little bit here and there, but it remained, the continuity remained.

That night the death was total. It was a date with death and the divine simultaneously.

Now this sutra.

THE BUDDHA SAID:

> *Look up to heaven and down on earth and they will remind you of their impermanency.*
>
> *Look about the world and it will remind you of its impermanency.*

*But when you gain spiritual enlightenment you shall then find
wisdom.*

The knowledge thus attained leads you anon to the way.

*Look up to heaven and down on earth and they will remind you of their imper-
manency* –look! You don't look, you never look. Before you look, you have an
idea. You never look in purity, you never look unprejudiced. You always carry
some prejudice, some opinion, ideology, scripture – your own experience or
others' experiences, but you always carry something in the mind. You are never
naked with reality. And when Buddha says, "Look up to heaven and down on
earth," he means look with a naked eye, with no coatings of opinions, ideas,
experiences, borrowed or otherwise.

Have you seen a naked eye? As far as humanity is concerned it is very rare
to come across a naked eye. All eyes are so dressed up. Somebody has a
Christian eye, somebody has a Hindu eye, somebody has a Mohammedan eye.
They look differently. When a Mohammedan reads the Gita he never reads the
same thing that a Hindu reads in it. When a Jaina reads the Gita he reads
something else again. A Hindu can read the Bible but he will never read that
which a Christian reads. The Bible is the same, so from where does this
difference come? The difference must be coming from the eye, the difference
must be coming from the mind.

Have you ever read a single page of a book without bringing your mind into
it, without corrupting it by your mind, by your past? Without interpreting it,
have you ever looked at anything in life? If not then you have not looked at all,
then you don't have real eyes. You have just holes not eyes.

The eye has to be receptive, not aggressive. When you have a certain idea in
the eye, in your mind, it is aggressive. It immediately imposes itself on things.
When you have an empty eye, naked, undressed – not Christian, not Hindu,
not Communist, just a pure look, innocent, just a primal innocence, as innocent
as an animal's eye or a child, a newborn child . . . A just-born child looks
around – he has no idea of what is what. What is beautiful and what is ugly, he
has no idea. That primal innocence has to be there; only then you will be able to
see what Buddha says.

You have been looking in life but you have not come to see that all is imper-
manence. Everything is dying, everything is decaying, everything is on a death
procession. People are standing in a death queue. Look around – everything
rushing towards death. Everything is fleeting, momentary, fluxlike; nothing
seems to be of eternal value, nothing seems to abide, nothing seems to hold,
nothing seems to remain. Everything just goes on and on and on, and goes on

changing. What else is it but a dream? Buddha says this life, this world that you live in, that you are surrounded with, that you have created around yourself, is but a dream – impermanent, temporary. Don't make your abode there, otherwise you will suffer. Because nobody can be contented with the temporary. By the time you think it is in your hands it is gone. By the time you think you have possessed it, it is no longer there. You struggle for it – by the time you achieve it, it has disappeared.

The beauty is fleeting, love is fleeting, everything in this life is fleeting. You are running to catch shadows. They look real; by the time you have arrived they prove mirages.

Look up to heaven and down on earth and they will remind you of their impermanency.

Look about the world and it will remind you of its impermanency.

It is one of the most fundamental principles of Gautama the Buddha – that one should become aware of the impermanent world we are surrounded with. Then immediately you will be able to understand why Buddha calls it a dream, maya, an illusion.

In the East our definition of truth is that which abides forever, and of untruth, that which is there this moment and next moment is not there. Untruth is that which is temporary, momentary, impermanent. And truth is that which is, always is, has been, will be. Behind these fleeting shadows find the eternal, penetrate to the eternal, because there can be bliss only with the eternal; misery only with the momentary.

But when you gain spiritual enlightenment . . .

That's why I was reminded of my own experience and I talked about it to you.

. . . But when you gain spiritual enlightenment you shall then find wisdom.

Wisdom cannot be found through scriptures. It is an experience, it is not knowledge. Wisdom is not knowledge; you cannot gather it from others, you cannot borrow it. It is not information. You cannot learn it from the scriptures. There is only one way to become wise and that is to enter into a live experience of life.

Something is said by Buddha and you hear it; something I say and you hear it – but you don't become wise by hearing it. It will become knowledge. You can repeat it, you can even repeat it in a better way. You can become very skillful, efficient in repeating it. You can say it in better language, but you don't have the experience. You have never tasted the wine yourself. You have simply seen some drunkard moving, wobbling on the road, fallen in a gutter. You have simply watched a drunkard, how he moves, how he stumbles, but you don't know what the experience is. You will have to become a drunkard – there is no other way. You can watch a thousand and one drunkards and you can collect all the information about them – but that will be from the outside, and the experience is inner. That will be from without, and you will collect it as a spectator. And the experience cannot be attained by seeing, it can be attained only by being.

Now the modern world has become very obsessed by seeing; the modern world is a spectator's world. People are sitting for hours in the movie houses, just watching, doing nothing. People are glued to their chairs for hours, six hours, eight hours even, just sitting before their TVs. You listen to somebody singing and you see somebody dancing and you see somebody making love – that's why people are so interested in pornography – but you are a spectator.

The modern man is the falsest man that has ever existed on the earth, and his falsity consists in thinking he can know by just seeing, just by being a spectator. People are sitting for hours watching hockey matches, volleyball matches, cricket matches – for hours! When are you going to play yourself? When are you going to love somebody? When are you going to dance and sing and be? This is a borrowed life. Somebody dances for you; maybe you can enjoy it, but how can you know the beauty of dance unless you dance? It is something inner. What happens when a person is dancing? What happens to his innermost core?

Nijinsky, one of the greatest dancers, used to say that moments come when he disappears, only the dance remains. Those are the peak moments – when the dancer is not there and only the dance is. That's what Buddha is talking about, when the self is not there. Now Nijinsky is moving into ecstasy and you are just sitting there watching the movement. Of course those movements are beautiful. Nijinsky's movements have a grace, a tremendous beauty, but it is nothing compared to what he is feeling inside. His dance is a beauty even when you are just a spectator, but nothing compared to what is happening inside him.

He used to say that there are moments when gravitation disappears. I can understand, because I have come across the feeling myself when gravitation disappears, and once upon a time it was only for moments that gravitation disappeared for me. Now I have lived for years without gravitation. I know what he means. Even scientists were very much puzzled, because there were moments in Nijinsky's dance when he would leap and jump – and those leaps were tremendous, almost impossible leaps. A man cannot leap that way; the gravitation does not allow it. And the most beautiful and amazing part was that when Nijinsky would be coming back from the leap he would come down so slowly that it was impossible. He would come so slowly, as if a leaf is falling from a tree ... very slowly, very slowly, very slowly. It is not possible, it is against the physical laws. The law of gravity does not make any exceptions, not even for a Nijinsky. He was asked again and again, "What happens? How do you fall so slowly? Because it is not within your power to control – the gravitation pulls you." He said, "It does not happen always, only rarely – when the dancer disappears. Then sometimes I am also puzzled and surprised, not only you. I see myself coming so slowly, so gracefully, and I know that the gravitation does not exist in that moment."

He must be functioning in another dimension where the physical law does not exist, where another law starts working that spiritualists call the law of levitation. And it seems absolutely rational and logical to have both the laws, because every law has to be counterbalanced by another in the opposite direction. If there is light there is darkness, if there is life there is death, if there is gravitation there must be a force of levitation that pulls you up.

There are stories that Mohammed went to heaven with his physical body; not only with his physical body, with his horse. Sitting on the horse, he simply went to heaven, upwards. It looks absurd, Mohammedans have not been able to prove it, but the meaning is clear. The story may have not exactly happened, but the meaning is clear. The meaning is to be understood, it is very symbolic. It simply says that there is a law of levitation, and if Mohammed cannot be pulled by levitation, then who will be pulled? He is the right person, a person who exists not. The ego is under the force of gravity, the no-ego is not – a weightlessness arises.

Nijinsky went mad because he was simply a dancer and he never knew anything about meditation, ecstasy, enlightenment. That became a trouble for him. If you don't understand, and if you don't move with awareness and suddenly you stumble upon something which cannot be explained by ordinary laws, you will go mad because you will be disturbed by it. It is so weird, it is so eerie. You cannot explain it. You start getting disturbed by it. He himself started getting disturbed by the phenomenon. Finally it was so staggering it disturbed his whole mind.

The force of the unknown, of the divine, is very destructive. If you don't go rightly you will be destroyed, because it is fire. Many people go mad if they don't move rightly. If they don't move with the right guidance they can go mad. It is not a child's play, one has to understand. And the divine ... if it happens like an accident you will not be able to absorb it. Your old world will be shattered and you will not be able to create a new order, a new understanding. Because for the new understanding you will need new concepts, a new framework, a new gestalt. That is the whole meaning of finding a master.

It is not just from gullibility that people become attached to masters, it has a scientific base to it. Moving into the unknown is a tremendous risk. One should move with somebody who has already moved into it. One should move hand in hand with somebody who knows the territory. Otherwise the thing can happen so shatteringly that you will be at a loss. Many people go mad if they don't know that somebody's help is needed. Somebody is needed like a midwife. You will be born, but somebody will be needed to watch over it. His very presence will be helpful; you can relax. The midwife is there, the doctor is there – you can relax. They don't do much – you can ask any doctor; they don't do much; what can they do? But their very presence relaxes the woman who is going into labor. She knows the doctor is there, the nurse is there, the midwife is there. Everything is okay. She goes, she relaxes, she is no longer fighting. She knows if something goes wrong people are around who will put it right. She can relax, she can trust.

The same happens to a disciple. It is a process of rebirth. A master is needed, but from the master don't go on collecting knowledge. From the master take hints and move into experience.

I talk about meditation. You can do two things. You can collect whatsoever I say about meditation, you can compile it. You can become a great, knowledge-able person about meditation – because every day I go on talking about meditation from different dimensions in different ways. You can collect all that, you can get a Ph.D from any university. But that is not going to make you wise, unless you meditate.

So whatsoever I am saying, try it in life. While I am here, don't waste time in collecting knowledge. That you can do without me, that you can do in a library. While I am here take a jump, a quantum leap into wisdom. Experience these things I am saying to you.

But when you gain spiritual enlightenment you shall then find wisdom.

Wisdom is only through one's own experience. It is never from anybody else. Wisdom always happens as a flower opens . . . just like that. When your heart opens, you have a fragrance – that fragrance is wisdom. You can bring a plastic flower from the market, you can deceive neighbors . . .

I used to live near Mulla Nasruddin. I used to see him every day pouring water into a pot that was hanging in his window, with beautiful flowers. I watched him many times. Whenever he would be pouring water, there was no water, in fact – the pot was empty. I could see that there was no water and the pot was empty, but he would pour twice every day, religiously. I asked Nasruddin, "What are you doing? You don't have any water and you go on pouring that which is not there! And I have been watching you for many days."

He said, "Don't get disturbed. These flowers are plastic flowers. They don't need water."

Plastic flowers don't need water, they are not alive. They don't need soil, they are not alive. They don't need fertilizers, they are not alive. They don't need any manure, they are not alive.

Real flowers are like wisdom. Wisdom is like real flowers, knowledge is plastic. That's why it is cheap. It is very cheap, you can get it for nothing because it is borrowed. Experience is a radical change in your life; you cannot be the same. If you want to become wise you will have to go through transformations, a million and one transformations. You will have to pass through fire. Only then, whatever is there which is ugly and useless will be burnt, and you will come out as pure gold.

The knowledge thus attained leads you anon to the way.

... And the wisdom only. The knowledge thus attained through one's own experience, through one's own enlightening experience, through one's own satori, samadhi, makes you capable of falling in tune with the way. The Buddha calls it dhamma, Tao. Then you are in harmony, what Pythagoras calls *harmonia*. Then you are suddenly not there, only the law is there, the dhamma is there, the way is there. Then you are simply with the whole. You go with it wherever it goes. Then you don't have any goal of your own. Then the whole's destiny is your destiny. Then there is no anxiety, no tension. Then one is immensely relaxed.

In fact, one is so relaxed that one is not! The ego is nothing but accumulated tensions through lives. When you are totally relaxed and you look within, there is nobody. It is simple purity, emptiness, vastness.

THE BUDDHA SAID:

You should think of the four elements of which the body is composed.
Each of them has its own name and there is no such thing there
known as ego. As there really is no ego, it is like unto a mirage.

Buddha says ego is just a concept, an idea; it does not exist in reality. When a child is born he is born without any "I". By and by he learns it, by and by he learns that there are other people and he is separate from them. Have you watched small children when they start speaking? They don't say, "I am thirsty." They say, "Bobby is thirsty." They don't have any "I". By and by they learn the "I", because they start feeling "thou". Thou comes first, then comes I, as a reaction to thou. They started feeling that there are other people who are separate from Bobby, and they are called "thou", you. Then by and by he starts learning the "I".

But it is just a utility. Useful, perfectly useful – use it. I'm not saying stop using "I", because that will create troubles. But know well that there is no "I" within you; it is just a linguistic convenience. Just as the name is a convenience so is the "I".

When a child is born he has no name. Then we call him Sam, and he becomes a Sam. Later on if you insult the name "Sam" he will start fighting – and he had come in the world without a name! And really he has no name, it is just a label – utilitarian, needed, but nothing true in it. He can as well be called Krishna or Mohammed or Michael or anything. Any name will do because he is nameless. That's why I change your names when I initiate you into *sannyas* – just to give you a feeling that the name can be changed, it does not belong to you. It can easily be changed. It has a utility in the world, but it has no reality.

The child learns that his name is Sam – the name is for others to call him. He cannot call himself Sam because that too will be confusing. Others call him Sam, he has to call himself something else, otherwise it will be confusing.

Ram Teerth used to call himself Ram, in the third person. It was very confusing. He was a beautiful man, and just not to use "I" – because the "I" has created so much trouble – just as a gesture, he used to call himself Ram. When he went to America he would say suddenly, "Ram is thirsty," and people would not understand. What does he mean? – "Ram is thirsty." They would look around – who is Ram? And he would say, "This Ram is thirsty." But this is confusing. You say, "I am thirsty," and things are settled. Because when you use the name it seems that somebody else is thirsty.

So there is a need for a name others can call you, and there is a need for something, a symbol, that you can call yourself. It is a need of the society, it has nothing to do with existence or reality.

You should think of the four elements of which the body is composed . . .

Buddha says the body is composed of fire, earth, water, air – these four things are there, they are real things, and there is nothing else. Behind these four things there is just pure space inside you. That pure space is what you really are – that zero space.

Buddha does not want to call it even a self, because the self carries again some distant reflection of the ego. So he calls it no-self, *anatta*. He does not call it *atma*, self, he calls it *anatma*, no-self. And he is right, he is absolutely right. One should not call it any name.

I have come across it. It has no name and it has no form. It has no substance and it has no center. It is just immense, pure, empty, full. It is pure bliss – *sat-chit-ananda*. It is truth, it is consciousness, it is bliss, but it has no sense of "I" in it. It is not confined by anything, it has no boundaries. It is pure space. To attain to that purity is what Buddha says is nirvana.

The word "nirvana" is beautiful. It means "blowing out a flame". There is a lamp, you go and blow out the flame of the lamp. Then, Buddha says, "Do you ask where the flame has gone now? Can anybody answer where the flame has gone now?" Buddha says it has simply disappeared into infinity. It has not gone anywhere, it has gone everywhere. It has not gone to any particular address, it has become universal.

Blowing out a flame is the meaning of the word "nirvana". And Buddha says when you blow out your ego, the flame of the ego, only pure space is left. Then you are nobody in particular, you are everybody. Then you are universal. Then you are this vast benediction, this bliss, this beatitude. Then you are it.

Enough for today.

Chapter 12:

Always on the Funeral Pyre

THE BUDDHA SAID:

*Moved by their selfish desires, people seek after fame and
glory. But when they have acquired it, they are already
stricken in years. If you hanker after worldly fame and
practice not the way, your labors are wrongfully applied
and your energy is wasted. It is like unto burning an
incense stick. However much its pleasing odor be admired,
the fire that consumes is steadily burning up the stick.*

THE BUDDHA SAID:

*People cleave to their worldly possessions and selfish
passions so blindly as to sacrifice their own lives for them.
They are like a child who tries to eat a little honey
smeared on the edge of a knife. The amount is by no
means sufficient to appease his appetite, but he runs the
risk of wounding his tongue.*

THE BUDDHA SAID:

*Men are tied up to their families and possessions more
helplessly than in a prison. There is an occasion for the
prisoner to be released, but householders entertain no
desire to be relieved from the ties of family. When a man's*

passion is aroused nothing prevents him from ruining himself. Even into the maws of a tiger he will jump. Those who are thus drowned in the filth of passion are called the ignorant. Those who are able to overcome it are saintly arhats.

The way of the Buddha is not a religion in the ordinary sense of the term, because it has no belief system, no dogma, no scripture. It does not believe in God, it does not believe in the soul, it does not believe in any state of moksha, liberation. It is a tremendous non-belief, and yet it is a religion. It is unique; nothing like it has ever happened before in the history of human consciousness, and nothing afterwards. Buddha remains utterly unique, incomparable. He says that God is nothing but a search for security, a search for safety, a search for shelter. You believe in God not because God is there; you believe in God because you feel helpless without that belief. If there is no God, you will go on inventing one.

The temptation comes from your weakness; it is a projection. Man feels very limited, helpless, almost a victim of circumstances – not knowing from where he comes and not knowing where he is going, not knowing why he is here. If there is no God it is very difficult for ordinary man to have any meaning in life. The ordinary mind will go berserk without God. God is a prop – it helps you, it consoles you, it comforts you. It says, "Don't be worried – the Almighty God knows everything about why you are here. He is the Creator; he knows why he has created the world. You may not know but the Father knows, and you can trust in him."

It is a great consolation. The very idea of God gives you a sense of relief – that you are not alone, that somebody is looking after affairs; that this cosmos is not just a chaos, it is really a cosmos; that there is a system behind it, there is logic behind it; that it is not an illogical jumble of things, that it is not anarchy. Somebody rules it; the sovereign king is there looking after each small detail – not even a leaf moves without his moving it. Everything is planned. You are part of a great destiny. Maybe the meaning is not known to you, but the meaning is there because God is there. God brings a tremendous relief. One starts feeling that life is not accidental; there is a certain undercurrent of significance, meaning, destiny. God brings a sense of destiny.

Buddha says: There is no God – it simply shows that man knows not why he is here. It simply shows man is helpless. It simply shows that man has no meaning available to him. By creating the idea of God he can believe in meaning, and he can live this futile life with the idea that somebody is looking after it.

Just think: you are on an airplane flight and somebody comes and says, "There is no pilot." Suddenly there will be a panic. No pilot?! No pilot simply means you are doomed. Then somebody says, "Believe the pilot is there – invisible, we may not be able to see the him, but the pilot is there; otherwise how is this beautiful mechanism functioning? Just think of it: everything is going so beautifully there must be a pilot! Maybe we are not capable of seeing him, maybe we are not yet prayerful enough to see him, maybe our eyes are closed, but the pilot is there. Otherwise, how is it possible? This airplane has taken off, it is flying perfectly well; the engines are humming. Everything is proof that there is a pilot."

If somebody convinces you of it, you relax again into your chair. You close your eyes, you start dreaming again – you can fall asleep. The pilot is there, you need not worry.

Buddha says the pilot exists not; it is a human creation. Man has created God in his own image. It is man's invention – God is not a discovery, it is an invention. And God is not the truth, it is the greatest lie there is. That's why I say Buddhism is not a religion in the ordinary sense of the term. A godless religion – can you imagine? When for the first time Western scholars became aware of Buddhism, they were shocked. They could not comprehend that a religion can exist without God. They had known only Judaism, Christianity and Islam. All these three religions are in a way very immature compared to Buddhism.

Buddhism is religion come of age. Buddhism is the religion of a mature mind. Buddhism is not childish at all – and it doesn't support any childish desires in you, it is merciless. Let me repeat it: there has never been a man more compassionate than Buddha but his religion is merciless. In fact, in that merci-lessness he is showing his compassion. He will not allow you to cling to any lie. Howsoever consoling, a lie is a lie. And those who have given you the lie are not friends to you, they are enemies – because under the impact of the lie you will live a life full of lies.

The truth has to be brought to you, howsoever hard, howsoever shattering, howsoever shocking. Even if you are annihilated by the impact of the truth it is good.

Buddha says: The truth is that man's religions are man's inventions. You are in a dark night surrounded by alien forces. You need someone to hang on to, someone to cling to.

And everything that you can see is changing – your father will die one day and you will be left alone, your mother will die one day and you will be left alone and you will be an orphan. From the very childhood you have been accustomed to having a father to protect you, a mother to love you. Now that childish desire will again assert itself: you will need a father figure. If you cannot find it in the sky, then you will find it in some politician. Stalin became the father of Soviet Russia – they had dropped the idea of God. Mao became the father of China – they had dropped the idea of God. But man is such that he cannot live without a father figure.

Man is childish; there are very few rare people who grow to be mature. My own observation is this, that people remain near about the age of seven, eight, nine. Their physical bodies go on growing older but their minds remain stuck there somewhere below the age of ten. Christianity, Judaism, Islam and Hinduism are the religions below the age of ten. They fulfill whatever are your needs; they are not too worried about the truth. They are more worried about you, they are more worried how to console you. The situation is such – the mother has died and the child is crying and weeping, and you have to console the child so you tell lies. You pretend that the mother has not died: "She has gone for a visit to the neighbors – she will be coming back. Don't be worried, she will be just coming." Or, "She has gone for a long journey. It will take a few days but she will be back." Or, "She has gone to visit God – nothing to be worried about. She is still alive; maybe she has left the body, but the soul lives for ever."

Buddha is the most shattering individual in the whole history of humanity. His whole effort is to drop all props. He does not say to believe in anything. He is an unbeliever and his religion is that of unbelief. He does not say "believe", he says "doubt".

Now, you have heard about religions that say "Believe!" You have never heard about a religion that says "Doubt!" Doubt is the very methodology – doubt to the very core, doubt to the very end, doubt to the very last. And when you have doubted everything, and you have dropped everything out of doubt, then reality arises in your vision. It has nothing to do with your beliefs about God; it is nothing like your so-called God. Then arises reality, absolutely unfamiliar and unknown.

But that possibility exists only when all the beliefs have been dropped and the mind has come to a state of maturity, understanding, acceptance that "Whatsoever is, is, and we don't desire otherwise. If there is no God, there is no God, and we don't have any desire to project a God. If there is no God, then we accept it."

This is what maturity is: to accept the fact and not to create a fiction around it; to accept the reality as it is, without trying to sweeten it, without trying to decorate it, without trying to make it more acceptable to your heart. If it is shattering, it is shattering. If it is shocking, it is shocking. If the truth kills, then one is ready to be killed.

Buddha is merciless. And nobody has ever opened the door of reality so deeply, so profoundly as he has done. He does not allow you any childish desires. He says: Become more aware, become more conscious, become more courageous. Don't go on hiding behind beliefs and masks and theologies. Take your life into your own hands, burn bright your inner light and see whatsoever is. And once you have become courageous enough to accept it, it is a benediction. No belief is needed.

That is Buddha's first step towards reality: all belief systems are poisonous; all belief systems are barriers.

He is not a theist – and remember, he is not an atheist either because, he says, a few people believe that there is a God and a few people believe that there is no God, but both are believers. His non-belief is so deep that even those who say there is no God, and believe in it, are not acceptable to him. He says that just to say there is no God makes no difference. If you remain childish, you will create another source of God.

For example, Karl Marx declared, "There is no God," but then he made history a God. History becomes the God; the same function is being done now by history that was done previously by the concept of God. What was God doing? God was the determining factor; God was the managing factor. It was God who was deciding what should be and what should not be. Marx dropped the idea of God, but then history became the determining factor. Then history became the fate, then history became kismet – then history is the determining factor. Now what is history? Marx says communism is an inevitable state. History has determined that it will come, and everything is determined by history. Now history becomes a super-God, but somebody or something is needed to determine reality. Man cannot live with an indeterminate reality. Man cannot live with reality as it is – chaotic, accidental. Man cannot live with reality without finding some idea which makes it meaningful, relevant, continuous, which gives it a shape that reason can understand; which can be dissected, analyzed into cause and effect.

Freud dropped the idea of God, but then the unconscious became the God – then everything is determined by the unconscious of man, and man is helpless in the hands of the unconscious. Now these are new names for God; it is a new mythology. The Freudian psychology is a new mythology about God. The name is changed but the content remains the same. The label has changed, the old label has been dropped and a fresh, newly-painted label has been put on it – it can deceive people who are not very alert. But if you go deeper into Freudian analysis you will immediately see that now the unconscious is doing the same work that God used to do.

So what is wrong with poor God? If you have to invent something – and man has always to be determined by something, history, economics, unconscious, this and that – if man cannot be free, then what is the point of changing mythologies, theologies? It makes not much difference. You may be a Hindu, you may be a Mohammedan, you may be a Christian, you may be a Jew – it makes not much difference. Your mind remains childish, you remain immature. You remain in search, you continue to search for a father figure, someone somewhere who can explain everything, who can become the ultimate explanation.

The mature mind is one who can remain without any search, who can be at ease even if there is no ultimate explanation of things.

That's why Buddha says, "I am not a metaphysician." He has no metaphysics. Metaphysics means the ultimate explanation of things – he has no ultimate explanation. He does not say, "I have solved the mystery." He does not say, "Here, I hand over to you what truth is." He says, "The only thing that I can give to you is an impetus, a thirst, a tremendous passion to become aware, to become conscious, to become alert; to live your life so consciously, so full of light and awareness, that your life is solved." Not that you come to some ultimate explanation of existence – nobody has ever come. Buddha denies metaphysics completely. He says metaphysics is a futile search.

So the first thing is that he denies God.

The second thing is that he denies moksha, paradise, heaven. He says your heaven, your paradise is nothing but your unfulfilled sexual desires, unfulfilled instincts being projected into the other life, the life beyond, the life after death. And he seems to be absolutely right. If you see the depictions of heaven and paradise in Islam, in Christianity, in Judaism, you will understand perfectly what he is saying. Whatsoever remains unfulfilled here you go on projecting in the hereafter. But the desire seems to be the same!

Hindus say there are trees they call *kalpavriksha* – you sit under them and whatsoever you desire, without any lapse of time, it is fulfilled. You desire a beautiful woman, she is there – immediately, instantly. In the West you have invented instant coffee and things like that just recently. India discovered a wish-fulfilling tree and down the centuries it has believed in it. That is *really* instantly fulfilling, without any time lapse at all. Here the idea arises, there it is fulfilled, and not even a single second passes between the two. The idea is its fulfillment! You desire a beautiful woman, she is there. You desire delicious food, it is there. You desire a beautiful bed to rest on, it is there.

Now, this is simple psychological analysis – that man is unfulfilled in life, and for his whole life he goes on trying to find fulfillment. Still he finds he cannot be fulfilled, so he has to project into the future. Not that in the future it can be fulfilled – desire as such is unfulfillable. Buddha has said that the very nature of desire is that it remains unfulfilled. Whatsoever you do, regardless of what you do about it, it remains unfulfilled – that is the intrinsic nature of desire. Desire as such remains unfulfilled. So you can sit under a wish-fulfilling tree – it doesn't make any difference. You can feel many times it is being fulfilled, and again desire arises. Ad infinitum it will go on arising again and again and again.

The Christian, the Muslim, the Jewish, the Hindu – all their heavens and paradises are nothing but unfulfilled projected desires, repressed desires, frustrated desires. Of course, they console people very much: "If you have not been able to fulfill your desires here, then you can do it there. Sooner or later you will reach God; the only thing you have to do is go on praying to him, go on bowing down before some image or some idea or some ideal, and keep him happy. Keep God happy and you will reap a great crop of pleasures and gratifications. That will be his gift to you – for your prayers, for your appreciation, for your continuous surrender, again and again touching his feet, for your obedience. That is going to be the reward."

The reward is, of course, after death, because even the cunning priests cannot deceive you in this life – even they cannot deceive you that much. They know that desire always remains unfulfilled, so they have to invent an afterlife. Nobody has known the afterlife, so people can be deceived very easily. If somebody comes and says to you, "God can fulfill your desire here and now," it will be difficult to prove it – because nobody's desire has ever been fulfilled here and now. Then their whole idea of God will be at stake. So instead, they have used a very cunning device; they say, "It will happen after this life."

Is your God not potent enough to fulfill your desires here? Is your God not potent enough to create wish-fulfilling trees on the earth? Is your God not powerful enough to do something while people are alive? If he cannot fulfill your desires here, what is the proof that he is going to fulfill them in the hereafter?

Buddha says: Look into the nature of desire. Watch the movement of desire – it is very subtle – and you will be able to see two things. One is that desire by its very nature is unfulfillable; and second, the moment you understand that desire is unfulfillable, desire disappears and you are left desireless. That is the state of peace, silence, tranquility. That is the state of fulfillment. Man never comes to fulfillment through desire; man comes to fulfillment only by transcending desire.

Desire is an opportunity to understand. Desire is a great opportunity to understand the functioning of your own mind – how it functions, what the mechanism of it is – and when you have understood that, in the very understanding is transformation. Desire disappears, leaves no trace behind, and when you are desireless, not desiring anything, you are fulfilled. Not that desire is fulfilled, but when desire is transcended there is fulfillment.

Now see the difference: other religions say, "Desires can be fulfilled in the other world." The worldly people say, "Desires can be fulfilled here." The communists say, "Desires can be fulfilled here. Just a different social structure is needed, just the capitalists have to be overthrown, the proletariat has to take over, the bourgeoisie has to be destroyed, that's all – then desires can be fulfilled here, heaven can be created on this earth here."

The worldly people say, "You can fulfill your desires – work hard." That's what the whole world goes on doing. Struggle, compete, cheat, by any means and methods acquire more wealth, more power. That's what the politicians all over the world go on doing: "Become more powerful and your desires can be fulfilled." That's what scientists say, that only a few more technologies have to be invented and paradise is just around the corner. And what do your religions say? They don't say anything different. They say, "Desires can be fulfilled but not in this life – after death." That is the only difference between the so-called materialists and so-called spiritual people.

Both are materialists – your so-called religious people and your so-called irreligious people are both in the same boat. Not a bit of difference! Their attitudes are the same, their approaches are the same.

Buddha is really religious in this way. He says desire cannot be fulfilled. You have to look into desire; neither here nor anywhere else has desire ever been fulfilled. Never! It has never happened and never it is going to happen, because it is against the nature of desire.

What is desire? Have you ever looked into your desiring mind? Have you encountered it? Have you tried any meditation on it? What is desire? You desire a certain house; you work for it, you work hard. You destroy your whole life for it – then the house is there, but is fulfillment there? Once the house is there, suddenly you feel very empty – you feel more empty than before, because before there was an occupation to achieve this house. Now it is there: immediately your mind starts looking for something else to get occupied with. Now there are bigger houses; your mind starts thinking of those bigger houses. There are bigger palaces . . .

You desire a woman and you have achieved your desire, then suddenly your hands are again empty. You start desiring some other woman. This is the nature of desire. Desire always stays ahead of you. Desire is always in the future, desire is a hope. Desire cannot be fulfilled because its very nature is to remain unfulfilled and projected in the future. It is always on the horizon.

You can rush, you can run towards the horizon, but you will never reach: wherever you reach you will find the horizon has receded, and the distance between you and the horizon remains absolutely the same. You have ten thousand dollars, the desire is for twenty thousand dollars; you have twenty thousand dollars, the desire is for forty thousand dollars. The distance is the same; the mathematical proportion is the same.

Whatsoever you have, desire always goes ahead of it.

Buddha says: Abandon hope, abandon desire. In abandoning hope, in abandoning desire, you will be here now. Without desire you will be fulfilled. It is desire that is deceiving you.

So when Buddha said that these so-called religious people are all materialists, of course the Hindus were very angry – very angry; they have never been so angry against anybody. They tried to uproot Buddha's religion from India, and they succeeded. Buddhism was born in India, but Buddhism doesn't exist in India anymore – because the religion of the Hindus is one of the most materialistic religions in the world. You can just look in the Vedas. All prayer, all worship is just asking for more, for more, from the gods or from God. All sacrifice is for the sake of more; all worship is desire-oriented. "Give us more, give us plenty – better crops, better rain, more money, more health, more life, more longevity – give us more!" The whole Veda is nothing but desire written large ... and sometimes very ugly. In the Veda not only do the so-called seers go on praying, "Give us more!" – they also pray, "Don't give to our enemies; give more milk to my cow, but let the enemy's cow die, or let its milk disappear."

What type of religion is this? Even to call it religion looks absurd. If this is religion, then what is materialism? And even so-called ascetic people who renounced the world ... and there were many in the days of Buddha. He himself had gone to many masters while he was searching, but from everywhere he came back empty-handed because he could not see that anybody had really understood the nature of desire. They themselves were desiring; of course, their desire was projected in the faraway future, another life, but still the desiring mind was the same; it was only a question of time. A few people desire before death, a few people desire after death, but what is the difference? That does not make any difference. They desire the same things – they desire and the desire is the same.

Buddha went to many teachers and was frustrated. He could not see religion flowering anywhere, blossoming – they were all materialistic people. They were great ascetics: somebody was fasting for months, somebody was standing upright for months, somebody had not slept for years – and they were just skeletons. You could not call them worldly and materialistic if you looked at their bodies. But look at their minds, ask them, "Why are you fasting? Why are you trying so hard? For what?" and there you would find the desire to attain to paradise, to heaven, to have eternal gratification in the afterlife. Listen to their logic and they all would say, "Here things are fleeting. This life is temporary. Even if you attain, everything is taken away when you die, so what is the point? This life is not going to be forever. We are searching for something which will remain forever. We are after immortality, we are after absolute gratification. People who are running after desires here in this life are fools, because death will take everything away. You accumulate wealth, and here comes death and all is left behind. We are searching for some treasure that we can take with us, that will never be lost, that cannot be stolen, no government can tax it – nobody can take it away, not even death."

You call these people religious? They seem to be even more worldly than the so-called worldly; they are more materialistic than the materialists. Of course, their materialism is garbed in a disguise. Their materialism has a flavor of the spiritual, but it is a deception. It is as if on a dung heap you have thrown some beautiful perfume. The dung heap remains a dung heap; the perfume can only deceive fools.

Buddha was not fooled, he could see through and through, and he could always see that the desire was there. If desire is there you are a materialist and you are worldly.

So he is not preaching any paradise to you, he does not believe in any paradise. Not that he does not believe in blissfulness, no. He believes in blissfulness, but that is not a belief – when all paradises are lost, when all desires drop, suddenly it is your innermost nature to be blissful. For blissfulness, nothing is needed – no virtue is needed, no asceticism is needed, no sacrifice is needed. Just understanding is enough.

The way of the Buddha is the way of understanding.

And the third thing before we enter the sutras: he does not believe in the soul – no God, no paradise, no soul. Now, this seems to be very difficult. We can accept there is no God – maybe it is just a projection; who has seen it? We can accept there is no paradise – maybe it is just our unfulfilled desire, dreaming about it. But no soul? Then you take the whole ground from underneath. No soul? Then what is the point of it all? If there is no soul in man, if there is nothing immortal in man, then why make so much effort? Why meditate? For what?

Buddha says this idea of the self is a misunderstanding. You are, but you are not a self. You are, but you are not separate from the universe. That separation is the root idea in the concept of self: if I am separate from you then I have a self; if you are separate from me then you have a self. But Buddha says existence is one, there are no boundaries. Nobody is separate from anybody else; we live in one ocean of consciousness. We are one consciousness – deluded by the boundaries of the body, deluded by the boundaries of the mind. Because of the body and the mind, and the identification with the body and mind, we think we are separate, we think we are selves. This is how we create the ego.

It is just like on the map you see India, but on the earth itself there is no India – only on the maps of the politicians. On the map you see the American continent and the African continent as separate but deep down, down under the oceans, the earth is one. All continents are together, they are all one earth.

We are separate only on the surface. The deeper we go the more the separation disappears. When we come to the very core of our being, suddenly it is universal. There is no selfhood in it, no soul there.

Buddha has no belief in God, in the soul, in paradise. Then what is his teaching? His teaching is a way of life, not a way of belief. His teaching is very scientific, very empirical, very practical. He is not a philosopher, not a meta-physician. He is a very down-to-earth man. Buddha says you can change your life – these beliefs are not needed. In fact, these beliefs are the barriers to the real change. Start with no belief, start with no metaphysics, start with no dogma. Start absolutely naked and nude, with no theology, no ideology. Start empty, that is the only way to come to truth.

I was reading an anecdote:

> A traveling salesman opened the Gideon Bible in his motel room. On the front page he read the inscription: "If you are sick, read Psalm 18; if you are troubled about your family, read Psalm 45; if you are lonely, read Psalm 92."
>
> He was lonely, so he opened to Psalm 92 and read it. When he was through, he noticed on the bottom of the page the hand-written words: "If you are still lonely call 888-3468 and ask for Myrtle."
>
> If you look deep down into your scriptures you will always find a footnote that will be more true. Look for the footnote on every scripture page – sometimes it may not be written in visible ink but if you search hard you will always find a footnote that is more real. Buddha says all your scriptures are nothing but your desires, your instincts, your greed, your lust, your anger. All your scriptures are nothing but creations of your mind, so they are bound to carry all the seeds of your mind. Scriptures are man-made. That's why religions try so hard to prove that *their* scripture at least is not man-made.

Christians say the Bible is not man-made; the Ten Commandments were delivered to Moses directly from God, directly from the boss himself. The New Testament is a direct message from God's own son, the only begotten son, Jesus Christ. It has nothing to do with humanity, it comes from above. Hindus say the Vedas are not man-made, they are God-made. And the same story goes on being repeated: Mohammedans say the Koran descended on Mohammed from heaven above. Why do all these religions insist that their scriptures, and especially *only* their scriptures, not anybody else's, come from God? Mohammedans are not ready to accept that the Vedas are God-made, neither are Hindus ready to accept that the Koran is God-made – only their Vedas are God-made and everything else is just manufactured by man. Why this insistence? Because they are aware that whatever man creates will have the imprint of man's mind and man's desires.

Buddha says all the scriptures are man-made – and he is right. He is not a fanatic at all; he does not belong to any country and he does not belong to any race; he does not belong to any religion, to any sect. He is simply a light unto himself, and whatever he has said is the purest statement of truth ever made.

A friend has sent me this beautiful anecdote:

> One of the religious leaders in Ireland was asked by his followers to select a suitable burial place and monument for his mortal remains. A "religious war" was in progress and his life had been threatened. Three separate plans had been submitted to him, and to the dismay of the committee he chose the least expensive. He was asked why he had made this selection, why he had chosen this humble resting place, when the other two designs were magnificent tombs.
>
> "Well, my dear friends," he told them, "I appreciate your generosity. But is it worth all this expense when I don't expect to remain in my tomb for more than three days?"

Now, this sort of stupidity you will never find in Buddha. This sort of dogmatic certainty you will never find in Buddha; he is very hesitant. There is only one other person who is also so hesitant and that is Lao Tzu. These two persons are very hesitant. Sometimes, because of their hesitance you may not be impressed by them. Because you are confused, you need somebody to be so confident that you can rely on him; hence, fanatics impress you very much. They may not have anything to say but they beat the table so much, they make such a fuss about it, their very fuss gives you a feeling that they must know. Otherwise how can they be so certain? The witnesses of Jehovah and people like that – stupid people, but they are so dogmatic in their assertions that they create a feeling of certainty, and confused people need certainty.

When you come to a Buddha, you may not be immediately impressed because he will be so hesitant. He will not assert anything. He knows better than that – he knows life cannot be confined to any statement, and all statements are partial. No statement can contain the whole truth, so how can you be certain about it? He will remain always relative.

Two great masters of India, Buddha and Mahavira, both were very deeply into relativity. Einstein discovered it very late; Einstein brought relativity to the world of science. Before Einstein scientists were very certain, dogmatically certain, absolutely certain. Einstein brought relativity and humbleness to science, he brought truth to science. The same was done by Buddha and Mahavira in India: they brought relativity, the concept that truth cannot be asserted totally, that we can never be certain about it, at the most we can hint at it. The hint has to be indirect; we cannot pinpoint it directly – it is so big, so vast. And it is natural that we fragile human beings should hesitate. This hesitation shows one's alertness.

You will always find stupid, ignorant people to be very dogmatic. The more ignorant a person is the more dogmatic. It is one of the greatest misfortunes in the world that the foolish are absolutely certain, and the wise are hesitant. Buddha is hesitant. So if you really want to understand him, you will have to be very alert in your listening, very open. He is not delivering truths to you wholesale. He is simply "hinting at" . . . he is giving indications at the most, and they too are very subtle.

As I told you, Buddha is very down-to-earth. He never flies high into meta-physics. He never introduces things in fact; he has no preface to his statements. He simply says them directly, immediately, as simply as possible. Sometimes his statements may not look to be of any profound depth – they are. But he does not beat around the bush, he does not make any fuss about it.

I have heard:

> She was a sweet young thing; he was a fast-rising account executive
> with the well-known Madison Avenue advertising agency, Bittner,
> Berman, Dirstein & Osman. Everyone thought it was an ideal
> marriage. But alas, there was a problem . . .with sex. The honeymoon
> hadn't even begun.
>
> "B-b-eing an advertising man," she sobbed to a friend, "all he
> does every night is sit on the edge of the bed and tell me how
> wonderful it's going to be!"

You can understand it about an advertising man: he simply goes on saying how wonderful it is going to be, but it never happens.

Buddha has no preface. He never advertises what he is going to say. He simply says it and moves ahead.

THE BUDDHA SAID:

> Moved by their selfish desires, people seek after fame and glory. But when they have acquired it, they are already stricken in years. If you hanker after worldly fame and practice not the way, your labors are wrongfully applied and your energy is wasted. It is like unto burning an incense stick. However much its pleasing odor be admired, the fire that consumes is steadily burning up the stick.

A very simple and matter-of-fact statement.

Moved by their selfish desires, people seek after fame and glory.

What is a selfish desire? In the Buddhist way of expression, a selfish desire is one that is based in the self. Ordinarily, in ordinary language, we call a desire selfish if it is against somebody else, and you don't care about others. Even if it harms others, you go ahead and you fulfill your desire. People call you selfish because you don't care for others, you don't have any consideration for others. But when Buddha says a desire is selfish, his meaning is totally different. He says: If a desire is based in the idea of self, then it is selfish.

For example you donate money, a million dollars for some good cause – hospitals to be made, or schools to be opened, or food to be distributed to the poor, or medicine to be sent to poor parts of the country. Nobody will call it a selfish desire. Buddha will say it is – if there is any motivation of self. If you are thinking that by donating a million dollars you are going to earn some virtue and you are going to be rewarded in heaven, it is a selfish desire. It may not be harmful to others – it is not, in fact everybody will appreciate it. People will call you a great man, religious, virtuous; a great man of charity, love, compassion, sympathy. But Buddha will say the only thing that determines whether a desire is selfish or not is motivation. If you have donated without any motivation, then it is not selfish. If there is any motivation hidden somewhere – conscious, unconscious – that you are going to gain something out of it, here or hereafter, then it is a selfish desire. That which comes out of the self is a selfish desire; that which comes as part of the ego is a selfish desire. If you meditate just to attain to your selfhood, then it is a selfish desire.

Buddha has said to his disciples: Whenever you meditate, after each meditation, surrender all that you have earned out of meditation, surrender it to the universe. If you are blissful, pour it back into the universe – don't carry it as a treasure. If you are feeling very happy, share it immediately – don't become attached to it, otherwise your meditation itself will become a new process of the self. And the ultimate meditation is not a process of self. The ultimate meditation is a process of getting more and more into un-self, into non-self – it is a disappearance of the self.

Moved by their selfish desires, people seek after fame and glory. But when they have acquired it, they are already stricken in years.

And Buddha says: Look, you can attain to fame, to glory, to power, to prestige, respectability, in the world – but what are you doing? Are you aware? You are wasting a great opportunity – for something absolutely meaningless. You are collecting rubbish and destroying your own life energy and time.

If you hanker after worldly fame and practice not the way . . .

Buddha always calls his approach "The Way" – dhamma – just the way, because he says, you needn't be bothered about the goal; the goal will take care of itself. You simply follow the way, not even with the motivation to reach any goal but just out of the sheer delight of meditating, of loving, of being compassionate, sharing. Out of sheer delight you practice the way. Not that you are going to gain any profit out of it; don't make it a business. Ordinarily the mind is a businessman . . .

> The old father was dying and his family was gathered around the bed waiting for him to take his last breath. As the old man wheezed away life, his oldest son said to one and all, "When Papa goes, if it's tonight, we can bury him early tomorrow from the big funeral parlor downtown. Since the funeral will be early in the morning, we won't be able to get in touch with too many people, so we won't need a lot of cars or the big room, and it won't cost too much."
>
> His daughter was standing there and she said to the brother, "You know, death to me is a very personal thing. Why do we have to call a bunch of strangers together to witness such a sad scene – if you two boys are there and I'm there, who needs anyone else?"
>
> The youngest son looked at them both and said, "I couldn't agree with you more. In fact, why do we need the expense of taking Papa to an undertaker? He is dying in the house, let's bury him from the house."
>
> All of a sudden the old man's eyes flew wide open. He looked at

his three children and shouted, "Give me my pants!"

They answered in a chorus, "Papa, you are a very sick man. Where do you want to go?"

He replied, "I'll walk to the cemetery – no need to pay for a hearse."

Their whole lives people simply go on saving, saving – for what? Life is slipping by; each moment, a precious moment is gone and it cannot be reclaimed. Buddha says: Don't waste it in foolish things.

Fame is foolish, it is pointless, meaningless. Even if the whole world knows you, how does it make you richer? How does it make your life more blissful? How does it help you to be more understanding, to be more aware? To be more alert, to be more alive?

If you are not practicing the way, then . . . *your labors are wrongfully applied and your energy is wasted. It is like unto burning an incense stick. However much its pleasing odor be admired, the fire that consumes is steadily burning up the stick.*

That's how life is, each moment burning. You are always on the funeral pyre because each moment death is coming closer, each moment you are less alive, more dead. So before this whole opportunity is lost, Buddha says, attain to a state of no-self – then there will be no death. Then there will be no misery, and then there will be no constant hankering for fame, power, prestige.

In fact, the more empty you are within, the more you seek fame as a sort of substitute. The poorer you are within, the more you seek riches; it is a substitute to somehow stuff yourself with something. I observe it every day. People come to me and whenever they have a problem with their love, they immediately start eating too much. Whenever they feel that their love is in a crisis, they are not being loved or they are not able to love, something has blocked their love energy, they immediately start stuffing themselves with things, they go on eating. Why? What are they doing with the food? They feel empty – that emptiness makes them afraid. They have to somehow stuff it with food.

If you are feeling happy inside, you don't bother about fame; only unhappy people bother about fame. Who bothers whether anybody knows you or not if you know yourself? If you know yourself, who you are, then there is no need. But when you don't know who you are, you would like everybody else to know who you are. You will collect opinions, you will collect people's ideas and out of that collection you will try to arrange some identity: "Yes, I am this person. People tell me I am very intelligent, so I am intelligent." You are not certain. If you are certain, who bothers what people say or not?

You go on looking into people's eyes to see your face – you don't know your face. You beg: "Say something about me. Say I am beautiful. Say I am lovely. Say I am charismatic. Say something about me!" Have you watched yourself begging? "Say something about my body, about my mind, about my understanding – say something!" You immediately grab hold of it if somebody says something. And if somebody says something that is shocking and shattering, you become very angry. He is destroying your image if he says something against you. If he says something in favor of you, he helps your image to be a little more decorated, it becomes a little more ornamental – you come home happy. If people applaud you, you feel happy. Why? You don't know who you are. That's why you go on seeking.

You go on asking people "Who am I? Tell me!" And you have to depend on them. The beauty of it – or the irony of it – is that those same people don't know who they are. Beggars begging from other beggars . . . they have come to beg from you, so there is a mutual deception.

You come across a woman; you say, "How beautiful! How divine!" And she says, "Yes, and I have never come across such a beautiful man as you." This is a mutual deception. You may call it love, but this is a mutual deception. Both are hankering for a certain identity for themselves. Both fulfill each other's desires. Things will go well until someday one of the two decides that enough is enough, and starts dropping the deception. Then the honeymoon is over . . . and the marriage starts! Then things go ugly. Then you think, "This woman deceived me", or "this man deceived me".

Nobody can deceive you unless you are ready to be deceived, remember. Nobody has ever deceived anybody – unless you were ready to be deceived, unless you were waiting to be deceived. You cannot deceive a person who knows himself, because there is no way; if you say something he will laugh. He will say, "Don't be worried about it – I already know who I am. You can drop that subject and go ahead with whatever you have to say. Don't be bothered about me – I know who I am."

Once you have an inner richness of life, you don't seek wealth, you don't seek power.

Psychologists have become aware that when people start becoming impotent, they start substituting some sexual, phallic symbols. If a person becomes impotent then he wants some phallic symbol to replace it. He may try to have the biggest car in the world – that is a phallic symbol. He would like to have the most powerful car in the world; now his own power is lost, his own sexual energy is gone and he would like a substitute. While pushing his car to the maximum speed, he will feel good – as if he is making love to his woman. The very speed will give him power. He will get identified with the car.

Psychologists have been watching the phenomenon for many years: people who have a certain inferiority complex always become ambitious. In fact, nobody goes into politics unless he is deeply rooted in an inferiority complex. Politicians are basically people who have to prove their superiority in some way; otherwise they will not be able to live with their inferiority complex.

What I am trying to point out is that whatever you miss within, you try to accumulate something outside as a substitute for it. If you don't miss your life within, you are enough unto yourself. And only then are you beautiful. And only then you *are*.

THE BUDDHA SAID:

> *People cleave to their worldly possessions and selfish passions so*
> *blindly as to sacrifice their own lives for them. They are like a child*
> *who tries to eat a little honey smeared on the edge of a knife. The*
> *amount is by no means sufficient to appease his appetite, but he*
> *runs the risk of wounding his tongue.*

Nothing is enough in this life to fulfill your desires, to fulfill your appetite. This world is a dream world – only reality can be fulfilling.

Have you watched? You feel hungry in the night and in your dream you go to the fridge and open it, and you eat to your heart's desire. Of course, it helps in a way – it does not disturb your sleep; otherwise, the hunger would not allow you to sleep, you would have to wake up. The dream creates a substitute: you continue to sleep and you feel, "I have eaten enough." You have deceived your body.

The dream is a deceiver. In the morning you will be still hungry, because a feast in a dream is equivalent to a fast. Feast or fast, both are the same in a dream because a dream is unreal. It cannot fulfill. To quench real thirst real water is needed. For fullfillment a real life is needed.

Buddha says: You go on taking the risk of wounding yourself, but no fulfillment comes out of this life. Maybe here and there you have a taste of honey – sweet, but very dangerous, unfulfilling. The honey is smeared on the edge of a knife and there is every danger you will wound your tongue.

Look at old people: you will not find anything else but wounds; their whole being is nothing but wounds, ulcers and ulcers and ulcers. When a person dies you don't see blossoming flowers in his being; you simply see stinking wounds.

If a person has really lived and not been deceived by his dreams and illusory desires, the older he grows the more beautiful he becomes. In his death he is superb.

Sometimes you may come across an old man whose old age is more beautiful than his youth ever was. Then bow down before that old man – he has lived a true life, a life of inwardness, a life of "interiorness". Because if life is lived truly, then you go on becoming more and more beautiful and a grandeur starts coming to you, a grace; something of the unknown starts abiding in your surroundings – you become the abode of the infinite, of the eternal. It has to be so because life is an evolution.

If when you are no longer young you become ugly, that simply means in your youth you tasted honey on too many knives – you have become wounded. Now you will suffer these cancerous wounds. Old age becomes a great suffering. And death is very rarely beautiful because very rarely have people really lived. If a person has really lived – like a flame burning from both ends – then his death will be a tremendous phenomenon, an utter beauty. You will see his life aglow when he is dying, at the maximum, at the optimum. In the last moment he will become such a flame; his whole life will become a concentrated perfume in that moment, a great luminosity will arise in his being. Before he leaves, he will leave behind him a memory.

That's what happened when Buddha left the world. That's what happened when Mahavira left the world. We have not forgotten them. Not because they were great politicians or great people of power – they were nobodies, but we cannot forget them; it is impossible to forget them. They had not done anything as far as history is concerned. We can almost omit them from history, we can neglect them from history and nothing will be lost. In fact, they never existed in the main current of history; they were by the side of it, but it is impossible to forget them. Their very last moment has left such a glory to humanity. Their last glow has shown us our own possibilities, our infinite potentialities.

THE BUDDHA SAID:

> Men are tied up to their families and possessions more helplessly than
> in a prison. There is an occasion for the prisoner to be released, but
> householders entertain no desire to be relieved from the ties of
> family. When a man's passion is aroused nothing prevents him from
> ruining himself. Even into the maws of a tiger will he jump. Those
> who are thus drowned in the filth of passion are called the ignorant.
> Those who are able to overcome it are saintly arhats.

Buddha says: Those who are lost into the filth of passion and never transcend it, those who never transcend as the lotus transcends the mud it is born into – they are the ignorant people, the worldly people. Those who transcend lust and desire, those who understand the futility of desire and become understanding about the whole nonsense that the mind creates and the dreams that it manufactures, they are the great arhats.

"Arhat", the very word means one who has overcome his enemies. Buddha says desire, desiring, is your enemy. Once you have overcome your desire, you have overcome your enemy, you have become an arhat. Arhat is the goal, to become desireless – because only when you are desireless is there benediction.

Our so-called religions are based in fear. Buddha's religion is based in an inner benediction. We worship God because we are afraid, because we don't know what to do with our lives. We are continuously trembling, scared – death is coming and we don't know what to do, how to protect ourselves. We need a protector; it is out of fear. Buddha's religion is based in an inner benediction, in an inner blessing – it has nothing to do with fear.

Let me tell you one anecdote:

> Henry went on his first hunting trip. When he got back to his office, his partner Morris couldn't wait to hear all about the trip. Henry told him, "Well, I went into the woods with the guide. You know me, two minutes in the woods I get lost. I'm walking extra quiet, when all of a sudden the biggest bear you ever did see is standing right in front of me. I turn around and run just as fast as I can and that bear, he is running even faster. Just when I feel his hot breath on my neck, he slipped and fell. I jumped over a brook and kept running, but I was losing my breath and sure enough there was that bear getting close to me again. He was almost on top of me when he slipped again and fell. I kept on running and finally I found myself in a clearing of the woods. The bear was running as fast as he could and I knew I didn't stand a chance. I saw the other hunters and shouted for help, and just then the bear slipped and fell again. My guide was able to take aim and he shot the bear and killed him."
>
> Morris said, "Henry, that was quite a story. You are a very brave man. If that would have happened to me, I would have made in my pants."
>
> Henry looked at him and shrugged, "Morris, what do you think the bear was slipping on?"

The so-called religions are just out of fear. And anything based on fear can never be beautiful. Your gods, your churches, your temples . . . if they have come out of your fear they stink. They are bound to stink of your fear.

Buddha's religion is not based in fear at all. That's why he says the first step is to drop all beliefs. Those beliefs are there because of the fear. Dropping the beliefs you will become aware of your fear, and that is good to become aware of your fear. You will become aware of your death. You will become aware of this whole infinite cosmos – nowhere to go, nobody to guide, nowhere to find any security. In that fear, in that awareness of fear, the only place left will be to start going withinwards – because there is no point in going anywhere else. It is so vast.

The interior journey starts when you have dropped all beliefs and you have become aware of the fear, death, desire. And once you are in, suddenly you see fears are disappearing; because in the deepest core of your being there has never been any death, there cannot be. Your innermost core is absolutely a non-self.

A self can die. The no-self cannot die. If there is something, it can be destroyed. That's why Buddha says there is nothing inside you – you are a pure nothing. That nothing cannot be destroyed. And once you have understood it, that death cannot destroy, that this nothingness is in itself so beautiful there is no need to go on stuffing it with money, power, prestige, fame . . . This nothingness is so pure and so innocent and so beautiful that you are blessed in it. You start dancing in that nothingness. That nothingness starts a dance. Buddha hints you towards that dance.

When Buddha was dying, Ananda started crying and he said, "What will I do now? You are leaving and I have not yet become enlightened."

Buddha said, "Don't cry, because I cannot make you enlightened – only you can do that miracle to yourself. Be a light unto yourself – *appa deepo bhava.*"

Buddha throws humanity into the interiormost core. Buddha says: Go within – and there is nowhere else to go. You are the shrine. Go within – there is no other god anywhere to worship. The more you move inwards, the more a worshipping consciousness will arise – without any object for worship. A prayer will arise that is not addressed to anybody – a pure prayer that comes out of bliss, out of being, out of inner benediction.

Enough for today.

Chapter 13:

There is Nothing Like Lust

THE BUDDHA SAID:

There is nothing like lust. Lust may be said to be the most powerful passion. Fortunately, we have but one thing which is more powerful. If the thirst for truth were weaker than passion, how many of us in the world would be able to follow the way of righteousness?

THE BUDDHA SAID:

Men who are addicted to the passions are like the torch-carrier running against the wind; his hands are sure to be burnt.

The lord of heaven offered a beautiful fairy to the Buddha, desiring to tempt him to the evil path. But the Buddha said: He gone! What use have I for the leather bag filled with filth which you have brought to me?

Then, the God reverently bowed and asked the Buddha about the essence of the way, in which having been instructed by the Buddha, it is said, he attained the srotapanna *fruit.*

The essence of the religion of Buddha is awareness. There is no prayer in it, there cannot be, because there is no God. And there cannot be any prayer in it because prayer is always motivated. Prayer is a form of desire, a form of lust.

Prayer has hidden deep down in it the very cause of misery. The cause of misery is that we are not contented as we are. The cause of misery is that we would like a different type of life, a different situation, a different world – and the world that is before us pales in comparison to our imagination. The cause of misery is imagination, desire, hope – and in prayer all those causes are present. There is no possibility for prayer in Buddha's religion; only awareness is the key. So we have to understand what awareness is.

When you pray, you ask for something. When you meditate, you meditate upon something. But when you are aware, you are simply centered in your being. The other is not important at all. The other is irrelevant. You are simply aware.

Awareness has no object to it. It is pure subjectivity. It is a grounding in your being, it is a centering in your being. Standing there inside your being, you burn bright. Your flame is without any smoke. In your light the whole life becomes clear. In that clarity is silence; in that clarity, time ceases. In that clarity, the world disappears because in that clarity there is no desire, no motivation. You simply are . . . not wanting anything whatever. Not wanting any future, not wanting any better world. Not wanting heaven, moksha. Not wanting God. Not wanting knowledge, liberation. You simply are.

Awareness is a pure presence, a centered consciousness. Buddha's whole effort is how to make you centered, grounded, a flame without smoke, a flame which knows no wavering. In that light, everything becomes clear and all illusions disappear and all dreams become non-existential. And when the dreaming mind stops, there is truth.

Remember it: only when the dreaming mind has stopped is there truth. Why? Because the dreaming mind continuously projects and distorts that which is. If you look at a thing with desire, you never look at the thing as it is. Your desire starts playing games with you.

A woman passes by, a beautiful woman, or a man passes by, a handsome man – suddenly there is desire: to possess her, to possess him. Then you cannot see the reality. Then your very desire creates a dream around the object. Then you start seeing the way you would like to see; then you start projecting – the other becomes a screen and your deepest desires are projected. You start coloring the object; then you don't see that which is. You start seeing visions, moving into fantasy.

Of course, this fantasy is bound to be shattered; when the reality erupts, your dreaming mind will be shattered. It happens many times. You fall in love with a woman – one day suddenly the dream has disappeared; the woman does not look so beautiful as she used to look. You cannot believe how you were deceived into it. You start finding faults with the woman. You start finding rationalizations – as if she tricked you into it, as if she deceived you; as if she pretended to be beautiful while she was not. Nobody is cheating you – nobody can cheat you except your own desiring and dreaming mind. You created the illusion, you never saw the reality of the woman. Sooner or later the reality will win over.

That's how all love affairs are always on the rocks. And lovers become afraid, by and by, to see the reality – they avoid it. The wife avoids the husband, the husband avoids the wife. They don't look directly at each other, they are afraid. They are already aware that the dream has disappeared: now, don't rock the boat. Now, avoid each other!

I have heard:

> A man was very much worried about his wife. He had heard rumors that she was moving with somebody else and naturally, he was disturbed. He asked a detective to follow the woman and to make a film showing with whom she was moving, what they were doing.
>
> Within a few weeks the detective was back with the film, and it was shown to the man. He watched it; again and again he would shake his head as if he could not believe it. The wife was swimming with somebody, was going to a movie, hugging, kissing, making love to the man, and he was shaking his head in tremendous disbelief. The detective could not contain himself: "Why does he go on shaking his head?"
>
> Finally, when the film was over, the man said, "I cannot believe it!"
>
> The detective said, "You have seen the film, what more proof do you need?"
>
> He said, "Don't misunderstand me. I cannot believe that my wife can make somebody so happy! Now I want you to try to find out what that man sees in my wife, because I have lived with her and I don't see anything at all. What does this man see in her?"

Husbands stop seeing things that they used to see in their wives. Wives stop seeing things in their husbands that they used to see. What happens? The reality is the same, only against the reality the dream cannot win for ever. Sooner or later the dream is shattered. And that happens in all directions.

You are after money, you are dreaming about money. You never look at the people who have money, you don't see them; you are just after money for yourself. You think when you have money everything will be beautiful. Then you will rest and then you will enjoy, and you will celebrate and sing and dance, and do whatever you always wanted to do when there was no money to do it and no opportunity to do it.

But have you ever looked at people who have money? They are not dancing, they are not celebrating. They don't look happy. It is possible that sometimes you may come across a beggar who looks happy, but it is impossible to come across a rich man who looks happy. It is almost impossible to find a rich man who is happy. Because the beggar can still dream, that's why he can be happy. The beggar can still hope, that's why he can still be happy. He can believe that tomorrow things will be better, or the day after tomorrow things are going to be better.

There is future for the beggar, but for a rich man the whole future has disappeared. He has attained whatsoever he wanted to attain, and there is nothing in it. When the money is piled up, he suddenly feels frustrated. Whatsoever he was seeing in the money, now he can no longer find in it. That dream has disappeared.

Man continuously dreams for power, prestige, respectability. And whenever he gets it, there is frustration. The happiest people are those who never attain to their desires. The unhappiest people are those who have succeeded in attaining their desires – then there is frustration.

The nature of desire is dreaming, and you can dream only when things are not there. You can dream about the neighbor's wife – how can you dream about your own wife? Have you ever dreamt about your own wife? It never happens. You can dream about somebody else's wife – and that man may be dreaming about your wife.

Whatsoever is far away looks beautiful. Come closer, and things start changing. Reality is very shattering.

Buddha says that to be aware means not to dream, to be aware means to drop this unconscious sleep in which we live ordinarily. We are somnambulists, sleepwalkers. We go on living, but our living is very superficial. Deep down there are dreams and dreams and dreams. An undercurrent of dreaming goes on – and that undercurrent goes on corrupting our vision. That undercurrent of dreaming goes on making our eyes cloudy. That undercurrent of dreams goes on making our heads muddled.

A person who lives in a sort of sleep can never be intelligent – and awareness is the purest flame of intelligence. A man who lives in sleep becomes more and more stupid. If you live in stupor, you will become stupid, you will become dull.

This dullness has to be destroyed. And it can be destroyed only by becoming more aware. Walk with more awareness. Eat with more awareness. Talk with more awareness. Listen with more awareness.

I have heard:

> Once there was a mother monkey who had a philosophic turn of
> mind. This would make her forgetful and often inattentive to her

baby, whose name was Charles. Like many modern mothers, she just did not take enough care, distracted as she was by her thoughts. Nevertheless, she went through the routine as her mother had done before her – but not in the same spirit. She just hitched him on her back and absently scaled the palms. So there it was, and as she rummaged amongst the more middling nuts, revolving matters in her mind, baby just slipped off, and with all his young life before him too.

On the way down, Charles, who also tended to brood, called up, "Mother, why are we here?"

"We are here," she observed, "to hang on."

We are here to hang on – all his life a sleepy person is doing only that. He goes on trying to hang on – with hope, with dream, with future. He goes on somehow hanging around, as if that is the only goal in life, as if just to be here is enough. It is not enough. Just to be alive is not enough – unless you come to understand what life is. Just to be here is not enough, unless you are so fully aware of being here that in that awareness is ecstasy, that in that awareness is contentment, that in that awareness is peace.

A man can live in two ways. One is just to go on hanging around. Or, to be more aware: why I am here, and who I am. Buddha says the whole of religion is nothing but a tremendous effort to become aware.

The first sutra:

THE BUDDHA SAID:

There is nothing like lust. Lust may be said to be the most powerful passion.

People can be divided in two categories very easily and very scientifically. People whose whole life is sex-oriented . . . whatsoever they do, whatsoever they say, is just superficial; deep down their obsession with sex remains. It starts when you are a small child not even aware of what sex is. Children start playing around, and children start learning things and it continues for the whole life. When people are dying in their old age, then too they remain sex-obsessed.

This is one of my observations, that when a person is dying you can see in his face, in his eyes, what type of life he has lived. If he is dying in a reluctant way, resistant – fighting against death, does not want to die, feels helpless, wants to cling to life – then his has remained a sex-obsessed life. In that moment of great crisis, in that moment of death, all his sexuality will surface in his consciousness. People die thinking of sex; ninety-nine per cent of people die thinking of sex. You will be surprised. Only rarely is there a person who dies not thinking of sex.

A person who dies thinking of sex is immediately reborn – because his whole idea is nothing but an obsession with sex. Immediately he enters into a womb. And this has to be so, because in the moment of death your whole life becomes condensed. Whatever you have lived for simply has to be encountered in the moment of death.

If you have lived a life of awareness, then death is very relaxed, peaceful, graceful; then there is an elegance and grace to it. Then one simply slips into it, welcoming it. There is no resistance – there is beauty. There is no conflict – there is cooperation. One simply cooperates with death.

A sexual person is afraid of death because death is against sex. This has to be understood: sex is birth; death is against sex because death will destroy whatsoever birth has given to you. Death is not against life. Let me remind you – in your mind this is the dichotomy, life and death, that is wrong – death is not directly opposed to life. Death is directly opposed to sex, because sex is synonymous with birth; birth is out of sex. Death is against birth; death is against sex. Death is not against life.

If you live a life of awareness, by and by the energy that was moving in sexuality is transformed. Not that you have to transform it – just by being aware, dreams disappear; exactly as you bring a burning torch into the room and the darkness disappears. Sex is like darkness in your being. It can exist only if you are unaware. And Buddha says:

There is nothing like lust. Lust may be said to be the most powerful passion.

It starts very early. If you listen to the Freudians . . . and they have to be listened to because they are more right than your so-called saints. Your saints may be telling you convenient and comfortable truths, but truth is never convenient and never comfortable. Only lies are convenient and comfortable. Freud is telling very uncomfortable truths.

Truth is uncomfortable because you have lived a life of lies. Whenever somebody says a truth it shocks you, it hits deep, it hits on your lies, it makes you uneasy, uncomfortable. You start protecting your lies. When Freud asserted this, that a child from the very beginning is sexual, he was opposed all over the world. All so-called religious people opposed him. Now, I cannot believe it, that a religious person can oppose such a tremendous truth.

A child is born in sex, has to be sexual. A child is out of sex, has to be sexual. And children start preparing for their sexual life. I was reading a beautiful story:

> A little four-year-old girl and a three-year-old boy walked hand in hand up to the front of their neighbor's house. "We are playing house," the little girl said when the neighbor opened the door. "This is my husband and I am his wife. May we come in?"
>
> The lady was enchanted with the scene. "Do come in," she said.
>
> Once inside, she offered the children some lemonade and cookies, which they gracefully accepted. When a second glass of lemonade was offered, the little girl refused by saying, "No thanks – we have to go now – my husband just wet his pants."

It starts very early, the husband and the wife and playing house! They are preparing. And it goes to the very end.

Another story:

> The octogenarian went to the psychiatrist to complain about her husband's impotence.
>
> "And how old is your husband?" the doctor asked.
>
> "He's ninety."
>
> "And when did you first notice his disinterest in you physically?"
>
> "Well," she said, "the first time was last night – and again this morning."

A ninety-year-old man, and the wife is worried about his impotence – and she has noticed it last night and this morning too. It goes on – the whole life is obsessed with sex, from beginning to end.

You gain energy by eating food, by breathing oxygen, by exercise; by living you create energy. Man is a dynamo. He continuously creates energy. And when this energy accumulates in your being, you are uneasy, you want to throw it out – because it feels like a burden. Sex is simply used as a relief. Now this is foolish.

On the one hand, you go on working hard – how to have better food, how to have more nourishment, how to have a better house, more rest – on one hand, you want to have better air, more sun, more of the beach, more of the sky, more greenery: you work hard. Then you accumulate energy, you generate energy – and then you are worried how to throw it somewhere, how to throw it down the drain. And when you have thrown it, again you are accumulating. This is a vicious circle.

From one end you go on accumulating energy, from another end you go on throwing it. This is your whole life! – gathering energy, throwing energy; gathering energy, throwing energy. If this is all, then what is the point of it all? Why should one live? It is a repetition, it is a vicious circle. When energy is lost you are hungry for the energy; when energy is there you are ready to lose it. You find ways and means to lose it.

Buddha says that this is the most powerful thing in man's life. And if life is lived according to this, then life is a wastage, is a sheer waste. Nothing comes out of it. So much running, and never arriving anywhere. So much work, and no fulfillment. In the end comes death, and one finds one's hands are empty. Can this be the sole purpose of life? If this is the sole purpose of life, then life has no meaning, then life in itself is just accidental.

One of the most profound thinkers of the West was G.K. Chesterton. He used to say that either man is a fallen God, or some animal has gone completely off his head. Only two are the possibilities: either man is a fallen God, or some animal has gone completely off his head. If sex is the only story, then some animal has gone completely off his head. There must be something more to it; there must be something more to life, otherwise it is meaningless. Your parents lived to give birth to you. You will live to give birth to a few more children, and they will live to give birth to somebody else, and this goes on and on – but what is the purpose of it all?

Buddha says: By becoming aware, you open another door to energy. Sexual energy moves downwards; sexual energy moves towards the earth; sexual energy moves according to gravitation. When you become aware, there comes a change, a change of direction. The more aware you become, the more the sexual energy starts moving upwards – it starts going against gravitation. It starts moving towards the sky. It starts moving on the lines of grace, not on the lines of gravitation.

If sexual energy moves downwards, it is a wastage. If sexual energy starts moving upwards, you start exploding new worlds, new plenitudes of being, new altitudes of consciousness.

Now, there are two possibilities to have this energy move upwards. You can force it upwards. That's what hatha yoga does. That's why standing on the head became meaningful. Do you understand the meaning of standing on the head? It is a trick to use gravitation for sexual energy to come towards the head – but still you live under gravitation. You stand on your head; head comes lower than the sex center; energy can start moving towards the head. But how long can you stand on your head? Again you will have to stand on your feet. You don't go beyond the law of gravitation. You simply use the law of gravitation.

In fact, you cheat the law of gravitation. That is doing something illegal in a legal way. But you don't change, you are not transformed. Your being remains the same.

Hatha yoga has developed many methods to prevent sexual energy from going downwards and to force it upwards – but they are all violent, a sort of enforced conflict. The growth is not natural. You can see it on the hatha yogi's face. His face will be always tense. You will not find grace there. You will not find beauty, grandeur. You will not find God there – you will find a subtle egoism. He has cheated – he has cheated nature itself. But you cannot cheat; it cannot be a real thing.

Buddha developed a totally different methodology – the methodology of elegance, grace. For that Buddha became the symbol. Have you seen statues of Buddha? – so graceful, so divine, so peaceful; not a single flaw, not a single tension on his face – so innocent. What did he do with his energy? He never enforced it, he never fought against it, and he never cheated nature.

Buddha became aware of one very subtle thing – now science knows it very well – that every law has its opposite whether you know it or not. If there is positive electricity there must be negative electricity, otherwise the positive cannot exist. If there is a law we call gravitation, the pull towards the earth, then there must be another law – whether we know it or not – that goes against gravitation. Laws are opposed to each other, and only because of their opposition do they create a balance. Because of their opposition and contrast, they create a situation where life becomes possible.

Man exists because woman exists. Man cannot exist alone and woman cannot exist alone. The downward exists because the upward exists, and the outward exists because the inward exists. Life exists because death exists. If sex exists then there must be a law which can go beyond sex. And if sex moves downwards, there must be a law which has to be sought and discovered that moves upwards, that helps energy to move upwards.

Buddha found that the more aware you become, energy automatically starts moving upwards.

In the human body there are many centers, and each center changes the quality of the energy. Have you not seen every day that electricity can be changed into so many forms? Somewhere it becomes light, somewhere it runs the fan, somewhere it runs the motor. Just different mechanisms are needed for it and it can be used in millions of forms. In the human personality there exist many centers. The sex center is the lowest. When energy moves into that center, it becomes a generative force; you can give birth to a child. It is the lowest use of the sexual energy. If it starts moving a little higher, then different qualities start coming to it. When it comes to the heart center, it becomes love. And love gives you a totally different world.

A man whose energy is moving at the sex center can never know many things. If a woman passes by, he will only see the physical form. If your energy is moving at the heart center, when a woman passes by you will be able to see her subtle body – which is far superior, which is far more beautiful. If a woman passes by your side and your energy is moving at the heart center, you will be able to feel her heart, not only her body. And sometimes it happens that a beautiful heart can exist in a very homely body. And the contrary is also true: a very ugly heart can exist in a very beautiful body.

If you can only see the physical body you will be in trouble sooner or later – because a man does not live with a woman's body; a man lives with the woman's heart. Life is of the heart. You can choose a woman who looks beautiful and is ugly, if her heart is not beautiful, if her subtle form is not beautiful – then you will be in trouble. You can choose a man who looks very handsome, very powerful, but may be just a beast, may not have any inner beauties, may not have any inner qualities, may be just a body and nothing else – then you are bound for trouble. Then sooner or later you will have to encounter the beast and you will have to live with the beast. And you will be wondering always that "What happened to such a beautiful man? What happened to such a beautiful woman?"

If your energy moves still higher, then the highest peak is *sahasrar* – where suddenly your innermost eyes open and you can not only see the body, you can see the heart, you can see the soul. A person whose *sahasrar* has opened looks into the world, but the world is totally different because he never sees just the body. Even if he looks at a tree, he looks at the soul of the tree. The form is not the only thing – it is there, but now it is luminous from an inner light.

A person who lives at the *sahasrar* lives in a totally different world. You may think that Buddha is walking with you on the road – he is walking on a different road, he is walking in a different world. He may be just walking alongside you, but that doesn't mean anything because his vision is different. His energy is at a different altitude. He looks at the world from a different clarity.

Buddha says that lust is the most powerful thing in man's life, because it is the reservoir of all his energies. But there is no need to feel despondent:

There is nothing like lust. Lust may be said to be the most powerful passion. Fortunately, we have but one thing which is more powerful. If the thirst for truth were weaker than passion, how many of us in the world would be able to follow the way of righteousness?

He says there is one thing that is higher than lust, that is the thirst for truth. There is one thing which is higher than life and that is the search for truth. People can sacrifice their life for it. They can sacrifice their passion for it. The highest passion is for truth; Buddha calls it the passion for truth – you can call it the passion for God – it means the same thing.

That's why the person who has lived only a sexual life cannot understand the story of a Meera, the story of a Chaitanya, the story of Christ, Buddha, Krishna – he cannot understand. What type of people are these? When Jesus was there, many were wondering: "What type of man is this Jesus? What manner of man?" because they know only one life, that is of lust and sex. And this man seems to be in a totally different world. It seems as if his whole sexual energy is arrowed somewhere high in the skies. His target seems to be somewhere else – it is not in this world. It is not visible: it is invisible. You cannot touch it. You cannot measure it. You cannot see it. But his life is of great passion, his life is of great adventure.

Buddha is not in favor of renunciation, remember. He is in favor of trans-formation. The energy that is moving into sex has to be moved towards truth.

Ordinarily, people just want to explore each other: a woman wants to explore a man; a man wants to explore a woman. It seems their whole life is just an exploration into each other's being. The thirst for truth means that one wants to explore into the being of this whole existence. It is a great passion – the greatest passion. And it has to be more powerful than sex, otherwise, Buddha says, how will anybody ever move towards it?

People have moved, but how do they come to know this thirst for truth? Let me explain it to you. And much depends on how you come to feel the thirst for truth. You can come by listening to me, you can come by reading a book, you can come by seeing a man of insight – but that will not be of much help, because that will be borrowed and thirst can never be borrowed. Either it is there, or it is not there – you cannot pretend that you are thirsty. By your pretensions thirst will not be created, and that creates much misery in the world.

Many people come to me and they say they would like to search and thirst will not be created, and that creates much misery in the world.

Many people come to me and they say they would like to search and seek what truth is. I ask them only one thing: has your life, as you have lived it up to now, proved an illusion? If it has not proved an illusion, then the real thirst for truth cannot arise. When you have seen the illusoriness of your life, only then does a real thirst arise – to know what truth is. If you are still in the illusion of life, if you are still enchanted by it, if you are still hallucinated by it, if you are still in that hypnosis of desiring and dreaming, then talking about truth will again be only another illusion, another desire. It will not help.

Truth cannot be one of your desires. Truth can only be there when all the desires have proved to be futile, and your whole energy is available and you don't know where to go, because the whole life seems to be meaningless. You are stuck. You are tremendously frustrated. You have failed and all your dreams have disappeared. You are shattered to the very roots. You are standing there throbbing with energy not knowing where to go. Then that energy becomes a pool and creates a new thirst in you: the thirst to know the truth. When the world has been known as an illusion, only then . . .

So experience the world as deeply as you can. Don't escape from anywhere – not even from sex. Never escape from anywhere. Just do one thing: wherever you are and wherever your dreams are moving, go with alertness, awareness. Even if you go into sex, make it a meditation, be watchful about what is happening. And by and by you will be able to see the illusoriness of it, the futility, the meaningless repetition, the boredom, the dullness, the death that goes on coming closer through it. The more you waste your energy, the closer you are to death.

I have heard:

> A traveling salesman was passing through a small hick town in the West when he saw a little old man sitting in a rocking-chair on the stoop of his house. The little man looked so contented the salesman couldn't resist going over and talking to him.
>
> "You don't look as if you have a care in the world," the salesman told him. "What is your formula for a long and happy life?"
>
> "Well," replied the little old man, "I smoke six packs of cigarettes a day, I drink a quart of bourbon every four hours, and six cases of beer a week. I never wash and I go out every night."
>
> "My goodness," exclaimed the salesman, "that's just great!
> How old are you?"
>
> "Twenty-five," was the reply.

You can go on wasting energy . . .

Each step taken in illusion is taken towards death. Each move which you take into lust you have taken towards death. So take it carefully and be aware. Be aware of what you really want through it. Is it just a habit? Is it just a natural hypnosis? Is it just that you go on doing it because you don't know what else to do? Is it just an occupation? Is it just a forgetfulness from the worries of life? Or what is it?

And don't go with any prejudice. Don't listen to what the saints have said. They may say it is bad, but don't listen to it – and they may be right, but you have to find it out by your own experience. Only then, and only then, do you start moving towards truth. Only your experience can bring you to truth; nobody else's experience.

Once you have seen the truth of it, that there is nothing in it, energy is relieved from the burden, energy is relieved from the old patterns, and energy goes on gathering inside you.

Scientists have discovered a law that quantitative change becomes qualitative at a certain stage. For example, if you heat water it evaporates only when the heat is one hundred degrees, never before it. At ninety degrees it may be hot, but not evaporating. At ninety-nine degrees it is very hot, but not evaporating. And just one degree more, at one hundred degrees, and a sudden jump, a leap, and the water starts moving.

And have you seen the change? Water naturally flows downwards, but when it evaporates it starts flowing upwards – it has taken a different route. And you have not done anything but simply heated it to a certain degree. A certain quantity of heat and a qualitative change happens. Water is visible; vapor becomes invisible. Water goes downwards; vapor goes upwards.

Exactly the same happens in the sexual energy: a certain amount, a certain quantity, has to be accumulated before the change happens. You have to become a reservoir of energy, and out of sheer quantity at a certain moment there is a jump; energy no more moves downwards – energy starts moving upwards, and exactly like vapor.

When energy moves downwards, sex is very visible. That's why scientists cannot discover what happens when the energy moves upwards – it becomes invisible. It becomes immaterial. It certainly moves, but there is no passage for it. If you dissect the body of a buddha, you will not find a certain passage for sexual energy to move upwards – there is no passage. A passage is not needed. If water moves downwards, a channel is needed; but when water becomes vapor, no channel is needed – it simply moves and becomes invisible. Exactly the same happens with sexual energy.

Awareness is heat. In India, we have called it precisely that: *tap* – *tap* means heat. *Tap* does not mean that you stand under the hot sun; it simply means you bring more fire of awareness inside you. That fire of awareness heats your sexual energy: this is the inner alchemy – and energy starts going upwards.

First your sex will become love, and then it will become meditation or prayer. If you follow the terminology of devotion, you can call it prayer; if you follow a more scientific terminology, then you can call it meditation. And once your energy is moving upwards, then you see things in a totally different light. I have heard:

> A little old man was sitting on a bus humming, "Dee dee dum dum, dee dee dum."
>
> The bus driver turned around and noticed a suitcase blocking the aisle. He turned to the old man and said, "Would you mind moving the suitcase?" to which the old man replied, "Dee dee dum dum, dee dee dum."
>
> In complete frustration, the bus driver jumped up and took the suitcase and threw it out the bus window and glared at the old man and shouted, "Now what do you have to say?"
>
> The old man looked at him and smiled and said, "Dee dee dum dum, dee dee dum – it's not my suitcase."

Once you have started moving, even death is not your death, even the body is not your body, even the mind is not your mind. You can go on singing: Dee dee dum dum . . . Even when death approaches you, you can go on humming – because the suitcase is not yours.

A man of awareness can die so easily, so peacefully. He lives peacefully, he dies peacefully. A man of sexuality lives restlessly, dies restlessly. It is your choice.

Buddha is not for repression – he cannot be, notwithstanding what Buddhist interpreters have said down the ages. I don't agree with them. The interpretation must be wrong – because I know it from my own experience that repression cannot help a person, repression can never become a transfiguration. Repression drags you down.

It is not repression: it is awareness. Of course, from the outside it may look like repression. You are rushing towards money; suddenly on the road you come across a treasure, and somebody else is passing by. He also looks at it but is not interested. What will you think about that man? You were afraid that he might claim the treasure, he might start asking that it has to be divided in two parts – but he simply goes on, he does not bother about it. You will think either he is mad, or he is a renunciate, he has renounced the world and repressed the desire for money.

You cannot understand that there can be a man who cannot see anything in money. You will think it is impossible because you see so much in it. Your whole life seems to be meaningless if there is no money. Money seems to be your whole life. How can you believe that there can be a man for whom money is simply meaningless? Only two are the possibilities: either the man is so stupid that he does not know the difference between money and no money; or he has repressed his desire – he has repressed his desire, his greed, his ambition.

When a man like Buddha happens in the world, people interpret it according to their own minds. He looks so far away, only two are the possibilities: those who are against him, they will say he is crazy; those who are for him, they will say he has disciplined his life, skillfully he has dropped his greed, lust. But both are wrong. Both have to be wrong because both are unable to understand a buddha. You can understand a buddha only when you are a buddha; there is no other way to understand. If you want to understand somebody who is standing on the peak of a Himalayan hill, you have to go to that peak – only then will his vision become your vision.

I would like to say that all the interpretations about Buddha are wrong – wrong in the sense that they all imply that it is as if he is teaching repression. He is not teaching repression. He is simply teaching awareness. In awareness, things change. Through repression, you may manage somehow but things remain the same.

I was reading about a church and about a priest:

> A topless girl tried to enter the church. The vicar stopped her at the door. "But, Vicar, you can't stop me from going to church," she protested. "I have a divine right."
>
> "They're both divine," he said, "but that is not the question – you'll have to go home and put on something that is more respectable."

Now she says, "I have a divine right," and the priest says, "They both are divine." The priest's repressed mind – he must be looking at her breasts. He says, "They both are divine, but still you will have to go home and put on something that is more respectable."

You can repress a desire, but you cannot uproot it. It will come in subtle ways. It will surface in many forms. It may take such disguises that you may not even be able to detect it. A repressed person is not a transformed person. He remains the same – he simply manages to be somebody else who he is not.

Buddha is not for repression. Buddha is for transformation. Repression is very easy. You can repress your sex – that's what so many saints are doing. You can drop out of the society, you can run away from women. You can go to the Himalayan caves and sit there, and you can think that you have attained to celibacy – but this is not celibacy. Sitting there in your Himalayan cave, you will still dream about women – even more so, because you will be so far away from women. Your fantasy will become more psychedelic and colorful. Of course, you will fight with it, but by fighting you can force the desire deep into your unconscious – you cannot uproot it. By fighting nobody is ever changed. Only by awareness is a person changed.

Awareness is not a fight. What is awareness? Awareness is neither accepting nor rejecting.

There is a famous saying of Tilopa: "Truly, because of our accepting and rejecting, we have not the suchness of things" – we miss the suchness of things. We cannot become aware of what reality is because we accept or we reject. When we accept, we indulge. When we reject, we repress. Buddha says: Don't accept, don't reject – just be alert, just see. Look, with no prejudice for or against.

If you can be in such an indifferent *udasin* – in such non-valuing, non-judging awareness – things start changing of their own accord.

Tilopa says:

> It never leaves this place
> and is always perfect.
> When you look for it,
> you find you can't see it.
> You can't get it, you can't be rid of it.
> When you do neither – there it is!
> When you are silent, it speaks.
> When you speak, it is silent.

"You cannot get it, you cannot get rid of it" – it is always there. "When you do neither, there it is."

Awareness is not something that you have to do. Awareness is not something that you have to force upon yourself, impose upon yourself. When you do nothing, it is there. Your doing is your undoing.

Fortunately, we have but one thing which is more powerful. If the thirst for truth were weaker than passion, how many of us in the world would be able to follow the way of righteousness?

The Buddha said:

Men who are addicted to the passions are like the torch-carrier running against the wind; his hands are sure to be burnt.

You can look: everybody's hands are burnt. But you never look at your own hands, you always look at others' hands and you say, "Yes, their hands seem to be burnt but I will be more clever. I am more clever; I will carry the torch and run against the wind and show you that I am an exception."

Nobody is an exception. Existence does not allow any exceptions. Your hands will also be burnt if you are running, rushing against the wind and carrying a torch, a burning torch. Lust is rushing against the wind. Nobody has come out of it unburned.

But people go on looking at each other. Nobody looks at himself. The moment you start looking at yourself you have become a sannyasin.

I was reading:

> Mrs. Cantor suspected her husband of playing around with the maid. Having to spend a few days with her sick mother, she told her small son, Harvey, to keep an eye on Papa and the maid.
>
> As soon as she returned she asked: "Harvey, did anything happen?"
>
> "Well," said the boy, "Papa and the maid went into the bedroom and took off their clothes and . . . "
>
> "Stop! Stop!" shouted Mrs. Cantor. "We will wait until Papa comes home."
>
> Papa was met at the door by his irate wife, cringing maid and confused son. "Harvey, tell me what happened with Papa and the maid," stormed Mrs. Cantor.
>
> "As I told you, ma," said Harvey. "Papa and the maid went into the bedroom and took off their clothes."
>
> "Yes! Yes! Go on, Harvey!" said Mrs. Cantor impatiently. "What did they do then?"
>
> Replied Harvey: "Why, mother, they did the same thing you and Uncle Bernie did when Papa was in Chicago."

Everybody goes on looking, everybody goes on seeing others' faults, flaws, foolishnesses. Nobody looks himself. The day you start looking at yourself you are a sannyasin; the day you start looking at yourself a great change is on the way. You have taken the first step – against lust, towards love; against desire, towards desirelessness – because when you see your own hands, you see that they have been burnt so many times, you are carrying so many wounds.

Looking at others is just a way of avoiding looking at oneself. Whenever you criticize somebody else, watch: it is a trick of the mind so that you can forgive yourself. People go on criticizing others; when they criticize the whole world they feel very good. In comparison they can think they are not worse than other people; in fact, they are better. That's why when you criticize somebody, you exaggerate, you go to the very extreme; you make a mountain out of a molehill; you go on making the mountain bigger and bigger and bigger, then your own mountain looks very small. You feel happy.

Stop this! This is not going to help you. This is very suicidal. Here you are not to think about others. Your life is yours. Thinking about others is not going to be of any benefit. Think about yourself. Meditate about your own self. Become more aware of what you are doing here – just hanging around? or are you really doing something? And the only thing that can be relied upon is awareness. Only awareness can you carry through death, through the door of death – nothing else.

A beautiful parable comes:

The lord of heaven offered a beautiful fairy to the Buddha, desiring to tempt him to the evil path. But the Buddha said: Be gone! What use have I for the leather bag filled with filth which you have brought to me? Then, the God reverently bowed and asked the Buddha about the essence of the way in which, having been instructed by the Buddha, it is said, he attained the srotapanna *fruit.*

A beautiful parable: Brahma came to Buddha. . . . Hindus have never forgiven Buddhists for inventing such beautiful tales, because Hindus think that Brahma is the creator of the world. And Buddhists say Brahma came to Buddha to be instructed on the path. Of course, as a test he brought a beautiful fairy.

It is significant because there are only two types of man: the man of sex and the man of truth. So if Buddha is really the man of truth then he cannot be deluded, then you cannot create any hallucination for him. The most beautiful fairy will not mean anything to him. And that is going to be the touchstone as to whether he has attained to truth. When a person is absolutely beyond sex, only then; otherwise his energy is still moving, still moving into the direction of lust, still going downwards.

The lord of heaven offered a beautiful fairy to the Buddha, desiring to tempt him to the evil path.

That temptation is a test, and temptation comes only at the very end. In all the world religions you must have come across stories like this. When Jesus is just close, arriving home, the devil tempts him. When Buddha has reached just very close, Brahma comes and tempts him. Such stories are there in the life of Mahavira, in the life of everyone who has attained to truth. There must be a meaning to these parables.

I don't mean to say that it happened exactly as it is told in the parable. These are symbolic parables; they are not historical facts – but they are very meaningful.

I was reading about Baal Shem, a Hasid mystic, the founder of Hasidism. A disciple came to him one day and said, "Master, how can I avoid temptation? How can I avoid the devil tempting me?"

Baal Shem looked at him and said, "Wait! There is no need for you to avoid any temptation, because right now temptation cannot be given to you – you are not worthy of it."

He said, "What do you mean?"

He said, "Temptation comes only at the last moment. Right now the devil is not worried about you. In fact, the devil is not chasing you at all – you are chasing the devil – so you don't be worried about temptation. It is not going to happen to you so soon. And when it happens, I will take care of it. I will tell you what to do."

The temptation comes only at the last moment. Why? Because when the sexual energy is coming to a point, the hundred-degree point, then the whole past, millions of lives lived in sexuality, pull you back. The devil is not a person somewhere – it is just your past. Many lives of mechanical sex pull you back. You hesitate for a moment whether to take the jump or not.

Just as when a river comes to the ocean she must be hesitating for a moment before she loses herself into the ocean, she must be looking backwards with nostalgia: the beautiful mountains, the snow-peaked mountains, the forests, the valleys, the song of the birds, the banks, the people, the journey – the past, thousands of miles. And suddenly now here comes a moment: you jump and you are lost for ever. The river must be thinking: "To be, or not to be?" – a hesitation, a trembling, a shaking to the very foundations.

That's what temptation is. When Buddha has come to the point where the energy is ready to take the ultimate jump and become non-sexual, when desire is ready to dissolve into desirelessness, when the mind is ready to die and the no-mind is ready to be born – it is such a great jump that it is natural one should hesitate. That is the meaning of the parable.

The Buddha said: Be gone! What use have I for the leather bag filled with filth which you have brought to me?

When a man has come to that point, then body is meaningless; then body is nothing but a bag, a skin bag, filled with filth. In fact, that's how the body is. If you don't believe it, go to the surgeon some time and see a body being opened – and then you will believe Buddha. Or go to the hospital to see a post mortem, when the whole body is dissected, and then you will see what he is saying.

In my town once it happened: a man was shot dead and there was a post mortem. I was just a small child – somehow I managed, I persuaded the doctor; his son was my friend so I succeeded in persuading him: "Just allow me to see, I would like to see." He resisted, "But why do you want to see?" I said, "I have come across the saying of Buddha that the body is nothing but a bag full of filth. Just let me have one glimpse!"

He allowed me, and he said, "Okay, you can stay." But I said, "Now there is no need to stay and I cannot stay anyhow." It was stinking so much, and the stomach was open –just filth and nothing else.

Each child should be brought to a post mortem. Buddha used to send his disciples to the burning place, where bodies are burnt, just to watch and meditate there. He said, "Unless you are completely aware of what the body is you will not drop your illusion about the beauty of the body and dreams about the body." He's right. He said:

Be gone! What use have I for the leather bag filled with filth which you have brought to me? Then, the God reverently bowed and asked the Buddha about the essence of the way . . .

The touchstone proved that Buddha was real gold.

Then, the God reverently bowed down . . .

In Buddhist mythology the gods are as lustful as man – even more so. Their whole life is nothing but one of lust. Brahma, the Lord of Heaven . . . *bowed down and asked about the essence of the way, in which having been instructed by the Buddha, it is said, he attained the* srotapanna *fruit.*

Srotapanna means one who has entered the stream – *srotapanna*: one who has entered into the stream – of consciousness, awareness, alertness. That is the essential message of Buddha: no prayer, no ritual; no priest, no temple – you are the priest, you are the ritual, you are the temple. Only one thing is needed. Buddha has reduced the requirement to the minimum; he is absolutely mathematical. He said only awareness is enough; if you can be aware, everything will take care of itself.

> Two drunks were weaving along the railroad tracks. One said, "I never saw so many steps in my life."
>
> The other said, "It's not the steps that bother me, it's the low railing."

The only thing that is needed somehow is to bring them out of their drunkenness.

Two other drunks were riding a roller coaster, when one turned to
the other and said, "We may be making good time, but I've got a
feeling we're on the wrong bus."

Everybody is on the wrong bus – unconsciousness is the wrong bus. Then wherever
you are makes no difference. And whatsoever you do makes no difference. In your
unconsciousness, whatsoever you do is going to be wrong. Wrong is that which is
done in unconsciousness, and right is that which is done consciously.

Edwin Arnold has written one of the most beautiful books about Buddha,
The Light of Asia. A few lines to sum up:

"This is peace – to conquer love of self and lust of life, to tear deep-rooted
passion from the breast, to still the inward strife; for love, to clasp eternal beauty
close; for glory, to be lord of self; for pleasure, to live beyond the gods; for
countless wealth, to lay up lasting treasure of perfect service rendered, duties
done in charity, soft speech, and stainless days: these riches shall not fade away
in life, nor any death dispraise. This is peace – to conquer love of self and lust of
life ..."

This is the whole essence of Buddha's message. Peace is not to be practiced:
it is a by-product of awareness. Love is not to be practiced: it is a by-product of
awareness. Righteousness is not to be practiced: it is a by-product of awareness.

Awareness is the remedy for all ills, because awareness makes you healthy,
whole, and of course holy.

Enough for today.

Chapter 14:

Become a Driftwood

THE BUDDHA SAID:

Those who are following the way should behave like a piece of timber which is drifting along a stream. If the log is neither held by the banks, nor seized by men, nor obstructed by the gods, nor kept in the whirlpool, nor itself goes to decay, I assure you that this log will finally reach the ocean. If monks walking on the way are neither tempted by the passions, nor led astray by some evil influences, but steadily pursue their course for nirvana, I assure you that these monks will finally attain enlightenment.

THE BUDDHA SAID:

Rely not on your own will. Your own will is not trustworthy. Guard yourselves against sensualism, for it surely leads to the path of evil. Your own will becomes trustworthy only when you have attained arhatship.

The way of the Buddha is known as via negativa – the path of negation. This attitude, this approach has to be understood.

Buddha's approach is unique. All other religions of the world are positive religions, they have a positive goal – call it God, moksha, liberation, salvation, Self-realization, but there is a goal to be achieved. And positive effort is needed on the part of the seeker. Unless you make hard effort you will not reach to the goal.

Buddha's approach is totally different, diametrically opposite. He says: You are already that which you want to become, the goal is within you, it is your own nature. You are not to achieve it. It is not in the future, it is not somewhere else. It is you right now, this very moment. But there are a few obstacles – those obstacles have to be removed.

It is not that you have to attain godhood – godhood is your nature – but there are a few obstacles which have to be removed. Once those obstacles are removed, you are that which you have always been seeking. Even when you were not aware of who you are, you were That. You cannot be other than That, you cannot be otherwise.

Obstacles have to be eliminated, dropped. So nothing else has to be added to you. The positive religion tries to add something to you: virtue, righteousness, meditation, prayer. The positive religion says you are lacking something; you have to be in search of that which you are lacking. You have to accumulate something.

Buddha's negative approach says you are not lacking anything. In fact, you are possessing too many things which are not needed. You have to drop something.

It is like this: a man goes trekking into the Himalayas. The higher you start reaching, the more you will feel the weight of the things you are carrying with you. Your luggage will become more and more heavy. The higher the altitude, the more heavy your luggage will become. You will have to drop things. If you want to reach to the highest peak, you will have to drop all.

Once you have dropped all, once you don't possess anything, once you have become a zero, a nothingness, a nobody, you have reached.

Something has to be eliminated, not added to you. Something has to be dropped, not accumulated.

When Buddha attained, somebody asked him, "What have you attained?"

He laughed. He said, "I have not attained anything – because whatsoever I have attained was always with me. On the contrary, I have lost many things. I have lost my ego. I have lost my thoughts, my mind. I have lost all that I used to feel I possessed. I have lost my body – I used to think I was the body. I have lost all that. Now I exist as pure nothingness. But this is my achievement.

Let me explain it to you, because this is very central.

According to Buddha's approach, in the beginningless beginning of existence there was absolute sleep; existence was fast asleep, snoring, what Hindus call *sushupti*, a state of dreamless sleep. The whole existence was asleep in *sushupti*. Nothing was moving, everything was at rest – so tremendously, so utterly at rest, you can say it was not existing at all.

When you move into *sushupti* every night, when dreams stop, you again move into that primordial nothingness. And if in the night there are not a few moments of that primordial nothingness, you don't feel rejuvenated, you don't feel revitalized. If the whole night you dream, and turn and toss in the bed, in the morning you are more tired than you were when you went to bed. You could not dissolve, you could not lose yourself.

If you have been in *sushupti*, in a dreamless state, that means you moved into that beginningless beginning again. From there is energy. From there you come rested, vitalized, new. Again full of juice, full of life and zest. That, Buddha says, was the beginning; but he calls it the beginningless beginning. It was like *sushupti*, it was tremendously unconscious; there was no consciousness in it. It was just like samadhi, with only one difference: in samadhi one is fully awake. In that *sushupti*, in that dreamless deep sleep, there was no consciousness, not even a single flame of consciousness – a dark night. It is also a state of *sat-chit-ananda*, but the state is unconscious.

In the morning when you become awake, then you say, "Last night was beautiful, I slept very deeply. It was so beautiful and so full of bliss." But this you say in the morning. When you were really in that sleep, you were not aware; you were absolutely unconscious. When you awake in the morning, then you look retrospectively backwards and then you recognize: "Yes, it was beautiful!"

When a person awakes in samadhi, then he recognizes that: "All my lives of the past, they were all blissful. I have been in a tremendously enchanted, magic world. I have never been miserable." Then one recognizes, but right now you cannot recognize – you are unconscious.

The primordial state is full of bliss, but there is nobody to recognize it. Trees still exist in that primordial state; mountains and the ocean and the clouds and the deserts, they still exist in that primordial consciousness. It is a state of unconsciousness.

This Buddha calls nothingness, pure nothingness, because there was no distinction, no demarcation. It was nebulous: no form, no name. It was like a dark night.

Then came the explosion. Now, scientists also talk about this explosion; they call it "the big bang". Then everything exploded. The nothingness disappeared and things appeared. It is still a hypothesis, even for scientists, because nobody can go back. For scientists it is a hypothesis, the most probable hypothesis at the most.

There are many theories proposed, propounded, but the "big bang theory" is accepted generally – that out of that nothingness things exploded, like a seed explodes, becomes a tree. And in the tree then millions of seeds; and then they explode. A single seed can fill the whole earth with greenery. This is what explosion means.

Have you observed the fact? – such mystery . . . a small seed, barely visible, can explode and fill the whole earth with forests. Not only the whole earth: all the earths possible in existence. A single seed! And if you break the seed, what will you find inside it? Just nothingness, just pure nothing. Out of this nothingness, the Whole has evolved.

For scientists it is just a hypothesis, an inference. For a buddha it is not a hypothesis – it is his experience. He has known this happening within himself. I will try to explain it to you, how one comes to know this beginningless beginning – because you cannot go back, but there is a way to go on moving ahead. And, just as everything moves in a circle, time also moves in a circle.

In the West, the concept of time is linear; time moves in a line, horizontal; it goes on and on and on. But in the East, we believe in a circular time. And the Eastern concept of time is closer to reality, because every movement is circular. The earth moves in a circle, the moon moves in a circle, the stars move in a circle. The year moves in a circle, the life moves in a circle: birth, childhood, youth, old age – again birth! What you call death is again birth. Again childhood, again youth . . . and the wheel goes on moving. And the year goes round and round: comes summer, and the rains, and the winter and again summer.

Everything is moving in a circle! So why should there be an exception – time? Time also moves in a circle. One cannot go backwards, but if you go on ahead, moving ahead, one day time starts moving in a circle. You reach to the beginningless beginning, or, now you can call it the endless end.

Buddha has known it, experienced it.

What the scientists call "the big bang" I call "cosmic orgasm". And that seems to me more meaningful. "Big bang" looks a little ugly, too technological, inhuman. "Cosmic orgasm" – the cosmos exploded into orgasm. Millions of forms were born out of it. And it was a tremendously blissful experience, so let us call it "cosmic orgasm".

In that orgasm three things developed. First, the universe; what we in the East call *sat*. Out of the universe developed life; what we call *ananda*. And out of life developed mind, what we call *chit*. *Sat* means being; *ananda* means celebrating the being – when a tree comes to bloom, it is celebrating its being. And *chit* means consciousness – when you have become conscious about your bliss, about your celebration. These three states: *sat-chit-ananda*.

Man has come up to the mind. The rocks are still at the first stage: universe – they exist but they don't flower, they don't celebrate; they are closed, coiled upon themselves. Some day they will start moving, some day they will open their petals, but right now they are caved within themselves, completely closed.

Trees, animals, they have come to the next stage: life – so happy, so beautiful, so colorful. The birds go on singing, and the trees go on blooming. This is the second stage: life. The third stage, only man has reached it: the state of mind, the state of *chit* – consciousness.

Buddha says: These three are like a dream. The first, the beginningless beginning, the primordial state, is like sleep – *sushupti*. These three are like a dream; these three are like a drama that goes on unfolding. If you move beyond mind, if you start moving towards meditation, that is towards no-mind, again another explosion happens, but now it is no longer explosion – it is implosion. Just as one day explosion happened and millions of things were born out of nothingness, so when implosion happens, forms, names disappear – again nothingness is born out of it. The circle is complete.

The scientists talk only about explosion, they don't talk about implosion yet – which is very illogical. Because if explosion is possible, then implosion is also possible.

A seed is thrown into the earth. It explodes. A tree is born, then on the tree again seeds are born. What is a seed now? When the seed explodes, it is a tree. When the tree implodes, it is again a seed. The seed was carrying a tree; it opened itself and became a tree. Now the tree again closes itself, caves in, becomes a small seed.

If explosion happened in the world, as scientists now trust, then the Buddhist idea of implosion is also a reality. Explosion cannot exist without implosion. They both go together. Implosion means again mind moves into life, life moves into universe, universe moves into nothingness – then the circle is complete. Nothingness moves into universe, universe moves into life, life moves into mind, mind again moves into life, life again into universe, universe again into nothingness . . . the circle is complete.

After implosion, when it has happened, when everything has again come to nothingness, now there is a difference. The first nothingness was unconscious; this second nothingness is conscious. The first was like darkness; the second is like light. The first was like night; the second is like day. The first we called *sushupti*; the second we will call *jagriti* – awareness, fully awake.

This is the whole circle. The first scientists call "the big bang theory" because there was so much explosion and so much noise. It was a big bang. Just a moment before everything was silent, there was no noise, no sound, and after one moment, when the existence exploded, there was so much sound and so much noise. All sorts of noises started.

What happens when the explosion disappears into an implosion? The soundless sound. Now there is no longer any noise. Again everything is silent.

This is what Zen calls the sound of one hand clapping. This is what Hindus have called *anahatnad omkar* – the soundless sound.

The first Hindus have called *nadavisphot* – big bang, the sound exploded. And the second is again when the sound moves into silence; the story is complete. Science is still clinging to the half story; the other half is missing. And one who watches this whole play – from *sushupti*, dark night of the soul, to dream, and from dream to awareness – the one who watches it all is the witness: the fourth state we call *turiya* – the one who witnesses all. That one known, you become a buddha; that one known, experienced, you become arhat – you have attained.

But the whole point to be understood is this: that all the time, when you are asleep or dreaming or awake, you are That. Sometimes not aware, sometimes aware – that is the only difference – but your nature remains the same.

T.S. Eliot has written a few beautiful lines:

We shall not cease from exploration
and the end of all our exploring
will be to arrive where we started
and know the place for the first time.

This is the meaning of Buddha's renunciation, his path of via negativa. You have to come to the point from where you started. You have to know that which you are already. You have to achieve that which is already achieved. You have to achieve that which, in the nature of things, cannot be lost; there is no way to lose contact with it. At the most we can become unconscious about it.

Religion means becoming conscious of that which you are. It is not a search for something new; it is just an effort to know that which has always been there, is eternal. From the beginningless beginning to the endless end it is always there.

Because the path is negative, there are a few difficulties about it. It is very difficult to be attracted to Buddhism, because ordinarily the mind wants something positive to cling to, the mind wants something to achieve – and Buddha says there is nothing to achieve, rather, on the contrary, you have to lose something. Just the idea of losing something is very unappealing, because our whole concept is of having more and more and more. And Buddha says having is the problem. The more you have, the less you are; because the more you have, the less you can recognize yourself – you are lost.

Your emptiness, your space is covered too much by things. A rich man is very poor – poor because he has no space left, poor because everything is occupied, poor because he does not know any emptiness in his being. And through emptiness you have the glimpses of the primordial and the ultimate – and they are both the same.

It is very difficult to be attracted to Buddhism. Only very, very rare people who have a quality of tremendous intelligence can be attracted to it. It cannot become a mass religion. And when it became, it became only when it lost all its originality, when it compromised with the masses.

In India Buddhism disappeared, because the followers of Buddha insisted for its purity. There are people who think that it is because Hindu philosophers and Hindu mystics refuted Buddhism, that's why Buddhism disappeared from India – that is wrong. It cannot be refuted. Nobody has ever refuted it. There is no possibility of refuting it, because in the first place it is not based on logic.

If something is based on logic, you can destroy it by logic. If something is based on logical proof, you can refute it. Buddhism is not based on logic at all. It is based on experience – you cannot refute it. It is very existential. It does not believe in any metaphysics – how can you refute it? And it never asserts anything about any concept. It simply describes the innermost experience. It has no philosophy so philosophers cannot refute it.

But this is true, that Buddhism disappeared from India. The cause of its disappearance, the basic cause is: Buddha and his followers insisted for its purity. The very insistence for its purity became an unbridgeable gap. The masses could not understand it – only very rare people, very, very cultured, intelligent, aristocratic, few, a chosen few could understand it, what Buddha means. And those who understood it, in their very understanding they were transformed. But for the masses it was meaningless. It lost its hold on the masses.

In China it succeeded. In Tibet, in Ceylon, in Burma, in Thailand, in Japan, it succeeded – because the missionaries, the Buddhist missionaries who went out of India, seeing what had happened in India, became very compromising, they compromised. They started talking in the positive language. They started talking about achievement, bliss, heaven – from the back door they brought everything that Buddha had denied.

Again the masses were happy. The whole of China, the whole of Asia was converted to Buddhism – except India. In India they tried to give just the pure, without any compromise; that was not possible. In China, Buddhism became a mass religion, but then it lost its truth.

Let me tell you one anecdote:

> A junior devil has been sent to earth to look around and see how things are progressing. He quickly returns to hell, horrified, and obtains an interview with Beelzebub, the chief devil himself.
>
> "Sir," he splutters, "something awful has happened! There is a

man with a beard walking around on earth, speaking Truth, and people are beginning to listen to him. Something has to be done immediately."

Beelzebub smiles pleasantly, puffing on his pipe but making no comment.

"Sir! You don't realize the seriousness of the situation," continues the distraught junior devil. "Pretty soon all will be lost!"

Beelzebub removes his pipe slowly, taps it out on the ashtray, and sits back in his swivel-chair, hands behind his head.

"Don't worry, son," he counsels. "We will let it go on a little longer and, when it has progressed far enough, we will step in and help them to organize!"

And once a religion is organized, it is dead – because you can organize a religion only when you compromise with the masses. You can organize a religion only when you follow the desires of the common mass. You can organize a religion only when you are ready to make it a politics and you are ready to lose its religiousness.

A religion can be organized only when it is no longer a religion. That's to say: a religion cannot be organized as religion. Organized, it is no more religion. A religion basically remains unorganized, remains a little chaotic, remains a little disorderly – because religion is freedom.

Now the sutras:

THE BUDDHA SAID:

Those who are following the way should behave like a piece of timber which is drifting along a stream. If the log is neither held by the banks, nor seized by men, nor obstructed by the gods, nor kept in the whirlpool, nor itself goes to decay, I assure you that this log will finally reach the ocean.

A very significant sutra. The first thing Buddha says: Surrender! The most basic thing is: surrender to reality. The more you fight, the more you are in conflict with it, the more you will create obstructions. The more you fight with reality, the more you will be a loser. Of course, through fighting you can attain to the ego, you can become a very strong ego, but your ego will be the hindrance.

Those who are following the way should behave like a piece of timber which is drifting along a stream.

They should be completely surrendered to the river of life, completely surrendered to the river of existence. In deep surrender, the ego disappears. And when the ego is not there, for the first time you become aware of that which has always been there.

The ego functions as a blindfold on your eyes. The ego keeps you blind; it does not allow you to see the truth. It creates too much smoke and the flame tends to be lost in it. The ego is like too many dark clouds around the sun – the sun gets lost. Not that those clouds can destroy the sun, but they can hide it.

Those who are following the way should behave like a piece of timber . . .

. . . they should become driftwood. Have you watched a piece of timber moving in the river? – with no idea of its own, not even trying to reach anywhere, not even knowing where this river is going. If it moves north, the timber moves north. If it moves south, the timber moves south. The timber is totally in tune with the river. This tuning with the river is what surrender is all about.

But the idea of becoming driftwood has no appeal. People come to me and they say: "Help us to have more will power. Help us to become more self-confident. Why are we missing will power? How can we have a stronger will?"

Everybody – if you watch inside yourself you will find the same desire hidden there: how to have more will power. Everybody wants to become omnipotent, omniscient, omnipresent; everybody wants to become powerful. Somebody wants to become powerful through having more money; of course, money brings power. Somebody wants to have power by becoming a prime minister or a president of a country; of course, politics brings power. Somebody wants to become powerful by becoming virtuous, because virtue brings respectability. Somebody wants to become powerful by becoming religious, because religion gives you a halo of power, of divine forces. Somebody wants to gain power by becoming more knowledgeable; knowledge is power. But it seems that everybody wants to be powerful; this seems to be the ordinary desire of the human mind.

And Buddha says, become a driftwood – what does he mean? What does he want to convey? He is saying: Drop this idea of becoming powerful. That is your hindrance. That's why you have become powerless – the very idea that "I should become powerful" proves nothing but your impotence. All impotent people want to become omnipotent; they would like to have all the power there is in their hands – but why? Ego is an illness, a megalomania.

Buddha says become a driftwood – powerless, helpless. Watch timber going down the stream: how helpless, no struggle, no conflict, simply cooperates. In fact, to say "cooperates" is also not right. The driftwood is not there in any ego sense, so there is no point in saying it cooperates. It has no conflict, it has no cooperation. It is simply not there. Only the river is there. The timber is completely surrendered.

This is how a disciple should be. And when somebody becomes so much surrendered, Buddha says he has become a *srotapanna*. *Srotapanna* means one who has entered the stream.

In the East, the concept of surrender has been developed very minutely, in details. But this example of a driftwood is almost perfect; you cannot improve upon it. Sometimes, sitting by the side of the river, watch timber flowing down. See how peacefully, how relaxed, how very trusting the driftwood is. No doubt. If the river is going south, it must be good to go to the south. None of its own desire, no private goal – "The river's goal is my goal." The river is already going towards the ocean. The river is going to dissolve into the vast infinity of the ocean. If you can surrender to it, that will be enough.

Coming to a master and surrendering to a master is nothing but entering into the stream. The master is one who is surrendered to the river of existence. It is difficult for you to see the river of existence, it is very invisible. It is not material, it is very immaterial. It is difficult to hold it in your hands, but when you stand by the side of a buddha at least you can hold Buddha's hand.

And he has become a driftwood. He is floating in the river. You cannot see the river right now; you don't have that much refined consciousness yet. Your eyes are not yet ready to see that river. But you can see Buddha, you can hold his hand. You can see Christ, you can hold his hand.

Buddha is surrendered to the infinite river of life – you can at least take courage and be surrendered to Buddha. By surrendering to Buddha you will be surrendering to the river to which Buddha is surrendered. A master is just a midway passage, a door.

That's why Jesus goes on saying again and again, "I am the door." Jesus is reported to have said: "Nobody achieves unless he passes through me." Christians have misinterpreted it. They think nobody reaches to God unless one follows Christ. That is not the meaning. When Jesus says: "Nobody reaches unless he passes through me," he is saying, "unless he passes through one who has already attained." He is not talking about Jesus the son of Mary and Joseph; he is talking about Christ – not about Jesus. He is talking about a state of consciousness.

"Christ" is the name of a state of consciousness. "Buddha" is also a name for a state of consciousness. When somebody is enlightened, he is no more – he is just a door. If you surrender to him, you will be able to surrender in a roundabout way, in an indirect way, to the stream of life itself.

To become a disciple means to be ready to float with the master. And if you can float with a man, with a master, you will start enjoying, you will start cele-brating – because all anxiety will disappear, all anguish will disappear. And then you will be ready to surrender totally.

First a little taste is needed. That taste can come through a master – the taste of Tao, the taste of dhamma, the taste of the way.

Those who are following the way should behave like a piece of timber which is drifting along a stream. If the log is neither held by the banks . . .

Now, Buddha says, a few things have to be remembered. You should surrender, surrender should be total, but there are a few obstacles which have to be continuously watched.

If the log is neither held by the banks, nor seized by men, nor obstructed by the gods, nor kept in the whirlpool, nor itself goes to decay, I assure you that this log will finally reach the ocean.

Now, you can start clinging to the master. Rather than surrendering you can start clinging – and both look alike, but the difference is vast. To cling to a master is not surrendering to him. To cling to a master means you are still clinging to your ego, because all clinging is of the ego.

Clinging is of the ego. To what you cling is immaterial. If you cling then you are trying to save yourself. I watch it. If I say to somebody to "do this", if it is just according to his desire he says, "Osho, I am surrendered to you. Whatsoever you say I will do." And if it is not according to his desire, then he never says, "I am surrendered to you." Then he says, "It is difficult." And then he brings a thousand and one reasons why he cannot do it. Now he is playing a game with himself.

You cannot deceive me; you can only go on deceiving yourself. When it fits with your desire, then you say, "I am surrendered to you – whatsoever you say." When it does not fit your desire, then you completely forget about surrender. But the real question arises only when it doesn't fit with your desire. If you can say yes then too, when your ordinary mind goes on saying no, then there is no clinging, then it is real surrender. Otherwise, you can hide behind the master – and that hiding itself can become a protection, a security.

A master is a danger. A master is insecurity personified. A master is an adventure.

Buddha says:

This log will finally reach the ocean – only if it is not held by the banks, nor seized by men, nor obstructed by the gods.

Buddha does not believe in any gods. He says people who believe in gods are only obstructed by their ideas; their very idea of God becomes their obstruction.

Sometimes it is the banks, sometimes the people around you. Sometimes the gods, the philosophies, theologies, sometimes your mind's own whirlpool – and sometimes you yourself can go to decay. If you are not alert and intelligent, you are already decaying, you are already dying. Every day your intelligence becomes more and more dull. Watch a child: how intelligent! how fresh! And watch an old man: how dull, rigid, dead! Every moment intelligence is slipping by, life is getting out of your hands.

So Buddha says these things have to be remembered. If these things are remembered, and you are not caught by anything, just surrender to the stream and the stream will take you to the ocean.

If monks walking on the way are neither tempted by the passions, nor led astray by some evil influences, but steadily pursue their course for nirvana, I assure you that these monks will finally attain enlightenment.

If monks walking on the way are neither tempted by the passions . . . because the passions are of the body, the passions are of the senses. They are very stupid!

People come to me and they say, "What to do? I go on eating too much, I go on stuffing myself – I cannot stop! The whole day I am thinking about food." Now the person who is saying this is simply saying that he has lost all intelligence. Food is needed, but food is not the goal. You need food to exist, but there are many people who exist only to eat more and more and more.

Somebody is continuously obsessed with sex. Nothing is wrong with sex, but obsession is always wrong. With what you are obsessed is not the question – obsession is wrong, because then it starts draining your energy. Then you are continuously moving in a whirlpool of your own making, and you go on round and round and round, and you waste your energy.

And one day suddenly you find death has come and you have not lived at all, you have not known even what life is. You have been alive and yet you have not known what life is. You have been here and yet you don't know who you are. What a wastage! And what a disrespectful way of living! I call it sacrilege.

It is good to eat, it is good to love, but if you are eating twenty-four hours a day you are mad. There is a balance. When the balance is lost then you are falling below human standards.

If monks walking on the way are neither tempted by the passions . . .

Temptation is there – and it will be greater when you start walking on the path. Ordinarily it may not be so, but when you start walking on the path, the body will struggle. That's how it happens.

People who have come to meditate here, they were never aware that they were obsessed with food. Meditating, suddenly one day, a great obsession arises about food. They feel continuously hungry; they are surprised because it has never been so. What has happened? Out of meditation? Yes, it can happen out of meditation, because when you are moving in meditation the body starts feeling you are going distant, you are going away. The body starts tempting you. The body will not allow you to become a master.

The body has remained master for many, many lives; you have been a slave. Now, suddenly you are trying to change the whole state: you are trying to make the slave the master, and the master the slave. You are trying to stand on your head – to the body it looks exactly like that, that you are turning things upside down. The body revolts, the body fights, the body resists. The body says, "I will not allow you so easily."

The mind starts fighting! When the body starts fighting you will feel a great obsession for food arising in you. And when the mind starts fighting, you will feel a great obsession with sex arising in you. Sex and food, these two are going to be the problems. These are the two basic passions.

The body lives out of food. When you start moving in meditation the body wants more food to become stronger so it can fight you more. The body wants all strength now, so that it can resist the aggression that has come upon it. The effort that you are making to conquer it, to become a master of it, has to be destroyed. The body needs all energy that is possible. The body becomes mad in eating.

The body survives because of food, and when the survival is at stake the body starts eating madly. The mind exists through sex. Why does the mind exist through sex? Because the mind exists by projecting in the future; the mind is a projection in the future. Let me explain it to you.

You are a projection of your mother's and father's sexuality. Your children will be your projection in the future. If you don't eat you will die. If you drop sexuality your children will never be born. So two things are clear: if you drop sexuality, nothing is at stake as far as you are concerned; you will not die by dropping sexuality. Nobody has ever been heard to die by becoming celibate. You can live perfectly well. Only if you drop food you will die – within three months, at the most you can survive three months if you are perfectly healthy, then you will die. Dropping food will be death to you. Dropping sex has nothing to do with you. Maybe your children will never be born; that will be a death to them – death before they are even born – but not death to you.

Through sex the race survives; through food, the individual. So the body is concerned only with food. This body is concerned only with food, but your mind is concerned with sex – because only through sex, the mind thinks, will it have a sort of immortality. You will die, that seems certain. You cannot deceive yourself – everybody some day is dying and every time the bell tolls it tolls for thee. Every time death happens, you become shaken: your own death is coming close by. It will come. It is only a question of time, but it is to come; there is no way to escape from it. And wherever you escape to, you will find it waiting for you.

I have heard a very famous story, a Sufi story:

A king dreamt. In the night in his dream he saw Death. He became afraid. He asked, "What is the matter? Why are you making me so frightened?"

Death said, "I have come to tell you that tomorrow by sunset I am coming, so get ready. It is just out of compassion so that you can prepare."

The king was so shocked, his sleep was broken. It was the middle of the night; he called his ministers and he said, "Find people who can interpret the dream, because time is short. Maybe it is true!"

Then the interpreters came, but as interpreters always have been, they were great scholars. They brought many big books and they started discussing and disputing and arguing. And the sun started rising, and it was morning. And an old man who was a very trusted servant to the king, he came to the king and he whispered in his ear, "Don't be foolish! These people will quarrel for ever and ever, and they will never come to any conclusion."

Now, everybody was trying to assert that his interpretation was right, and the king was more confused than ever. So he asked the old man, "Then what am I supposed to do?"

He said, "Let them continue their discussions. They are not going to conclude so soon – and the sun will be setting, because once it has risen the sunset is not very far. Rather, take my advice and escape – at least escape from this palace. Be somewhere else! By the evening reach somewhere as far away as possible."

The logic looked right. The king had a very fast horse, the fastest in the world. He rushed, he escaped. Hundreds of miles he passed. By the time he reached a certain town the sun was just about to set. He was very happy. He patted his horse and he said, "You did well. We have come very far."

And when he was patting his horse, suddenly he felt somebody was standing behind him. He looked back – the same shadow of

Death. And Death started laughing. And the king said, "What is the matter? Why are you laughing?"

Death said, "I was worried because you were destined to die under this tree – and I was worried how you would manage to reach.

Your horse is really great! It did well. Let me also pat your horse. That's why I came in your dream: I wanted you to escape from the palace because I was very worried how it would happen, how you would be able to reach. The place looked so far away, and only one day was left. But your horse did well, you have come in time."

Wherever you go you will find death waiting for you. In all the directions death is waiting. In all the places death is waiting. So, that cannot be avoided – then mind starts imagining some way to avoid it.

First it spins philosophies that "the soul is immortal", that "the body will die – I am not going to die." You are even more fragile than the body. This ego that thinks "I will not die" is more flimsy, more dreamlike than the body. The body is at least real; this ego is absolutely unreal. So you spin philosophies: "The soul will never die – I will remain in heaven, in paradise, in moksha." But deep down you know that these are just words, they don't satisfy.

Then you find some other way: to earn money, make a great monument, a great palace – do something historical, leave a place in history! But that too seems to be meaningless. In such a big history, even if you make all the efforts you will become only a footnote, nothing much. And what is the point of becoming a footnote in a history book? You will be gone all the same; whether people remember you or not does not matter. In fact, who bothers to remember? Ask school children who have to read history: the great kings . . . and they must have made great effort somehow to enter into the history books, and now children are just not bothered at all. They condemn. They are not happy that these great kings existed. They would have been more happy if nobody had existed and there was no history to be read and crammed. So what is the point?

Then the mind has a very subtle idea. The idea is: "I will die but my children can live; my child will be my representative. He will live and somehow, deep down in him; I will live, because he will be my extension." It will be your sex cell that will live in your child – in your son, in your daughter. Of course, then sons became more important, because the daughter will move into somebody else's life stream, and the son will continue your life stream. The son became very important; he will be your continuity. And the mind starts getting obsessed with sex, goes mad with sex.

Whenever you come closer to meditation, these two things are going to happen: you will start stuffing yourself with food and you will start stuffing yourself with sexuality. And you will start becoming a maniac.

BUDDHA SAYS:

*If monks walking on the way are neither tempted by the passions,
nor led astray by some evil influences, but steadily pursue their
course for nirvana, I assure you that these monks will finally attain
enlightenment.*

You have to be alert not to be distracted by your passions, not to be distracted from the Way, not to be distracted from your meditation. Whatsoever the cause of distraction, it has to be avoided. You have to bring your energy again and again to your innermost core. You have to make yourself again and again relaxed, surrendered, non-tense.

THE BUDDHA SAID:

*Rely not upon your own will. Your own will is not trustworthy.
Guard yourselves against sensualism, for it surely leads to the path
of evil. Your own will becomes trustworthy only when you have
attained arhatship.*

This is a very significant statement. Buddha never said that you need a master, but in a subtle way he has to concede it – because a master is needed.

Buddha was against masters, because the country was so cheated, exploited in the name of the guru-disciple relationship. There were so many charlatans and frauds – there have always been and there will always be. And Buddha was very much worried about it, that people were being exploited, so he said there is no need for anyone to become anybody's disciple. But how can he avoid a very basic thing? There may be ninety-nine percent frauds – that doesn't matter. Even if one right master exists, he can be of tremendous help.

So in a very indirect way, in a roundabout way, Buddha concedes. He says: Rely not upon your own will. He says: If you rely upon your own will you will never reach anywhere. Your own will is so weak. Your own will is so unintelligent. Your own will is so divided into itself. You don't have one will; you have many wills in you. You are a crowd!

Gurdjieff used to say you don't have one "I", you have many small "I"s. And those "I"s go on changing. For a few minutes one "I" becomes the sovereign, and then it is thrown out of power; another "I" becomes the sovereign. And you can watch it! It is a simple fact. It has nothing to do with any theory.

You love a person, and you are so loving. One "I" dominates: the "I" that loves. Then something goes wrong and you hate the person – in a single moment love has turned into hatred. Now you want to destroy the person – at least, you start thinking how to destroy the person. Now the hatred has come in: another "I" which is totally different is on the throne.

You are happy, you have another "I". You are unhappy, again . . . it goes on changing. Twenty-four hours, day in, day out, your "I"s go on changing. You don't have one "I".

That's why it happens that you can decide tonight: "Tomorrow morning I will get up at three o'clock; whatsoever happens I am going to get up." You set the alarm and at three o'clock you stop the alarm and you are annoyed by it. You think, "One day – what does it matter? Tomorrow . . ." and you go to sleep. And again when you get up at eight o'clock in the morning you are angry at yourself. You say, "How could it happen? I had decided to get up. How did I continue to sleep?"

These are two different "I"s: the one that decided and the one that was annoyed with the alarm are different "I"s. Maybe the first is again back in the morning and repents. You become angry and then you repent. These are two different "I"s, they never meet! They don't know what the other is doing. The "I" that creates anger goes on creating anger, and the "I" that repents goes on repenting – and you never change.

Gurdjieff used to say that unless you have a permanent, crystallized "I" you should not trust yourself. You are not one; you are a crowd, you are polypsychic.

That's what Buddha says: *Rely not upon your own will.* Then on whom to rely? Rely on somebody who has a will, who has an integral "I", who has attained, who has become one in his being, is no longer divided, who is really an individual.

Rely not upon your own will. Your own will is not trustworthy. Guard yourselves against sensualism, for it surely leads to the path of evil. Your own will becomes trustworthy only when you have attained arhatship.

When you have come to know who you are, when you have become a realized soul, when the enlightenment has happened, then your "I" becomes trustworthy – never before it. But then there is no point. Then you have come home. It is of no use now. When there was need it was not there. So you need somebody to whom you can surrender, you need somebody with whom trust can arise in you. That is the whole relationship of a master and a disciple.

The disciple has yet no will of his own, and the master has. The disciple is a crowd and the master is one unity. The disciple surrenders. He says, "I cannot trust myself, hence I will trust you." Trusting the master, by and by, the disciple's crowd inside disappears.

That's why I say that when I tell you to do something and you want to do it, and you do it, it is meaningless – because it is still according to your "I", your will. When I say to do something, and it is against you, and you surrender and you say yes, then you are moving, then you are growing, then you are becoming mature. Then you are coming out of the mess that you have been up to now.

Only by saying no to your mind do you say yes to the master.

Many times I simply say that which you would like, because I don't see that you will be able to do that which I like. I have to persuade you slowly. You are not ready to take a sudden jump. First I say change your clothes, then I start changing your body. Then I start changing your mind.

People come to me and they say, "Why should we change clothes? What is the point?" They are not even ready to change their clothes; more cannot be expected of them. They say they are ready to change their souls, but they are not ready to change their clothes – look at the absurdity of it. But with the soul there is one thing: it is invisible, so nobody knows.

But I can see your soul, I can see where you are standing and what you are talking about; I can see through your rationalizations. You say, "What is there in clothes?" but that is not the question. I also know there is nothing in the clothes, but still I say change. I would like you to do something according to me, not according to you. That's a beginning. Then, by and by, first I take hold of your finger, then your hand – hmm? – then of your totality. You say, "Why are you holding my finger? What is the point of holding my finger?" I know what the point is – that is the beginning. Very slowly I have to go. If you are ready then there is no need to go slow, then I can also go in a sudden leap, but people are not ready.

BUDDHA SAYS:

Rely not upon your own will. Your will is not trustworthy.

Find a person in whose presence you feel something has happened. Find a person in whose presence you feel a fragrance of the divine, in whose presence you feel a coolness, in whose presence you feel love, compassion, in whose presence you feel a silence – unknown, inexperienced, but it surrounds you, overwhelms you. Then surrender to that person. Then, by and by, he will bring you to the point where surrender will not be needed – you will realize your own innermost core of being, you will become an arhat. The arhat is the final stage of enlightenment.

You become yourself only when all the selves that you have been carrying all along are dissolved. You become yourself only when there is really no self left but a pure nothingness. Then the circle is complete. You have come to the ultimate nothingness, fully aware. You have become a witness of the whole play of life, existence, consciousness.

This state is possible if you don't create obstacles. This state is certainly possible if you avoid obstacles. I can also assure you that if you become a driftwood and don't cling to the banks, and don't get attached to whirlpools, and don't start decaying in your unawareness, you are sure, absolutely sure, to reach the ocean.

That ocean is the goal. We come from that ocean and we have to reach to that ocean. The beginning is the end – and when the circle is complete there is perfection, there is wholeness, there is bliss and benediction.

Enough for today.

Chapter 15:

Just Working for Peanuts

THE BUDDHA SAID:

*O monks, you should not see women. [If you should have
to see them] refrain from talking to them. [If you should
have to talk] you should reflect in a right spirit: "I am now
a homeless mendicant. In the world of sin I must behave
myself like unto the lotus flower whose purity is not defiled
by the mud. Old ones I will treat as my mother; elderly
ones as elder sisters; younger ones as younger sisters; and
little ones as daughters." And in all this you should harbor
no evil thoughts, but think of salvation.*

THE BUDDHA SAID:

*Those who walk in the way should avoid sensualism as
those who carry hay would avoid coming near the fire.*

The magnificent temple that Buddha built consists of three floors; his teaching
has three dimensions to it, or three layers. And you will have to be very patient
to understand those three layers. I say so because they have been misunderstood
down the centuries.

The first floor of Buddha's teaching is known as Hinayana; the second floor
is known as Mahayana, and the third floor is known as Vajrayana. Hinayana
means "the small vehicle", "the narrow way". Mahayana means "the great
vehicle", "the wide way". And Vajrayana means "the supreme vehicle", "the
ultimate way", "the transcendental way". Hinayana is the beginning and
Vajrayana is the climax, the crescendo.

Hinayana starts from where you are. Hinayana tries to help you to change
your mechanical habits; it is just like hatha yoga – very body-oriented, believes

in great discipline; strict, almost repressive – at least it looks repressive. It is not repressive, but the whole work of Hinayana consists in changing your centuries-old habits.

Just as a tightrope walker starts leaning to the left if he feels that he is going to fall towards the right, to balance one has to move to the opposite. By moving to the opposite, a balance arises – but that balance is temporary, momentary. Again you will start falling into the new direction, then again you will need balance and you will have to move to the opposite.

Sex is the basic problem, and all the habits that man has created are basically sex-oriented. That's why no society allows sex total freedom. All the cultures that have existed – sophisticated, unsophisticated, Eastern, Western, primitive, civilized – all cultures have tried in some way to control sexual energy. It seems to be the greatest power over man. It seems that if man is allowed total freedom in sex, he will simply destroy himself.

Skinner writes about a few experiments he was doing with rats. He was testing a new theory, that electrodes could be put into the human or animal brain, attached to particular centers in the brain and you can just push a button and that center will be stimulated.

There is a sex center in the brain. In fact, you are more controlled by the sex center in the brain than the actual sex center of your body. That's why fantasy works so much. That's why pornography has so much appeal. The pornography cannot appeal to the sex center itself; it stimulates the brain center attached to the sex center. Once the mind is active, the sex center, the physiological sex center, immediately starts being active.

He fixed electrodes into rats' brains and taught them how to push a button whenever they wanted sexual stimulation and an inner orgasm. He was surprised; he was not expecting that this was going to happen. Those rats completely forgot everything – food, sleep, play – everything they forgot. They continuously pushed the button! One rat did it six thousand times and died – he died pushing the button. Six thousand times! He forgot everything else . . . then nothing else mattered.

Sooner or later, some Skinner or somebody else is going to give you also a small box to keep in your pocket, and whenever you feel sexual just push a button and your brain center will become active and will give you beautiful orgasms, and nobody will ever know what is happening inside you. But you will almost follow the rat – then what is the point of doing anything else? You will kill yourself.

Sex is such a great attraction that if there were no limitations on it . . . First there is a limitation that body puts on it. A man cannot have too many orgasms in a day; if you are young, three or four; if you become older, then one; when you become a little older still, then even that becomes difficult – once a week, once a month. And, by and by, your body puts so many limitations on it.

Women are freer that way. The body has no limitation. That's why, all over the world, the woman has been completely repressed. She has not been allowed freedom; she has not been allowed even the freedom to have orgasms in the past – because a woman can have multiple orgasms. Within seconds she can have many orgasms, six, twelve; then no man will be able to satisfy a woman. Then no man will be able to satisfy any woman. Then only group sex will be able to satisfy. A woman will need at least twelve partners, and that will create tremendous complexities.

That's why, down the centuries, for thousands of years, women were brought up in such a way that they have completely forgotten that they can have orgasm. Just within these fifty years women have again started learning what orgasm is. And with their learning, problems have arisen all over the world. Marriage is on the rocks. Marriage cannot exist with women having the capacity of multiple orgasm. And man only has capacity for one orgasm. There can be no compatibility between the two. Then monogamy cannot exist. It will become difficult.

This society and the pattern that it has evolved up to now is doomed. Man has released some energy that has always been kept under a certain rigid control. But the attraction has always been there – whether you repress, whether you control, discipline, that doesn't make any difference. The attraction is there – twenty-four hours, deep down like a substratum, sexuality goes on like a river flowing. It is a continuum. You may eat, you may earn money, you may work, but you are doing everything for sex.

Somewhere, sex remains the goal . . . and this pattern has to be changed, otherwise your energy will go on being drained, your energy will go on being dissipated, your energy will go on moving into the earth. It will not rise towards heaven. It will not have an upward surge.

Hinayana works just exactly where you are. You are continuously obsessed with sex? – Hinayana tries to remove this obsession. It gives you a certain discipline, a very rigid discipline, how to drop out of it.

Hinayana says there are four steps to drop out of sex. The first is called purifying. The second is called enriching. The third is called crystallizing. The fourth is called destroying.

First you have to move your total energy against sex, so that sexual habits developed in many lives no longer interfere – that is called purifying. You change your consciousness, you shift. From sexual obsession you move to anti-sexuality.

The second step is called enriching. When you have moved to non-sexuality, then you have to enjoy non-sexuality; you have to celebrate your celibacy. Because if you don't celebrate your celibacy, again sex will start pulling you backwards. Once you start celebrating your celibacy, then the pull of sex will be completely gone, and gone for ever.

You are obsessed with sex because you don't know any other sort of celebration. So the problem is not sex really; the problem is that you don't know any other celebration. Nature allows you only one joy, and that is of sex. Nature allows you only one enjoyment, that is of sex. Nature allows you only one thrill, and that is of sex.

Hinayana says there is a greater thrill waiting for you – if you move towards celibacy. But the celibacy should not be violently forced. If you violently enforce it you will not be able to enjoy it. One has to be just aware of the sexual habits, and through awareness one has to shift by and by towards celibacy.

Celibacy should be brought very slowly. All that brings you again and again to sexuality has to be dropped slowly, in steps. And once you start enjoying the energy that becomes available, when you are not obsessed with sex, just that pure energy becomes a dance in you – that is called enriching. Now, your energy is not wasted. Your energy goes on showering on yourself.

Remember, there are two types of celibates. One has simply forced celibacy upon himself – he is a wrong type, he is doing violence to himself. The other has tried to understand sexuality, what it is, why it is; has watched, observed, lived through it, and, by and by, has become aware of its futility, by and by has become aware of a deep frustration that comes after each sexual act.

In the sexual act you have a certain thrill, a moment of forgetfulness, a moment of oblivion. You feel good – for a few seconds, only for a few seconds, you drop out of this routine world. Sex gives you a door to escape into some other world – which is non-tense; there is no worry; you are simply relaxed and melting. But have you observed? After each sexual act you feel frustrated.

Sex has promised so much, but it has not been supplied. It is difficult to find a man or a woman who does not feel a little frustrated after the sexual act, who does not feel a little guilty. I am not talking about the guilt that priests have imposed upon you. Even if nobody has imposed any guilt upon you, you will feel a little guilt – that is part, a shadow of the sexual act. You have lost energy, you feel depleted, and nothing has been gained. The gain is not very substantial. You have been befooled, you have been tricked, by a natural hypnosis – you have been tricked by the body, you have been deceived. Hence comes a frustration.

Hinayana says: Watch this frustration more deeply. Watch the sexual act and the way your energy moves into the sexual act; become aware of it – and you will see there is nothing in it. And frustration. The more you become aware, the less will be the enjoyment and the more will be the frustration. Then the shift has started taking place: your consciousness is moving away, and naturally, and spontaneously. You are not forcing it.

The second step becomes available, *enriching*. Your own energy goes on feeding your being. You no more throw it into the other's body, you no more throw it out. It becomes a deep accumulation inside you. You become a pool. And out of that feeling of energy you feel very cool. Sex is very hot. The enriching stage is very cool, calm, collected. There is a celebration, but it is very silent. There is a dance to it, but it is very graceful; there is elegance to it.

Then comes the third step, *crystallizing*. When this energy inside you has started an inner dance, by and by, slowly, enjoying it more and more, becoming more and more aware of it, a certain chemical crystallization happens in you. Exactly the same word was used by Gurdjieff in his work: crystallization. Your fragments fall together, you become one. A unity arises in you. In fact, for the first time you can say "I have an 'I.'" Otherwise there were many "I"s; now you have one "I", a big "I" which controls everything. You have become your master.

And the fourth step is *destroying*. When you have one "I", then it can be destroyed; when you have many "I"s, they cannot be destroyed. When your energy has become one and is centered, it can be killed, it can be completely destroyed. When it is a crowd it is difficult to destroy it. You destroy one fragment, there are a thousand other fragments. When you rush after those other fragments, the first one grows again. It is just like the way trees grow branches: you cut one, three branches sprout out of it.

You can destroy sexuality totally only when it has become a crystallized phenomenon; when a person has accumulated too much energy and has become one, is no longer fragmentary, no longer split, no longer schizophrenic; then Buddhists have a special term for it – they call it "Manjushree's sword".

It is said that when Manjushree reached to this third stage – he was a disciple of Buddha, a great disciple of Buddha – when he reached to this stage of crystallization, in one single moment he took his sword and destroyed it completely, utterly, in a single moment. It is not a gradual process then. That has become known down the centuries as "the sword of Manjushree".

When a person reaches to the third state, he can just raise a sword and destroy it completely – in one single attack. Because now the enemy is there, now the enemy is no longer elusive, now there are no longer many enemies – just one enemy confronting you. And the sword is just the sword of perfect awareness, mindfulness, self-remembering. It is a very sharp sword.

When Buddha destroyed his own sexuality, it is said he roared like a lion – because for the first time the whole absurdity of it became clear. And so many lives wasted! So many lives of sheer stupidity, gone for ever. He was so happy he roared like a lion.

These are the four steps, and today's sutras are concerned with these four steps. Before we enter into the sutras, a few more things have to be understood.

The second vehicle is Mahayana. When your sexual energy is no longer obsessed with the other's body, when you are completely free of the other's body, when your energy has a freedom to it, then Mahayana becomes possible – the second floor of Buddha's temple.

Mahayana makes it possible for you to be loving. Ordinarily we think sex makes people loving – sex can never make people loving. In fact, it is sexuality that prevents love from growing – because it is the same energy that has to become love. It is being destroyed in sex. To become love, the same energy has to move to the heart center. Mahayana belongs to the heart center.

Hinayana works at the sex center, *muladhar*. Mahayana works at the heart center – it says love and prayerfulness have to be developed now. Energy is there, now you can love. Energy is there, now you can be prayerful. Mahayana is loving effort. One has to love unconditionally – the trees and the rocks and the sun and the moon and the people – but now love has no sexuality in it. It is very cool, it is very tranquil.

If you come near a person whose energy is moving in his heart center, you will suddenly feel you are moving under a deep cool shade, no hot energy. You will feel suddenly a breeze surrounding you. The person of love, the person who lives at the heart center, is to a traveler like a shady tree, or cool running water, or a breeze fragrant with many blossoms.

Mahayana is not afraid of sex. Hinayana is afraid of sex. Hinayana is afraid of sex because you are too obsessed with sex; you have to move to the opposite. Mahayana is not afraid of sex – it has attained to the balance; there is no fear of the opposites. Mahayana is when the tightrope walker is balanced; he neither leans to the left nor to the right.

Then the third and the final stage, the third floor of Buddha's temple, is Vajrayana. "Vajra" means diamond – it is the most precious teaching; certainly very difficult to understand. Vajrayana is Buddhist Tantra.

Vajrayana is called "vajra", the diamond, because the diamond cuts everything. The diamond vehicle, the way of the diamond, Vajrayana, cuts everything completely, through and through – all materiality, all desire, all attachment. Even the desire to be born in heaven, the desire to be in a peaceful state, the desire to become a buddha, the desire to have nirvana, enlightenment

– even these beautiful desires are cut completely. Vajrayana knows no difference between the world and nirvana, knows no difference between ignorance and knowledge, knows no difference, no distinctions – all distinctions are dropped – knows no distinction between man and woman.

Now let me explain it to you.

On the stage of Hinayana, man is man, woman is woman. The man is attracted towards the woman, and the woman is attracted towards the man – they are outgoing; their attraction is directed somewhere outside them. Of course they will be slaves – when your attraction is directed somewhere outside you, you cannot be independent of it. That's why lovers never forgive each other, they cannot. They are annoyed. You love a person and you are irritated by the person at the same time. There is a reason for it. There is constant fight between lovers and the reason is that you cannot forgive the lover because you know you are dependent on him or her. How can you forgive your slavery? You know your woman makes you happy, but if she decides not to make you happy, then . . . ? Then suddenly you are unhappy. Your happiness is in her hands and her happiness is in your hands. Whenever somebody else controls your happiness, you cannot forgive them.

Jean-Paul Sartre says: "The other is hell" – and he is right. He has a great insight into it. The other is hell because you have to depend on the other. Sex cannot make you free; somehow it takes you away from yourself; it takes you farther and farther away from yourself. The goal is the other.

Gurdjieff used to say sex is one-arrowed – the arrow is moving towards the other. Exactly the same metaphor has been used by Vajrayana: sex is one-arrowed – it goes towards the other. Love is double-arrowed – it goes to the other and to you also. In love there is balance.

One arrow going towards the other, then you have to work with Hinayana. Two-arrowed: one arrow going towards the other, one arrow coming towards you – you have attained to balance; that lopsidedness is no longer there.

A man of love is never angry with the other, because he is not really dependent on the other. He can be happy alone too; his arrow is double-arrowed – he can be happy alone too. Of course, he still shares his happiness with the other, but he is no longer dependent on the other. Now it is no longer a relationship of dependence: it is a relationship of interdependence. It is a mutual friendship. They share energies, but nobody is anybody's slave.

In Vajrayana the arrow completely disappears. There is no you and no other; I and thou, both are dropped. The mechanism has to be understood.

When you are looking for a woman or for a man, you don't know one very important factor: that your woman is within you and your man too. Each man is both man and woman, and each woman is both woman and man. It has to be so, because you are born out of two parents. One was man, one was woman; they have contributed to your being fifty percent each. You have something of your father and you have something of your mother. Half of you belongs to the male energy; half of you belongs to the female energy – you are both.

In Hinayana you have to work hard to bring your energy to the inner woman or the inner man; that is its whole work.

Carl Gustav Jung became aware of this fact – of this fact of bisexuality, that no man is pure man and no woman is pure woman. In each man a woman exists, and in fact every man is searching for that woman somewhere outside. That's why suddenly one day you come across a woman and you feel, "Yes, this is the right woman for me." How do you feel it? What is the criterion? How do you judge? It is not rational, you don't reason it out. It happens so suddenly, like a flash. You were not thinking about it, you have not reasoned it out. Suddenly if somebody asks you, "Why have you fallen in love with this woman?" you will shrug your shoulders. You will say, "I don't know – but I have fallen in love. Something has happened."

What has happened? Jung says you have an image of woman inside you; that image somehow fits with this woman. This woman seems to be similar to that image in some way or other. Of course, no woman can be absolutely similar to the inner woman – that's why no lover can ever be absolutely satisfied. A little similar, maybe: the way she walks; maybe her sound, her voice; maybe the way she looks, maybe her blue eyes; maybe her nose, maybe the color of her hair. You have an image inside you that has come from your mother, from your mother's mother, from your mother's mother's mother – all the women that have preceded you have contributed to that image. It is not exactly like your mother, otherwise things would have been simple. Your mother is involved in it, your mother's mother is also involved, and so on and so forth. They all have contributed little bits.

And it is the same with your man: your father has contributed, your father's father, and so on and so forth. From your father to Adam, and from your mother to Eve, the whole continuum has contributed to it. Nobody exactly knows, there is no way really to know whom you are seeking. A man is searching for a woman, a woman is searching for a man – the search is very vague. There is no clear-cut image, but somewhere in your heart you carry it; in the dark corner of your soul you keep it, it is there. So many times many women and many men will appear to fulfill something of it, but only something. So each lover will give you a little satisfaction and much dissatisfaction. A part that fits will satisfy, and all other parts which don't fit will never satisfy.

Have you watched it? Whenever you fall in love with a man or a woman, you immediately start changing the man and the woman according to something that you also don't know what . . . Wives go on changing their husbands their whole lives: "Don't do this! Be like this, behave like this!"

> Just the other day, Mulla Nasruddin's wife was saying to me, "Finally, I succeeded."
> I asked, "About what?"
> She said, "I have stopped Mulla Nasruddin biting his nails."
> I said, "Biting his nails? Fifty years you have been married together – Mulla is seventy – now you have been able after fifty years?"
> She said, "Yes!"
> I asked, "But how did you succeed, tell me?"
> She said, "Now I simply hide his teeth so he cannot bite."

People go on trying to change each other. Nobody ever changes – I have never seen, I have never come across it. People even pretend that "Yes, we have changed," but nobody can change. Everybody remains himself. The whole effort is futile, but the urge to change is there. Why is the urge to change there?

The urge to change is for a real necessity. The woman is trying to make her husband fit with some vague image inside her. Then she will be happy – that he does not drink, that he does not smoke, that he does not go after other women . . . and a thousand and one things . . . that he always goes to the temple, that he listens to the saints. She has a certain image – she wants her husband to be a hero, a saint, a great man. The ordinary human being does not satisfy her.

And the husband is also trying in a thousand and one ways. He brings beautiful clothes, diamonds, rubies and pearls, and goes on decorating his wife. He is trying to find a Cleopatra. Somewhere he has some image of a beautiful woman, the most beautiful woman. Now he tries – even from his very childhood.

I have heard:

> The old man asked his precocious six-year-old how he liked the new little girl next door.
> "W-e-l-l," said the kid, "She's no Elizabeth Taylor, but she's nice."

Even a small child is thinking about Elizabeth Taylor. "She's no Elizabeth Taylor, but she's nice." And this conflict continues. The reason is that we are always looking for someone – who is not – outside.

Hinayana turns you from looking outside. It says: close your eyes to the outside. Mahayana makes you more alert and aware, fills your inner chamber with more light, so that you can see the inner woman. And Vajrayana makes it possible for you so that you can have an inner orgasm with your man inside or your woman inside. That inner orgasm will satisfy you, nothing else. These three steps are of tremendous meaning.

So don't be worried about these sutras that we will be discussing today.

Just two days ago, one woman wrote to me, "Osho, what is happening to me? When you were talking about the Hassid I was so flowering, so floating with it – each talk – and I would go happy and dancing and joyous. And now you are talking about Buddha, since then I am very depressed. I love my man and he is a very beautiful man, and the Buddha says nothing is there in the body, it is just a bag full of filth. I don't want to hear things like that."

I know nobody wants to hear, but they are true. And unless you pass through the Buddha you will never reach to the Hassid. Hassidism is Vajrayana, it is the ultimate flowering. Listening to Hassidism you feel very happy; when I talk about Tantra you feel very happy – you think you are all *tantrikas*. It is not so simple, it is not so cheap. To be a *tantrika* is the ultimate flowering of religiousness – don't deceive yourselves. It is hard, arduous, to reach to that point.

Vajrayana is Tantra, Buddhist Tantra, pure Tantra. But just look at the arrangement of things! Hinayana is the first step, and Hinayana seems to be absolutely repressive. But Buddha says that unless you change your old patterns, you can go on rationalizing and you can go on living in your unconscious, robotlike life, and you can go on repeating it again and again. You have done it many times.

How many times have you fallen in love with a beautiful man or a beautiful woman, and how long does it last? One day Buddha proves to be right: your beautiful woman, your Elizabeth Taylor, one day suddenly you find is a bag full of filth – and he is saying it from the very beginning. But, of course, when you are on your honeymoon these sutras will not appeal to you.

Never take Buddhist sutras when you are going on a honeymoon. But when you are approaching the divorce court these sutras will be very relevant! You will immediately see what he is saying. One day comes the ultimate divorce. The ultimate divorce is the day when you simply understand the whole absurdity of searching for the other.

Divorces have happened many times to you, but you again and again forget. One divorce is finished – even if it is not finished, the court proceedings may still be on – you are again falling into another love affair. It may be in fact that because you have fallen into another love affair, that's why you are asking for the divorce. Before you are out of the first prison, you have already entered the next.

You have become so accustomed to living in chains that freedom tastes bitter.

To that woman who is feeling depressed I would like to say this, that that depression shows something is hitting deep in the heart. Buddha has some truth – you cannot avoid it. You would like to avoid it. Who wants truth? People like lies. Lies are very comfortable; truth is always destructive, shattering. But don't make any judgement too soon – this is Buddha's first layer of teaching. The second layer is more relaxed. The first layer is of great struggle. Hinayana is struggle, sheer force of will – because that is the only way you can get out of the mess you have been for so long – a sheer struggle to get out of it. The second step is perfectly relaxed, Mahayana is very relaxed and graceful. The third step is of tremendous celebration. On the third step you transcend all discipline.

This is the beauty of the Buddha's path; it is very scientific. Each step is a must. If you lose one step, the whole building will collapse, the whole temple will disappear.

Hinayana is very great discipline; Mahayana is relaxed discipline. And Vajrayana is no discipline – one has come to such a point where he can have total freedom. But you have to earn that total freedom.

Hinayana is based in the body, the material part of your being. When you are in your body, you can enjoy life only in drops. In fact, in the East, semen is called *bindu* – *bindu* means a drop. You can enjoy sex only drop by drop. And you are so vast that this enjoyment drop by drop is more frustrating than fulfilling.

I have heard:

> The oversized elephants were picketing the zoo. A lion happened to be strolling by and asked, "Why are you picketing?" and one of the elephants answered, "We're tired of working for peanuts."
> This is what sex is – just working for peanuts.

In Tibet they have a metaphor for it; they call it *preta*. Preta means a hungry ghost. A hungry ghost they depict in a certain way: he has a belly like an elephant, and a neck so thin like thread, and a mouth so small like the eye of a needle. Of course, he has to remain hungry for ever and ever, because of that small mouth like an eye of a needle. He goes on eating twenty-four hours, but he has a belly like an elephant – so he goes on eating and eating and eating and always is hungry.

That's how sexuality is. You are vast; you have no boundaries, no limits. Unless your bliss also is as vast as your being it is not going to give you any contentment. And sex is just drip, drip, drop, drop . . . You can just entertain yourself; you can go on hoping against hope – but it is not going to fulfill you. Sex creates neurosis, it is neurotic, because it can never satisfy you. Now, go to the madhouses of the world and just watch the mad people, and you will always find that somewhere or other there is a sexual problem. That's what Freud says, that all pathology is somehow connected with sex. Too much sex obsession becomes neurotic.

If you live in the body, you are bound to become neurotic. You have to go a little deeper and higher than the body.

The second layer Buddhists call the heart; you can call it mind but the heart is a better word. The heart includes the mind; it is bigger, more satisfying, more space is available. You feel more free. Love is more free than sex. In love there is less conflict than there is in sex. Then there is a still higher . . . the vast open sky of Vajrayana. Buddha gives it the name of compassion. You live in passion and you have to reach to compassion.

Passion is obsession, neurosis. Compassion is when your energy has flowered. You are so contented within yourself, you are so enough unto yourself, now you can share, you can shower your bliss. Now you have to give. Neurosis is when you go on demanding and nobody is ready to give to you, and you are a hungry ghost. Your demands are great, and all that the world provides is just peanuts.

When, at the stage of Vajrayana, you are vast, full of energy, a great reservoir of energy, a pool, a tremendous pool, then you can give. In sex you ask. Passion means demand, passion means begging. Have you not watched it? Whenever you are sexually attracted to a woman, you go around her and wag your tail – you are a beggar. In compassion you are an emperor, you share, you give; you give because you have. In sex you ask because you don't have. And this sex continues from the childhood to the very end. Children are getting ready for it, for this absurd journey. Old people are tired, sitting by the roadside – very jealous of those who are still not tired and are young; feeling very jealous. Out of their jealousy they start preaching; out of their jealousy they start condemning.

Remember, a saint never condemns. If he condemns then he is not a saint – he is still interested in the same things, it is just that now he is jealous. Have you not watched this jealousy? A young boy climbing up a tree, and you immediately say, "Get down! You may get hurt or you may fall down." Have you watched? – in your voice there is something of jealousy. You cannot climb the tree now; you are old, your limbs are more rigid; they have lost their flexibility. You are jealous but you cannot say you are jealous. You hide your jealousy.

Whenever a person starts condemning sex, somewhere he must be carrying jealousy. Buddha is not condemning, he is simply factual. He simply says whatsoever is the case. And he wants you to come out of it because your destiny is bigger, higher is the potentiality.

A woman, an old woman, reached the insurance company's office. "But lady, you can't collect the life insurance on your husband – he isn't dead yet," said the insurance man.

"I know that – but there's no life left in him."

When no life is left in you, you start hiding the fact; you start becoming religious. Your religion may be just a garb. Buddha is not saying that you have to become religious when you are old. Buddha is saying you have to become religious when the passion is alive, when the fire is alive – because only when the fire is alive can it be transformed, you can ride on the energy.

Buddha introduced something absolutely new into the Indian consciousness. In India, *sannyas* was for old people – old, dead; almost dead, one foot in the grave, then people used to take *sannyas*. The Hindu *sannyas* was like that – only for old people. When you have nothing left in you, then try *sannyas*; that was the last item. Buddha introduced a new element. He said that is foolish – only a young person can be really religious, because when the energy is there you can ride on it. He introduced *sannyas* to young people.

And, of course, when you introduce *sannyas* to young people you have to make sure that they don't go on moving towards sex. For old people you need not bother too much. So in Hindu scriptures, there exists nothing like Hinayana – because there is no need! Only old people become sannyasins, so what is the point? There is no need to be worried about them. They can live as they want. But when a young person becomes a sannyasin, then much care has to be taken. He has energy, he has fire, and that fire can misfire too; it can lead him in wrong directions. And he is very fresh, inexperienced. For him these sutras are very helpful.

Mulla Nasruddin tells this story:

> My mother-in-law is a widow; she is eighty-two years old. One night, just to get her out of the house, I arranged a date for her with a man who is eighty-five years old. She returned home from the date very late that evening, and more than a little upset.
>
> "What happened?" I asked.
>
> "Are you kidding?" she snapped. "I had to slap his face three times."
>
> "You mean," I answered, "he got fresh?"
>
> "No," she replied, "I thought he was dead!"

Now if you initiate such dead people into *sannyas*, then there is no need for these sutras.

Buddha had to make it certain, because he took on a great danger. He was very courageous, he introduced thousands of young people into *sannyas*. He had to make it absolutely certain that their energy moves from body to heart, from heart to soul. Every care had to be taken.

The first sutra:

THE BUDDHA SAID:

> O monks, you should not see women. [If you should have to see
> them], refrain from talking to them. [If you should have to talk],
> you should reflect in a right spirit: "I am now a homeless
> mendicant. In the world of sin I must behave myself like unto the
> lotus flower whose purity is not defiled by the mud.
> Old ones I will treat as my mother; elderly ones as elder
> sisters; younger ones as younger sisters; and little ones as
> daughters." And in all this you should harbor no evil thoughts, but
> think of salvation.

THE BUDDHA SAID:

> Those who walk in the way should avoid sensualism as those who
> carry hay would avoid coming near the fire.

> To initiate a young man is to initiate somebody who is carrying hay
> – he should avoid fire.

Now, try to understand. These simple words are not so simple – they have many depths and layers.

First: they are addressed to monks, not to ordinary people. "O monks," Buddha says. The word "monk" is very beautiful; it means one who has decided to live alone. Monk, the very word, means solitary. Words like monopoly, monogamy, come from the same root. "Monogamy" means one husband; "monopoly" means one man's power; "monastery" means where monks live, those who have decided to live alone.

Ordinarily, you are seeking the other. The monk is one who has decided that the search for the other is futile, one who has decided to be alone. Enough he has searched into relationship, but that which he was searching he could not find there. Frustration was the only gain. He has failed – he has tried, but in vain. Now he decides, "Let me try alone. If I cannot be happy with others, let me try to be happy alone. If I cannot be happy in relationship, then let me be out of relationship, let me drop out of the social structure. I will try now to be alone. I have tried outside, now let me try inside. Maybe that which I am desiring is there."

To be a monk means a decision that "Love has failed, relationship has failed, society has failed, now I will try meditation, now I will try my innermost core. Now I am going to be my only world, the only world there is. I will close my eyes and remain into myself." To be a monk is a great decision. The path of the monk is the path of the lonely, the solitary.

One day or other, everybody comes to feel that – that relationship has failed. You may not be courageous enough to drop out of it – that is another thing. Or you may be not intelligent enough – that's another matter. Great courage is needed; even a little chutzpah, what Jews call chutzpah, even that is needed. Not only a little courage, but a little dare-devilishness – otherwise one cannot get out of the old pattern; the familiar is so familiar. And the familiar . . . maybe it is uncomfortable, but still it is familiar. One has become accustomed to it.

People go on smoking knowing well that disease is there, knowing well that cancer is approaching– they go on coughing, go on suffering, and go on asking how to drop it. Now there is no pleasure in it, but still they cannot drop it – just an old habit, just a mechanical habit. They are not intelligent people. When you ask how to stop smoking, you are declaring you are stupid. You don't have any intelligence, and you don't have any courage to move into some new pattern of life. Yes, a little chutzpah will be good. Let me explain it to you, what chutzpah is.

> A man entered into a bank with a gun. He forced the cashier to give him $50,000. Of course, there was no choice for the cashier because the man was standing there and he was saying, "Give me it immediately, otherwise get ready to die!"
>
> He delivered him $50,000. He went to the next window and tried to open an account with the money.

This is chutzpah! Or there is an even better story.

> A man killed his mother and father, was caught red-handed, and appealed for mercy. And when the magistrate said, "Mercy, for you? What are your reasons?" he said, "Now I am an orphan."

This is chutzpah! Courage is needed, great courage is needed. And to be religious is almost to be madly courageous. Otherwise, there are millions of habits; one is entangled completely. It is not that you have one chain on your body – millions of chains. And things become more complicated because you have decorated the chains and you think they are ornamental. In fact, you have made them golden and they seem valuable. You don't think they are chains. The prison you have decorated so long and so beautifully that you have forgotten that it is a prison, you think it is your home.

A day is bound to come in everybody's life when a person realizes that "All that I have tried has failed." Courage is needed to recognize that "I have failed utterly." Let me repeat it: only a courageous person can accept that "I have failed completely." Cowards always go on rationalizing. They say, "Maybe we have failed in this, but we will try another. Once more," they say, "then we are finished. One marriage more, then we are finished."

That's what psychologists call the gambler's psychology. He goes on losing, but he thinks, "One time more . . . maybe this time I am going to win." If he starts winning, then too he cannot leave, because he thinks, "Now I am winning. Now I am fortunate, now God is with me, fate is with me – I should not lose this opportunity. One stake more . . ."

If he is losing, he goes on playing. If he is winning, he goes on playing. And the final result is always failure. Whether you win or lose in the middle makes no sense: ultimately failure comes into your hands.

Courage is needed to recognize that "I have failed". The monk is one who has recognized the fact that "all my life-ways have failed", that "all my ideas have failed", that "my mind has proved impotent. Now I am going to make a drastic change in my life. I am going to bring a radical transformation. I will turn inwards." This turning inwards makes a man a monk.

A monk is a rebellious person. He completely drops out of the society, out of relationship.

Buddha says: You can come back to the society at the third stage, when you are a Vajrayanist, when you have come to the third stage of flowering – but not before it.

So remember, these words are not uttered for householders. These words are not uttered for those who are still in the world and still dreaming. These words are uttered to a specific group of people who have dropped out of the world, and who have decided to search within, to explore their own souls. They have explored others' bodies – because as far as others are concerned you can explore only the body; you cannot get deeper than that. These people have turned away from that. Now they are trying to explore their heart, they are trying to explore their transcendental witnessing self.

O monks, you should not see women.

Don't see women! You will be surprised: Buddha used to say to his monks that even in dream this sutra has to be followed – even in dream you have to remain so alert!

This sutra is a sutra of awareness. The actual thing happened in this way: one of Buddha's great disciples, Ananda, was going to another town to preach. He asked Buddha, "Bhagwan, if I meet a woman on the way, how am I supposed to behave?" This is the story of this sutra being born.

Buddha said, "You should not see women. You close your eyes. You avoid seeing them" – because the eye is the first contact with the other. When you see a woman or when you see a man, you touch the other's body with your eyes. The eye has its own touch.

That's why you are not expected to stare at somebody. If you stare, that shows you are uncivilized, unmannerly. There is a certain time limit: three seconds you can look; that is allowed. But more than that means you are uncivil, unmannerly, ungentlemanly. If you look at a woman for three seconds it's okay; beyond that the woman will start feeling uncomfortable. And if you go on staring, she will report to the police, or she will start screaming or shouting or she will do something. Because seeing is not just seeing – eyes touch; not only touch, there are ways to penetrate the other's body with the eye. The eyes can function like knives. And the eyes can be lustful, then the other feels you have reduced her or him to an object of lust – and who are you to reduce somebody? This is offensive.

In Hindi we have a very beautiful word for such a person, we call him *luchcha*. *Luchcha* means one who goes on looking at you – exactly this; literally *luchcha* means one who goes on staring. *Luchcha* comes from a Sanskrit root *lochan*. *Lochan* means "the eye". *Luchcha* means one who goes on eyeing you, staring at you, and whose stare becomes like a knife, whose stare becomes lustful, whose stare becomes violent; who uses his eyes as if eyes are sex organs – that man is a *luchcha*.

. . . *You should not see women.* When Buddha is saying this, he is saying you should not stare. Of course, when you are walking on a road in a town, sometimes you may have to see a woman – but that is not the point. You should not stare, you should not try to look; there should not be any deliberate effort to look at a woman; it should not be deliberate. You simply pass on.

Buddha used to say to his disciples: You should not look, really, more than four feet ahead. The eyes should remain just four feet ahead – more is useless, more is unnecessary, a wastage of energy. Just walk silently, looking four feet ahead; that's enough.

And don't stare, because the stare simply shows that deep down lust is boiling. And once you see something, immediately desire arises. If you don't see, desire does not arise. You are walking on the road; you were not thinking of diamonds, for years you may not have thought, and suddenly you find a diamond there by the side just waiting for you. Suddenly it catches your eyes – desire arises. You look all around: is anybody seeing or not? You have become a thief. And you had not been thinking about a diamond; there was no desire at all. Just the eye contact and the desire has arisen from the unconscious. It must have been in the unconscious, otherwise it cannot arise.

Buddha says that you know well your unconscious is full of sexuality, so better not to stare; otherwise that which is in the unconscious will be stirred again and again. And that which is stirred again and again is strengthened. That which is stirred again and again and never allowed to rest and disappear becomes stronger. And a monk is one who has decided to drop out of relationship.

. . . *You should not see women.* It is said Ananda asked, "But if a situation arises in which one has to see a woman, then what?" So Buddha said:

[If you should have to see them], refrain from talking to them.

Because if you don't talk to a woman, you cannot relate to her. Relationship arises with talking. Communication arises with talking. You can sit by the side of a woman for hours, and if you have not talked there is no bridge; you are as distant as stars. You can sit by the side, even your bodies touching, but if you have not talked there exists no bridge, your personalities remain far away.

You can see in a commuter train so many people crowding the compartment, everybody touching everybody's body, but nobody talking. They are far away from each other. Once you talk, distance disappears; words bring you together.

> The shy character noticed a blonde in a low-cut dress sitting next to
> him alone at the bar. He gathered all his courage and sent a drink to
> her. She silently nodded her thanks. He repeated the same gesture six
> times. Finally, the drinks in him spoke up and he got up all the
> courage he could muster and mumbled, "Do you ever make love to
> strange men?"
>
> "Well," she smiled, "I never have before – but I think you've
> talked me into it – you clever, silver-tongued devil, you."

Now, he has not talked much – just one sentence . . . Even a single gesture of communication can create relationship. If you don't talk you remain separate. That's why with people, if you are sitting silently, that shows something has gone wrong. If the husband is silent and the wife is silent, then it seems that something has gone wrong. That means communication has broken, the bridge is broken. When they are laughing and talking, then there is a bridge, there is communication.

Animals have sex but no sexuality. Man has sex plus sexuality. Sex is physical, sexuality is mental – and when you talk, your talk can be sexual. Animals have sex; that's a physiological act. They don't talk, they don't have any language; but man has language, and language is one of the most powerful instruments in the hands of man. You communicate through it, you relate through it. You seduce through words, you insult through words; you show your love through words, you show your hate through words. You repel or attract through your words.

Buddha knows that the word is very potential.

In the Bible they say, "In the beginning was the Word." Maybe it is so or maybe not – but in the very beginning of every relationship there is a word. Maybe in the beginning of the world it was so, maybe not, but in every relationship it is so – relationship starts with a word. Can you start any relationship without a word? It will be difficult, very, very difficult. Silence will surround you like a citadel.

So Buddha says, if some situation is there – for example, a monk is passing and there is an accident and a bullock cart has fallen by the side in a ditch, and a woman is there, hurt, broken – what is the monk supposed to do? Should he go without helping? No, compassion is needed. Buddha says help but don't talk, see but don't talk.

Ananda asked, "But there can be certain situations in which one has to speak."

If you should have to talk, says Buddha, then you should reflect in a right spirit: "I am now a homeless mendicant . . ." Never forget that you have fallen out of relationship. The old habits are strong. The pull of the past is strong. So remember that you are a mendicant, that you are a monk, that you are a *bhikkhu*.

In the world of sin I must behave myself like unto the lotus flower whose purity is not defiled by the mud.

So, Buddha says, if you have to see, if you have to talk, if you have to touch, okay, but remember one thing, that you should remain like a lotus flower, transcendental to the mud – you should remain aware. Your awareness is your only shelter.

Have you watched? Whenever you are aware, you are alone. Whenever you are aware you are cut away from the whole world. You may be in the marketplace, but the marketplace disappears. You may be in the shop, in the factory, in the office – if you are aware, suddenly you are alone.

When I entered into my high school, I had a very eccentric teacher, a Mohammedan teacher – I loved him. I loved him because he was very eccentric; he had a few whimsical ideas. For example he would not allow any student to say, "Yes sir", when the attendance was to be taken. He would insist: "Say, 'Present sir.'" We used to annoy him by saying "Yes sir", but he would not allow it. Unless you said "Present sir", he would not allow you inside the class. He would force you to stand outside. Now, this was just whimsical. It doesn't matter whether you say "Yes sir", or you say "Present sir". But I started feeling that he had some point in it, and I started meditating on it. And whenever he would call my name, I would say "Present sir", and I would not only say it – I would feel that "I am simply present, aware, alert." And I had beautiful moments; just for a half minute. I would become so present that the class would disappear, that the teacher would disappear. He also became aware of it.

One day he called me; he said, "What do you do? What are you doing? Because when you say 'Present sir' I see a sudden change on your face, your eyes go blank. Are you playing some trick upon me?" Because it was known in the school that before I entered the school, if some boy was to be called to the principal's office then the boy was in trouble. When I entered the school, the dictum had to be changed. Whenever I was called to the principal's office, the whole school would know: "The principal is in trouble!"

So he said, "What? You are creating some trouble? And I feel very awkward when you say 'Present sir'. You change so tremendously, as if you are transported into another world. What exactly do you do? You embarrass me. If you continue doing this, then I will allow you to say 'Yes sir.'"

I said, "Now it will not make much difference – I have learned it. And I am going to use it my whole life. And I am thankful to you that you insisted. The word *present* opened a door."

You try it! Walking on the road, suddenly become present. Just say to some unknown person, "Present sir", and be present really; just become a flame of awareness. Suddenly you will see you are not in the world. You have become a lotus flower, the mud cannot touch you. You become untouchable, you become something of the beyond, incorruptible.

Buddha said: If you have to see, if you have to talk, even if you have to touch, then be present, remember, be mindful that you are a mendicant, that you are pure awareness.

And he says:

Old ones I will treat as my mother . . .

Have you looked at the psychology of man? Can you ever think of making love to your mother? Even thinking is impossible. Something suddenly cuts the whole idea. The whole thing seems ugly – making love to your mother, or making love to your sister? The whole thing seems to be impossible, inconceivable. But your sister is as much a woman as anybody else's sister. Somebody else will fall in love with your sister – they are bound to – but you never fall in love with your sister. Who loves his own sister? The moment you say "sister", some distance arises. Then sexual approach becomes impossible. The very word functions like a conditioning – you have been conditioned. From the very childhood you have been conditioned; it has been repeated so often that the relationship between a sister and a brother is a holy relationship, that to think of sex is unthinkable.

Buddha says that one who has become a monk has to create, at least in the beginning, these barriers, so he does not slip into old habits. He must have been a great psychologist, he must have known the laws of conditioning. He must have known whatever was known by Pavlov in modern times; he must have known everything about the conditioned reflex. It is a conditioned reflex: the moment you say "sister" something simply disappears. Sex becomes irrelevant. You call somebody "mother" and sex becomes non-existential.

BUDDHA SAYS:

> *"Old ones I will treat as my mother; elderly ones as elder sisters;*
> *younger ones as younger sisters; and little ones as daughters."*
> *And in all this you should harbor no evil thoughts. But think*
> *of salvation.*

And take each situation as a challenge for your awareness, as a challenge you have to work through towards your salvation.

THE BUDDHA SAID:

> *Those who walk in the way should avoid sensualism as those who*
> *carry hay would avoid coming near the fire.*

This is the first step. The second step: you are allowed to be loving – because old habits are broken, now there is no fear. In the third step you are allowed to be completely free of all discipline, because now your awareness has become a permanent phenomenon in you; now there is no need to think that "this woman is my mother, or this woman is my sister".

In the third step of Vajrayana, you have come in contact with your inner woman; your attraction for the outer woman has disappeared. The very moment you have come in contact with your inner woman, you have met the perfect woman you have been always seeking and seeking and never finding. You have met your inner man – you have found the perfect man. Yin and yang, they have become a circle, they have joined together.

That is the theory of *ardhanarishwar* in Hindu mythology. In Shiva, half is man and half is woman. And Shiva is said to be the greatest god – *mahadeva*. All other gods are small gods; Shiva is the "great god". Why is he called the great god? Because he has come to meet the inner woman, he has become ultimate unity; the woman and the man have disappeared.

The same phenomenon has happened in a Buddha. You see what grace surrounds Buddha, what feminine beauty – and what strength, what power! Power comes from the man and grace comes from the woman. Buddha is both – tremendously powerful and yet tremendously fragile, like a flower. He can face the storm, is ready to face the whole world, and yet so open, so vulnerable, so soft, so delicate – almost feminine. Look at Buddha's face – so feminine. In India we have not even put a mustache and beard on him, just to show that the face has become absolutely feminine. Not that he was not growing a beard, not that he was lacking in some hormones, but we have not put one. We have not put a beard on Mahavira, on the twenty-four *tirthankaras*, on Ram, on Krishna – we have not put that. Not that they all were lacking in hormones; even if one or two were, maybe, all of these people cannot lack hormones. They must have grown beards, and they must have grown beautiful beards – but it is a symbol that the man has come to meet the woman inside, the man and the woman have mingled and merged and become one.

This is the meaning of the name that I have given to these talks on these forty-two chapters – "The Discipline of Transcendence". It starts with the discipline of Hinayana, then with the relaxation of Mahayana, then the no-discipline of Vajrayana. But one has to begin from the beginning, one has to start by sowing the seeds, then comes the tree, and then the flowering.

Enough for today.

Chapter 16:

Away with the Passions!

THE BUDDHA SAID:
There was once a man who, being in despair over his inability to control his passions, wished to mutilate himself. The Buddha said to him, "Better destroy your own evil thoughts than do harm to your own person. The mind is lord. When the lord himself is calmed, the servants will of themselves be yielding. If your mind is not cleansed of evil passions, what avails it to mutilate yourself?"

THEREUPON, THE BUDDHA RECITED THE GATHA:
Passions grow from the will; the will grows from thought and imagination. When both are calmed, there is neither sensualism nor transmigration.

THE BUDDHA SAID,
This Gatha was taught before by Kashyapabuddha.

THE BUDDHA SAID:
From the passions arises worry, and from worry arises fear. Away with the passions, and no fear, no worry.

Man is in misery, and man has remained in misery down the centuries. Rarely can you find a human being who is not miserable. It is so rare that it almost seems unbelievable. That's why buddhas are never believed. People don't believe that they ever existed. People can't believe it. They can't believe it because of their own misery. The misery is such, and they are entangled into it so deeply,

AWAY WITH THE PASSIONS!

that they don't see that any escape is possible. They think the buddhas must have been imagined – they are dreams of humanity. That's what Sigmund Freud says, that buddhas are wish-fulfillments. Man wants to be that way, man desires to be out of misery, man would like to have that silence, that peace, that bene-diction, but it has not happened. And Freud says there is no hope – it cannot happen by the very nature of things. Man cannot become happy.

Freud has to be listened to very keenly and very deeply. He cannot be simply rejected outright; he is one of the most penetrating minds ever. When he says that happiness is not possible, and when he says that hoping for happiness is hoping for the impossible, he means it. His own observation of human misery led him to this conclusion. This conclusion is not that of a philosopher. Freud is not a pessimist. But observing thousands of human beings, getting deeper into their beings, he realized that man is made in such a way that he has a built-in process of being miserable. At the most he can be in comfort, but never in ecstasy. At the most we can make life a little more convenient – through scientific technology, through social change, through a better economy, and other things – but man will remain miserable all the same.

How can Freud believe that Buddha ever existed? Such serenity seems to be just a dream. Humanity has been dreaming about Buddha. This idea arises because Buddha is so rare, so exceptional. He is not the rule. Why has man remained in so much misery? And the miracle is that everybody wants to be happy, you cannot find a man who wants to be miserable, and yet everybody is in misery. Everybody wants to be happy, blissful, peaceful, silent; everybody wants to be in joy, everybody wants to celebrate – but it seems impossible. Now, there must be some very deep cause, so deep that Freudian analysis could not reach it, so deep that logic cannot penetrate it.

Before we enter into the sutras, that basic thing has to be understood: man wants happiness, that's why he is miserable. The more you want to be happy the more miserable you will be. Now this is absurd, but this is the root cause. And when you understand the process of how the human mind functions you will be able to realize it.

Man wants to be happy, hence he creates misery. If you want to get out of misery you will have to get out of your desire for happiness – then nobody can make you miserable. Here is where Freud missed. He could not understand that the very desire for happiness can be the cause of misery. How does it happen? Why in the first place do you desire happiness? And what does it do to you, the desire for happiness?

The moment you desire for happiness, you have moved away from the present, you have moved away from the existential, you have already moved into the future – which is nowhere, which has not come yet. You have moved into a dream. Now, dreams can never be fulfilling. Your desire for happiness is a dream. The dream is unreal, and through the unreal, nobody has ever been able to reach to the real. You have taken a wrong train.

The desire for happiness simply shows that you are not happy right at this moment. The desire for happiness simply shows that you are a miserable being. And a miserable being projects in the future that some time, some day, some way, he will be happy. Out of misery comes your projection. It carries the very seeds of misery. It comes out of you – it cannot be different from you. It is your child: its face will be like you; in its body your blood will be circulating. It will be your continuity.

You are unhappy today and you project that tomorrow will be happy – but tomorrow is a projection of you, of your today, of whatever you are. You are unhappy – the tomorrow will come out of this unhappiness and you will be even more unhappy. Of course, out of more unhappiness you will again desire more happiness in the future. Then you are in a vicious circle: the more unhappy you become, the more you desire happiness; the more you desire happiness, the more unhappy you become. Now it is like a dog chasing its own tail.

In Zen they have a certain phrase for it. They say it is "whipping the cart". If your horses are not moving and you go on whipping the cart, it is not going to help. You are miserable; then anything you can dream about and anything that you can project is going to bring more misery. So the first thing is not to dream, not to project. The first thing is to be here now. Whatsoever it is, just be here now, and a tremendous revelation is waiting for you. The revelation is that nobody can be unhappy in the here now.

Have you ever been unhappy here and now? Right this moment you are sitting there; is there any possibility of being unhappy right now? You can think about yesterday and you can become unhappy, or you can think about tomorrow and you can become unhappy, but right this very moment – this throbbing, beating, real moment – can you be unhappy right now, without any past, without any future?

You can bring misery from the past, from your memory. Somebody insulted you yesterday and you can still carry the wound, you can still carry the hurt and feel unhappy about it. Why? Why did it happen to you? Why did the man insult you? And you have been doing so much good for him, and you have been always a help, always a friend – and he insulted you! You are playing with something that is no more. The yesterday is gone. Or you can be unhappy for tomorrow. Tomorrow your money will be finished – then where are you going to stay, what are you going to eat? Tomorrow your money will be finished! Then unhappiness enters in. Either it comes from yesterday, or it comes from tomorrow, but it is never here now.

Right this moment, in the now, unhappiness is impossible. If you have learned this much, you can become a buddha. Then nobody is hindering your path. Then you can forget all the Freuds. Then happiness is not only possible, it has already happened – it is just in front of you! And you are missing it because you go on looking sideways.

Happiness is where you are; wherever you are, happiness is there. It surrounds you. It is a natural phenomenon. It is just like air, just like sky. Happiness is not to be sought: it is the very stuff the universe is made of. Joy is the very stuff the universe is made of. But you have to look direct, you have to look in the immediate. If you look sideways then you miss.

You miss because of you. You miss because you have a wrong approach.

This is the most fundamental truth Buddha brought to the world. This is his contribution. He says: Go on dying to the past and never think of the future, and then try to be miserable – you will fail. You cannot be miserable. Your failure is absolutely certain; it can be predicted. You cannot manage, however efficient you are in being miserable, however trained, you cannot create misery this very moment.

Desiring happiness helps you look somewhere else, and then you go on missing. Happiness is not to be created, happiness is just to be seen. It is already present. This very moment you can become happy, tremendously happy. This is how it happened to Buddha. He was the son of a king, he had everything – but was not happy. He became more and more unhappy – the more you have, the more unhappy you become. That is the misery of a rich man. That's what is happening in America today. The richer they get the more unhappy they become; they are completely at a loss what to do.

Poor people are always certain about what to do. They have to earn money, they have to build a good house, they have to buy a car, they have to send their children to the university. They always have a program waiting for them. They are occupied, they have a future. They have hope: "Some day or other . . ." They remain in misery, but the hope is there. The rich man is in misery and the hope has also disappeared. His misery is double. You cannot find a poorer man than a rich man; he is doubly poor. He remains projected into the future, and now he knows the future is not going to supply anything – because whatever he needs, he already has it. He becomes troubled, his mind becomes more and more anxious, apprehensive. He becomes anguish itself. That's what happened to Buddha.

He was rich. He had everything that it was possible to have. He became very unhappy. One day he escaped from his palace, left all the riches, his beautiful wife, his newly born child – he escaped. He became a beggar. He started seeking happiness. He went to this guru, to that guru; he asked everybody what to do to be happy – and of course there were a thousand and one people ready to advise him, and he followed everybody's advice. And the more he followed their advice, the more confused he became. Buddha tried whatsoever was said to him. Somebody said: "Do hatha yoga" – he became a hatha yogi. He did yoga postures and he did them to the very extreme. Nothing came out of it. Maybe you can have a better body with hatha yoga, but you cannot become happy. Just a better body, a healthier body, makes no difference. With more energy you will have more energy at your disposal to be unhappy – but you will be unhappy. What else will you do with the energy? If you have more money, what are you going to do with it? – you will do that which you can do. And if a little money makes you so miserable, more money will make you more miserable. It is simple arithmetic.

Buddha dropped all yoga. He went to other teachers, the raja yogis, who teach no body postures, who teach only mantras, chantings, meditations. He did that too, but nothing came out of it. He was really in search.

When you are really in search then nothing can help, then there is no remedy. Mediocre people stop somewhere on the way; they are not real seekers. A real seeker is one who goes to the very end of the search and comes to realize that all search is nonsense. Searching itself is a way of desire – Buddha recognized it one day. One day he had left his palace, he had left his worldly possessions; after six years of spiritual search, he dropped all search. The material search was dropped before, now he dropped the spiritual search. This world was dropped before, now he dropped the other world too.

He was completely rid of desire . . . and that very moment it happened. That very moment there was benediction. When he was completely rid of desire, when he had lost all hope, the future disappeared – because the future exists because of your hope. Future is not part of time, remember. Future is part of your hope, desire; future is part of your greed.

Future is not part of time. Time is always present. Time is never past, never future. Time is always here. The now is infinite; the time never goes anywhere and never comes from anywhere. It is already here and always here. It is your greed, it is your desire, it is your hope that in some way, in some situation, you are going to be happy.

All desire dropped, all hope dropped, all hope abandoned, suddenly Gautama Siddhartha became a buddha. It was always there but he was looking somewhere else. It was there, inside, outside. It is how the universe is made. It is blissful, it is truth, it is divine.

Man remains miserable because man goes on missing this fundamental truth about his desiring. This has to be understood, then these sutras will be very simple.

THE BUDDHA SAID:

> There was once a man who, being in despair over his inability to
> control his passions, wished to mutilate himself. The Buddha said
> to him, "Better destroy your own evil thoughts than do harm to
> your own person. The mind is lord. When the lord himself is
> calmed, the servants will of themselves be yielding. If your mind is
> not cleansed of evil passions, what avails it to mutilate yourself?"

Many things to be understood. First, a great misunderstanding exists about Buddha that he was anti-body. That is absolutely wrong. He was never anti-body. He was not *for* the body, that's true; but he was never anti-body. This sutra will make it clear. He says:

> There was once a man who, being in despair over his inability to control
> his passions, wished to mutilate himself.

And there have been many persons like that, not only one person. Millions of people have destroyed their bodies in the search for truth, God, ecstasy, or whatsoever you call it. Millions of people have concluded that the body is the enemy. There is a certain logic in it. People think it is because of the body that you are in misery. People think it is because of the body that you have sexuality; it is because of the body that you have greed; it is because of the body that you need money; it is because of the body that you need relationship. People think it is because of the body that the whole trouble arises, so why not destroy the body? Why not commit suicide?

There have been many religious sects that are suicidal, which really teach suicide; which say, "This body has to be dropped. If you are courageous enough, then in one leap drop this body. If you are not courageous, then slowly, in parts, cut the body, drop the body." There was a very popular sect in Russia before the revolution – it was very popular – that used to teach people to cut their sexual organs. And there were thousands and thousands of people who followed it, just to mutilate the sexual organs. The idea is that by cutting the sexual organ you will go beyond sex. This is simply foolish, because sexuality does not exist in the sexual organs, it exists in the mind. You can remove the sexual organs and sex will still exist; in fact, now it will become more neurotic because there will be no way to fulfill it.

There have been sects all over the world that teach fasting. Once in a while – once a month, say – fasting can be of help, can be very healthy, can be a cleansing process. But to go on long fasts is destroying the body. But there have been sects . . . in Buddha's time there was a sect of the Jainas that was obsessed with the idea of fasting. "Go on fasting – one month, two months, three months – and if you die while you are on a fast, you will reach the highest heaven."

Why did this idea of fasting become so deep-rooted? Food and sex seem to be the two obsessions of man. And people who wonder, "How to get out of the misery?" think these two things are the reasons why they are miserable. In fact, just the opposite is the case.

I have heard that one airline received this letter: "Gentlemen – may I please suggest that your pilots do not turn on the little light that says 'Fasten Seat Belts', because every time they do, the ride gets bumpy."

Now you can misunderstand the effect for the cause, and the cause for the effect – and it seems logical! This man who wrote the letter must have seen it again and again: whenever it is announced that you should fasten your seat belts, suddenly the ride gets bumpy, rough. He had watched it happen many times. He must have been a professor of logic. Seeing it again and again, that whenever the light comes on, and the announcement is made, immediately something goes wrong . . . His suggestion is very logical – and yet, absurd. The announcement comes only because the ride is going to be bumpy. The announcement is not the cause; the announcement does not create it. It is going to be bumpy and the announcement is to protect you.

But it happens in ordinary life too. Your mind is sexual – the cause is there – and the body simply follows it. But when the body follows, only then you become aware. You are not yet so aware that you can see it when it is in the mind. When it enters into the body, it becomes very tangible – then you become aware. Your awareness is not sharp. You cannot catch it in the cause; when it has already moved into the effect, then you catch it. You catch it when it is already beyond control. You catch it only, you become alert about it only, when it has already become solidified.

There are three states of any idea arising in you. First, the idea is wordless; it is not formulated in thoughts. That is the subtlest thing. If you can catch hold of it there, you will become free of it. The second stage is when it has entered into words; it is formulated – there is a thought arising in you. People are so sleepy that they don't become aware even at the second stage. When the thought has become a thing, when it has already entered into the gross body and the body has become possessed by it, then you become aware. It simply shows your unawareness.

Hence Buddha says if you really want to get rid of the misery, the pain, that life that is almost like hell, you have to become more and more aware. The more aware you become, the deeper the cause you can see. The deeper the cause known, the more capable you become to get out of it. If you can catch some desire when it has not even entered into your conscious mind, and it is still just a feeling with no words, just in the unconscious striving to get to the conscious, there it is very simple to stop it.

It is just like you can brush away a small seed very easily, there is no trouble about it, but when it has taken root and has become a great tree it will be difficult to uproot it.

First the idea arises in the innermost core. Then it enters into the mind. Then it enters into the body. You feel it only when it has entered into the body. There are even more sleepy people who don't even feel it there. When it has entered into the world, *then* they feel it. For example, anger arises first in your deepest core, wordless, undefined. Then it comes to be a thought. Then it enters in your body; adrenaline and other poisons are released in the bloodstream – you are ready to kill somebody or beat somebody, bite somebody. You are getting mad, but you may not even be aware of it. When you hit somebody it has entered into the world – that is the fourth stage. Then you become aware: "What have I done?"

Haven't you observed it many times? When you have hit somebody – your child, your friend, your wife – then suddenly you become aware. "What have I done? I never wanted to do it! It happened in spite of me," you say. This simply shows your unawareness.

Go deeper and catch hold of anything arising in the first step. And then it is so easy – just like you can destroy a seed very easily, but to destroy a tree will be difficult. And when the tree has sent its millions of seeds into the air, then it is almost beyond your control. The winds have taken the seeds to faraway fields; now it is impossible to find out where they have fallen. Now the tree is not one; it has created many possibilities of its own being. It will be replicated in many fields.

Buddha says that destroying the body is not going to help. If your eyes make you desirous of beautiful women or beautiful men, it is not going to help if you destroy your eyes.

There is a story in India about a saint, Surdas. I don't think it is true. If it is true then Surdas is not a saint; he can only be a saint if the story is untrue. I am ready to say that the story is untrue; I cannot say Surdas is untrue. He is so authentic, his insight is so pure –the story must be wrong.

The story is that Surdas left the world, and he was moving through a town. He saw a beautiful woman and he followed her almost as if a magnet was pulling him. Started feeling guilty too! He is a sannyasin, he has renounced the world – what is he doing? But he was incapable of controlling himself, so the story goes. He went to the woman, he asked for food – but that was just an excuse. Then he started to go to the same woman every day – just to have a look at her face, just to have a look into her eyes, just to have a little contact. He started dreaming about her. The whole day he was continuously thinking and fantasizing, and was waiting for the next day when he would be able to go to the woman again.

Then, by and by, he became aware that he was getting into a trap. And the story says that because it was his eyes that made him aware of the beauty of the woman, he destroyed his eyes and became a blind man.

I say, and I say it categorically, this story is simply invented – because this is so foolish! Surdas cannot do it; the story must have been invented by blind people. It must have been invented by the stupid people who always go on inventing stupid things. It is stupid because the eyes cannot do anything – it is the mind. It is the mind that approaches through the eyes. It is the mind that approaches through the hand. When you hit somebody or you kill somebody, it is not the hand that is the murderer, it is you. And it is not going to help if you cut off your hand. You cannot go to the court and say to the magistrate, "It was just my hand."

It happened once in a court that a man argued this way. He said, "It is my hand that has killed." The magistrate was also very clever and cunning – they have to be clever and cunning because they have to deal with clever and cunning people. They have the same logic. The magistrate said, "You are right, you are absolutely logical: you have not killed, your hands have killed. So your hands will remain in prison. You can go home, but the hands cannot go." So the hands were chained and the magistrate said, "Why don't you go now?"

The man said, "How can I go without the hands?"

And the magistrate said, "If you cannot go without the hands, how can the hands do something without you? You are partners. And in fact, the hand is simply a servant – you are the master."

There was once a man who, being in despair over his inability to control his passions wished to mutilate himself.

Buddha is not against the body; he is not anti-body. He cannot be! – because the body is so innocent. It has never done anything wrong. It is so pure; you cannot find a purer thing in existence. Yes, one thing is certain, that whatsoever you want to do, the body follows you. It is a servant and very obedient. Even if you are going to murder somebody, the body follows; it never says no. If you are going to the temple to pray, the body follows. It never says no. Whether you are going to commit a crime or going to pray in the temple, the body follows you so obediently, like a shadow.

No, the body is never responsible.

And one thing has to be understood about the body. The body is a unique thing in the world; nothing can be compared to it. It has one unique situation and that is that it is the only object in the world that you can look at from both sides, from without and from within. If you look at a rock, you look from the outside. If you look at the moon, you look from the outside. Except for the body, *your* body, everything else you look at from the outside. Your body is the only object in the world you can look at from without and you can look at from within.

Hence, the body is the door to the within, the body is the door for the inner journey – how can Buddha be against it? And you can see Buddha's body – so beautiful, so graceful – how can he be against it? Look at Buddha's statues . . . he must have loved his body, he must have had tremendous compassion for his body. His body is flowerlike – it is a rose flower or a lotus. No, he cannot be against the body. And if people interpret that Buddha is against the body, those people are putting their own interpretations on him.

> The Buddha said to him, *"Better destroy your own evil thoughts than do harm to your own person. The mind is lord. When the lord himself is calmed, the servants will of themselves be yielding."*

Buddha's whole effort is to make you aware that whatsoever you are, the cause is your mind. If you are miserable, the mind is functioning in a wrong pattern. If you are happy, the mind is functioning in the right pattern. Happiness is nothing but the humming of the mechanism of mind when it functions perfectly. When the mind is simply in tune with the universe, you are happy. When the mind goes against the nature, against the natural law – what Buddha calls dhamma – when the mind goes against Tao, when the mind goes against the current, when the mind tries to swim upstream, then there are problems, there is misery. When the mind simply follows the stream like a driftwood, just goes with the stream wherever it is going, it is happy. And one day it reaches to the ultimate, the oceanic bliss. There is no need to reach to it, there is no need to make any effort – effortlessly it happens.

So Buddha says the basic question is not of the body, and it is not of the soul.

The soul has no problems, and the body also has no problems. The problem is just in between the two. This mind that links the body and the soul is the problem; this mind that bridges the unknown to the known, the invisible to the visible, the formless to the form – this bridge is the only problem. If you can solve the mind, suddenly you are at home.

The mind is the problem. What can we do to change the mind? What can we do to have a better functioning mind? Again a desire arises, and again you are in the trap of the mind.

If I teach to you that you should become desireless and you will be happy, immediately a desire arises in the mind: how to become desireless? Immediately you start looking for clues, methods, techniques, how to become desireless. Now, to become desireless is again a desire. If I say mind is the problem, you immediately ask how to solve it, how to dissolve it, how to get rid of it – but the one who is asking the question is mind itself, and the one who is going to try is mind itself. So whatever you do you will never get out of the mind by *doing* anything. Still your question is relevant: then what should we do?

We should look into the nature of the mind and not try to do anything. Just a great insight into the nature of your mind is all that is needed. Let me try to explain it to you.

Buddha says, "Desire, and you will be miserable." Suddenly a desire arises: "How to be desireless . . . because we want to be happy and we don't want to be miserable." Desire arises, and new misery arises. When Buddha says desire creates misery, he means simply to watch how desire arises, how it creates misery. Just go on watching.

Each desire brings its own misery. You are passing down the road and you see a beautiful car just passing by – a flash – and a desire arises to possess this car. Now you become miserable. Just a moment before you were perfectly okay, there was no misery, and here this car passes and misery arises. Buddha says, "Watch." Just a moment before, you were humming a song and going for a morning walk, and everything was beautiful. The birds were singing and the trees were green, and the morning breeze was cool and the sun was fantastic – everything was beautiful. You were in a poetic world full of joy and verve and gusto, and you were juicy and you were part of this beautiful morning. Everything was simply just as it should be . . . and here comes a car. It is not that the owner of the car has come to disturb you; he may not even be aware of you. He is not trying to create any misery for you – don't be angry at him. It is not that the car is creating misery in you, because how can the car create misery in you? It is your desire.

Seeing the car a desire arises: "I should become the possessor of the car; this car has to be in my garage." And suddenly the trees are no longer green, birds are no longer singing, the sun is no longer there – it is already sunset. The sunrise has disappeared from the morning; everything is dismal and dark. You are full of desire, you are surrounded by smoke. You have lost contact with life – immediately! Just a flicker of desire and you are millions of miles away from beauty, from truth, from joy.

Just watch. Buddha says simply watch. Stand by the side of the road and watch – what has happened? Just a small desire arising and you are thrown into hell, and you were almost in heaven. You change from heaven to hell so many times in twenty-four hours, and you don't watch.

People come to me and they ask, "Is there any heaven? Is there any hell?" And I am surprised because they go on shunting like a freight train between heaven and hell – continuously! Just a second is needed, a split second – in no time they are in hell and in no time they are in heaven. Just watch how desire brings hell, how desire is hell. And then don't ask how to attain to desireless-ness, there is no need. If you have looked into the nature of desire and you have felt it brings misery, that very understanding will be the dropping of desire. Just go on watching. If it is not dropping that simply shows that your insight is still not deep enough, so make your insight deep.

And it is not a question that somebody else can enlighten you about – it is your desire and only you can watch. I cannot watch your desire. You cannot watch anybody else's desire. It is your private world. Hell or heaven are private things. And within a split second you can shift from one to another.

Just watch . . .

Buddha's word is "watch". Be watchful. Don't create any desire for desire-lessness, otherwise you are simply behaving in a very stupid way – now you are creating a new desire and this will create misery. Simply go into the nature of the desire, look deep into it. Watch how it creates darkness, how it brings misery, how suddenly it takes you, overpowers you. Just go on watching.

One day it is going to happen: a car will pass by and before the desire has arisen you will become watchful, and suddenly a laughter will come to you. You have become watchful; the desire has not arisen. It was just going to appear, it was just ready to jump upon you and take you to hell – but you were watchful. You will feel so happy. For the first time you will have a key. You will know now that just in being watchful the desire has not arisen, the car has passed. The car has nothing to do with desire. Desire arises because you are unconscious, unaware, sleepy; you are living the life of a somnambulist, drunk.

Awareness is desirelessness. Awareness of the desire brings desirelessness. And this key has to be used to open many locks.

If you are greedy, don't ask how to get rid of it because that is greed again, under another name, in another form. You have heard saints, mahatmas, you have read scriptures, and they say if you are greedy you will go to hell. Now greed arises to go to heaven. And those scriptures go on saying that in heaven everything is just beautiful, fabulous. They create greed. Now you ask how to get rid of greed because a new greed has arisen in you: how to achieve heaven? How to enter paradise? How to live there for ever and ever, eternally, ecstatically, blissfully? This is a new greed!

This is not the way. The Buddha's way is really the best that has ever been brought to earth. The Buddha's way is the most penetrating and the most revolutionary way possible. He says watch greed. Just watch greed and see what it is and how it creates misery for you. In that watching, a light will start arising in you; your inner flame will burn bright, and the darkness of greed will disappear. And the same with violence, the same with anger, the same with possessiveness – and the same with all that makes you miserable.

Once you taste something, whatsoever it is, the desire arises again and again to repeat it. Whatsoever you have known in your past, you go on asking for again and again in the future. Your future is nothing but your modified past. Your future is nothing but the desire to repeat your past. And, of course, if you live a bored life, nobody else is responsible for it but you. You ask for boredom! And boredom is misery. You ask for boredom because you ask for repetition. Something happened; for example, you were sitting, and the first star of the evening was becoming visible. You watched, and it was a quiet evening; it was cool and birds were returning to their nests. It was silent and it was very musical and you were in tune. Just watching the star becoming visible you felt beautiful. Now, you have tasted something and you will gather it like a treasure. This treasure will make you miserable.

First, you will hanker for it again and again. That hankering will create misery. And it cannot be repeated by your hankering, remember – because it happened only because there was no hankering in you. You were simply sitting there not knowing what was going to happen. It happened in a state of innocence. It happened in a state of non-expectation. It happened because you were not looking for it. That is a basic ingredient in it. You were not looking, you were not asking. In fact, you were not desiring – you were simply there. Suddenly you became aware: the first star! And in that moment when you became aware of the first star, you were not thinking that it was happiness, remember that too. That comes later on; that is a recapitulation. In that moment you were simply there – not happy, not unhappy, nothing. These words don't mean anything. Existence is so vast that no word about it is meaningful.

But then it is gone and there remains a memory. And you say again and again, "It was beautiful – how beautiful! How divine!" Now a desire arises to repeat it every evening. Next day you are waiting again, but now the whole situation has changed – you are waiting for it, you are looking for it; you want to repeat the old experience. Now this is something new, which was not present in the previous experience. So it won't allow you. You are looking for it too much. You are not relaxed, you are tense, you are afraid you may miss the first star. You are apprehensive. You are worried whether it is going to be again or not. It is not going to be.

First, it is not possible now because you have lost that innocence, that inexperienced state where no memory existed, where the past was not, where the future was not. Secondly, if some day it is repeated it will be boring because it will be a repetition. You have already known it. The beauty is in the new, it is never in the old. The beauty is in the fresh, it is never in the dead. The beauty belongs to the original, never to the carbon copy. The beauty is when an experience is firsthand, not secondhand. Now, if it happens at all it will not make you happy; it will be a secondhand experience. And remember, existence is never secondhand. Existence is always fresh.

To know godliness in the beauty of the evening, or in the beauty of a bird on the wing, means you have to be absolutely innocent. The past has to be completely dropped and the future is not to be allowed to interfere. Then, and only then, there is beauty and there is benediction, there is blessing, there is happiness and bliss.

Once you experience something, you start asking for it, you become a beggar. Then it will never happen, and you will carry the memory like a wound.

Have you watched it? Watch it: whenever you are happy, in that moment you don't know it is happiness. It is only afterwards, when the experience is gone, faded away, is no more, then mind comes in and starts looking for it, starts comparing, evaluating, judging, and says, "Yes, it was beautiful! so beautiful!" When the experience itself was present, mind was not present.

Happiness is when mind is not.

And when mind comes in, happiness is no longer there. Now there is only a memory, a dead memory. Your lover is gone; you are just carrying a letter written by your lover. The flower has faded; now it is just an image in your mind. This image will not allow happiness to enter again in your being – this image will be the barrier, will be the rock.

Buddha says: Don't carry the past and don't ask for the future – just be here now. Then there is no-mind.

And the body simply follows that no-mindness. Right now the body follows the mind, and the mind is the culprit – and you go on punishing the body. It is

321

almost like a small child who comes running into the room and hits his head on the door, becomes angry at the door, starts beating the door – as if the door is the culprit. Not only children but even grown-up people do such things. You are writing and your fountain pen is not flowing well; you become angry and you throw it on the floor – you punish the fountain pen! And still you think man is rational? Still you believe man is a rational being?

When you come home angry, have you watched? You open the door in such anger, you bang it. Now, the door has not done anything to you . . .

It happened once:

> A man came to see a Zen master; he banged the door, he threw his shoes on the floor. He came to the master and bowed down, touched his feet. The master said, "I cannot accept your greeting. You first go and ask the door to forgive you, and the shoes."
>
> The man said, "What are you talking about?! Do you want me to become a laughingstock?" And there were so many people sitting around . . .
>
> The master said, "If you don't do this, then I am not going to allow you to be here – you simply get out! If you can insult the door and if you can insult the shoes, then you have to ask for their forgiveness. When you insulted them, did you not feel that you were doing something ridiculous? Is it only now, when I ask you to apologize, that you feel ridiculous? Go and do it!"
>
> The man went. At first he felt a little foolish, and people were watching . . . but he asked to be forgiven. He said, "Sir, please, I was not conscious and I have done something wrong unconsciously, forgive me." And he was talking to the shoes and to the door, and when he came back he was a totally different man. The master took him close and hugged him. The man said, "It is tremendous! When I was asking to be forgiven, first I felt foolish, then suddenly I felt so good – I have never felt this way. I actually felt that they had forgiven me. I felt their compassion and their sympathy and their love."

You go on behaving in such unconscious ways. That unconscious manner of your behavior is all that Buddha means by the word "mind." Mind is your sleep. Mind is your absence. And if the body follows this mind, this sleepy, drunk mind, don't get angry at the body.

> *"The mind is lord. When the lord himself is calmed, the servants will of themselves be yielding."*

When the mind is calm it becomes no-mind. No-mind and a calm mind mean exactly the same thing; they don't mean two different things. A calm mind, a cool mind, is a no-mind – because mind is the fever. Mind is the continuous anxiety, tension, the disease – yes, the disease is the mind. When the disease has disappeared, you function from a state which is of no-mind, and then the body follows it.

The body is a follower. If you have mind, the body follows the mind; if you have no-mind, the body follows the no-mind.

But don't start fighting with the body. Don't be stupid.

"If your mind is not cleansed of evil passions, what avails it to mutilate yourself?" Thereupon the Buddha recited the Gatha: Passions grow from the will, the will grows from thought and imagination: when both are calmed, there is neither sensualism nor transmigration.

The Buddha said, This Gatha was taught before by Kashyapabuddha.

Buddha says, "There have been millions of buddhas before me and there will be millions of buddhas after me." This is something very new in the world of religions. Mahavira says, "There have been only twenty-three *tirthankaras* before me, and there will be no *tirthankara* any more." Mohammed says, "There have been only four prophets before me and there will be no prophet any more after me." Jesus says, "I am the only begotten son of God." Buddha is rare. He says, "There have been millions of buddhas before me, and millions of buddhas will be after me." And this seems to be truer.

Only twenty-three *tirthankaras* in the whole infinity? Then what about Ram, then what about Krishna? They are not included in the Jaina *tirthankaras*. Mohammed says, "There have been only four prophets before me" – then what about Mahavira, and what about Krishna, what about Buddha? They are not included in it. Jesus says, "I am the only begotten son." This looks absurd, that God should have only one son. And what has he been doing afterwards, using birth control? This looks absurd, and it creates fanaticism. Then the Christians think they are superior because they are the followers of the only son that God has. Others are prophets, at the most, if they recognize them at all, but theirs is the only son of God. That creates ego, a feeling of superiority.

Hindus say they have only twenty-four avatars. A few centuries ago they had the idea of ten avatars, and then they expanded it a little because Jains were claiming twenty-four *tirthankaras*. There was great competition, so they said, "Okay, we will also have twenty-four." The number twenty-four became standard; even Buddhists started saying that there are only twenty-four buddhas. And when *tirthankaras* are twenty-four and buddhas are twenty-four, to have only ten avatars looks a little poor – so Hindus extended their idea. They dropped the idea of ten avatars; they also claimed to have twenty-four avatars. But what about Mahavira, what about Adinatha? They are not included.

Buddha includes all. He is tremendously inclusive and he creates no superiority; he says millions of buddhas have been before and millions will be afterwards. The world has never lacked buddhas – and that is how it should be! Because to be a buddha is just to be aware of your nature. It is nothing special. It looks special because you have not tried it; otherwise it is your own treasure, it has only to be claimed.

And look at the beauty of it: Buddha claims nothing special for himself. He says many buddhas have lived, millions, and there are millions to come. Look at the beauty of his declaration – about himself he is saying, "I am just one in millions – nothing special about me!" This is how a really religious person should be: nothing special, very ordinary. When there are millions of buddhas, then how can you be special? You can be special if there is a limited number.

There was much conflict, because when Mahavira claimed that he was the twenty-fourth, there were eight others who were claiming that they were the twenty-fourth. There was trouble! Nobody was ready to believe in the others, and there are no ways to prove it really. How can you prove who is the real *tirthankara*? A few chose Goushalak and followed him; a few chose Mahavira and followed him. A few chose others – Ajit Keshkambal, Sanjay Vilethiputta, and there were other claimers – how do you decide? Christians say Jesus is the only son of God – and the Jews crucified him. How do you decide? They thought he was a cheat.

The Jews are also waiting for a Messiah, they have been waiting for centuries – but they never allow anybody to become that Messiah because then for whom will they wait? They are hoping and hoping and hoping, and they have waited so long that now it has become habitual for them – they won't allow anybody to be the Messiah. Jesus claimed to be; many others have claimed after Jesus, but whoever claims, "I am the Messiah" has to be destroyed, has to be rejected, has to be proved a cheat. The Messiah is certainly going to come, but they won't allow anybody to claim it. Centuries of waiting and they have become addicted. Now they will wait – even if God comes they will crucify him, because they will say, "Who wants you? We love waiting, we exist in our hope." They go on hoping.

But everybody tries to prove himself special . . . Jews think they are the chosen race, that God has chosen them specially; Hindus think they are the chosen race; Jainas think they are the chosen ones. Buddha is rare. Buddha says there were millions of buddhas before, countless. In fact, he has said that if you count the grains of sand in the Ganges, there have been more than that many buddhas before, and there will be more later on. This makes his own stature very ordinary, but this is his beauty. Not to claim any extraordinariness is what extraordinariness is. And when you claim, when you claim you are superior, you are simply showing that you suffer from an inferiority complex.

Now, Mohammed says there will be no prophet any more. Why are you closing the door? Now if somebody claims "I am the prophet", Mohammedans will kill him, because Mohammed has closed the door. But who is he to close the door? The door belongs to nobody or it belongs to all. How can he close it? And why in the first place this idea? Mahavira thinks he is the last, Mohammed thinks he is the last, Jesus thinks he is the last – then what do you mean? You simply don't allow evolution, you don't allow any new idea to evolve. You close the door, you make a closed dogma so that nobody can disturb it.

Buddha keeps all doors open, he says there are millions . . . He remembers this Gatha from some past Buddha; Kashyapabuddha was his name. He says:

This Gatha was told by Kashyapabuddha.

Passions grow from the will, the will grows from thought and imagination: when both are calmed, there is neither sensualism nor transmigration.

The will means the ego. The will means to fight against existence. Whenever you see somebody fighting upstream, you say, "He is a man of willpower." What do you mean by willpower? All "will" is against existence. You fight with it, you try to do something that is not in the nature of things. You try to force something. If you are violent with nature, then you have will.

Many people come to me and they say, "Osho, somehow help us to have more will power." Why? Am I your enemy? Should I help you to become more mad? Will power? But in the West, will power is very important because the whole West thinks that to have a strong ego is a must; you should have will power, you should develop will power. Thousands of books exist in the market on how to develop will power and they sell because people want to be more and more refined in their egos.

Buddha says: *Passions grow from the will* . . . desires grow from the will. The "I", the ego, is the root of your mind. Your whole mind is centered around the "I".

The will grows from thought and imagination . . . Thought comes from the past; imagination means movement in the future. Whatsoever you have experienced, thought, learned, that is your ego. And whatsoever you want to experience in your future, would like to have in your future, is your will. These are two aspects of the same phenomenon.

When both are calmed . . . when thought is no longer there, means when past is no longer there, and when imagination, projection, dreaming, future is no longer there: *When both are calmed, there is neither sensualism nor transmigration.* Buddha says then all sensualism disappears; then one is no longer greedy for senses and the experience of the senses.

Remember that by the disappearance of sensualism he does not mean that your sensitivity disappears – you become tremendously sensitive. A sensual person is not a sensitive person; a sensual person is gross, rough, very primitive. A sensitive person is very highly developed; he is receptive. A sensual person is after pleasure, and the sensitive person is one who knows bliss is here and he is open to it, and he goes on being showered by the divine bliss. He soaks it up like a sponge. He is sensitive.

The sensual person is always after something, trying to achieve – money, power, prestige. The sensitive person is simply alive here now, enjoying the beauty that is available. When tomorrow comes then tomorrow will take care of itself.

That's what Jesus means when he says, "Think not of the morrow." That's what Jesus says when he shows to his disciples the lilies in the field and says, "Look, how beautiful they are! And they toil not. They are simply here; they don't worry about what is going to happen tomorrow. Even Solomon, in all his glory, was not so beautiful," says Jesus, "as these poor flowers of the lilies."

A sensitive person is a flowerlike person, open to existence, enjoying it – enjoying it tremendously but not seeking anything. His search has dissolved. He is not chasing anything.

I have heard:

> A man lost everything at the casinos in Vegas. He tried every one in town and each was a disaster. All he had left now was a Kennedy fifty-cent piece. He kept tossing it in the air as he walked along the street trying to figure out a way to get another stake, when his coin slipped out of his fingers and fell into a grating in the middle of the street.
>
> The man was after it like a shot, but before he could grab it he was hit by a taxi and carried off to the hospital with a broken leg.
>
> He was out in a couple of months, and with the settlement from

the insurance company he started back to the casinos. On the way, he limped past the same grating where he had lost his coin. He started to look down to see if he could find it when he was hit by another taxi, and he was back in the hospital with his other leg broken.

"How could you get knocked twice in exactly the same place?" the nurse asked him. "I mean, what in the world made you go back to that stupid grating?"

"That was my good luck charm," he explained, "and I didn't want to lose it."

People go on chasing, and go on being hit every time. Their whole life becomes just wounds and wounds and wounds, but again and again they go on chasing the same things – as if they don't see what is happening to them.

A man of sensitivity remains wherever he is, and truth seeks him. A man of sensualism rushes from here to there, from there to somewhere else, chasing and chasing. And this is the beauty of the whole process: if you are chasing truth you will never find it because you don't know where it is. If you are chasing happiness you will never meet it, because you don't know the where-abouts, you don't even know the face of happiness – even if you come across her, you will not be able to recognize her. The person who is sensitive simply sits wherever he is and happiness comes to him, and bliss comes to him, and truth comes to him.

THE BUDDHA SAID:

From the passions arises worry, and from worry arises fear. Away
with the passions, and no fear, no worry.

Observe it. These are not theories. These are facts of life. Buddha is not a theor-etician, not a metaphysician – not at all. He is just a scientist of the basic facts of life. He talks only about a fact. You need not believe in it. You have simply to watch and you will find the truth of it.

He says: *From passions arises worry* . . . Whenever desire arises, worry arises: how to get it? How to reach it, how to achieve? You are worried. When you are worried there are a thousand and one alternatives. Then more worry arises: which will be the right alternative to reach to it? Which will be the right path? And then fear arises: whether you will be able to reach? There are so many competitors in the world, and so many people have tried and failed. Look at Alexander and Genghis Khan and Nadir Shah – and so many people have tried, and tried so powerfully, tried hard, and still they have failed.

What is the guarantee that you will succeed? Then fear arises. These are simple facts!

> A man comes into a store to buy a suit. The salesman tries one jacket on him after another. He says to the customer, "Turn around, let's see it in this light; now let's look at it in the rear-view mirror; now from this angle, now this angle." Still the man asks to try on other jackets.
>
> Finally the boss comes up to them and picks out a jacket. The customer puts it on and buys it immediately. Says the boss, "See how easy it is to make a sale?"
>
> "Okay," says the salesman, "you made the sale – but who made him dizzy?"

Once a passion is there it will make you dizzy – worries, apprehensions; what to choose, what not to choose; where to go, how to go; what will be the right technique, the right method, the right approach? And then the fear: whether you will be able to make it? A constant fear. One becomes dizzy. Passion is the salesman and then comes the devil, the boss. Then you are thrown in hell. Desire makes you dizzy. And nobody can be certain, nobody.

I was reading a beautiful anecdote:

> Father O'Malley and Rabbi Cohen were playing golf. On the third hole, Father O'Malley hit one into the rough, and he hollered, "Oh, shit!" And he looked up to heaven and said, "Dear Lord, I'm terribly sorry. It was an oversight." On the fifth hole he made another terrible shot into the rough. Again he shouted, "Oh, shit!" Again he looked up to heaven and said, "Dear Lord, again please excuse me. I'm terribly sorry." On the ninth hole, same thing again, into the rough. He hollered "Oh, shit!"
>
> Just then there was a bolt of lightning and Rabbi Cohen was struck and killed. A loud rumbling was heard in heaven and a voice saying, "Oh, shit!"

Even God can miss, so what is the guarantee of your ever being successful? One goes on being afraid, trembling, shaking with fear.

Passions create worry; worry creates fear – away with the passions, and no fear, no worry.

But people have only passions in their lives; that's why they have only worries and fear and nothing else. They come to me – so many people – and they want to get some peace of mind, they want a way to get out of their worries. But if you tell them, "Get out of your passions," then they are not ready to follow you. They want some mantra, some cheap thing, so they can go on desiring, they can go on chasing their passions – and still remain unworried.

A politician used to come to me, and he would always say, "Somehow help me to have some peace of mind."

I said, "Being a politician you should not ask for it – it never comes in the way of a politician. Peace of mind? If it can happen to a politician, then are the saints fools? What are they doing? Then why should they leave ambition? It can never come. Ambition creates tension, worry. You get out of your politics!"

And he would say, "You may be right, but right now I cannot get out of it."

I told him, "Then you be at ease with your tensions, accept them. You are trying to do something which is not possible. You want to eat the cake and have it too."

Then he started going to Maharishi Mahesh Yogi. For many days he didn't turn up. One day, suddenly we met in a train. I asked him, "You have not been coming to me for many days."

He said, "What is the point of coming to you? You say get out of politics. Mahesh Yogi is better. He says, 'Wherever you are, I will make you more efficient. You are a politician? You will become a better politician – just do TM.'"

Now that fits, that completely fits. You are not to change anything; just repeating some foolish thing – blah, blah, blah – and that's all. Twenty minutes you repeat it and wherever you are, all success is guaranteed to you, all efficiency is guaranteed to you. Even thieves are doing TM, smugglers are doing TM, politicians are doing TM. The smuggler thinks that if he does TM he will never be caught, he will become more efficient.

Meditation is not so cheap. Meditation is a total transformation of your being. And a great understanding is needed and a great intelligence.

Buddha's sutras are only for those who are really intelligent people and who really want to get out of the misery that they have created around themselves. It is only for those who are really fed up with misery and are ready to get out of the trap.

It is up to you, it depends on you. You have created it! Once you understand how you have created it, it will disappear – because then you will not be able to create it any more.

Enough for today.

Chapter 17:

The Eightfold Way

THE BUDDHA SAID:

Those who follow the way are like unto warriors who fight single-handed with a multitude of foes.

They may all go out of the fort in full armor; but among them are some who are faint-hearted, and some who go halfway and beat a retreat, and some who are killed in the affray, and some who come home victorious.

O monks, if you desire to attain enlightenment, you should steadily walk in your way, with a resolute heart, with courage, and should be fearless in whatever environment you may happen to be, and destroy every evil influence that you may come across; for thus you shall reach the goal.

Gautama the Buddha has no leaning towards abstraction, philosophy or metaphysics. He's very practical, down-to-earth practical. He's very scientific. His approach is not that of a thinker; the approach is existential. When he attained and became a buddha, it is said that the god of the gods, Brahma, came to him and asked him, "Who is your witness? You declare that you have become a buddha, but who is your witness?" Buddha laughed, touched the earth with his hand, and said, "This earth, this solid earth is my witness."

He is very earthy; he made the earth his witness. He could have said the sky, but no . . . he could have said the sun or the moon or the stars, but no . . . He touched the earth and said, "This solid earth is my witness." His whole approach is like that.

Before we enter into these sutras his basic steps have to be understood.

Buddha's way is called "the eightfold way". He has divided it into eight parts. Those divisions are arbitrary, just utilitarian. The way is one. It is not really divided, it is just so that you can understand it easily. And this is very fundamental – if you can understand these eight steps or eight divisions of the way, the way will open just in front of you. You are already standing on it, but not aware; your mind is wandering somewhere. The way is in front of you. So try to understand these eight steps as deeply as possible.

The first is *right view.*

And all these eight steps are concerned with rightness – right view, right intention, right speech, right morality, right livelihood, right effort, right mindfulness, and the eighth, the ultimate, right samadhi. The word "right" has to be understood first because the Sanskrit word *samyak* is so meaningful, is so pregnant with meaning that it cannot be translated. "Right" is a very poor translation for it for many reasons.

First, the word "right" immediately gives the idea as if it is against the wrong. *Samyak* never gives that idea. *Samyak* is not against the wrong, Buddha's "right" is not against the wrong, because he says, "Wrongs are many, right is one – so how can the right be against the wrong?" Health is one, diseases are many. There are not as many healths as there are diseases, so health cannot be against disease – otherwise there would be so many healths. Somebody is suffering from TB and then he becomes healthy, somebody is suffering from cancer and he becomes healthy, and somebody is suffering from flu and he becomes healthy. These three healths are not three healths. The diseases were different but health is one, and the one cannot be against the many.

Exactly the same is true about right and wrong. Right is one. Wrongs are millions; you can go on inventing wrongs. Right cannot be invented; it does not depend on you. Right is a state of affairs where you are in tune with the whole. That is the meaning of health too: when you are in tune with the whole you are healthy. The music flows between you and the whole, there is no obstruction. You feel a well-being. There is no noise, everything is in harmony. When the individual is in tune with the universal then right exists, health exists. When you fall out of tune then so many wrongs arise – there is no limit to them, they are endless. And you can invent new wrongs.

Humanity has invented many new diseases that were not prevalent before. In the old scriptures, ayurvedic scriptures, many diseases are not mentioned. People think they are not mentioned because ayurveda was not yet enough of a science to diagnose those diseases. That is not true; ayurveda became a perfect science. But those diseases were not in existence, so how can you diagnose a disease that doesn't exist? They were non-existential. There were a few diseases which existed only for rich people, very rich people. They were called royal diseases. Tuberculosis was called "royal". It was not an ordinary disease. Now the whole world has become royal; now the whole world suffers from richness, affluence. Leisure has made many new diseases available.

Cancer is a very new disease. It can exist only when the mind is very worried, when worry becomes like a wound. And around that subtle wound in the psyche arises a disease in the body corresponding to it. That's what cancer is and that's why cancer seems to be incurable. There is no way to cure it from the body side. It can be cured only from the mind side because basically it arises there.

Each age has its own diseases, each age has its own vices, and each age invents its own sins. But virtue is ageless, timeless. Sainthood has nothing to do with any age, any time period. It is not historical, it is existential.

Buddha says: Right is that which is not your invention. It is already there. If you go away from it you are wrong, if you come close to it you are right. The closer you are the more right you are. One day, when you are exactly home, you are perfectly right. *Samyak* and samadhi both come from the same root *sam*. *Samyak* is the step towards samadhi. If you don't understand *samyak*, you will not be able to understand samadhi. So, seven steps ultimately lead to the final step. "Samadhi" means now everything has fallen in tune with existence. Not a flaw exists; the music is utterly perfect.

But there is no better word for *samyak* in English than "right", so you have to understand it. "Right" in the Buddhist meaning of the term means balanced, centered, grounded, harmonious, tranquil – all of these things. The basic thing can be understood even if there is no synonymous term in English to translate it. But remember, it has nothing to do with wrong. Wrong is a human invention, right is divine. Right is not something that you have to do – you were born right. Wrong is something that you have to do; you were not born wrong. Every child is born in harmony. That's why children are so beautiful. Have you ever seen a baby who is ugly? It doesn't happen. All babies are beautiful, but all grown-ups are not. So something somewhere must have gone wrong – because *all* babies are beautiful. They have a grace, a tremendous elegance which has nothing to do with any practice, because they have had no time to practice anything. They come into the world without any rehearsal. They are just there – so happy, so silent, so harmonious, such grace surrounds them, as if the whole of existence is protective towards them. Then, by and by, they learn the ways of man and become wrong. Then ugliness appears. Then beautiful eyes can become horrible; then a beautiful face can become criminal; then a beautiful body can lose all grace. Then a beautiful intelligence . . . Every child is born intelligent; that's how things are. An intelligent child can become stupid, mediocre. These are human achievements.

The wrong is a human achievement, the right is divine. You are not to do anything for it, you have only to stop all that you have been doing to create the wrong. And when there is right, you don't feel you are right. That's why, I repeat again, it is not *against wrong*. When you are in the right you are simply natural. You don't have any feeling of being righteous, you don't have any feeling that you are a great saint. If you have that feeling then you are still wrong somewhere because the "no" is a jarring note. It does not allow the music to flow.

"Right" means balanced, non-tense, centered; you are not a stranger in existence. That's what "right" means: you are at home. This existence is your family, you are not an alien. In the West, and in the East too, the modern mind continuously talks and thinks about alienation, that man has become an outsider, that man has become a stranger, that we seem to be just like accidents on earth. Existentialists have the right word for it: they say we have been thrown here. Thrown, dumped, expelled, punished! This existence is against us, and you can prove it – so many diseases, and death is there; so many frustrations, failures. People go on saying man proposes and God disposes. So of course man is doomed, doomed from the very beginning, is born with great desires and without any possibility of any fulfillment, ever. How can this existence be your home? It can't be your family.

The right is when you start feeling that you are at home. Nothing is alien, nothing is strange.

Buddha says: If *you* are, you are wrong – because whenever you are, you are separate from existence. When you are not you are right. Listen to this paradox; it is one of the most beautiful paradoxes. Buddha says: When you are, you are wrong. The very separation, the "I am", creates a barrier. Then you don't melt, then you become frozen, then you are like an ice cube, dead, closed. Then you have a boundary. When you start melting, and you start feeling, "Existence is, and I am just a part of it" and you relax, and there is a let-go, you disappear. Then you are right. When you are not, you are right.

These eight steps are just indicators, by and by, of how to come to that tremendous courage, that ultimate courage where you take the quantum leap and you simply disappear. When the self disappears, the universal self arises.

The first is right view.

Buddha says: Look at things without any opinion; otherwise you never look at reality. Look at things without any philosophy, without any prejudice, without any dogma, creed, scripture. Just look. Look at things as they are. Be factual; don't create a fiction. If you are looking for something with a prejudice, you will find it – that is the trouble. If you are already full of a belief you will find it because the mind is so creative, so imaginative, so capable of auto-hypnosis, that whatsoever it believes it can create. Buddha says: Go to reality without any belief. Belief is the barrier.

You must have watched it.

If you are born a Hindu – that means if you are being conditioned from your childhood by Hindus – it means you are a victim of Hinduism. The same applies to Mohammedans and Christians, Jews, Jains, communists – the whole of humanity is a victim of this school or that, of this prejudice or that, of this belief or that. If you are born a Hindu and have been conditioned in certain dogmas, and you start meditating, you will start seeing visions of Krishna, Rama – it depends on what you have been taught, who has been enforced and engraved in your mind – but Christ will never come to you. Christ comes to a Christian, Buddha comes to a Buddhist, Mahavira comes to a Jaina. To a Jaina, Mohammed can never come; it is impossible. Even to conceive of the idea is impossible. Even in a dream, Mohammed will not come to a Jaina. What is happening? Are these Buddhas, Mahaviras and Christs really coming, or is your own belief creating them? Your own belief is creating them.

To a communist, nobody comes. His belief is that all religion is nonsense, an opium for the people, a dangerous poison to be got rid of as soon as possible – then nobody comes. It depends on you. If you have a belief, that very belief becomes a dream; and if you are very, very sensitive, receptive, that dream can look more real than the reality. In fact, this happens every day, even in non-religious people. You dream in the night and when you dream the dream looks so real. You have dreamed your whole life and every morning you cancel it as unreal. But again, next night you dream, and the dream again seems real.

The dreaming faculty lives on belief. If you have a strong belief then the dreaming faculty joins with the belief, pours its energy into the belief, makes the belief a reality, and you start having visions. Buddha is not in favor of any visions – because he says: "That which is, needs no visions. It needs simply clarity to see." Your mind need not have any dreams, great dreams of great saints, heaven and hell; these are all your creations.

"Right view" is having no prejudice, having no belief, having no opinion whatsoever. Difficult . . . Buddha's path is arduous; he demands too much. It almost seems to be a superhuman feat. But it is possible – and that is the only way towards truth.

If you have any opinion you will impose your opinion on the truth. You do it every day. If you come to me with the opinion that this man is good, you will go convinced that this man is good; if you come with the opinion that this man is bad, you will go convinced that this man is bad. Your belief will always find that which it wants to find. Belief is very selective.

I have heard:

> The boy had been brought into court again charged with stealing auto hubcaps. The magistrate determined to appeal to his father: "See here," said the judge. "This boy of yours has been in this court many times charged with theft, and I am tired of seeing him here."
>
> "I don't blame you, Judge," said the father. "And I am just as tired of seeing him here as you are."
>
> "Then why don't you teach him how to act? Show him the right way and he will not be coming here."
>
> "I have already shown him the right way," said the father, "but he just does not seem to have any talent for learning. He keeps getting caught!"

Now, the right way is different for the judge and for the father. The father himself is a thief. He also wants the boy to learn "the right way" so that he is never caught again. But his right way is *his* right way.

> For a holiday, Mullevy decided to go to Switzerland to fulfill a lifelong dream and climb the Matterhorn. He hired a guide, and just as they neared the top the men were caught in a snowslide.
>
> Three hours later a Saint Bernard plowed through to them, a keg of brandy tied under his chin.
>
> "Hooray!" shouted the guide. "Here comes man's best friend."
>
> "Ah," said Mullevy. "And look at the size of the dog that is bringing it!"

It depends on how you look at things. You can look at the same thing, and you may not be seeing the same thing. If you are listening to me in trust, you listen differently. If you are listening to me with disbelief, you listen to me differently. If you are listening as a disciple, you listen differently. If you are listening just as an outsider, a visitor – just by the way, you have come with a friend – you listen differently. What I say is the same, but how you interpret it will depend on you. Right listening will be that you listen as nobody, neither for nor against, with no prejudice – just listening. If you can see things without any idea in the mind, then Buddha says it is right view.

Right view needs no conceptualization. That's why Buddha says: Don't ask me any theoretical question. He does not say anything about God because it is pointless to create a theory. He tries to open your eyes. He says: To know the truth, you need eyes – just as you cannot teach a blind man what light is like, howsoever you try. You cannot teach a blind man anything about the light. Of course, you can teach as much as you want and he may learn all the information that you deliver to him, but still, in reality, he will not be able to conceive what light is. He cannot.

It happened that a blind man was brought to Buddha. Buddha was passing through a village, and the people of the village were getting tired of this blind man because he was very logical and very philosophical. He was so argumentative that he used to prove that the light exists not. He would say, "You just bring it, I would like to touch it" . . . or "You bring it so I can taste it" . . . or "You bring it, at least let me smell it . . . bring it and beat it like a drum so I can hear it."

Of course, you cannot beat light like a drum, and you cannot taste it, smell it, or touch it. The blind man would laugh, laugh with victory and say, "You fools! You are trying to prove something to me which is not. I have four senses. Prove it! I am ready, I am open." They could not prove it, so the blind man started thinking that they were just trying to befool him about this light: "The whole business is just a deception, a fraud. In fact, they want to prove that I am blind. They are insulting me. I am not blind, because light exists not. So what is the point? If light exists not, the eyes need not be there. Eyes are just a fiction." He would say, "You are all blind, but you are dreaming about something that exists not."

They brought the man to Buddha, and Buddha said, "Don't bring him to me. I know a physician – because he needs no conviction, he needs a vision of light. He needs eyes. He needs treatment, he needs no theory about it. But I know a physician."

Buddha had a beautiful, very learned physician. He was given to him by an emperor, to look after Buddha's body. The blind man was taken to the physician. He treated him, and within six months he was able to see.

By that time Buddha had moved to another town. The man came running and dancing; he was ecstatic. He fell at Buddha's feet and he said, "You have convinced me."

Buddha said, "Don't talk nonsense. I have not done anything. Your eyes have convinced you, and there is no other way."

Buddha used to say, "I am not a philosopher, I am a physician. I would like to treat your inner eyes, and the first step is right view." "Right view" really means a mind without views. If you have any view, it is wrong view. If you don't have any view, then you are simply open, clear. Then your window is completely open, you don't have any hindrance; whatsoever is available you will be able to see. Buddha never says anything about that which you will see; he only talks about how to treat your blindness, how to get out of your blindness.

Mulla Nasruddin's son, studying political science, asked his father, "Dad, what is a traitor in politics?"

"Any man who leaves our party," said the Mulla, "and goes over to the other one, is a traitor."

"Well, what about a man who leaves his party and comes over to yours?" asked the young man.

"He would be a convert, son," said Nasruddin, "a real convert."

When a Hindu becomes a Christian, to Hindus he is a traitor and to Christians he is a convert. When a Christian becomes a Hindu, they welcome him; he has come to his senses, he has realized what truth is. But to Christians, he is a traitor.

If you live with views you cannot see the truth of anything. Your view always comes as a barrier. It obstructs, it distorts, it does not allow you to see things as they are. And godliness, or truth, is that which is. To know the real you need not have any views. In fact, if you really want to know the real, you have to drop all views. That is the first renunciation Buddha teaches: drop all views and "right view" will arise. All views are wrong views. The Hindu, the Christian, the Buddhist – all views are wrong views. A person without views, without opinions, a person with not a thought to cling to, a person who is just a mirror, reflects reality.

The woman heard the preacher go through the commandments, and after every commandment she joined the rest of the audience in shouting, "Amen!" When he came to the commandment, "Thou shalt not commit adultery," she said, "Now he is beginning to meddle."

Something looks absolutely right until it doesn't fit with you – as if you are the touchstone of truth, as if you are the criterion of truth. The moment it is not fitting with you, you think it is wrong. This is a wrong approach, and if you have this approach you will never arrive to that which is real. If something is not fitting with you, then don't be in a hurry to settle the matter – don't decide that it must be wrong because it doesn't fit with you. It need not fit with you.

Existence has no obligation to fit with you, reality has no obligation to fit with you. If it is not fitting with you, then a man of right understanding will change himself rather than deny the reality.

So whenever it hurts, whenever reality hurts and you feel that you are not fitting, it is you who are not fitting, not the reality. And a man who has no views will never find that there is any conflict between him and the reality. He will always fit with the reality and reality will fit with him – just like a glove fits on the hand. This is right view.

The second step is *right intention.*

We live result-oriented, we live goal-oriented, we live with intention, with desire: "Things should be like this, then I will be happy. If they are not like this then I'm going to be unhappy." That's why we are so frustrated. Buddha says your frustration comes from your intentions. Your intentions seem to be going against reality; then you are frustrated.

Drop intentions, drop desires, and just move moment to moment with reality, wherever it leads. Just become a driftwood; just float with the stream and you will never be frustrated. Frustration comes whenever there is conflict between you and the real. And remember, the real is going to win; you cannot win against the real. Nobody can win against existence; that's not possible, that doesn't happen. You can win only with existence. Whenever you succeed remember, somehow accidentally you must have been with existence. All success simply means that unknowingly you must have stepped into a harmony with existence, and that's why you have succeeded. Failure means that unknowingly you must have stepped against it. Failure is an indication, success is an indication.

A man who has learned this drops all his intentions. He has no private desires. He says exactly what Jesus said on the cross: "Thy will be done." He surrenders. Buddha has no concept of God. His approach is more scientific than Jesus.' Jesus is more poetic. Buddha is not a poet, he's very mathematical. He says only one thing can be understood, and that is that you drop all your intentions. When you don't have any intentions, you have the right intention.

And you have to remember this paradox in all the eight steps. "Right intention" means no intention on your part. Then the universe flows through you. Then the universe goes on fulfilling its intention through you. You become a vehicle.

> "Please," the little man prayed, "you know me. I am always praying
> to you and yet I have had nothing but bad luck, misery, sickness and
> despair all my life. And look at the butcher next door. He's never
> prayed in his life, and yet he has nothing but prosperity, health and

joy. How come a believer like me is always in trouble and he is always doing good?"

Suddenly a big booming voice sounded in his ear, "Because the butcher is not always nagging me, that's why!"

Now, your prayer can be just nagging. What are your prayers? – your prayers are your intentions, the desires that you would like fulfilled. What are your prayers? – your prayers are always *against* what is. And look at the absurdity – you are praying to God, and the prayer is basically against God because if it is not against what is happening then there is no point in praying. You are ill – if you trust God that means you know that God wants you to be ill. This is how you are at this moment, this is what God's will is. You accept it. Then your prayer is only of gratitude. You don't beg for anything, you simply thank God: "Thank you for making me ill. Thank you, because I know it must be needed. I may not understand, but I know you give me whatsoever is needed, whenever it is needed." You don't go to the temple or the church or the mosque and ask for help. If you ask, you are going against God.

That which has happened already cannot happen against the will of the whole, whatever it is. If it is a dark night, then you must be in need of a dark night.

A Sufi mystic used to say in his prayer every day, "Thank you, my Lord – you always give me whatsoever is needed." His disciples were very annoyed by this, because they had seen him many times when he was poor, hungry, nowhere to rest in the night. And still, he would pray to God five times a day, and he would say, "Thank you. How grateful I am – whatsoever I need you always give me."

One day it was too much. For three days they had been hungry; nobody had even offered them food. For three days they had been sleeping under the trees, outside a town, and the townspeople were very antagonistic and ready to kill them. On the morning of the fourth day the mystic was praying again and he was saying, "Thank you. Whatsoever I need you always give me." One disciple could not contain himself. He said, "Stop all this nonsense! There is a limit to everything. What are you thanking God for? For three days we have been hungry, thirsty, no shelter. Nights are cold and we are freezing and you are thanking God! For what! What has he given you!"

The mystic laughed and said, "For these three days I needed to be hungry, needed to be without any shelter. It was part of my growth. These three days have done me tremendous good, they have been a great blessing. That's what was needed, and existence always gives whatsoever is needed."

In fact, whatever existence gives is what is needed. But when you pray, your prayer is always nagging. You are complaining, you are grumpy, grouchy. You are saying, "Nothing is right, everything is wrong. Put it right! Otherwise I am going to become an atheist. If you exist, then do these things." Is your prayer a sort of bribery? Do you praise God just to persuade him to fulfill your desires?

Buddha says the real religious person has no intention of his own – and that is his right intention. He does not live a private life, he does not live a separate life. He moves with the universe, he's one with the universe. He has no separate goal, no separate destiny. The destiny of the whole is his destiny. Then the man becomes holy.

The man who has no intention of course lives moment to moment. He cannot project into the future. To whatsoever is needed in this moment, he responds accordingly. He is spontaneous and he is responsible. When I use the word "responsible" I use in its original sense. He is response-able; he can respond, and he can respond totally, because he has no intention of his own. He can simply say, "Yes!" and he can say it totally. He will not hold back anything. His yes will not be a reluctant yes. It will be like a flower . . . blooming, releasing its fragrance to existence.

The man of right intention lives a life without any tension. Look at the word "intention" – it is made of tension. All intention will create tension. It is made of two words, "in", and "tension". When your inner reality is tense, it is "in tension". When your inner reality is relaxed and there is no tension – you are not going anywhere, you are not chasing anything, you are not after anything, you are just here and now, relaxed – that state of no-tension or no-intention is what Buddha calls "right intention". Because then suddenly the universe starts flowing through you. You become like a hollow bamboo. You become a flute.

The third is *right speech*.

Buddha says, "Say only that which is." Never move into fictions; only say that which is true and real. Only say that which you have experienced. Never talk about others' experiences. If you have not known truth, please don't say anything about truth – because whatsoever you say will be a falsification, will be sacrilege, will be a sin. Whatsoever you say will be wrong. If you have known, only then speak; otherwise not. The world would be more beautiful, less confused, if Buddha's dictum were listened to. Right speech – he says, "Say only that which you have experienced, which is grounded in your experience, rooted in your experience." Never say anything else.

Just think about it . . . how many things we go on saying that we have never experienced, that we don't know anything about. You may have heard, you may have read, but that doesn't make you capable of uttering anything. It is all borrowed, and the borrowed is never the truth. Say only that which is. Be factual, not fictitious.

Buddha has not created any mythology. His statements are bare of all poetry and fiction, all ornaments. He never decorates his statements; they are nude, they don't have any dressing. He says if you start playing with fictions there is no end. And the many religions in the world are ninety-nine percent fiction. Hindus say there is one hell, one heaven. Jainas say there are seven hells and seven heavens. And there was a teacher, Gosal, in the days of Mahavira. Somebody asked him, "What do you say? Because Hindus believe in only one heaven, one hell. And the disciples of Mahavira say that they have not gone deep enough, but their master has gone deeper and he says there are seven hells and seven heavens."

Gosal laughed. He said, "That's nothing! I know there are seven hundred hells and seven hundred heavens."

Now, you can go on playing; there is no end to it, and there is no need to prove it. In the name of religion fictions can continue; all sorts of foolish things can be said in the name of religion. There is no way to judge whether they are true or not. There is no way to make them valid or invalid; you cannot prove them and you cannot disprove them. That's why all sorts of nonsense continues. There are three hundred religions on the earth and every religion has its own fiction. They are all fictitious. And if you know they are just fictitious, then there is no problem. If it is understood, if you want to enjoy a fiction, then you can enjoy them.

Do you know that Krishnamurti goes on reading detective novels? He never reads the Gita, he never reads the Koran, never reads the Bible. He goes on reading detective novels. Nobody has asked him why, and he has never answered, but I know why – because it is all the same. Whether you read a detective novel or you read the Bible or the Koran makes no difference. There are religious detective novels and there are secular detective novels. You may be surprised that a man of the qualities of Krishnamurti should read detective novels, but it is very indicative. He's simply saying that everything is a fiction, and if you want to read a detective novel then why not read a twentieth-century detective novel? Why go backwards and read rotten, primitive things? Why not the newest, the latest model?

Buddha says: Right speech means don't be fictitious, don't be esoteric. Just be absolutely honest and authentic. There were many times when questions were asked of Buddha and he would remain quiet, he would not answer. He would say, "This is not needed for your spiritual growth. This is unnecessary." Somebody would ask, "Who created the world?" And he would say, "Don't ask – because if A created or B created or C created it, what difference does it make to you? Or if nobody created it and it has been there without anybody's help, what difference does it make? You just ask something real, empirical. You ask something that can be of some help to you. Don't ask foolish questions."

Now see – he says these questions are foolish because the answers won't help you in any way to grow. And there are people who go on fighting about these things. Somebody says God created the world; somebody says it happened in six days; somebody else says God is still creating, the creation continues and it has never been finished, the full stop has not come yet . . . and they go on fighting and quarreling. It seems they want to fight, so any excuse will do. And these are beautiful excuses because there is no way to end them. You can go on and on and on, ad infinitum. Then there are people who ask, "Who created God?" Now they think they are also asking a pertinent question.

All these questions are irrelevant, and Buddha says: Only say that which you know, and only say that which is helpful, and only say that which is beneficial. Don't be frivolous and don't be fictitious. Be sincere in your utterances.

It happened:

> The local political leader was invited to speak to the inmates of a mental asylum. The politician had begun his talk and had been going for about ten minutes when a fellow in the back stood up and yelled, "Oh, you don't know what you are talking about! Besides, you are talking too much. Why don't you shut up and sit down!"
>
> "I will wait a minute until you send that man out," the politician said to the superintendent.
>
> "Send him out?" the superintendent asked. "Certainly not! That poor man has been here for eight years, and that is the first time he has ever said anything that made any sense, sir."

Have you listened to your politicians' speeches? They go on talking and talking – and without saying a single thing. That's what diplomacy is – to go on saying things without saying anything, otherwise you will be caught. So roundabout and roundabout people go on. In the end you cannot come to any conclusion. There is no conclusion! They simply play with words. Words have their own charm, and if you watch you will be able to see. Sometimes you say a word, then that word leads to another word – the words have their own charm – then you go to the other word that leads you into another word, and finally you end up somewhere you had never wanted to go. Words have their own charm, their own magic. Ask the novelists, poets; they know about it. The novelist starts a story, but it never ends according to his idea. By and by, the characters start asserting their own personalities. By and by, the words weave together in certain ways and lead in certain directions. All great novelists have known it and said. "It's so – we start the novel but we never end it. It ends in its own way."

You try to write a story. First you plan in the mind, you have a bare blueprint when you start. The moment you start, things start happening that you never intended. Then you are led astray and astray, and the novel or the story ends somewhere you had not even dreamt about. What happens? Words have a magic of their own. One word leads to another, and one can go on and on.

Buddha says: Be mindful. Don't be led astray by words. Say that which you really want to say, don't be frivolous.

> Just the other night Mrs. Mulla Nasruddin came to me. She said, "Do you know? I can stand at the door and by just looking at my husband's face I can tell whether he is lying or not."
>
> I was surprised. I said, "How on earth can you do that?"
> She said, "If his lips are moving, he's lying."

Mulla Nasruddin is a politician. If his lips are moving, that's enough! Then he must be lying. What else can he do?

Remember one thing: you have to be careful about what you take in, and you have to be careful about what you bring out. Only then can you have a life which is centered. People are careless; they go on stuffing themselves with whatsoever they find. Anything! They go on stuffing – into the body, and into the mind, too. Be careful.

If your neighbor comes and starts gossiping, you listen very attentively. If the neighbor was throwing some rubbish into your garden, you would start fighting, but if he throws some rubbish into your head you are perfectly welcoming of it. You don't see it: once somebody has been allowed to put rubbish in your head, what will you do with it? Sooner or later it will come out through your mouth and enter somebody else's head. You cannot keep it inside. That's why people have so much difficulty in keeping a secret. Tell somebody not to tell anybody anything, and you can be certain he will tell. Tell your wife, "This is very secret . . . don't tell anybody," and you can be certain that within twenty-four hours the whole town will know. Of course she will also say the same thing when she tells the story to the servant: "Don't say this to anybody, it is very secret." And the servant will say the same to his wife, and it will go on and on and on. Within twenty-four hours you will see that the whole town knows about it. There is no better way to spread a thing around – just go on telling people, "Don't say it to anybody." Certain it is – they will have to say it. Because whenever there is a secret it becomes difficult to keep it inside. It wants to come out.

Don't go on taking just anything in, and don't go on throwing just anything out on people. If you are too full of rubbish, go to the riverbank, go to the forest and just talk to the trees. Nothing will be harmful in it, because they won't listen. You can talk, you can unburden yourself, you can unwind and come back. But don't do that to human beings – they are already too burdened.

Buddha says: Right speech means very sincere speech.

The Bible says: In the beginning was the word . . . and then everything else came in. Buddha says if you drop the word, there will be reality, the beginning. If you become silent, then whatsoever you say will have significance.

Have you watched it? If you fast for one day, the next day your hunger has a different passion to it. If you fast then you have a fresh hunger arising in you. If you go on stuffing yourself every day, continuously, and never fast, you completely forget the language of hunger, the freshness, the beauty, the aliveness of hunger. Fast one day, and next day you will have a fresh hunger arising, and you will have a different sense of taste. The food may be the same but it will be more tasty, because it is hunger that makes it tasty.

And the same happens with words. Keep silent, and then say something, and you will see – that something has power in it. Silence is like a fast; it brings life to your words. And in this world only those people who have kept themselves in deep silence have been of tremendous import, and their words have been of lasting, eternal value.

Buddha was silent for many months, Mahavira was silent for twelve years. Whenever Jesus would feel that he was tired, he would go to the forest and he would say to his disciples, "Leave me. Leave me alone." He would be in silence for forty days, and then he would come back. And then his words would have a value to them; each word would be like a diamond.

If you really want your words to have value, then learn silence. Keep more and more silent; then one day you will know what right speech is.

The fourth is *right morality*.

Buddha says that the morality that comes from without is not the right morality. The morality that comes from within is the right morality.

All that we think is moral is not really moral, it is just conditioned by the society. You have been taught to behave in a certain way and you behave that way – but that behavior is the behavior of a slave. It is not that of a free man, it is not out of freedom. And how is morality possible out of slavery?

Buddha says morality is possible only when you are totally free, without any conditioning. Not that you have to do certain things, not that it is your duty, not that you have to follow a certain rule; but that you have become conscious, you have become aware. And out of that awareness you behave in a certain way. Awareness is right morality; unawareness is wrong morality.

You can be truthful. You may not be a thief, and you may not fool around with others' wives, and you may not be a deceiver, but if it is just because society has forced these things on you, you are not moral. You may be a good citizen, but morality is a greater thing; it is not so cheap. You may be good to the society; society does not want anything more than that. If you don't create any trouble that's enough; if you don't create any mischief that's enough – you are a good citizen. But to be moral means something more than being a good citizen. It means being a good human being; it has nothing to do with society. It has something to do with your inner integrity.

Buddha says become more conscious. Live through consciousness rather than living through conscience.

Conscience is created by the society. If you are born in a Jaina family you will not eat meat, but it does not mean that you are non-violent. How can you be non-violent just by not eating meat? But from your very childhood you have been taught not to eat meat and it has become nauseating. The Jaina cannot even look at meat: even seeing meat he starts feeling nauseous, he starts feeling sick.

When I was a child, in my home even tomatoes were not allowed. I asked my mother, "Why are tomatoes not allowed?" She said, "They look like meat. One starts feeling sick if one looks at tomatoes." Tomatoes, poor tomatoes . . . you cannot find more innocent people than tomatoes! But I had never tasted tomatoes in my childhood. When I went to a hostel, only then did I gather courage to eat tomatoes. And the first day, when I ate them, I could not sleep the whole night. My whole stomach was rumbling, and I was afraid I had committed a great sin. In the morning I vomited – just conditioning.

The French language has only one word for both consciousness and conscience. That is right; Buddha would have agreed with it. It has only one word for both conscience and consciousness. Buddha also says your consciousness should be your conscience. You should become more aware. You should start seeing more things as they are, and then non-violence will arise. It is stupid to kill animals just for your food. It is not a sin, it is stupid. It has nothing to do with sin. You are not going to be thrown into hellfire.

Buddha says that it is not because of fear that should you be moral, but because of understanding. And not because of greed should you be moral – because your ordinary religions are based on fear and greed, just the ordinary trick of reward and punishment. Just as you do with your children your religions have been doing with you: "If you do this you will go to heaven, if you do this you will go to hell" – fear and greed. They are playing on human fear and greed – and they say that one should not be afraid, and one should not be greedy? Their whole structure is based on the same fear and greed.

Buddha says: Have no fear and have no greed. Just look into things, and out of your awareness a responsibility arises. You start behaving gracefully, you don't do foolish things. That's all. If you are doing things out of fear, you will never be able to be totally moral because deep down, beyond the fear, you will know. And the desire to do the opposite, to be the opposite, will remain.

It happened:

> During a religious meeting an attractive young widow leaned too far over the balcony and fell. But her dress caught on a chandelier and held her suspended in mid air. The preacher, of course, immediately noticed the woman's predicament and called out to his congregation, "The first person who looks up there is in danger of being punished with blindness."
>
> Mulla Nasruddin, who was in the congregation, whispered to the man next to him, "I think I will risk one eye."

An enforced morality cannot be total; one is always willing to risk one eye, at least. Who knows? It may be true, it may not be true . . .

And the so-called moral people will always need holidays, because it will be tiring. It is based on conflict; one part of your being says something, and morality says something else. You are divided, you are split. Because of this split the whole humanity is a little schizophrenic – one part going south, one part going north. And you are always in an ambiguity, and you are always undecided, wavering – where to go? What to do? Your instincts say something and your conditioning says just the opposite. You can enforce anything upon yourself, but really, it will never be part of you.

An egoist can be told by the society to become humble, and he can try to become humble. But an egoist is an egoist: now humility will hide his ego.

I have heard:

> A rabbi addressed his congregation. They were very moved by his sermon and one man stood up and said, "I'm Joe Smith. I came to this land without a cent. Now I am worth five million, but when I hear your words, I am nothing."
>
> Another man stood up and said, "I started out without a cent, too. Now I am worth ten million, but when I hear your words, Rabbi, I am nothing, absolutely nothing."
>
> Then another man rose and said, "I work for the post office. I make eighty dollars a week, but when I hear your words I am nothing, utterly nothing." And the first millionaire said to the second, "Look who wants to be nothing."

Just a postman, trying to become nothing? Then nothingness needs that you first become a millionaire. That's why in India, such a religious country, not even once has a simple person been declared an avatar, a *tirthankara*. No, not yet; it has not happened – because if you are poor, what will you renounce? All the twenty-four *tirthankaras* of the Jainas come from royal families, sons of kings. Buddha himself comes from a royal family; Rama, Krishna – everybody comes from a royal family.

Why? Why not Kabir? Why not Farid? Why not Dadu? Nothing is lacking. Only one thing is missing: they don't have anything to renounce. "Look who is trying to be nothing!" First you have; to renounce you must have much, you need much; you have to *have*. A simple person is not really a humble person, only an egoist is a humble person. And then he tries, through his humbleness, to say that he is the most humble person in the world. But the same thing in a different garb continues.

Your morality never transforms you.

So Buddha says: Right morality is from within, from awareness – not out of fear, not out of greed.

The fifth step is *right livelihood*.

Buddha says life should be simple, not complex. Life should be based on needs, not on desires. Needs are perfectly okay: you need food, you need clothes, you need a shelter, you need love, you need relationship. Perfectly good, nothing wrong in it. Needs can be fulfilled. Desires are basically unfulfillable. Desires create complexity. They create complexity because they can never be fulfilled. You go on and on working hard for them, and they remain unfulfilled, and you remain empty.

The first thing about livelihood is that it should be based on needs, not on desires. Then a very small quantity of things is enough.

Secondly, it should not be violent. You should not do something just because you can get some money out of it. You can kill somebody and get some money, you can be a butcher and you can make your livelihood, but that is inhuman . . . and very unconscious. Better ways are possible. One should be creative in one's livelihood, one should not be destructive.

The businessmen were discussing a compatriot.

> "He used to work for me," said the first one. "I would not trust him
> with my money. He would lie, steal, cheat; anything for a buck."
> "How do you know him so well?"
> "How?" said the first. "I taught him everything he knows."

One should be a little more alert. Money is not all, and one should not destroy one's own life just in accumulating money. Poverty can be tremendously beautiful. If you are just living by your needs, poverty can be a tremendous contentment. In fact, you will never find rich people contented. Sometimes you can come across a beggar with a contented face, but never a millionaire.

The more you chase, the more you feel the horizon is far away. The faster you run, the closer you come to your death, but never to any fulfillment. The shadow of death, the fear of death, the fear that you are going to miss again, destroys all contentment.

The sixth is *right effort*.

Buddha says never strain, and never be lazy; one has to balance between the two. Then there is right effort; effort which is basically effortless.

Have you seen children playing? They play but there is no effort, there is no strain. They enjoy it. Have you seen a painter painting, a poet writing his poetry, a musician playing on his instrument, or a dancer? There is no effort. If there is effort then the dancer is not a real dancer. Then the dancer is just trying to earn something out of it. Then he is result-oriented, goal-oriented. Then the activity itself, the dance itself, is not his joy.

When Buddha says "right effort" it means everything that you do should be a joy unto itself. It should be an intrinsic value. It should be playful.

And *right mindfulness* is the seventh step.

"Mindfulness" is Buddha's word for meditation. By mindfulness he means you should always remain alert, watchful. You should always remain present. Not a single thing should be done in a sort of sleepy state of mind. You should not move like a somnambulist, you should move with a sharp consciousness.

Buddha used to say: Not even your breath should be allowed to go out and in without your consciousness. He said to his monks, "Always go on watching the breath coming in, the breath going out. If you move, go on watching your feet moving. If you are talking, be watchful. If you are listening, be watchful. If you are eating, be watchful." Never allow any act to be done without awareness, and then nothing else is needed. This awareness will spread all over your life; it will be a twenty-four-hour thing. There is no need to keep separate hours for meditation. And Buddha says that meditation cannot be separate from life; it has to spread and mix with life, it has to be one with life.

And the eighth, the last step is: *right samadhi* – when you are totally absorbed into the center of existence . . .

These seven steps will bring you to it, but still he says "right samadhi". That means there is a possibility of a wrong samadhi too? Yes, there is a possibility. If you fall into unconsciousness, if you fall into a coma, that is wrong samadhi; it is not right. It should bring you to total awareness, to perfect awareness. You should not fall into a coma, you should not become unconscious.

One can become unconscious. One can go inside so deeply that one can forget the outside. We ordinarily live outside, we have forgotten the inside. Inside we are unconscious; outside there is a little consciousness. We are out-moving, out-going. Then one day you just stand on your head, you change the whole process . . . you start forgetting the outside and you start becoming aware inside. A moment comes when you are totally inside and you have forgotten the outside. Buddha says that this is wrong samadhi. It is the same person just standing in a reverse posture.

Buddha says right samadhi is when, in and out, you are totally aware – not at the cost of the out. In or out, you are aware. Your light of consciousness is burning so bright that it fills you with light, and it fills your outside also with light. In fact, in right samadhi the inner and the outer disappear; there is only light. Right samadhi is not inner, right samadhi is transcendental to both inner and outer. Right samadhi is transcendental to duality, to division.

Now the sutra. This sutra simply says how a seeker should be.

THE BUDDHA SAID:

Those who follow the way are like unto warriors who fight single-handed with a multitude of foes. They may all go out of the fort in full armor; but among them are some who are faint-hearted, and some who go halfway and beat a retreat, and some who are killed in the affray, and some who come home victorious.

O monks, if you desire to attain enlightenment, you should steadily walk in your way, with a resolute heart, with courage, and should be fearless in whatever environment you may happen to be, and destroy every evil influence that you may come across; for thus you shall reach the goal.

These eight steps are the work.

And Buddha says there are many types of people: a few are cowards who never go on the way; a few go fully armored but come back as they start feeling difficulties arising; a few go half the way half-heartedly, then turn back; a few go a little further but are killed. Because they could never gather their energy, they could never become integrated, they can be easily destroyed. They were not ready enough to go into the battle – maybe outwardly they were full of armor, maybe outwardly looking very strong, but inwardly hollow, empty. There are only very few who go into the battle, win the battle, and come back home.

That coming back home is what samadhi is, and these seven steps before samadhi are the battle, the way. Move slowly, otherwise you may be killed.

For example: if a person of false morality goes into the battle he will be killed. You have to be authentically moral. "Authentically moral" means that you have to be moral from within. Those false faces learned from the outside won't help. You will remain hollow inside. And you have to move step by step. You cannot jump steps; otherwise those missing gaps will become dangerous.

That's why I talk about these eight steps, this eightfold path. This sutra is meaningful only if you understand these eight steps. "Coming home" means samadhi. That means you have come to the very center of existence.

Let me read it again.

Those who follow the way are like unto warriors who fight single-handed with a multitude of foes.

Foes are many, and you are alone. So you have to be perfectly ready, otherwise you will miss the goal.

They may all go out of the fort in full armor; but among them are some who are faint-hearted . . .

If you have not lived the right view, right intention, right speech, you will remain faint-hearted. You will remain a weakling, you will remain impotent.

. . . And some who go halfway and beat a retreat . . .

If you have not practiced right morality and right livelihood, this is going to happen. You will go half the way. You will be a runner, an escapist.

. . . And some who are killed in the affray . . .

Some go full-heartedly but are killed. If you have not practiced right effort and right mindfulness, this is going to happen. But there are only a few . . . *who come home victorious.*

If you have practiced all the seven steps you will come home victorious, you will attain to samadhi.

. . . You should steadily walk in your way, with a resolute heart, with courage, and should be fearless in whatever environment you may happen to be, and destroy every evil influence that you may come across; for thus you shall reach the goal.

Enough for today.

Chapter 18:

Remember the Middle

One night a monk was reciting a sutra bequeathed by Kashyapabuddha. His tone was so mournful and his voice so fainting, as if he were going out of existence. The Buddha asked the monk, "What was your occupation before you became a homeless monk?" Said the monk, "I was very fond of playing the guitar." The Buddha said, "How did you find it when the strings were too loose?" Said the monk, "No sound is possible." "How when the strings were too tight?" "They crack." "How when they were neither too tight nor too loose?" "Every note sounds in its proper tone."

The Buddha then said to the monk: Religious discipline is also like unto playing the guitar. When the mind is properly adjusted and quietly applied, the way is attainable; but when you are too fervently bent on it, your body grows tired; and when your body is tired, your spirit becomes weary; when your spirit is weary, your discipline will relax; and with the relaxation of discipline there follows many an evil. Therefore, be calm and pure, and the way will be gained.

Man's whole misery consists in his being off-center. There is a maladjustment between the hub and the wheel, there is a maladjustment between you and reality, and that maladjustment manifests itself in a thousand and one ways. The farther you are away from reality, the more miserable. Hell is the farthest point from reality. The closer you are to reality, the more close you are to heaven. When there is no maladjustment between you and reality, you are heaven itself.

It is not a question of going anywhere, it is a question of how to get in tune with reality again. It is a rediscovery – because in the mother's womb each child is centered in reality. In the mother's womb each child is profoundly blissful. Of course he is unaware of it, not knowing anything about it. He's so one with his bliss that there is no knower left behind. Blissfulness is his being, and there is no distinction between the knower and the known. So of course the child is not aware that he is blissful. You become aware only when you have lost something.

Mulla Nasruddin was saying to his son one day, "You don't know what happiness is until you get married – and then it is too late."

It is so. It is very difficult to know something without losing it, because when you have not lost it you are so totally one with it. There is no distance; the observer and the observed are one, the known and the knower are one. Every child is in a profoundly blissful state.

Psychologists also agree with this. They say that the whole search of religion is nothing but a way to again find the womb of the mother. They use it as a criticism of religion, but to me it is not criticism at all. It is simply true. Yes, the search for religion is again a search for the womb. The search for religion is again a search to make this whole existence a womb.

The child is in absolute tune with the mother. The child is never out of tune with the mother, he does not even know that he is separate from the mother. If the mother is healthy the child is healthy; if the mother is ill the child is ill; if the mother is sad the child is sad; if the mother is happy the child is happy; if the mother is dancing the child is dancing; if the mother is sitting silently the child is silent. The child has no boundaries of his own yet. This is the purest bliss, but it has to be lost.

The child is born, and suddenly he is thrown off center. Suddenly he is uprooted from the earth, from the mother. He loses his moorings and he does not know who he is. There was no need to know it when he was with the mother. There was no need to know – he was all, and there was no need to know, there was no distinction. There was no "you", so there was no question of "I". The reality was undivided. It was *advaita*, pure *advaita*, pure non-duality.

But once the child is born, the umbilical cord is cut and he starts breathing on his own. Suddenly his whole being becomes a quest to know who he is. It is natural. Now he starts becoming aware of his boundaries, his body, his needs. Sometimes he is happy, sometimes unhappy, sometimes he is fulfilled, sometimes not fulfilled; sometimes he is hungry and crying and there is no sign of mother anywhere; sometimes he is on the mother's breast, again enjoying oneness with the mother. But now there are many moods and many climates and he will start, by and by, to feel the separation. A divorce has happened; the marriage is broken.

He was absolutely married to the mother; now he will always be separate. And he has to find out who he is. The whole life one goes on trying to find out who one is. This is the most fundamental question.

First the child becomes aware of "mine", then of "me", then of "you", then of "I". This is how it proceeds. This is precisely the procedure, exactly in this order. First he becomes aware of "mine". Watch it, because this is your construction, the structure of your ego. First the child becomes aware of "mine" – this toy is mine, this mother is mine. He starts possessing. The possessor enters first; possessiveness is very basic. Hence all the religions say: become non-possessive because with possession starts the road to hell. Watch small children – very jealous, possessive, each child trying to snatch everything from everybody else and trying to protect his own toys. You will see children that are very violent, almost indifferent to others' needs. If a child is playing with his toy and another child comes you can see an Adolf Hitler, a Genghis Khan, a Nadirshah. He will cling to his toy; he is ready to hit, he is ready to fight. It is a question of territory, a question of domination. Possessiveness enters first; that is the basic poison. The child starts saying, "This is mine."

Now look – nothing can be "mine" in reality, in truth. We come empty-handed, we go empty-handed. This whole business of "mine" and "thine" is just a dream. But once the child says, "This is mine," now he is entering into a mal-adjustment with reality. So you will find that the more you have this idea of "mine", the more you will be miserable, the more you will suffer. It is everywhere – "This house is mine; this woman is mine; this man is mine" – and everywhere you immediately claim and possess, misery enters. Two persons are in love. If it is just a beginning the "mine" has not started – because if "mine" has not started, the mind has not started. Once the "mine" starts, the ego is on the way. The ego is the crystallized "mine". And once the "mine" starts, love is lost. Love is beautiful only when there is no "mine". But it enters immediately, because that has become our very structure. That is our foundation in this world. We are wrongly based.

I have heard . . .

> This playboy was six and he was playing with the girl next door who was five.

"Want to wrestle?" he asked.

She said, "I can't wrestle. I am a girl."

He continued, "Want to play ball?"

She replied, "I can't play ball. I am a girl."

Finally he said, "Okay, wanna play house?"

She said, "All right. I will be the father."

From the very beginning it is a question of who dominates whom, who possesses whom. Hence all the religions – Eastern, Western – all the religions that have existed on earth emphasize non-possessiveness, non-attachment because that will take the very earth from beneath your feet. If you become non-possessive the ego cannot exist. If you become aware of this basic flaw of your being, this claim for "mine", you will be surprised that all your misery can be dropped by dropping this single word. This is not just a word, it is your whole style of life. The wrong style of life is based on "mine". The right style of life knows no "mine", no "thine".

Once we say "mine" we are making ourselves separate from the whole. Now this separation will grow, and each step will take you farther away. Once the "mine" enters then you are a competitor with everybody. Once the "mine" enters, your life will be a life of competition, struggle, conflict, violence, aggression.

The next step of "mine" is "me". When you have something to claim as yours, suddenly through that claim arises the idea that now you are the center of your possessions. The possessions become your territory, and through those possessions arises a new idea: "me".

Once you are settled with "me", you can see clearly that you have a boundary, and those who are outside the boundary are "you". The other becomes clear; now things start falling apart.

The universe is one, it is a unity; nothing is divided. Everything is connected with everything else, it is a tremendous connectedness. You are connected with the earth, you are connected with the trees, you are connected with the stars; stars are connected with you, stars are connected with the trees, with the rivers, with the mountains. Everything is interconnected. Nothing is separate; nothing can be separate. Separation is not possible. Each moment you are breathing – you breathe in, you breathe out – continuously there is a bridge with the existence. You eat, existence enters into you; you defecate, it becomes manure. The apple on the tree will become part of your body tomorrow, and some part of your body will go and become manure, will become food for the tree . . . a continuous give and take. Not for a single moment does it stop. When it stops, you are dead.

What is death? – separation is death. To be in unity is to be alive, to be out of unity is to be dead. So the more you think, "I am separate," the less sensitive you will be, more dead, dragging, dull. The more you feel you are connected, the more this whole existence is part of you and you are part of this whole existence. Once you understand that we are members of each other, then suddenly the vision changes. Then these trees are not alien; they are continuously preparing food for you. When you breathe in you take oxygen in, when you breathe out you give carbon dioxide; the trees breathe in carbon dioxide and breathe out oxygen – there is a continuous communion. We are in tune. The reality is a unity. With the idea of "me", "you", we are falling out of the reality. And once a wrong conception settles inside, your whole vision becomes upside down.

I have heard:

> The young New Yorker was in Texas for the very first time. Seeing a herd of buffalo, he asked his host what they were.
>
> "They are just wild pigs," said his host. "Everything in Texas is big."
>
> A little later the visitor saw a flight of eagles and asked what they were.
>
> "They are just sparrows," said his host. "Everything is big in Texas."
>
> Later that night the visitor went looking for the toilet and fell into the swimming pool. "For Pete's sake!" he cried "Nobody pull the flush!"

Once you have a wrong conception of things, then that conception will distort everything. If "everything is big in Texas", then the swimming pool must be a toilet! It is natural – one wrong conception leads to another wrong conception and one small wrong conception leads to a bigger wrong conception. If you go on settling with this, one day you simply don't know what reality is. You are simply clouded by your own conceptions.

"Me", then "you", and then as a reflection arises "I" – "I" is the subtlest, the most crystallized form of the possessiveness. Once you have uttered "I", you have committed sacrilege. Once you have said "I", you are broken completely from existence – not really broken, otherwise you would die, but in your ideas you are completely broken from reality. Now you will be in a continuous fight with reality. You will be fighting your own roots, you will be fighting with yourself.

That's why Buddha says, be a driftwood. You can be a driftwood only if you have dropped the idea of "I" – otherwise you cannot be a driftwood, struggle will persist. That's why it becomes so difficult when you come to meditate. If I say to just sit silently, you cannot do that – such a simple thing. One would think it is the simplest thing; there should be no need to teach it. One should simply sit and be. But you cannot sit because the "I" cannot allow you a moment of relaxation. Once a moment of relaxation is allowed, you will be able to see reality. Once reality is known, the "I" will have to be dropped, then it cannot persist. So the "I" never even allows you a holiday. Even if you go to the hills, to the summer resorts, the "I" never allows you a holiday even there. You take your radio, you take your TV set; you take all your problems and you remain occupied. You had gone somewhere to relax, but you continue your whole pattern in the same way. You don't relax.

The "I" cannot relax. It exists through tensions. It will create new tensions, it will create new worries, it will constantly manufacture new problems, it won't allow you any rest. Even a minute's rest and the whole house of the "I" starts toppling down – because the reality is so beautiful and the "I" is so ugly. One continues to fight his way unnecessarily. You are fighting for things that are going to happen of their own accord. You are unnecessarily fighting, you are desiring things that are going to be yours if you don't desire. In fact, by desiring you will lose them.

That's why Buddha says: Float with the stream. Let it take you to the ocean.

"Mine", "me", "you", "I" – this is the trap. And this trap creates misery, neurosis, madness.

Now the problem is that the child has to go through it, because he does not know who he is and he needs some sort of identity – maybe a false identity, but it is better than no identity. He needs some identity. He needs to know exactly who he is, so a false center is created. The "I" is not your real center. It is a false center – utilitarian, make-believe, just manufactured by you. It has nothing to do with your real center. Your real center is the center of all. Your real self is the self of all. At the center, the whole existence is one – just as at the source of light, the sun, all rays are one. The farther away they go, the farther away they are from each other.

Your real center is not just your center, it is the center of the whole. But we have created small centers of our own, homemade, manufactured by ourselves. There is a need . . . because the child is born without any boundary, with no idea of who he is. It is a survival necessity. How will he survive? He has to be given a name, he has to be given an idea of who he is. Of course this idea comes from the outside – somebody says you are beautiful, somebody says you are intelligent, somebody says you are so vital. You gather the things that people say. Out of all that people say about you, you gather a certain image. You never look into yourself, at who you are. This image is going to be false – because nobody else can know who you are, and nobody else can say who you are. Your inner reality is not available to anybody else except you. Your inner reality is impenetrable to anybody else except you. Only you can be there.

The day you realize that your identity is false, put together; you have collected opinions from people . . . Sometime just think, just sit silently and think who you are. Many ideas will arise. Just go on watching from where they come and you will be able to find the source. Some things come from your mother – much; about eighty to ninety percent. Something comes from your father, something comes from your schoolteachers, something comes from your friends, something from the society. Just watch and you will be able to sort out from where it comes. Nothing comes from you, not even one percent comes from you. What type of identity is this in which you have not contributed at all? And you are the only one who could have contributed, in fact, the whole hundred percent.

The day you understand this, religion becomes important. The day you realize this you start seeking for some technique, some method to enter into your being to know exactly, really, existentially, who you are. No more collections of images from the outside, no more asking others to mirror your reality – but to face it directly, immediately, to enter into your nature and to feel it there. What is the need to ask anybody? And whom are you asking? They are as ignorant about themselves as you are about yourself. They don't know themselves, how can they know you?

Just see how things are functioning, how things go on functioning, how things go on happening. One falsity leads to another falsity. You are almost swindled, duped. You are conned, and those who have swindled you may not have done it knowingly. They may have been swindled by others. Your father, your mother, your teachers, have been duped by others – their fathers, their mothers, their teachers. And they have duped you in turn. Are you going to do the same to your children too?

In a better world, where people are more intelligent, more aware, they will teach the child that the idea of identity is false: "It is needed, we are giving it to you, but it is only for the time being, before you yourself discover who you are. It is not going to be your reality. And the sooner you find out who you are, the better. The sooner you can drop this idea, the better – because from that very moment you will really be born, and you will be really real, authentic. You will become an individual."

The ideas that we gather from others give us a personality, and the knowledge that we come to know from within gives us individuality. Personality is false, individuality is real. Personality is borrowed. Reality, individuality, your authenticity, can never be borrowed. Nobody can say who you are.

Your body can be seen by others. They can say whether your body is beautiful or not, and that too depends – because no ultimate criterion for beauty exists. That depends on the idea of the person, on what he thinks is beautiful. Two persons never agree. It is almost like "like" and "dislike". You may fall in love with a woman and you may think she is the most beautiful woman in the world – and your friends may laugh at you. I'm not saying they are right, I'm not saying you are right. I'm simply saying that there is simply no criterion. You may think the woman is horrible and your friend is mad, but there is no criterion. There is no objective way to know who is beautiful, what is beautiful. It depends on your mind, your conditioning.

I have overheard . . .

A male elephant was watching a female elephant wiggle by. Said he, almost charmed, "Wow! A perfect 250 by 210 by 400!"

For an elephant, of course, those are the proportions of beauty – not for a man. And as you are laughing about the proportions, elephants laugh about your ideas of beauty.

In fact even a single individual's idea of beauty goes on changing. In childhood you have different ideas of beauty, in youth different ideas, in old age different ideas. And then it depends on your necessity, your need.

I have heard that there was an advertisement in a farmer's magazine. The farmer had advertised that he wanted to meet a woman about thirty years of age. He himself was forty-one. Object: marriage. But one condition had to be fulfilled – the woman had to have a tractor, and she had to send a picture of the tractor!

It depends on your need, on your ideas, on your philosophy, religion, conditioning, culture. Somebody can say something about your body; that too is not objective. Somebody can say something about your mind – a teacher can say you are very intelligent – but that too depends, because there is no way to decide who is intelligent. The very idea of an intelligence quotient, measuring the intelligence, has failed. Psychologists were thinking that they would be able to measure intelligence, but it has failed. Now it is out of date. It does not mean much.

Who is intelligent? – a child who is efficient in mathematics, or a child who is very good in painting? Who is intelligent? – a child who can compose poetry, or a child who can make an engine or a machine? Who is intelligent? There is simply no way to say. Of course, ordinarily, the mathematician, the mechanic, the technologist will be thought intelligent – because they have more utility. A painting has not much utility. A poem has no survival value; you cannot merchandise it, in the marketplace nobody will bother about it. But if you can create a gadget, a mechanical device, many people will be interested in it. But how to decide?

In a different society . . . for example in ancient China, three thousand years ago, a person who could compose poetry was thought to be more intelligent than the person who could devise a machine, because the society existed on different principles. Lao Tzu had said that machines are not needed; Lao Tzu had said that machines are a way to cheat nature, to exploit nature; they are aggressive. Man does not need any mechanical things – poetry, painting, sculpture and music are more valuable. A child who was a born musician was thought to be more intelligent than a mathematician because what will you do with a mathematician? Of what use is mathematics? But in the modern world the mathematician is more useful, has more utility, has more market value.

But this is not going to be so for long. Sooner or later, a few countries will come to such affluence that again they will need music, poetry, sculpture. People would like to listen to great music, would like to see dance, would like to enter into the realms of beauty, would like to become more deeply in tune with reality. Who will bother about a mathematician, a technologist, an engineer? Sooner or later this is going to change. It depends on the needs of the society.

People can say something about your body, something about your mind, but that too is not of any value. Who can say anything about your soul? – not even your mother who has given birth to you, not even your father.

When Buddha became enlightened he went back home. The father was very angry, naturally so. It is very difficult to satisfy a father, because whatever you do will go against his ambitions. It is very difficult to satisfy a father. If you don't have any personality, if you don't have any individuality, if you don't have any unique intelligence, then you are dull. You may be obedient, but then the father is not satisfied because of your dullness, stupidity. You are obedient, okay; but what is the point of your being obedient? You have nothing to give. If you are intelligent, unique, have something to give, then you cannot be obedient. Intelligence is always rebellious. Only dull and stupid people are obedient.

In the world today there is so much rebellion only because there has been an explosion of intelligence. Each generation is more intelligent than the previous one, hence more rebellion, more disobedience, more chaos in the world. You can watch it in your children. Just observe your children impartially. Were you so intelligent when you were a child? Now look at children; they are so intelligent. You may not see it, because it hurts. You may not see it, you may deny it, but just watch – and it has to be so. It is natural that consciousness goes on evolving. So when a child is intelligent he's rebellious, and the father is not satisfied. When the child is obedient but he is not intelligent, then too he is not satisfied. It is difficult to satisfy a father.

Even Buddha could not satisfy his father. Buddha's father must have thought that he had become a hippie. Maybe the term was not there, so he must have thought it in some other terms, but that's exactly what he was saying to Buddha when he came. He was very angry, annoyed, and he said, "What have you done? You are a king's son, and you are living like a beggar? Drop all this nonsense and come back home. I am your father. Though you have pained me, and you have been a pain in my neck, still my heart is that of a father and I can forgive you. My doors are still open. You can come back."

Buddha laughed. He said, "You don't know me at all. I have entered into a great kingdom."

The father, of course, became more furious. He said, "Stop all this! I know you well. I have given you birth." Buddha said, "There you are mistaken, there you err. You have given birth to my body, but not to me; and you don't know me at all. Even as I am standing in front of you, you are not seeing me. You are so full of your idea that you are the father and I am your son. That idea is functioning like a barrier. Just look at me! The son that has left your house has not come back – that person is gone, that person is dead. I am a totally new being. I come with a new identity, I come with a new realization – I come as awareness. I had gone as unconsciousness, I had gone as Gautama Siddhartha, your son. Now I come as Buddha, as enlightened, just enlightened. I had gone with a false identity, now I come with a real realization of who I am. Look at me!"

In fact, there is no way for anybody else to see your reality. You have to go into it yourself. It cannot be done by servants; you cannot pay somebody to do it for you.

A great Sufi saint was called by Caliph Omar to pray in his court. He went, but he said, "I cannot do it. There are a few things you have to do for yourself. You have to breathe for yourself; nobody else can do it. You have to make love to your woman yourself; nobody else can do it for you. And you have to pray for yourself; I cannot do it. Sorry." He said, "I can pray, but that will be prayer for myself. It will not be for you."

There are things which nobody can do for you. And at least one thing can *never* be done by anybody else and that is to give you the answer to who you are. No, you have to dig deep into your own being. Layers and layers of identity, false identity, have to be broken.

There is fear when one enters into oneself, because chaos comes in.

Somehow you have managed with your false identity. You have settled with it. You know your name is this or that; you have certain credentials, certificates, degrees, universities, colleges, prestige, money, heritage. You have certain ways to define yourself. You have a certain definition, howsoever workable – but it works. Going in means dropping this workable definition . . . there will be chaos.

Before you can come to your center, you will have to pass through a very chaotic state. That's why there is fear. Nobody wants to go in. People go on teaching, "Know thyself." We hear them, but we never really listen. We never bother about it. There is a very certain idea in the mind that chaos will be let loose and you will be lost in it, you will be engulfed in it. Because of the fear of that chaos, we go on clinging to anything from the outside. But this is wasting your life.

The day you become courageous enough to enter into your being, you have become a sannyasin. *Sannyas* means that now you are taking your life into your own hands. Now you are trying to live the life that is yours, authentically. Now you are no longer playing roles. Now you will not allow anybody else to write the story of your life. Now you are ready to unfold that which you have always carried like a seed within you. Chaos is the problem; so when people become religious they begin to find some way to avoid the chaos. That has to be understood before we can enter into this sutra.

A certain identity is there. For example you are rich, you have a lot of money – that is your identity. When a person starts thinking, "How to know myself?" and when he comes to listen to the truths always explained by the sages: that "mine", "me", "you," "I", have to be dropped, he thinks, "Okay, so I will drop all my riches and I will become poor." He drops one identity – the identity of being rich – but he has moved to the other extreme. To avoid one wrong he has moved to its opposite wrong. And this is a fundamental thing to understand – if you move against a wrong too much, you will enter another wrong. One wrong opposed by another thing cannot be corrected; the opposite is also wrong. Just in the middle somewhere is truth.

When you are rich you have an identity. You drop that, you become poor, you become a beggar; now you have another identity. The first one was borrowed from the society and the second is also borrowed from the society. Now everybody will say that you have renounced the world, you are a great seeker; you have dropped out of the world, you are simply great. You were great because you had money and now you are great because you have renounced the money – but the identity is still coming from the outside. First you were rich, now you are poor; now poverty is your richness. You were egoistic, you became

361

humble; but now humbleness is your ego. One can move from one disease to another disease very easily, just like the pendulum can swing from one extreme to another extreme.

Buddha says extremes are what wrong is. To be an extremist is to be in the wrong. Be in the middle, be balanced – *samyak* – and that's where right is. Just be in the middle, don't move from one polarity to another.

That's what people are doing. Somebody is rushing after women, then one day he decides it is futile and he starts running away from women. But the running continues! First he was chasing women and now he's afraid some woman may be chasing him. And that's how it happens – if you chase a woman, she runs. If you start running from her, she starts chasing you! Life is very mysterious . . . but the running continues. It is a game. Only one can be the chaser and one has to be the chased. Either you are the chaser or the woman becomes the chaser, but the game continues.

Buddha says: Stop in the middle.

This sutra is part of a very famous story in Buddha's life The story is about a prince named Srona.

Srona was a prince, and he lived the life of an Epicurean – eat, drink, be merry. He had lived as deeply in indulgence as possible. He had never known anything about discipline, he had never heard anything about awareness. Women, wine – that was all, that was his whole life, confined to two words, women and wine. The whole day he was drunk and the whole night he was indulging in sexuality. He was a maniac. But by and by the extreme started tiring him. By and by he became alert to what he was doing to his life.

When you indulge too much, one day, if you are a little intelligent, you start feeling the whole futility of it.

One day, when Buddha was passing through his town, Srona heard about him. He had been thinking for many days, "There must be another way of life, and there must be more to life than the way I am living it." Hearing that Buddha had come, he went to see him. And Srona was an extremist. Seeing Buddha – his silence, his grace, his peace – he was touched. His heart was overwhelmed. He bowed down to Buddha and he said, "Give me *sannyas* this very moment!"

Buddha said, "Wait. Don't be in such a hurry."

"But," he said, "I cannot wait. I don't know what waiting is. When I want to do something, I want to do something. And enough is enough! I have lived a life of debauchery and I have been simply wasting myself. It has been suicidal. Now I cannot go back home. Please accept me."

Even Buddha's disciples said, "Why don't you accept him? You never say no to anybody. Why are you hesitating?" Ananda said, "Why are you hesitating? He is great prince, well known, and he is ready. He is ready to surrender totally."

Buddha said, "I am hesitating because I am afraid that this may be just another extreme. This man has been just indulgent. Now he may renounce and just move to another extreme – and renunciation is in the middle."

But Srona persisted; he wouldn't go. He was sitting there from the morning till the evening. He was a man of that type. The more Buddha said no, the more he became insistent. Next morning, Buddha accepted him as a disciple. This sutra is about Srona.

The story says that when Srona became a *bhikkhu*, a monk, immediately he turned to the other extreme – the extreme that Buddha had been apprehensive about. Buddha's *bhikkhus*, his monks, used to take one meal every day; Srona would take only two meals every week. The *bhikkhus* would move from one town to another and they would walk on the road. But Srona would never walk on the path. He would walk in the forest, or on the rocks, his feet would start bleeding; there were wounds on his feet and legs. Buddha's *bhikkhus* were very tranquil people, silent people – because the whole teaching is to remain in the middle. They were never indulgent and they were never ascetic, but this Srona became a great ascetic. When everybody would be sitting under the trees, he would stand in the hot sun. He had a beautiful body, he was a beautiful young man but his skin became dark, black, and within a few months it was impossible to recognize him. When people from his capital would come they would be surprised; he had changed so much. He had become thin, his eyes had lost luster, his face had lost all grace; he had started becoming ugly. And he was always ill, because the body has a limit of tolerance to certain things. But Srona was not worried; in fact, he was enjoying it. And the other monks started feeling that he was some great soul. Everybody started feeling that he was superior to them. Now a new ego was arising in Srona.

This sutra is about Srona.

One night a monk was reciting a sutra bequeathed by Kashyapabuddha. His tone was so mournful and his voice so fainting, as if he were going out of existence.

Of course he must have become very sad, he must have become very low and depressed, he must have lost all joy. He was torturing himself. He must have been a little masochistic. He was destroying himself and enjoying the violence. He must have become very serious, he must have become very deeply ill, all well-being disappeared. He was not a flowering; in fact, the tree was dying. He was reciting this sutra given by Kashyapabuddha. When you recite a sutra you have to recite it in joy – otherwise it is meaningless. When you pray, if you cannot pray joyfully it is meaningless – don't waste your time, because your prayer never reaches anywhere unless it rides on the horse of joy. Unless you can celebrate, your prayer is never heard. Only through celebration does it reach to existence because existence understands only one language, and that is celebration. Existence does not understand English, it does not understand Sanskrit, it does not understand Arabic. Existence understands only one language – the language of flowers, the language of clouds, the language of peacocks, the language of the cuckoos, the language of joy, the language of greenery, of rivers rushing to the ocean, glaciers gliding down from the mountains. Existence knows dance, knows what singing is. Words are not meaningful, only music. The whole understands sounds, it does not understand words.

Language is man-created, joy is from existence. So whenever you meditate, you pray, or you recite a sutra or you recite the Koran, do it in joy. Otherwise don't do it. There is no need because it is just useless. You are wasting your time.

I have heard about a Sufi mystic, Hassan.

> He passed by a mosque, and a man was reciting the Koran. His voice was so horrible, and he was doing it in such a terrible way, and he was so sad and so serious – as if all his laughter had dried up. His voice sounded like a ghost's voice.
>
> Hassan said, "What are you doing?"
> He said, "For God's sake, I am reciting this Koran."
> Hassan said, "For God's sake, stop!"

Unless you do it in joy, please don't do it. For God's sake, never do it. It is better to be an atheist and not to believe in God than to do something in sadness, depression, than to do something ugly and call it prayer.

But you can do only that which you are. Joy you cannot manage suddenly. Unless it is bubbling, unless it is welling up in your being, unless it runs like sap, you cannot manage it. And it is not a question of managing your face, because existence is not looking at your face; it is looking at your heart . . . you cannot deceive. Unless joy is in your being, it will not reach – your prayer will never be heard.

That's why I insist that if you can dance and sing, that will do. There is no need to actually verbalize any prayer – let your prayerfulness be exhibited in dance, let it be exhibited in singing. There is no need. You can play guitar or you can play on the flute – that will do. You are using something universal.

His tone was so mournful and his voice so fainting, as if he were going out of existence. The Buddha asked the monk, "What was your occupation before you became a homeless monk?" Said the monk, "I was

*very fond of playing the guitar." The Buddha said, "How did you find it
when the strings were too loose?" Said the monk, "No sound is possible."*

When the strings are too loose, sound is not possible . . .

*"How when the strings were too tight?" "They crack." "How when they
were neither too tight nor too loose?" "Every note sounds in its proper tone."*

*The Buddha then said to the monk: Religious discipline is also like
unto playing the guitar. When the mind is properly adjusted and
quietly applied, the way is attainable.*

In fact, when the mind is just in the middle, neither too loose nor too tight
– balanced, tranquil, still, neither moving left nor right – when the pendulum of
the mind has stopped just in the middle, time disappears. The clock stops. In
that very moment, the way is attainable. In fact, the way is *attained*. This *is* the
way – to be in the middle is the way. You are missing the way because you are
not in the middle, and the way is in the middle. In life's situations, in every
situation, one has to be alert not to go to the extreme. Otherwise, sometimes
the strings are too loose and the music does not arise, and sometimes they are
too tight and they crack, and instead of music they create just noise. Music is
possible only when things are just in the middle. There is a point when the
strings are neither tight nor loose.

You must have seen it: whenever Indian musicians play, first they try to bring
their instruments to the middle. The drummer will drum his tabla and will feel
whether it is in the middle or not; otherwise he will tighten something or loosen
something. The veena player will tighten or make loose his strings.

It happened once:

A viceroy was invited by a nawab of Lucknow, and to welcome him
he had asked his best musicians to play something for the viceroy.
And of course, as it is done traditionally, the musicians started
tightening and loosening their instruments. The nawab asked the
viceroy, "What type of music do you like most?" Just to be polite the
viceroy said, "Exactly this music that is going on" – just to be polite,
because he could not understand what was going on. So then, just to
be polite, the nawab ordered the musicians to continue. For three
hours they simply continued tuning their instruments.

There is a point when the strings are neither loose nor tight – and only a master
knows it. It is easy to play on a guitar; it is difficult to bring the guitar to the
tuning where music is born, and naturally born, effortlessly born. A man

becomes a master, or a maestro, when he can tune his instrument. Playing is not so difficult; tuning is more difficult because for tuning you have to learn what the exact middle is. You have to be very alert, very sensitive. Your ear has to be very, very sensitive. Only then can you know where the middle is.

AND BUDDHA SAYS:

> *Religious discipline is also like unto playing the guitar. When the mind is properly adjusted and quietly applied, the way is attainable. But when you are too fervently bent on it, your body grows tired; and when your body is tired, your spirit becomes weary; when your spirit is weary, your discipline will relax; and with the relaxation of discipline there follows many an evil.*

> *Therefore, be calm and pure, and the way will be gained.*

In every life situation, you have to remember it. This sutra is of tremendous import – because mind tends to move to the polar opposite. And if you move to the polar opposite you are again as far away from the middle as you were before.

Somebody is an egoist – now he becomes a humble man. But the real man of awareness is neither an egoist nor humble. He does not know the language of humility and ego. Humbleness is just the opposite of ego. In fact is not really opposite; it is the same language. When you say somebody is humble, what do you mean? You are saying that he is not an egoist – that means that from the peak of ego he has moved into the valley of humbleness. But if you come across a buddha you cannot say he is humble and you cannot say he is an egoist. He simply is. He has not dropped from the peak to the valley. He has just come onto plain ground. That is one of the most difficult things to understand.

A Jesus is not humble in the sense that other saints are humble. A Jesus is not an egoist in the sense that people are egoists. He simply does not know what ego and humbleness are; he has dropped out of that duality. He simply is, and he responds out of his isness. Sometimes he will look very egoistic to you; that is your interpretation. Sometimes he will look very humble to you; that too is your interpretation.

For example, Christians will talk about those stories in which Jesus looks very humble – that he touched and washed the feet of his disciples, and that is so humble. But they avoid a few other stories where he doesn't look so humble. He chased the money lenders out of the temple with a whip in his hand – somehow they avoid that story because there he was not humble at all. He was in a rage. He was a rebel, a revolutionary.

In fact, he's neither humble nor egoistic.

The same is true about all those who have attained. Krishna was working as a chariot driver to Arjuna; that is his humbleness. Hindus talk about it very much – "What humbleness!" Anti-Hindus will not talk about it; they will say, "What egoism! Krishna says to Arjuna, 'Forget all religions and come to my feet' – what egoism! What more can you ask? This is the peak of egoism." But in fact he is neither. If the situation demands, he can become a driver to his own disciple. He can take the horses to the river, give them a bath, wash them, massage them . . . the horses of his disciple. And then in another moment he can say to Arjuna, "Forget all I said. Drop all religions, drop all your ideologies. Come to my feet." Now, this is very paradoxical.

But a real man of realization is neither humble nor egoistic. Whatsoever the situation, he responds totally.

Remember, Buddha says whenever you are in the middle, you are on the way. Whenever you are leaning towards the right and left, you are going astray.

And keeping in the middle is what he means by being calm, because whenever you lean to the left or to the right you become excited. So never be a rightist and never be a leftist. Just be in the middle and you will be nowhere, and you will be nobody – because in the middle all excitement is lost. One is simply calm.

And that's what he means by being pure – when you lean to the left, the left corrupts you. When you lean to the right, the right corrupts you. When you don't lean, when you are simply in the middle, nothing corrupts you. You become incorruptible. You are pure.

Therefore, be calm and pure and the way will be gained.

I told you that a child learns "mine", "me", "you", "I". Now, you can move to the opposite and you can say, "Nothing is mine." You can say that there is no ego in you, and you don't possess anything – "me" exists not – and you are also a divine form, a form of the formless. But if it is just moving to the other extreme then nothing is gained. If it is an understanding from the middle, then something is gained. But from the middle you will not say, "I don't possess anything" – remember it; to say this is possible only if you still think that something can be possessed. One day you think you can possess, another day you deny it and you say, "I don't possess anything. I renounce everything." But in your renunciation also possession comes in. How can you renounce the world if you don't possess it?

A real man of understanding never renounces anything. He simply understands: "Nothing is there to possess, so how can I renounce?"

It is said about a Japanese emperor that he renounced his kingdom and went to a Zen master. He bowed down at his feet and said in tremendous humbleness, "I have renounced the kingdom."

The Zen master said, "Then it is better that you go and possess it again, claim it again. It is better that you go."

The emperor was very disturbed. He said, "What do you mean? I have really renounced it."

The master said, "If you have really renounced it, then how can you say that you have renounced it? Real renunciation is simple understanding that nothing belongs to you. There is nothing to renounce."

Renunciation is possible only if in the first place you think possession is possible. Non-attachment is possible only if in the first place you accept that attachment is possible. A real man of understanding comes to know that attachment is not possible. Attachment is false, possession is false; it is not possible. It is impossible to possess. Then what is the point of renouncing? What is the point of becoming non-attached? Attachment simply disappears. If attachment disappears and there is nothing left behind, not even non-attachment, not even the idea of non-attachment, then you are pure and calm. If attachment disappears but now it is replaced with non-attachment, you have moved to the other extreme. When violence disappears, it is not that now there is non-violence in you. What is the point of non-violence? Violence has disappeared and non-violence with it. The dualities go together. Now suddenly you are left alone, pure. If you get into one, you get into the other too.

"Well, young man, I understand you want to become my son-in-law," said the father to his daughter's boy-friend, Mulla Nasruddin.

"No sir, not exactly," replied Nasruddin. "But if I marry your daughter, I don't see how I can get out of it."

If you marry someone's daughter you become a son-in-law too, at the same time. It is not possible to choose one out of the two; they go together. In fact to call them two is not right. They are one phenomenon just looked at from two sides.

When you become violent, non-violence comes in. When you become non-violent, violence waits behind it. They go together. All dualities go together. When sex disappears, celibacy disappears too – remember it. If you start claiming that you have become a celibate then sexuality still exists and any day it can explode. You are sitting on a volcano. When sex has gone what is the meaning of celibacy? Then it is simply meaningless, the word is meaningless. "Celibacy" can carry any meaning only in reference to sex.

Buddha says that when the dualities are gone, you are simply in the middle – silent, calm, pure. The way is attained. The way is the middle way.

Finally, so that you can remember it always, let me condense the whole thing into one sentence:

Whenever you are tired, frustrated, finished with something, remain alert –
the mind will tend to go to the opposite.

When the strings are too loose, the mind will tend to make them too tight –
and there again you miss. And when the mind is too tight, when the strings are
too tight, one day you will get tired of that too, because the music will not be
coming out of it. Then the mind will tend again to make them too loose. This is
how life goes. One life after another you go on moving from one pole to
another. You become a volleyball – kicked from this side to that, kicked from
that side to this. If you want to get out of this game, this game of samsara, this
game of the world, then be in the middle. Whenever a moment comes to decide,
be very alert; never go to the other extreme. Remember to remain in the middle.

If you can learn to remain in the middle you have learned all that is there to
learn, and all that is worth learning. Buddha's way is called *majjhim nikai*, "the
middle way". He is one of the most penetrating seekers of truth. He has made
something very profound, discovered something which you can use. It is not a
ritual, it is not a prayer. It is something to do with your awareness. His whole
field of work is awareness.

So remain in the middle. If you have been eating too much, don't start
fasting. That is very simple. That's how people go on. I know many people: the
first two or three months they will fast and diet, and then they will rush into
food. And then they will become obsessed; for two or three months they will
eat too much. Again, whatsoever the fast has done to their bodies is undone.
Again they are ready to fast. This way they go on – volleyballs kicked from here
to there.

Right food, right quantity, eaten with awareness, is enough. You need not eat
too much, you need not fast.

Remember the middle and you will always be right.

Enough for today.

Chapter 19:

The Discipline of Transcendence

THE BUDDHA SAID:

When a man makes utensils out of a metal which has been thoroughly cleansed of dross, the utensils will be excellent. You monks, who wish to follow the way, make your own hearts clean from the dirt of evil passions, and your conduct will be unimpeachable.

Even if one escapes from the evil creations, it is one's rare fortune to be born a human being. If one be born a man, it is one's rare fortune to be perfect in all the six senses. Even if he be perfect in all the six senses, it is his rare fortune to be born in the time of a buddha. Even if he be born in the time of a buddha, it is his rare fortune to see the enlightened. Even if he be able to see the enlightened, it is his rare fortune to have his heart awakened in faith. Even if he have faith, it is his rare fortune to awaken the heart of intelligence. Even if he awakens the heart of intelligence, it is his rare fortune to realize a spiritual state which is above discipline and attainment.

O children of Buddha! You are away from me ever so many thousand miles, but if you remember and think of my precepts, you shall surely gain the fruit of enlightenment. You may, standing by my side, see me always, but if you observe not my precepts, you shall never gain enlightenment.

Consciousness is like a lake. With waves it becomes the mind, without waves it becomes the soul. The difference is only of turmoil. Mind is a soul disturbed, and soul is mind silenced. The mind is just the ill state of affairs, and the soul is the healthy state of affairs. Mind is not something separate from the soul, as waves are not separate from the lake. The lake can be without waves, but the waves cannot be without the lake. The soul can be without the mind, but the mind cannot be without the soul. When there are great winds and the lake is disturbed, there is turmoil. And the lake loses one quality in that turmoil, and that is the quality of reflection. Then it cannot reflect the real. The real becomes distorted. There may be a full moon in the sky, but now the lake is not capable of reflecting it. The moon will still be reflected, but in a distorted way. It will be reflected in thousands of fragments. It will not be any unity; it will not be collected, integrated. It will not be one. The real is one. But now the lake will reflect many millions of moons; the whole surface of the lake may be filled with silver. Everywhere, moons and moons – but this is not true. The truth is one: when the mind reflects it, it becomes many; when consciousness reflects it, it is one.

Consciousness is neither Hindu nor Mohammedan nor Christian. If you are a Hindu you are still in the mind, distorted. If you are a Mohammedan you are still in the mind, distorted. Once the mind has settled and the waves are no longer there, you are simply a consciousness – with no adjective attached to it, with no conditioning attached to it. And then truth is one. In fact, even to say that truth is one is not right – because one is meaningful only in the context of many. Truth is so one that in the East we have never called it "one"; we call it "non-dual", not-two.

Why have we chosen a roundabout way in calling it "not two"? We want to say that it is difficult to say it is one, because one implies two, three, four. We simply say "not two". We don't say what it is, we simply say what it is not. There is no "manyness" in it – that's all. We have to express it via negativa, by saying that it is not two. It is so one and it is so alone . . . only it exists and nothing else. But that is reflected in consciousness when the mind is no longer there. When I say "the mind is no longer there", remember, I am not talking about mind as a faculty. Mind is not a faculty. It is simply a disturbed state, consciousness wavering, shaking, trembling, not at home.

What winds blow on the consciousness that disturb it? Buddha says the name of that wind is passion, desire.

Watch, and you will see the truth of Buddha's saying. It is a fact, it has nothing to do with any theory. Buddha is not interested in abstract systems; he simply says that which is. He's not formulating a philosophy. Always remember it, never forget it – he is very experimental, existential. His whole approach is just to say something that you can immediately experience. And your experience will prove that he is right; there is no other way to prove right or wrong. There is no way to argue about it.

Just sometimes sit silently; even if for a single moment desire stops, you will see that all turmoil has disappeared. Sitting silently, not desiring anything; sitting silently, not moving into the future; sitting silently, contented – in that single moment you will be able to understand what Buddha means. Suddenly you will see that there are no waves at all. All the waves have gone. The waves arise only when you desire, when you are discontented with the present and you hope for the future.

Desire is a tension between the present and the future. In that tension, waves arise. Then you are shattered – and consciousness is very fragile. Consciousness is very soft – just a slight desire, just a flicker of desire and the whole lake is disturbed. Go sometimes, watch, sit by the bank of a lake. See . . . there are no ripples. Throw a small pebble, a very small pebble in the biggest of lakes, and the small pebble will start creating ripples and those ripples will go on spreading to the farthest bank. Just a small pebble creates so much disturbance. Just a slight desire and disturbance comes through the back door.

Desire is disturbance, passion is a fever. In passion you are not yourself. In passion you are beside yourself. In passion you are not centered, you lose your balance. In passion you do things you cannot even imagine that you could have done. Many murderers have said in the courts, down through the centuries, that they have not committed the crime; it *happened*. They were in such rage, they were almost insane. They have not done it deliberately, it has just happened. They are not criminals, they are victims of their own rage.

You may think they are trying to deceive you; you may think they are now trying to escape from punishment. No, it is not so. Murder is impossible if you are conscious, if you are silent, if you are centered. It happens only when you are not, when you are so clouded, when there are only waves and waves and the surface of the lake is completely disturbed – then it happens. All that is wrong happens only when you are disturbed. Ordinarily religious people say, "Cultivate character." Buddha says, "Cultivate consciousness." Ordinary religious teachers say, "Do good." Buddha says, "Be silent and good will be done." The good follows silence as your shadow follows you – and there is no way to do good unless you are silent. You can do good, but only wrong will happen if you are not silent. That's why the so-called do-gooders go on doing a thousand and one mischiefs in the world. Your so-called do-gooders are the most mischievous people, but they are doing good for your sake, they are doing it for your good, and you cannot even escape from them.

Everybody knows that good parents are dangerous parents. A parent that is too good is bound to be a wrong parent – because he will encage you. Too much good is destructive. A good mother will destroy you, because the mother herself is not centered. Her good is enforced, she is *trying* to do good. The good is not natural and spontaneous, it is not like a shadow, it is full of effort – it is violent. Your so-called mahatmas go on crippling people, destroying people, destroying their freedom in many ways. They go on trying to dominate – by subtle methods, in subtle ways, but the whole desire is to dominate. And it is very easy to dominate somebody when you are good. He cannot even rebel against you. Against a bad mother you can escape, but what to do against a good mother? She's so good that you start feeling bad. Watch it – everybody has passed through that state, and it has to be understood. Otherwise you will never be able to accept yourself.

Whenever there is a child, there is bound to be some conflict between the child and the parents – particularly between the child and the mother in the beginning, and then later on with the father. It is natural, because the mother has her own way, her own ideas, her own philosophy of how life should be lived. And the child is almost wild; he knows no society, no culture, no religion. He's coming directly from existence; he's as wild as existence. He has nothing but freedom, so there is bound to be some conflict. And the child has to be initiated into the walls of the society. He cannot be left alone – that too is true. So conflict is natural. If the mother is very good then the child is in a difficulty, a very great anguish and anxiety. The anxiety is that the child loves his freedom and knows, intrinsically, that freedom is good. Freedom is an intrinsic value. There is no need to prove that freedom is good – freedom is good, it is self-evidently good. Everybody is born with that desire. That's why we called the ultimate goal in the East "total freedom", moksha, where the intrinsic desire is completely fulfilled and one has no limitations of any sort. One is absolutely free, unconditionally free.

Every child is born with that intrinsic desire to be free, and now everywhere there is bondage. The mother says, "Don't do this, don't do that, sit here, don't go there." And the child feels pulled and pushed from everywhere. Now, if the mother is bad, there is not much difficulty; the child can think that the mother is bad and deep in his heart he can start hating her. Simple, it is arithmetical – she is destroying his freedom and he hates her. Maybe for political reasons he cannot express it, so he becomes a diplomat. He knows that she is the rottenest woman in the world, but he goes on paying lip service. But if the mother is good then the problem arises. Then the child is at a loss to figure it out. The mother is good . . . and freedom is good: "Now, if Mother is good then I must be wrong, and my freedom must be wrong. If I am good and my freedom is good, then Mother must be wrong." Now, to think that the mother is wrong is impossible – because she is really good, and she goes on caring, loving, and doing a thousand and one things for the child. The mother is really good, the child knows that she is good. So there is only one possibility to decide, and that is, "I must be wrong. The mother is good, I must be wrong."

Once the child starts thinking, "I must be wrong," he starts rejecting himself. I ordinarily never come across a person who accepts himself totally. And if you don't accept yourself totally you will never grow – because growth is out of acceptance. If you go on rejecting yourself, you are creating a split. You will be schizophrenic. The part that you reject will hang around your neck like a great burden, a great sorrow, a great anxiety, a tension. You cannot throw it away, because it is part of you; it cannot be divided. At the most you can throw it into unconsciousness. You can become unaware of it, you can forget about it, you can believe that it is not there. That's how the unconscious is created.

The unconscious is not a natural thing. The unconscious is that part of your being that you have rejected and you don't even want to face it, you don't want to encounter it, you don't want to see that it exists at all. It is there; deep down in your being it goes on manipulating you. And it will take many types of revenge, because it also needs expression.

Now this is the whole misery of human beings. A "good" mother can create the idea of a "bad" child. The child himself starts rejecting himself. This is a division, a split in personality. The child is getting neurotic, because to feel good with oneself should be a natural and easy thing.

That's what your religious preachers go on doing, what your priests go on doing. Go to the mosque, go to the temple, go to the church, and they are there thundering, condemnatory, ready to throw you into hell, ready to reward you with heaven if you listen to them, if you follow them. Of course you cannot follow because their demands are impossible, and their demands are impossible because they don't show you the *way* to be good. They simply say, "Be good."

The way to be good has nothing to do with being good. The way to be good has something to do with centering, with awareness. Being good has nothing to do with your character. A really good person has no character at all; he is characterless. And when I say "characterless" I mean he has no armor around him. He has no defenses around him, he's simply open. He's as characterless as a flower. He's neither good nor bad, he's simply there – alert, conscious, responsible. If something happens he will respond, but he will respond directly. He will respond from here, he will respond out of the now. He will not respond out of the past. "Character" means you go on carrying the things that you have learned in your past. "Character" means the conscience that has been preached to you and forced upon you. Conscience is a prison for consciousness.

Buddha brought a revolution into the world of religion, the greatest ever. The revolution was that he emphasized consciousness and not conscience. He emphasized awareness and not character. Of course, character comes automatically, but it comes like a shadow. You are not to carry it; it is not a burden. Have you ever watched? – your shadow goes on following you and you are not burdened, and you need not care about it. You need not think about it. Even if you forget completely it will be there. You cannot lose it.

Buddha says character is real only when you cannot lose it. If you are afraid that you can lose it, then it is conscience and not consciousness.

So the first thing to be understood before we enter into these sutras is that a man becomes blind by passion, by desire. And why does he become blind by passion and desire? Because desire and passion bring two things – first, a discontent with the present. It is the very root of desire. If you are not discontented with the present, desire cannot exist. Desire can come into existence only with discontent.

Just see . . . If you are sitting here and you are contented in this moment – and I don't see why you should not be contented in this moment – then there is no desire. And when there is no desire, there is such calm, such quiet. The silence becomes so solid that you can almost touch it, you can taste it, you can hold it in your hands.

Whenever there is contentment, there is no desire. When there is no desire you are at home, relaxed. In that relaxed state, there is no mind. Mind is the accumulated tensions. Mind is not a faculty, mind is just a bundle of all your desires, all the waves that you go on creating. One passion is lost; before it is lost you get involved in another passion. One desire is finished, and even before it is finished you start planning for another trip in the future.

So you go on rushing into the future and you go on missing the present. Presence is possible only in the present. And when you are present there is no mind. This state of no-mind is the goal, the Buddhist goal. When there is no tension, no thought, no desire, no passion, a great well-being arises in your soul; it wells up. That's what benediction is. You feel tremendously happy, and you feel happy for no reason. You feel tremendously high – but this high has no cause to it. It is not that you have taken some drug, or alcohol; it is not that you have been chanting a mantra – because a mantra also changes your chemistry. The constant repetition of a certain sound brings changes in your body chemistry. It is a drug. A mantra is a drug, a very subtle drug. It creates certain waves in your being. And if you go on chanting a certain mantra – *Aum . . . Aum*

... *Aum* – by and by, the sound "Aum" changes your whole body chemistry.

Or you can go on a fast. And look at the absurdity: people who preach fasting are against drugs, but fasting is a chemical change. It is as much a drug as any other drug. When you fast what are you doing? – you are not giving certain chemicals to your body – chemicals which, if not given, the balance of inner chemicals will be changed. It is the same. Either you take some drug – that changes your inner proportion of chemicals; or you stop taking food – that changes your inner balance of chemicals. When people feel high, when Mahatma Gandhi says that he feels very high when he is on a fast, he's not talking about anything different from what Timothy Leary says. Both are saying the same things; both are talking about chemistry. Though ordinarily we don't see fasting as a drug, it is a drug – it can make you high, it can make you weightless.

Or you can go on chanting. Chanting creates changes in the physical body chemistry. That's why a few sounds have become very important. Down through the centuries many people have tried many mantras, and found that a few mantras succeeded and a few failed. Those that have succeeded are the mantras which immediately bring changes to your chemistry. You might call it Transcendental Meditation but it is still a drug. Now, Maharishi Mahesh Yogi is very much against drugs, and TM itself is a subtle drug.

Or, you can change your body chemistry through postures, yoga; you can change your body chemistry through certain types of breathing – but all changes are basically chemical. When you breathe deeply you bring more oxygen to the body, and more oxygen in the body starts changing your chemistry – you start feeling high. When you don't breathe deeply more carbon dioxide collects in the lungs. The proportion changes; you feel dull, you feel low, you feel depressed. Yes, that word is right – you feel "pressed" by something. It is carbon dioxide that brings depression; you are under a rock.

But these are all physical, chemical changes; they don't go deeper than that. Buddha says that just being aware, just being aware and contented . . . He does not even preach a certain pattern, a rhythm of breathing. He says let the breathing be natural. He does not preach fasting; he preaches right food, the right quantity of food. He does not preach vigilance in the night. There are many sects, particularly Mohammedans, who stay awake the whole night. That too changes the body chemistry. Buddha simply says just one thing is needed, and that is that you should not move into the future, you should remain present here now. You should remain contented with the moment. Move with the moment, don't go ahead, don't jump ahead. Let there be no passion. "Passion" means jumping ahead of yourself. Then you create anxiety, then you create frustration, then you create worry, and then a thousand and one waves arise on the surface of your consciousness. You become a mind. When these waves disappear, you are again a consciousness.

Try it sometime . . . Gurdjieff used to give a method to his disciples. He used to call it the "Stop Exercise". He taught his disciples to sometimes, suddenly, stop the whole world. By stopping yourself, you can stop the whole world. You are walking on the road – suddenly, with a jerk, you stop. For a half-second you simply remain unmoving. That sudden non-moving will also help the mind to stop – because the mind takes time. If you stop slowly, then the mind will not stop; it will get adjusted. If you suddenly stop then there is a shock and the mind stops. In that moment of sudden stopping you will be able to see that the whole world has stopped, because all the waves have disappeared.

Try it – just dancing, suddenly stop! Running, suddenly stop. Swimming, suddenly stop. Talking, suddenly stop – and for a single moment be absolutely unmoving, as if you have become a statue – and you will see that your mind has stopped. For a split second, of course, then again it takes possession of you. But in that single moment you will see that it is so silent that it will become a glimpse, it will become a great support. And you will know that this is how reality is. In that single moment, that which is will reveal itself to you. That's what godliness is, or truth, or nirvana.

THE BUDDHA SAID:

When a man makes utensils out of a metal which has been thoroughly cleansed of dross, the utensils will be excellent. You monks who wish to follow the way, make your own hearts clean from the dirt of evil passions, and your conduct will be unimpeachable.

Cleanse your heart from the dross of passion. And in fact, to do it, nothing much is needed. It is not really the case that you have become impure. You are simply disturbed, that's all; that's what impurity is. Whenever you are undisturbed, impurity disappears. Impurity is not something that has entered into your being. It is just on the surface, like waves. So if you want it to happen, it can happen right now. And don't play with explanations. Don't say, "How can it happen right now? I have many karmas to settle first." All nonsense, tricks of the mind to postpone. The mind says, "How can I do it right now? First I have to settle many, many lives' karmas." But do you know how many lives you have been here? Millions of lives! If you have really to settle those karmas, you will again take millions of lives to settle them. And after you have settled them millions of lives will have again passed – and in these lives again you would be creating many karmas. There is no way to avoid it. If you are alive you will do something or other. You will eat something, karma is created. You will breathe, karma is created. You will walk, karma is created. You will sleep, karma is created. Any action is karma. So this is a vicious circle. For millions of lives you have existed; now to settle those karmas, again millions of lives will be needed. And even after that, nothing will be settled because in these millions of lives again you will be creating karmas. Then you cannot get out of this mess. Then there is no way out.

Buddha says there is a way out. It is not a question of settling the past karmas, it is simply settling the present state of mind, that's all.

It is just here now. If you understand, the settlement can happen. You have never done anything; you have been simply dreaming. The action or the actor, the doer and the doing – all are dreams. Buddha says your innermost core is simply empty. It has never done anything. It cannot do. It is a witness, by its very nature.

Watch it. Find out whether what he says is true or not. Try it in your life. You were a child, now you are no longer a child; then you were a young man, now you are no longer young; now you have become old; the childhood body has gone, the childhood mind has disappeared. Then you had another body in your youth – that has gone. The vigor, the vitality, the youth, the beauty – everything has disappeared. You had a different type of mind – too ambitious, too desirous, too egoistic. Now all that is a story of the past. Now death is coming; you can hear the sound of its coming closer every day. You can feel that every day the distance is becoming smaller and smaller. But watch one thing: you have remained the same. Your innermost core has not changed a little bit, it has not changed at all. When you were a child, it was the same consciousness watching from behind. You were young; it was the same consciousness, watching. Then you became old; it is the same consciousness.

It is as if consciousness is a mirror. A child stands before the mirror, the mirror reflects the child; a young man stands before the mirror, the mirror reflects the young man; an old man stands before the mirror, the mirror reflects the old man – but the mirror is neither a child, nor a youth, nor old. And when all have gone there is simply a mirror reflecting nothing, just being there.

Your consciousness is a mirror.

This metaphor of the mirror is tremendously meaningful. It will be very helpful on the way if you can understand it. The consciousness is just standing behind, watching. It is a witness. Things come and go . . . just like a movie. You sit in a movie house; on the screen many things come and go. Sometimes you get identified, too. Sometimes you become identified with an actor. Maybe he is beautiful, powerful, has a charm, a grace of personality, is impressive, has some charisma – you get identified, you forget yourself. For a moment you start thinking as if he is you. Sometimes it happens that there is a very sad scene and you start crying, Your eyes are wet –and there is nothing on the screen, just light and shadow passing. And you know it, but you have forgotten for a moment. If you become aware of it, you will start laughing at yourself: "What are you doing? Crying, weeping?" But it happens when you read a novel, too. At least there is something on the screen, but reading a novel there is nothing – no screen, no actors, nothing; just in your own fantasy the novel goes on and on, and sometimes you feel very happy, sometimes you feel very sad. The climate of the novel starts possessing you.

This is exactly what is happening in life. Life is a great stage, a great drama. And it is very complex – because you are the actor, and you are the director, and you are the film and you are the screen, and you are the projector and you are the audience, too. You are all the layers: one part playing the role of an actor, another part directing, another part functioning as a screen, another part working as a projector, and behind it all is your real reality – the witness who is just watching.

This watcher . . . Once you start feeling its existence, once you start getting settled with it, more and more in tune with it, then you will see what Buddha means when he says consciousness is a mirror. The mirror is never contaminated, it only appears to be. You can put a heap of dung before a mirror and of course it will reflect it. But still the mirror is not contaminated, it is not polluted. It doesn't become impure because a heap of manure or dung is reflected in it. It remains pure. Remove the dung and the mirror is there in all its purity. Even when the dung was reflected the mirror was not contaminated. So whatever is impure is really a reflection; it is mirrored. And Buddha says: If you get cleansed of this dross, the dirt of evil and passions, your conduct will be unimpeachable.

So the emphasis is not on conduct. The emphasis is on the mirrorlike purity of consciousness.

THE BUDDHA SAID:

Even if one escapes from the evil creations, it is one's rare fortune to be born a human being.

These are the seven great rare fortunes. Buddha talks of them many times, in many ways. They have to be understood; they are of great import.

First, it is a rare fortune to be born as a human being. Why? Why is it not a rare fortune to be born as a dog, or as a buffalo? Or as a donkey, or as a tree, or as a rock? Why is it a rare blessing to be born as a human being? Because except for human beings, the whole of nature is fast asleep. You also are not awake. Let me repeat it: the whole of nature is asleep except for man, and man is also not awake, but just in the middle.

Sometimes it happens in the morning that you go on tossing and turning in the bed. You know that now it is time to get up, and still there is sleep. It is a midway state. You can hear the milkman talking to your wife, you can hear the children rushing and getting ready for school, you can hear the bus stop outside the house to take the children, and still dreaming also continues. You still feel sleepy, the eyes are closed. Sometimes you drift into sleep, sometimes you drift out of it. This is the state of human beings.

And Buddha says it is a rare blessing – because the whole of nature is very deeply asleep, so deeply asleep that there is not even a dream. It is in a state of *sushupti*, dreamless sleep. Man has come to the second state, the state of dreaming. At least there is a certain dream. Dream means that you are not fast asleep anymore. You are certainly not awake, because when you become awake you become a buddha. You are somewhere in between the animals and the Buddha. You are hanging in a limbo.

And Buddha says it is a great opportunity, a rare blessing – because if you make a little effort you can become awake. A dog cannot become awake, no matter how much effort he makes. A tree cannot become awake; howsoever hard it tries, it is not possible. If a tree tries hard, it will become a dog. If the dog tries hard, the dog may become a man. But awakening happens only when you are a human being. The way towards enlightenment opens only from the human being. And in the East we think – and the thought has much validity in it – that even devas, angels, gods, are not as blessed as a man. Why? Because man stands on the crossroads. Even if gods have to become liberated, they will have to be born as men.

Animals are fast asleep, man is just at the midway point, and the gods are in their dreams too much. The world of the gods is a dreamworld, a fantasy. They live in a fantasy. Man lives just midway, and there is a possibility that he can move towards more awakened states of being. He can become an awakening.

. . . it is one's rare fortune to be born as a human being.

So don't miss this great opportunity. It is after very great struggle that you are born as human beings. It is simply ridiculous to waste it. For millions of lives you have been moving towards this state. Now that you have come to it, you may destroy it just by eating, drinking and being merry. You may simply lose the whole opportunity. There are people who if you tell them to meditate they will say, "Where is the time? We don't have any time." And then you can see them playing cards in a club, and you ask, "What are you doing?" They say, "Killing time" – the same people! When it is a question of meditating they say, "But there is no time," and when it is a question of drinking, of gambling, of going to a movie, or just sitting glued for hours before the TV, they have enough time. Then they say, "We are killing time."

Are you killing time, or is time killing you? Who has ever been able to kill time? Otherwise, with so many people who have been killing time, by this time, time would have died! Nobody has been able to kill time. Time kills everybody, each moment time is bringing death. In India we have the same word for both: time we call *kal* and for death we also have the same name, *kal* . . . because time brings death.

Time is death. Each moment you are slipping into death. Each moment death is coming closer and closer and closer. All clocks are in the service of death. The whole of time is serving death. It is a rare opportunity to be a human being, and it is very easy to lose it. Buddha reminds us. The second thing he says:

Even if one be born a man, it is one's rare fortune to be perfect in all the six senses.

There are people who may be born as human beings but are blind, or deaf, or dumb, or mentally retarded. Then too it is impossible – nobody has ever heard of any mentally retarded person becoming a buddha. It has never been heard of, it is not possible. Great intelligence is needed. It is very difficult to become aware if your senses are missing because for awareness, sensitivity is a must. A man who has eyes and a man who has no eyes are in different states, altogether different states. The man who has eyes is more sensitive, because eyes are the most sensitive part of the body. Eighty percent of your sensitivity belongs to the eyes. A man who is blind is enclosed in a subtle darkness, and there is no way to get out of it. He lives surrounded in a very subtle prison. It is very difficult to escape it.

Your outer eyes give you some glimpses, some visions, and you can start thinking about the inner eyes too. But a person who has no outer eyes cannot have any conception of what a third eye can be, of what inner eyes can be. If the "out-sight" is missing, the "in-sight" will be missing; they exist in a pair. That's why when you see a blind man great compassion arises in you. Just watching a blind man one feels very, very compassionate. Why? The man is missing so much. He is human, and yet eighty percent of color experience, light, is missing. His whole life is colorless; he does not know what green is. Just think about yourself – if you had never known green, if you had never known a rose, if you had never seen a rainbow, if you had never seen the sunrise and the sunset, if you had never seen the face of a beautiful woman or a man, if you had never seen the beautiful, innocent eyes of a child, if you had never seen the face, the grace of one who has attained, how much you would be missing. You would be more like a rock, less like a human being.

Buddha is not against the senses; this sentence will prove it to you. Buddha says sensation, and the lust for sensation is bad, but the senses are good. To be sensitive is an absolute necessity, so become more sensitive.

Let me make it clear to you. If you use your eyes just to reach for lust and you go on looking out of lust, then your eyes will become, by and by, dull. Lustful eyes are always dull. Lustful eyes are always ugly. If a man looks at you with lustful eyes, you suddenly feel offended – he's trespassing. His eyes function like a knife into the heart. He's not a cultured man, he's not gentlemanly at all.

It happened:

> Mulla Nasruddin entered an office, and the receptionist was a
> beautiful woman. He looked at her with such lustful eyes, and then
> he asked, "Where is the bathroom?" The woman said, "Go directly to
> the end of the passage. You will find a room with a sign –
> "Gentlemen" – but don't let that sign prevent you. Just go in."

When you look at a woman with lustful eyes you are not a gentleman. In fact, you are a little inhuman. When the eyes are sensitive, with no lust, they have a depth. When the eyes are not sensitive but only hungering for sensation, they are shallow. You will find them muddy, they will not be transparent. When the eyes are tremendously sensitive, then they have a depth, a transparent depth. You can look into them and you can reach to the very heart of the person. The person becomes available through the eyes, and through the eyes you can see what type of person you are encountering.

Eyes are very indicative. That's why criminals will never look directly into your eyes, they will avoid it. Guilty people will look sideways, they will not look directly because they are not innocent. They know that their eyes can reveal their guilt, their eyes can say things they don't want to say. If you can watch the eyes of a man, you have the very key to his personality.

And the same is true about the other senses. Just think of a deaf person who has not heard Wagner, who has not heard Ravi Shankar, who has not heard the birds singing in the morning, for whom cuckoos don't exist, who has not heard somebody singing a love song or a sad song, for whom a flute is just a hollow bamboo. Just think how poor he is.

Buddha says that the first blessing is that you are born as a human being, the second blessing that you are born with six senses. Now use this opportunity; become more and more sensitive.

And how can you become more sensitive? When you don't lust, you become more sensitive. When you lust, your sensitivity is lost; you become shallow. By and by, a person who does not lust gathers so much energy. If a person is without lust, all the senses become clear windows – no smoke, no barriers. And the inner and outer meet through that sensitivity.

Even if he be perfect in all the six senses, it is his rare fortune to be born in the time of a buddha.

And Buddha says: You may be a human being, you may be born with all senses perfect, but if you are not born in the time of a buddha you will miss the contact with the unknown. You may see the trees, you may see the flowers, you may see the stars, but these are nothing compared to a man of enlightenment – because he represents the unknown in the world of the known. He brings a ray of the beyond into the darkness of the earth. He's the real flowering of consciousness.

"It is rare," Buddha says, "to be born in the time of a buddha." In fact, it is a great blessing just to occupy the same time, the same space, as a buddha occupies – because something of his vibration is bound to touch you. His presence is bound to become a showering of benediction. Even if you never go to him, even if you are against him, even if he passes through your town and you don't have any time to visit him, even then his coolness will bring something to you, something unasked for. He will reach you uninvited. Whenever a buddha exists humanity takes a turn, an upward turn. Whenever a buddha enters into history, history is never again the same – the total perspective changes.

And when Buddha is present it is very easy if you meditate, because his energy is moving. You can simply ride on his wave. When you are doing your meditations alone and a buddha is not present, you are fighting with such great barriers, single-handed; it is almost impossible, improbable, that you will be the conqueror. With Buddha it is almost like this. Ramakrishna used to say, "When the wind is blowing in the right direction, you simply leave your boat in the stream and the wind will take it. Just wait for the right direction; then you need not make any effort. You simply sit in the boat, the wind will take it." When

Buddha is blowing and the whole existence is in a rising-upwards, then everything is going towards the divine. You can simply join hands and you can ride on the wave very easily. You can simply leave your boat in the stream, and the stream is already flowing.

Hence Buddha is right when he says that to be born in the time of Buddha is a rare opportunity.

Even if he be born in the time of a buddha it is his rare fortune to see the enlightened.

But difficulties are there. You may be born in the time of Buddha but you may never go to see him – because just the very idea that somebody is enlightened is against your ego. You cannot believe that somebody is enlightened and you are not. It is impossible that somebody has gone ahead of you. You cannot believe it because of your ego, and you will find a thousand and one reasons not to go to a buddha. You will find arguments that he is wrong, that he is a megalomaniac, that he is making false claims, that he is not really a buddha – "What is the proof?" People used to go to Buddha and ask, "What is your proof? Who is your witness?"

Now these are foolish questions. Who can be a witness? Buddhahood happens in such deep aloneness that nobody can be a witness. It is not an act in the world, it is an act out of the world. Who can be a witness? It happens in tremendous aloneness. It happens at the innermost core; nobody can see it. A Buddha has to be self-proclaimed; there is no other way. And who will certify that he is a buddha? People used to go to him and they would find a thousand and one ways to prove that whatsoever he was saying did or did not coincide with the old scriptures. It never coincides; it cannot, in the very nature of things. Because whenever somebody becomes enlightened he brings a different vision into the world which had never existed before.

Each enlightened person brings a new gift to the world which had not existed before. So if you look in the Vedas you may not find it; if you look in the Upanishads you may not find what Buddha is saying. It will look a little rebellious, unorthodox. An enlightened person is rebellious, is unorthodox, because truth is rebellious and truth is unorthodox. So whenever a buddha comes, people just start looking in their old scriptures to see whether there is a proof and it never happens.

When Christ came Jews started looking in their old scriptures, and they never became convinced that this man was the Messiah for whom they were waiting. They crucified him. Why? – because they could not figure it out. People believe in scriptures. Scriptures are dead things, and scriptures are made by you, collected by you, interpreted by you. Nobody knows what the scriptures really mean. Nobody can know – because words are there, but the content has to be given by you.

I have heard . . .

> Mulla Nasruddin went to his doctor and said, "I am very worried. A week ago, I came home to find my wife in the arms of another man who talked me into going out for a cup of coffee. The next five nights, exactly the same thing happened."
>
> "My good man," said the doctor, "it is not a doctor you want. It is a lawyer."
>
> "No," insisted the Mulla, "it is a doctor I want. I have just got to know if I am drinking too much coffee."

Now it depends . . . how you take a certain thing, how you interpret it. Interpretation is bound to come from your mind.

Listen to an anecdote.

> It was their honeymoon night, and the bride had put on a sheer nightgown and crawled into bed, only to discover that her devout Catholic husband was about to go to sleep on the couch. It was the month of Lent, when Catholics are supposed to drop at least one of their enjoyments.
>
> "George," she called out, "are you not going to make love to me?"
>
> "I can't, honey," he replied, "because it is Lent."
>
> "Why, that's awful!" she exclaimed, bursting into tears. "To whom? and for how long?"

Now the passionate mind, the lustful mind, has its own interpretations. Words don't matter much; you project your ideas on the words. If you are looking for something you will be able to see it. If you are not looking for something you may not be able to see it. And the natural tendency of the human mind is to first deny that somebody has arrived. It is offensive to the ego. That's why it is very difficult for you.

If somebody comes and says that your neighbor is a murderer, you immediately believe it. You don't bother about any proofs. You say, "I have known him for a long time and I have always thought that he was murderous." If somebody comes and says, "That man is a thief, immoral," this and that, you never bother about any proofs. If people bothered about proofs there would not be so much gossiping in the world. Who bothers about proofs? When somebody is being condemned you immediately believe it because that gives you a feeling that you are better than the other person. But if somebody comes and says, "One man has become a meditator, a great meditator," immediately there is suspicion. You listen to it but you don't want to listen. You say, "It is not possible. I know that man; he is a cheat. How can he meditate? I know him from his very childhood, we were together in school. No, he cannot be. What is the proof?" you ask. Whenever somebody talks about somebody else being good, you ask for the proof because it hurts your ego: "So, somebody else has become good before me?"

When a buddha walks on the earth he's claiming the impossible, that which only rarely happens. He's saying he has become a buddha, and of course only he can say that. There is no other way to prove it or disprove it. His statement is not provable or disprovable – and your ego feels offended.

Buddha says it is a rare fortune to be born in the time of a buddha, and still more rare a fortune to see the enlightened – and it is not a question of physical eyes. Many people saw the Buddha passing from one town to another, but they were not people who had *seen* him. Only those few rare individuals who became his disciples had seen. Because it is impossible to see a buddha and not to become a disciple. If you have seen, then you have seen; and then you cannot be the same again. Then your whole life is upside down. Then you are in a chaos, then you are reborn. Then there is going to be a complete collapse of your past, a new birth – and of course all the pain that is always involved in a new birth.

. . . Even if he be able to see the enlightened, it is his rare fortune to have his heart awakened in faith.

You can see with your physical eyes, but that is not much. Unless trust arises in you . . .

Try to understand this word "faith", It does not mean belief. "Belief" means a dogma; "belief" means believing in a dogma. For example, Christians believe in the Trinity – the Father, the Son, and the Holy Ghost. This is a belief. Or, Hindus believe in the three faces of God; that is a belief. When you encounter a buddha and you trust the person, then it is faith. Faith is personal; belief is theoretical, conceptual. Faith is like love – you fall in faith as you fall in love. It is not a belief, it is not that Buddha has convinced you about something. No, his being has convinced you about his own being. He has convinced you not to believe in a dogma, he has convinced you that "something has happened here in this man". You have become convinced of the fact that here is a man who is transformed, transfigured, who is no more of this world. It is a conviction, a personal conviction. It is not an argument, it is not theology – it is a love affair.

There are two types of people: one person comes and he says, "What you say convinces me. Your argument is superb. Your reason appeals to me." Now, this person has come as a believer. He has not really come. Some day he can find somebody who can "unconvince" him because there can be better arguments. There is always the possibility, because logic is a double-edged sword; it cuts both ways. The argument can be used to destroy the conviction, the same argument can be used to make it. Logic is like a prostitute, or like a lawyer. It can go with anybody, with whosoever pays.

It happened:

> In a coffee house there was always a great discussion going on. One philosopher said one day, "If you will give me Aristotle's system of logic, I will force my enemy to a conclusion. Give me the syllogism and that's all I ask."
>
> Another philosopher said, "If you give me the Socratic system of interrogation I will run my adversary into a corner and defeat him immediately. That's all I ask."
>
> Mulla Nasruddin, hearing all this said, "My brother, if you give me a little ready cash, I will always gain my point. I will always draw my adversary to a conclusion because a little ready cash is a wonderful clearer of the intellect."

Logic is not very fundamental; it is superficial. If somebody comes and he says that he believes in what I say, then it is not faith. But there are a few rare people who say, "We don't know what you are saying, we don't even understand much. We enjoy what you say, but that is not the point. We have fallen in love with you." A faith has arisen; now nobody can destroy this faith, because it is illogical.

You cannot destroy faith because it is not based on logic. Anything based on logic can be destroyed – if you can pull on the logic it will collapse. It has a cause; pull the cause away and the effect will disappear. But a faith is uncaused. It is just like falling in love. If you go to Majnu and prove to him that Laila is not the most beautiful woman in the world, and logically you go on proving it, he will say, "Don't unnecessarily trouble yourself. Nobody can prove it."

It actually happened that the king of Majnu's town called him, and felt very kindly towards him. Majnu had been crying and weeping, screaming in the streets in the night. He would just call, "Laila! Laila!" And the king felt very compassionate. He called him and he said, "You are a fool. I have seen your Laila; she is an ordinary girl. In fact, because you were crying so much I thought she must be very beautiful, so I myself became interested. But when I saw her I simply laughed. You are a fool! And I have so much compassion for your foolishness. You are a good young man; don't waste your life."

He called twelve beautiful women from his harem and he said, "You choose any one." They were the best, the most precious of his kingdom. Majnu looked and he said, "Nothing compared to Laila." And he said to the king, "Sir, if you really want to see Laila, you will need my eyes. Majnu's eyes will be needed. There is no way to see Laila and her beauty except through Majnu's eyes."

A disciple is a Majnu. He is a madman; he has fallen in love. Buddha says: "His heart awakened in faith. . . ." The presence of Buddha is his appeal; the grace that surrounds Buddha has touched his heart. It is not Buddha's logic, it is not his philosophy. Even if Buddha remained silent it would not make much difference; the disciple would be convinced all the same. Even if Buddha started contradicting himself it would not make any difference. That's why you see that I go on contradicting myself. Those who come through intellect by and by disappear. My contradiction helps me to throw the weeds out of my garden. Those who have come through love don't bother. They say, "Okay, you enjoy contradicting yourself, but we love you. You cannot deceive us." They say, "You can go on contradicting but you cannot force us to run away from you."

Those who come to a buddha through belief, sooner or later, will have to leave – because truth is paradoxical. Only theories are non-paradoxical. Truth contains all the contradictions of life. Truth is very illogical, very irrational.

Even if he have faith, it is his rare fortune to awaken the heart of intelligence.

And then Buddha says: But this is not the end. When your heart is full of love, and full of faith and trust, this is not the end. This is just the beginning. Now you have to help your intelligence to come up and take possession of you. Faith is the door; you should enter through it but you should not remain at the door. Otherwise, you never enter into the palace. Finally, you have to come to your own experience. It is good to trust in a buddha, it is good to have faith, but that is not enough – because your faith in Buddha is still not your experience. What has happened to Buddha must happen to you too. Then the second step happens: your own intelligence arises. Now it is not only love towards Buddha. Now from your own experience you have become a witness, it is not only unfounded faith. In the beginning faith is unfounded, but in the end it becomes absolutely founded. The foundation is not supplied by logic, the foundation is supplied by your experience. When it has become your own experience you don't say, "I trust in Buddha." You know it is right, it is true.

So Buddha says: First you trust. Trust means simply that you have come across a man who is far away from you. You have come across a person who has shown you your own future, your destiny. It is as if a seed has come to a tree, and the seed has become aware that the tree is possible. The tree says, "Once I was also a seed just like you." Now trust arises in the seed. If he had never seen the tree, he would never have dreamed about it. How can a seed dream about a tree? He has never seen one. That's why to be born in the time of a buddha is a great blessing – because there exists a tree, and your seed can start dreaming. When the first impact of the tree falls on the seed, he trusts. His own future becomes full of possibilities now. It is not going to be just a repetition of the past, it will be something new. He is thrilled – that thrill is faith. He's thrilled to the very roots. Now, for the first time, he knows there is meaning; now, for the first time, he knows there is destiny. Something is going to happen: "I'm not just an accident. I'm carrying a great message. It has to be translated, it has to be decoded. I have to become a tree and bloom, and spread my fragrance to the winds."

Seeing a buddha, you have seen your own possible buddhahood. That's what faith is . . . but it is not enough. Then you have to work hard to make it real. The seed has to fall into the earth, die into the earth, be born as a sprout. And a thousand and one difficulties have to be crossed – winds are there, thunder is there, animals are there, and the new sprout is very fragile, very weak. With infinite potentiality to become strong, but right now it is not strong – it will need somebody's help; it will need a gardener. That is the meaning of a master.

When you choose a master, you choose a gardener. And you say, "Protect me until I have become strong enough to go my own way." But faith is just the door.

Even if he have faith, it is his rare fortune to awaken the heart of intelligence.

And the last:

Even if he awakens the heart of intelligence, it is his rare fortune to realize a spiritual state which is above discipline and attainment.

The whole goal of discipline is to come to a point where discipline can be dropped. The whole goal of spiritual practice, *sadhana*, is to come to a moment when all *sadhana* can be dropped and you can be simply spontaneous. Then you have flowered.

For example, if you have to continue meditation, and one day you stop your meditation and the mind jumps back, then this is not a great state. A moment should be longed for when you can even drop your meditation but nothing differs; it remains the same. Whether you do meditation or you don't, you remain meditative. Meditation has become your innermost core, part of your being, no longer something imposed from the outside. Not that you have to force yourself to be good; not that you have to repress your temptations to be bad, no. Now there is no temptation, no enforcement. One has gone beyond discipline. This is what Buddha calls "The Discipline of Transcendence". This is the seventh fortune, the last, the ultimate.

To be born as a human being is just the beginning, and then you have to come to this point where all discipline can be dropped. Then you have become a God, then you have become as spontaneous as nature, then there is no tension, then you don't have any character, then you are as innocent as a child. Your awareness is perfect now, your awareness is enough now. Nothing else is needed.

The Buddha said:

O children of Buddha, you are away from me ever so many
thousands of miles. But if you remember and think of my precepts,
you shall surely gain the fruit of enlightenment. You may, standing
by my side, see me always. But if you observe not my precepts, you
shall never gain enlightenment.

And Buddha says: Never stop anywhere unless you have attained to the seventh – the state of a disciplined no-discipline, the state of effortlessness, the state of Tao, dhamma, the state which Kabir calls *sahaj*, spontaneous. But you have to work hard for it.

So Buddha says, "You can remain with me, and if you don't follow what I am saying, if you don't bring it to your heart, to your intelligence, to your being, then you are thousands of miles away from me. But you may be thousands of miles away from me – if you are following what I have said, you are close to me and your enlightenment is absolutely certain, assured, promised.

To be close to a buddha . . . there is only one way to follow his footprints. To be close to a buddha means to become more and more aware, become more and more alert. Bring a little buddhahood to yourself. The goal is that you also have to become a buddha. Only then will you be able to understand exactly what is the meaning and significance and the grandeur of being awakened.

This consciousness exists within you right now, this very moment. You may not be able to see it. I can see it. It is there like a mirror, and you get identified with all that reflects in the mirror. Drop your identifications: start seeing that you are not the body; start seeing that you are not the mind; start seeing that you are not the emotions, not the thoughts; start seeing that you are not pleasure and pain; start seeing neither old nor young; start seeing neither success nor failure. Remember always that you are the witness. By and by, this mirrorlike quality will explode into your being.

The day you recognize that you are a mirror, you are free. You are freedom. This is what moksha or nirvana is all about.

Enough for today.

Chapter 20:

The Ten Grounds of the Way

The Buddha asked a monk: "How do you measure the length of a man's life?"

The monk answered, "By days."

The Buddha said: "You do not understand the way."

The Buddha asked another monk: "How do you measure the length of a man's life?"

The monk answered, "By the time that passes during a meal."

The Buddha said: "You do not understand the way."

The Buddha asked a third monk: "How do you measure the length of a man's life?"

The monk answered, "By the breath."

The Buddha said: "Very well, you know the way."

Very simple question, and a very simple answer. But much is implied in the question. And the answer also shows much about the monk – his understanding, his state of mind.

When Buddha asks, "How do you measure the length of a man's life?" he is raising a question that can only be answered by depth. Man's life can be measured only by depth. It looks paradoxical: length can be measured only by depth.

In fact, the deeper you live, the longer you live. The length of your life depends on your depth. The quantity of your life depends on your quality. The monk could not understand it. He simply said, "By days." His simple answer also showed much about himself. "By days" means by time; "by days" means by the fleeting; "by days" means by the flux, the changing. He measures life by the momentary – not by the eternal, not by the timeless.

Life exists in time, but life does not belong to time. It penetrates time, and one day it disappears from time. It is just like when a ray of sun penetrates water, and when it penetrates the water its angle changes. That's why if you put a straight stick into water it will look curved. It will not look straight because the angle of light changes. When the ray of light enters into the medium of water, it does not belong there, it has come from beyond. It will go back, it will be reflected back – because everything returns to its source, has to return to its source. Only then is the circle complete, and there is contentment.

When Buddha asked, "How do you measure the length of a man's life?" and the monk replied, "By days," he showed his understanding. He does not know anything beyond time; he thinks life is just that which consists of time. Being born, getting married, living, then old age, then death – days go on flicking by, just like numbers on a gasoline pump. But this is not life; this is just the very periphery.

Have you observed that if you look inside, time exists not? If you look outside there is time, but if you look inside there is no time. Have you not felt it sometimes, sitting silently with closed eyes – that inside you have not aged at all? Inside you remain the same as when you were a child, or as when you were young. Inside nothing has changed: the face is wrinkled by age, the hairs have gone gray, death is approaching – this is all from the outside. If you look in the mirror then of course there are signs that much time has passed, that very little is left, that sooner or later you will be gone. But look within: there has never been any time there. You are exactly the same as you ever were when you were running in a garden or on the sea beach and collecting colored stones and seashells. Just remember . . .

Inside you are exactly the same this moment too. Time is a fallacy as far as the inner world is concerned, because in the inner world nothing ever changes. It remains the same, its taste remains the same.

In the inner world time is simply irrelevant. And life is in the inner. It expresses itself in the outside, but it does not belong to the outside. It wells up from your within. It moves outwards like ripples, it pulsates outwards, but it arises from your innermost core.

When Buddha was asking, "How do you measure the life of a man?" in a very simple question he was asking a very complicated philosophical question too. And the monk was deceived. The monk said, "By days." But there is no day, no night. Time is a utilitarian concept, it is needed outside. When you are alone time is not needed. It is a relationship between you and others; it is a relative concept. Try to find out, and you will be surprised to discover that believing in time you have been believing in an illusion – because that which does not correspond to your inner reality cannot be real.

It is just like money – if you go to the market it has value; if you simply sit alone with your money it has no value. The value comes only when you relate with others, because the value is just an agreement between you and the others. That's why money has a beautiful name, it is called currency. "Currency" means that when money moves it has value; when it does not move it has no value. If you go on keeping it in your pocket always and always, it is meaningless. You can keep anything else instead of it; it will be the same.

Money has value when it changes hands. From one hand to another – then there is value. Its value is in being a currency, a moving force. When it moves from you to somebody else it has value. Again, if it is stuck there it loses value. That's why miserly people are the poorest in the world. They have money but they don't know that money has value only when it is a currency. You can hide it in your treasure chest; you will remain poor.

Time is also a currency between two people, between relationships, between societies. But in the inner world, when you are alone, it is simply meaningless. All the concepts of time, if looked at deeply, look very stupid. But people don't look deeply into things because to look deeply creates anxiety. Then you become very anxious. Then settled things are unsettled, and whenever something is unsettled one feels anxious. One wants to be settled again.

People say time passes. But where does it pass to? From where does it come? You say it comes from the future and goes into the past? That means the future exists before it has become present? Otherwise, from where is it coming – from nowhere, from nothingness? And then you say it goes into the past – that means it goes on collecting in the past. It is still there? It still exists? Then what is the difference between present, past, and future, if they all exist? Then they are all present. Then there is no past and no future.

You say a moment that has passed is past, and a moment that has yet to come is future. You stand on a road, you have walked two miles; that distance has been traveled. But those two miles actually exist; you can look back and those two miles are still there and if you want to go back you can go back. But can you go back in time?

Look back – nothing exists. Except for this present moment, on both sides there is simply smoke and nothing else. The past simply disappears, and the future appears out of nothing. And then a problem arises: if in the beginning there is nothing, and in the end again there is nothing, how can there be something between two nothings? It is impossible.

Time is not a valid concept at all. It is just utilitarian. It is accepted, it has utility. Every morning you come to the discourse at eight o'clock; if there were no time it would be difficult. When would you come, how would you manage? And how would there be a possibility of me meeting you? It would become difficult. But remember it is just an agreement, it is not truth.

Truth is timeless. Time is a human invention, truth is eternal. In fact, time does not pass, we pass. We come and go; time remains. Then time is not time; then it is eternity.

Buddha was asking all these things in a simple question. The monk said, "By days." Buddha said, "You do not understand the way."

The man's understanding was very superficial. We can call it the understanding on the level of the body. Of course, the body has a clock in it. Now the scientists call it the biological clock. That's why if you eat every day at one o'clock, your lunch time, then every day at one o'clock the body will say you are hungry. The body has a clock. You need not actually look at the clock. If you listen to your body, the body will tell you, "Now it is time to sleep because every day you go to sleep at this time."

And you can even put an alarm in your body-clock. When you are going to sleep you can repeat your own name loudly, three times. If your name is Rama, You can say, "Rama, listen. I have to get up at five o'clock. Help me." Talk to your body and go to sleep, and exactly at five o'clock your body will wake you. The body has a clock. That's why each month, after four weeks, twenty-eight days, the monthly period comes to a woman. The body manages very exactly unless something has gone wrong with the body – the woman may have disturbances; otherwise, it is exactly twenty-eight days. If the clock is functioning well there will never be any problem: twenty-eight days means twenty-eight days. After nine months the body is ready to give birth to a child, exactly after nine months. If the woman is healthy and there is no complication in her body, it will happen exactly when the nine months are complete. The body carries a clock and functions perfectly well.

The body, of course, is measured by days. And the body shows every sign of passing time. Young, old, you can see it on the body. The body carries the whole biography.

This man's understanding was very physical, very superficial.

The Buddha asked another monk. "How do you measure the length of a man's life?"

The monk answered, "By the time that passes during a meal."

His understanding goes a little deeper. He is less physical and more psychological. To enjoy a meal you need a mind, to indulge you need a mind, to be sensual you need a mind. This man's understanding was a little deeper. What was he saying? He was saying that a man's life is measured by the pleasures, indulgences, sensuality, experiences that he has gathered in his life. The man is saying, "How long you live is not the point, but how much you enjoy the pleasures of life."

There is a story about Nero, the Roman emperor. He must have been of the exact same type as this second monk. He always had two physicians with him. He would eat, and the physicians would help him to vomit. Then he would eat again. You cannot go on eating; there is a limit. So when Nero would feel that now the stomach was full, he would order the physician to help him vomit; then he could eat again. He would eat ten, twelve times a day.

And don't think that this is very far-fetched: I have come across a few people who do it.

There was one woman who told me this after she had been here for at least two years. She said, "I am ashamed, but I have to tell you that every day, when I eat, I vomit immediately." I said, "Why?" She said, "So that I can eat more. But then I vomit again."

Now vomiting has become a habit. Now she cannot resist; when she eats she has to vomit. It has become a mechanical habit. It took almost six months to break her habit.

Nero must have done it. Ordinarily, you may not be vomiting but you can go on eating too much. There are people who live to eat. It is good to eat, it is good to eat to live, but once you start living for eating then you are in a very confused state. Eating is a means, not the end.

This monk says, "By the time that passes during a meal."

He must have been a glutton. He must have understood only one language, and that is of taste. He must have been a food addict. He says that if we count real life, then real life means those moments in which we are enjoying, indulging. It may be food, it may be sex, or other gratifications. Many people are of that type. Their philosophy seems to be, "Eat, drink, be merry, and there is nothing else in life."

There was a great philosopher in India, Charvak. This was his message to his disciples: "Eat, drink, and be merry. And don't bother about the other life, and the soul, and God; this is all nonsense. These are just theories invented by the priests to exploit you." He was the first Marxist. Marx came three thousand years later; Charvak was the first communist. But if life is just eating, drinking, indulging, then it cannot have any meaning. That's why in the West a new problem has become very important, and the problem is, "What is the meaning of life?" All intelligent people are asking that. Why? The problem has become almost epidemic. It is no longer academic; everybody is asking what the meaning of life is. And they are asking at the wrong time – when they have enough to eat, enough to drink, and enough to be merry. Why are they asking this question?

In fact, when you have all that this world can give to you, then arises the question, "What is the meaning of it?" Yesterday you ate, today you are eating, tomorrow also you will eat – so what is the point? Eating and defecating – on the one hand you go on stuffing yourself, on the other hand you go on emptying yourself. Is this your whole life? And in between there is a little taste on the tongue . . . It seems absurd. The effort seems to be too much, and the result seems to be nothing, almost nothing.

Man needs to have a meaning, but the meaning can come only from the higher. The meaning always comes from the beyond. Unless you feel related to something higher, you feel meaningless. Meaning arises when you feel that you are part of a divine plan, a divine flow. When you feel that you are part of a great whole, then you have meaning. A brick in itself has no meaning, but when it becomes part of a great palace, part of the Taj Mahal, it has meaning. It has contributed something to the beauty of the Taj Mahal; it is not futile, it is significant.

When a feeling of godliness is not there, man starts trying to find a new meaning to his life: become part of a party, the great Communist Party, or the great Fascist Party. Become part of something . . . then Stalin and Hitler become gods. Then you join hands with them so that you can feel a little meaning – that you are not alone, that you are not just accidental, that you have some mission to fulfill. Maybe you are here to bring communism to the world, a classless society; or you are here to bring the kingdom of the Aryans. Then one becomes part of a Hindu religion, Christian, Mohammedan. One finds some way, somewhere, to become part of something. And people go to foolish lengths. They become Rotarians and Lions just to have a feeling that they are part of an international organization. You are somehow chosen, you are a Rotarian; not just everybody can be a Rotarian. Only very few people can be Rotarians, but you are a Rotarian, so you have a meaning. But what a foolish meaning! What does it matter whether you are a Rotarian or not? It really does not bring meaning to your life, it simply deceives you.

You can eat well, you can live well, you can have all the pleasures of life – still you will remain empty. This man, the second monk, said that life is to be measured by pleasure, by indulgence, by sensuality. But Buddha said, "You do not understand the way" – because the way cannot be understood by the body-oriented mind, and the way cannot be understood by the mind-oriented mind. Neither can it be understood through time, nor can it be understood through experience. The way is beyond time and beyond experience.

> *The Buddha asked a third monk. "How do you measure the length of a man's life?"*
> *The monk answered, "By the breath."*
> *The Buddha said: "Very well, you know the way."*

Now in an English translation, saying "by the breath" does not seem to so significant as it appeared to Buddha when the monk said, "By prana." "Breath" is an English translation of "prana", but prana is much more meaningful than breath. The actual translation, closer to truth, would be "spirit", not "breath". And the word "spirit" exists in such words as "inspiration", "expiration". "Spirit" seems to be closer to home, but still not exactly true. So let me first explain to you what prana is; then you will be able to understand. Otherwise it looks a little absurd. The man says, "By the breath," and Buddha says, "Very well, you know the way."

The first thing: if you look at yourself you will find there is the body, the outermost circle around you. Then there is your mind, the second circle within the first circle. And then you will come to a bridge – that bridge is your breath, prana. Through that bridge you are joined with the soul. That's why when a person stops breathing we say he is dead, the bridge is broken. Now the soul is separate and the body is separate. When a child is born the first thing he is expected to do is to breathe. Through breath the soul and body become joined together. And again, the last thing he will do when he dies will be to stop breathing. Again there will be a divorce; the body and soul will be separate.

Prana is the bridge, the glue by which you are glued together. A man can live without food for many days; you can live without water for many hours; but without breath you cannot live even for many minutes. Even seconds will seem difficult.

Breath is the bridge between matter and no-matter, between the form and the formless, between the world and the divine, or whatever terms you choose. Breath is the bridge, and much depends on the breath. How you breathe, what the quality of your prana is – much depends on it.

Watch . . . when you are angry you breathe in one way, when you are silent you breathe in another way. The pulse is different, the rhythm is different, the quality is different. When you are angry your breath is not rhythmic, not musical, not harmonious. It is bumpy. When you are in a passion, in sexual passion, again the breath is feverish. It is not in tune; something goes wrong with the breathing. When you are sitting silently, just being peaceful, not doing anything – no desire, no passion, no anger – just full of compassion, full of love, your breathing is very soft. Your breathing has a rhythm to it, a dance to it. It has no violence, no aggression; it is very delicate.

Have you watched it? When you are in passion your breath will have a bad odor to it; when you are peaceful your breath will have a sweet smell to it. Because you are at ease, the whole being is at ease, you are at home; the breathing will carry the message that you are at home.

There are moments of deep meditation when breathing almost stops. I say almost; it does not stop really. But it becomes so silent that you cannot feel it. You can feel it only if you put a mirror close to your nose. Then on the mirror you can feel it; otherwise you cannot feel it. Those are rare moments of blessing and benediction.

All the yoga systems of the world have worked on breathing, because it is through the breathing that you will pass from the body to no-body. It is through breathing that you will enter into the innermost core of your existence.

The monk is right when he says, "A man's life is to be measured by the way he breathes, by how he breathes." If you are afraid, your breathing is different; you are nervous, your breathing is different; you are sad, your breathing is different. With every mood your breathing changes. The breathing goes on showing where you are. If you can watch your breathing, you will learn the whole alphabet of your inner changing climates. You can see all the moods reflected in the breathing. Breathing is a great way to measure where you are, what you are, what you are doing. Buddha emphasized breathing very much, and his emphasis is unique. It is very different from Patanjali, it is very different from hatha yoga, it is different from all systems. He says don't use any system for breathing, because if you do something with breathing you will create something artificial. Let breathing be natural – you simply watch it. You don't do anything to it, you simply be a witness, you simply look at it.

Now, if you watch breathing, by and by you will see that you are different from the breathing. Certainly – because the watcher cannot be the watched, the subject cannot be the object, the observer cannot be the observed.

When you start watching your breathing – and Buddha says to continuously do it, walking, sitting, whenever you are not doing anything else just watch your breathing, go on seeing it – by seeing it, a great serenity will arise in you. Because you will be standing behind the breathing, and behind the breathing is your soul; you will be centered in your soul.

And if you watch the breathing you will learn. Subtle changes in breathing show where you are, and breathing continuously functions as a measuring rod. A slight change in breathing will be noted when your awareness is full and you can drop then and there, you can become more alert. If you feel your breathing is wavering a little, and you feel that this wavering is the wavering that comes when sex takes possession, then it is the moment to become more aware. If the wavering breath settles, you have passed through it. That desire that was going to possess you will not be able to possess you. By and by you become aware of what type of changes happen in breathing when you become angry. They are so subtle that if you can become aware when the breathing changes slightly the anger can be dropped from there – because it is right in the seed and the seed can be dropped easily. When things become big trees it is very difficult to drop them. You become aware of anger only when it has already possessed you; then diagnosis is too late.

In Soviet Russia they developed a new kind of photography called Kirlian photography. Kirlian photographers say that we can catch hold of a disease six months before it really happens to the person. And if that can be done, then there will be no need for anybody to be ill. The person himself is not aware that he will be falling a victim of tuberculosis in six months. How can you be aware of that? But before it enters into the body, first it enters prana. Before it enters the body, first it enters your energy. They call it "bioplasma" in Russia; it is exactly what we mean by prana – bioplasma, your vitality, your body electricity.

First it enters into the body electricity, and then it takes six months to be transformed into a physical phenomenon. Then it becomes solid in the body and then it is already too late. When you start treating it, it is already too late. If you could have caught it when it was in the bioplasma you could have destroyed it very, very easily. There would have been no problem in it. And the body would never have suffered, the body would not even have known about it.

Buddha says that anything that enters into the bioplasma first happens in your breathing. Anything that happens to your body, to your mind, first happens to your breathing. Maybe some day Kirlian photographers will be able to rediscover the fact that there is a certain association between the pulse of bioplasma and breathing. It has to be so – because when you breathe deeply you have a bigger aura. That has been photographed. When you breathe deeply you have more oxygen and more flowing energy, and your body has a bigger aura, more luminosity to it. When you breathe in a dull way, the whole of your lungs are not full of oxygen and you go on carrying much stale carbon dioxide; then your aura shrinks and becomes very small.

A really alive person has a very big aura, so big that when he comes close to you his aura touches your aura. And you will feel it – there are people with whom you will suddenly feel that you are attracted, pulled. They are irresistible, you would like to come close to them, closer and closer. Their aura has touched your aura.

Then there are people whose auras are almost dead, whose auras do not exist at all. They repel, they don't attract. They are like dead people; nobody feels attracted towards them.

Buddha says watch, become aware of your breathing.

His yoga is called *anapanasati* yoga – the yoga of watching the breath coming in and watching the breath going out. He says this is enough. So when the monk said, "By the breath," Buddha said, "Very well, you know the way."

The Buddha's way has ten grounds called *bhumis*. *Bhumi* means ground. Buddha has said that if you understand these ten grounds, and if you practice these ten grounds you will attain to the ultimate. I would like to go into these ten *bhumis*, these ten grounds. They are very practical.

The first *bhumi* is *pamudita*. It means joyousness. Now, you will be surprised. People have a misunderstanding about Buddha and his teaching – they think that he is a very sad, pessimistic thinker. He is not. His first grounding is joyousness. He says unless you are joyous you will never reach to the truth. Joyousness, delight, celebration; that is the meaning of *pamudita*. Be like a flower – open, dancing in the breeze, and joyous. Only joy can take you to the other shore.

If you are not joyous, your very sadness will function like a rock around your neck and will drown you. People are not drowned by anything else but their own sadness and pessimistic outlooks. Life has to be joyous; then life becomes spiritual. If your church is sad, then that church exists for death, not for life. A church, a temple, has to be joyous. If you come to a saint and he has no sense of humor, escape from him, beware! He can kill you, he will prove poisonous. If he cannot laugh, then you can be certain that he does not know what truth is. Truth brings a sense of humor; truth brings laughter; truth brings a subtle happiness for no reason at all.

Pamudita means joyous for no reason at all. You are sometimes joyous, but that is not *pamudita* – because it has a reason. Some day you have won the race and you are very happy. What will you do? It is not going to happen every day. What are you going to do tomorrow? Or you have won a lottery and you are very happy – but this is not going to happen every day.

> One day I saw Mulla Nasruddin very sad, sitting on his verandah. I asked, "What is the matter Nasruddin? Why are you so sad?"
>
> He said, "Two weeks ago one of my uncles died and left me fifty thousand dollars."

So I said, "This is nothing to be sad about. You should be happy."

He said, "Yes, I was. And then the next week another uncle died and left me a hundred thousand dollars."

So I said, "Why are you sad? You should be dancing!"

He said, "I know. But now . . . no more uncles left."

It cannot happen every day; uncles cannot keep on dying.

Your joyousness, if it is caused, is bound to turn into unhappiness sooner or later. It is on the way already; watch out. If you have a cause to be happy you are already getting into unhappiness, because the cause will disappear. Only uncaused joyousness can be yours; and then nobody can take it away.

Only sages and madmen are joyous for no reason at all. That's why there is a similarity between mad people and sages, a little similarity, an overlapping. Their boundaries overlap. Both are very different: the sage is aware, the madman is absolutely unaware. But one thing is certain, both are happy for no reason at all. The madman is happy because he is so unaware that he does not know how to be unhappy; he is so unconscious that he cannot create misery. To create misery you need a little consciousness. And the sage is happy because he is so fully aware; how can he create misery? When you are fully aware you create happiness for yourself, you become a source of your own happiness.

That's what Buddha means by *pamudita*, and he says this is the first ground.

The second ground is *vimal*. It means innocence, purity, simplicity.

Innocence . . . remember the word. If you become too knowledgeable, you lose innocence. If you become a pundit you lose innocence. So don't go on gathering beliefs and knowledge, otherwise your innocence will be corrupted. If you don't know, you don't know. Simply say, "I don't know." Accept your ignorance and you will be more innocent. And out of innocence, much happens. Never lose your childlikeness. I don't mean that you should be childish. To be childish and to be childlike are totally different. To be childish means to be irresponsible; to be childlike means to be simple, innocent, trusting.

The third ground is *pabhakari*. It means luminousness, light.

Feel yourself as a flame, live as if you are an inner burning light, move with the inner flame. Do whatsoever you do, but always feel as if you are made out of light, and by and by you will see a luminousness arising around you. It is already there! If you help, it will arise – and you will have an aura.

Now Kirlian photographers can even take photographs of it. It is now very tangible. Man is made of bio-electricity; everything is made of electricity. Electricity seems to be the basic component of all. Ask the physicists; they say matter consists of nothing but electricity, everything is nothing but different formulations and combinations of energy. And Buddha says man is light. Light means electricity. You have just to recognize the fact, you have just to cooperate with it, and you will become a great light – not only unto yourself; you will become a light to others too. And wherever you walk there will be light.

This is *pabhakari*, the third grounding.

The fourth grounding is *arsimati* – radiance, aliveness, vitality.

The spiritual seeker should not be dull and dead. But ordinarily you will find these people. That's why I am interested in telling you about these groundings – even Buddhists have forgotten. If you see a Buddhist monk you will see a pale, dead, dull person, sleepy, in a stupor, somehow dragging, somehow carrying the burden of life, not interested. Buddha says radiance, aliveness, vitality – this is the fourth grounding. Be alive! Because it is only on the wings of life that you will reach to truth. If you are dull you are lost. And be radiant – because when there is no anxiety for the future and no desire for the future, then your whole energy is available to you. Then you can burn your torch from both ends at once.

The fifth is *sudurjaya*. It means adventurousness, courageousness, challenge, welcomingness. Whenever there is a challenge, welcome it, don't avoid it. And whenever there is an adventure, don't escape. Go on the journey, go on the trip.

Nobody ever loses anything by being adventurous. I am not saying that the path of adventure is full of roses – it is not. Roses are few and far between, and there are many thorns. But one grows, one becomes crystallized when one accepts a life of adventure. Ordinarily people accept the life of security, of no adventure – a good job, a good house, a good wife, a good husband and good children, and people are satisfied. People are satisfied in living and dying comfortably, as if comfort is the goal. Then they never grow, then they never achieve to any peaks, then they never achieve what Maslow calls "actualization". They remain just possibilities.

It is as if a seed has chosen to hide in the house and is not ready to go into the adventure of falling into the soil. It is dangerous, because the seed will have to die. It is dangerous, because the seed does not know what will happen when he has disappeared. No seed has ever known what happens after the seed has died. How can the seed know? The tree may happen or may not happen. Buddha says *sudurjaya* – look at the far. *Sudur* – that which is very far, let that be your challenge. Don't be confined to the comfortable, to the familiar, to the secure; don't base your philosophy on the promises of a life insurance company. Have a little more courage, move into the unknown.

When you move into the unknown, the unknown moves to you. When you are ready to drop your securities, existence is also ready to reveal its mysteries. When you are ready to be nude and available, existence is also ready to be nude and available. It responds, it exactly responds to you. It never goes farther than you go. If you go towards the truth, the truth comes towards you; if you escape, it also escapes. *Sudurjaya*.

And then the sixth is *abhimukhi* – immediateness, face-to-faceness, encountering that which is. *Abhimukhi* is face-to-face immediateness. Don't bother about the past and don't bother about the future. Face the truth as it comes, encounter the fact as it comes, and with no preparation but with immediateness. A person who lives by preparation is a pseudo-human. In life there are no possibilities for rehearsals ... but we all live through rehearsals. Before you go home you start preparing what you are going to say to your wife. Can't you be immediate? Can't you wait for the moment when the wife is there, and let what happens happen? But coming home from the office you are preparing: what is she going to ask, and what are you going to answer? You go through a rehearsal, and then you are always clouded by your rehearsals. You cannot see that which is. You always see through your clouds and those clouds distort things.

Buddha talks about *abhimukhi*, immediateness – be alert and let there be response. Whatsoever the result, don't be afraid of it. People start rehearsing because they are afraid of the results, so they want to plan everything. There are people who plan everything, every gesture is planned. Then their life is like that of an actor – it is not real, it is not authentic, it is not true. And if your life is not true, then it is impossible for you to come to truth.

The seventh is *durangama* – far-goingness, accepting the call of the beyond. There is a beyond everywhere. We are surrounded by the beyond. That beyond has to be penetrated. It is within, it is without; it is always there. And if you forget about it ... as we do ordinarily, because it is very uncomfortable, inconvenient, to look into the beyond. It is as if one looks into an abyss, and one starts trembling, one starts feeling sick. The very awareness of the abyss and you start trembling. Nobody looks at the abyss; we go on looking in other directions, we go on avoiding the real. The real is like an abyss, because the real is a great emptiness. It is vast sky with no boundaries. Buddha says *durangama* – be available to the beyond. Never remain confined to the boundaries, always trespass the boundaries. Make the boundaries if you need them, but always remember you have to be able to step out. Never make imprisonments.

We make many sorts of imprisonments – relationship, belief, religion, they are all imprisonments. One feels cozy because there are no wild winds blowing. One feels protected ... although the protection is false, because death will come and will drag you into the beyond. Buddha says, before death comes and drags you into the beyond, go on your own.

A Zen monk was going to die. He was very old, ninety years old. Suddenly he opened his eyes and he said, "Where are my shoes?"

A disciple said, "Where are you going? Have you gone crazy? You are dying, and the physician has said that there is no more possibility; you have just a few minutes more."

The master said, "That's why I'm asking for my shoes. I would like to walk to the cemetery, because I don't want to be dragged. I will go on my own and I will meet death there. I don't want to be dragged. And you know me – I have never leaned on anybody else. It would be very ugly that four persons will be carrying me. No."

He walked to the cemetery. Not only that, he dug his own grave, lay down in it, and died. This is what Buddha means by *durangama* – such courage to accept the unknown, such courage to go on your own and welcome the beyond. Then death is transformed, then death is no longer death. Such a courageous man never dies; death is defeated. Such a courageous man goes beyond death. For one who goes on his own to the beyond, the beyond is never like death. Then the beyond becomes a welcome. If you welcome the beyond, the beyond welcomes you; the beyond always goes on echoing you.

The eighth is *achala*: centering, grounding, immovability. Buddha says one should learn to be centered, unmoving, grounded. Whatsoever happens, one should learn how to remain unwavering. Let the whole world go into disappearance, let the whole world dissolve, but a buddha will go on sitting under his Bodhi Tree, unmoved. His center will not be wavering, he will not go off-center.

Try it. By and by, you start coming closer to your center. And the closer you come the more happy you will feel, and a great solidity will arise in your being. Things go on happening, but they are happening outside; nothing penetrates to your center. If you are there, then nothing makes any difference. Life comes, death comes, success, failure, praise and insult, and pain and pleasure – they come and go. They all pass away, but the witnessing center always remains.

The ninth is *sadhumati* – intelligence, awareness, mindfulness. Buddha is very much in favor of intelligence, but remember that he does not mean intellect. Intellect is a heavy thing, intelligence is more total. Intellect is borrowed, intelligence is your own. Intellect is logical, rational; intelligence is more than logical. It is super-logical, it is intuitive.

The intellectual person lives only through argument. Certainly, arguments can lead you up to a certain point, but beyond that, hunches are needed. Even great scientists who work through reason come to a point where reason does not work, where they wait for a hunch, for some intuitive flash, for some light from the unknown. And it always happens: if you have worked hard with the intellect, and you don't think that intellect is all, and you are available to the beyond, someday a ray penetrates you. It is not yours; and yet it is yours because it is nobody else's. It comes from your innermost center. It looks as if it is coming from the beyond because you don't know where your intuitive center is.

Buddha uses intelligence in the sense of awareness, in the sense of mindfulness. The Sanskrit word *sadhumati* is very beautiful. *Mati* means "intelligence", and *sadhu* means "sage" – sagely intelligence; not only intelligence but *sagely* intelligence. There are people who may be rational but are not reasonable. To be reasonable is more than to be rational. Sometimes the reasonable person will be ready to accept the irrational too – because he is reasonable. He can understand that the irrational also exists. The rational person can never understand that the irrational also exists. He can only believe in the limited logical syllogism.

There are things which cannot be proved logically, and yet they are. Everybody knows they are, and nobody has ever been able to prove them. Love is; nobody has ever been able to prove what it is, or whether it exists or not. But everybody knows – love is. Even people who deny it – they are not ready to accept anything beyond logic – even they fall in love. When they fall in love then they are in a difficulty, they feel guilty. But love is.

And nobody is ever satisfied by intellect alone unless the heart also is fulfilled. These are the two polarities inside you: the head and the heart. *Sadhumati* means a great synthesis of both, head and heart. *Sadhu* means the heart and *mati* means the head. When the sagely heart is joined together with a sharp intelligence, then there is a great change, a transformation. That's what awareness is all about.

And the tenth is *dharma-megha* – grace showering, becoming a cloud of truth, love and grace. *Dharma-megha* . . .

Just a few days ago there were so many clouds raining, showering on the thirsty earth. Buddha says unless you become a showering of grace you will not attain to the ultimate. The nine grounds are to prepare you. The tenth ground is the beginning of sharing; you start showering. Whatever you get you have to share; then you will get more. Whatever you have, you have to shower, you have to give it to others, you have to distribute it. All that you attain in your being has to become your compassion. Then you will get more. The more you become a spendthrift of your inner energies, the more space will be created for the divine to descend in you, for truth to penetrate you.

That's why it is very difficult to know the truth and not to share it. It is impossible! Mahavira remained silent for twelve years, then suddenly one day he burst forth. What happened? For twelve years he was silent; he must have been moving into the nine grounds. Then came the tenth; he become a *dharma-megha*, he became a cloud of truth and started showering.

You cannot do anything about it. It is just like a flower opening and releasing its fragrance to the winds. It is just like a lamp burning and showering its light all around. There is no way to prevent it; you cannot be miserly about truth.

Buddha attained to truth, then for forty-two years continuously he moved from one place to another – continuously talking, continuously saying what had happened to him. One day he was asked, "You teach us to be silent but you go on talking."

Buddha said, "I have to talk to teach you to be silent. Be silent, so that one day you can also talk." Be silent, because in silence you will gather the juice. The flower remains closed until the right moment has come when the fragrance is ready. Then it opens its petals, not before.

Be silent, be aware, be adventurous – one day all of these nine *bhumis*, these nine grounds, will prepare you to become a cloud. Then you will shower on people and you will share.

Truth has always been shared in different ways. Meera danced; she knew how to dance the truth. Buddha never danced. Chaitanya sang; he knew how to sing. Buddha never sang. It depends on the individual. Whatever capacities you have, whatever creative possibilities you have, when truth comes into you it will find your possibilities, your creativities.

Just the other night a man was saying to me, "It is very difficult; the more I become meditative, the more I like to compose music." He's a composer and he had stopped doing it. Now he thinks that this is a disturbance: "What is happening? Whenever I am feeling meditative, immediately great ideas arise in me and I would like to compose. Now, what to do? Should I stop it?"

There is no need to stop. Meditation brings your creativity to an expression. Whatsoever is hidden in you will be revealed; whatsoever you are carrying within you will be sung, will be danced – whatsoever it is. You will become a *dharma-megha*.

These three answers from the three monks show three types of understanding: the bodily, the psychological, and the spiritual. Breath means spirit – that's why I call the third understanding spiritual. If you have the first understanding then these ten *bhumis* are not for you. If you have the second type of understanding, then too these ten grounds are not for you. If you have the third understanding, then these ten grounds are for you. And unless you can become a *dharma-megha*, remember, your life was in vain. You lived without any purpose, you lived fruitlessly, barrenly. In fact, you lived not; you only appeared to live.

So meditate on this small story of Buddha's, his asking, and the answers . . . just meditate on it. I will tell you a few anecdotes to show you how we understand.

A minister asked a little girl what she thought of her first church service.

"Well," she said, after giving the matter some thought, "the music was nice, but the commercial was too long."

The couple were married forty years. She decided to get a check-up at the hospital. When she came home, she was ecstatic.

"The doctor says I am in perfect health," she bragged to her husband. "In fact, he said I can have sex twelve times a month."

"Wonderful!" said the husband. "Put me down for two."

The girlie show was touring army camps overseas. At one outpost, arrangements were being made to feed them before leaving.

"I say," said the officer in charge. "Would you like to mess with the officers?"

"Don't mind if we do, dear," said the leading lady, "but can't we have something to eat first?"

Even words don't carry the meaning they have; you put meaning into them. Each time you utter a word, watch. Each time you listen to a word, watch. Each time you make a gesture, watch and you will see that whatsoever your level of understanding, it is expressed in all the ways.

Seated in a restaurant, a priest was scrutinizing the beauty of a young lady escorted by her male companion. A layman kidded him about his female interest.

"Just because I am on a perpetual diet does not mean I can't study the menu once in a while!" said the priest.

Whatever in you is repressed, rejected, thrown into the basement, also goes on reflecting in your ways. Even sometimes when you avoid something, then too, in your very avoidance your understanding is shown.

The famous story of two Zen monks . . .

Crossing a ford they came across a woman, a very young and

beautiful woman. She wanted to cross but she was afraid. So one monk took her on his shoulders and carried her to the other shore. The other monk was furious, the other monk was fiery: "It is prohibited! A Buddhist monk should not touch a woman. Now this is too much. Not only touching: he has carried the woman on his shoulder!" The monk remained quiet, but he was boiling within.

Miles passed. When they reached the monastery, when they were entering the door, the other monk turned to the first and said, "Look, I will have to talk to the master. I will have to report it. It is prohibited!"

The first monk said, "What are you talking about? What is prohibited?"

He said, "Have you forgotten? You carried that young beautiful woman on your shoulders. You should not touch women!"

The first monk laughed and he said, "Yes, I carried her, but I left her on the other bank, miles back. Are you still carrying her?"

Yes, the other monk was still carrying her.

Remember that your understanding is shown in every way, and if you watch correctly, your very watchfulness will take you to a further step.

One unfortunate sailor was shipwrecked on a desert island in the South Pacific. Fortunately food and water were plentiful, and the weather was perfect. So he survived in comparative comfort for six months, after which time, to his intense excitement, he spotted a small craft on the horizon. As it drifted in closer and closer, he could see that it was a ship's life raft containing one passenger. And as it got even closer he saw this passenger was a young woman. Eventually the raft splashed up on the beach and he went towards her. She was a beauty – tall and glowing and blonde.

"Hello! hello!" said the poor lonely sailor. "Are you shipwrecked too?"

"Yes, I am," she replied.

"I have been here for six months," he said.

"Six months!" she exclaimed. "Well, then I am sure I have something you have been missing."

"Don't tell me you've got a cigarette on you!" he cried joyously.

Your own desire, your own understanding, your own greed is always there in each response, in each reaction. If you watch closely you will become aware that you go on showing your understanding or misunderstanding in each moment of your life.

Buddha's questions are very simple, and the monks who answered may not have thought at all that they had any metaphysical significance. They may even have laughed at the ridiculous questions Buddha was asking them. But with very simple questions he had provoked their layer of understanding. The significance of the story is great. I never ask you any questions, but the questions you ask me are enough. They show everything about you. When I read your question, I am less concerned about your question than I am concerned with the questioner. I am more concerned with the questioner.

That's why I insist that you should always write your name under the question, you should always sign it – because a question in itself means nothing. It becomes meaningful only when I know who the questioner is. My answer is not for the question but for the questioner. One may ask a question and I may answer it in one way, another asks exactly the same question, with the same words, but I will not answer in the same way – because it is not the question that is important, it is the questioner.

Your question shows your understanding. Your question shows your confusion, your question shows where you are. And I have to answer you where you are – remember it. Many people come; somebody asks a question, others listen. You are allowed to listen, but those answers that I am giving to that particular person are not given for you. Remember it, otherwise there will be great misunderstanding. It happens sometimes that a questioner says something, I explain it to him, I help him to understand his problem; another comes and he says, "That is exactly my question and you have already answered." I say, "No, don't be deceived so easily. You two are so different. In fact, there are no two similar persons in the world, so how can your questions be similar? Just ask your question and forget what I have said to the other."

Then many times people become puzzled, because they see that I can contradict myself.

Just the other night one person asked about fear: "I am afraid." I talked to him about death because I could see why he was afraid. Death was in his eyes, death was around him, he was shadowed by death. I talked much about death rather than about fear, and he understood it. I said to him, "Accept death and fear will disappear."

The next person said, "Now there is no need to ask. I have also fear in me and you have answered." I looked at the person; his fear had no relationship with death at all. His fear was fear of loneliness; it was a totally different dimension of fear. I said, "Forget all that I have said to the other person. It was

not your question and it was not answered for you. Tell me about your fear."
And by and by it became clear that his fear had nothing to do with death. His
fear was fear of being left alone; fear that maybe his aloneness would always be
there.

The first was afraid of death, the second was afraid about whether love
would happen or not. His fear was concerned with love – whether he would
remain always alone, or would somebody be there who would love him? And
would he be able to love? Would there be a possibility that he would be together
with somebody and this constant wound of loneliness would disappear? He was
not worried about death, he was worried about life. His fear was not concerned
with death, his fear was concerned with life and relationship and communication and communion, love. They were totally different, but they both used the
word "fear".

When I give different answers to different people, naturally you can collect
all the answers and you will think: "This man is mad!" They will be contradictory. They are bound to be contradictory. My approach is individual; my
approach is person-to-person. I try to relate with you as individuals.

Enough for today.

Chapter 21:

Provisions for the Journey

THE BUDDHA SAID:

Those who study the doctrine of the buddhas will do well to believe and observe all that is taught by them. It is like unto honey; it is sweet within, it is sweet without, it is sweet throughout; so is the Buddha's teaching.

O monks, you must not walk on the way as the ox that is attached to a wheel. His body moves, but his heart is not willing. But when your hearts are in accord with the way, there is no need of troubling yourselves about your outward demeanor.

Those who practice the way might well follow the example of an ox that marches through the deep mire carrying a heavy load. He is tired, but his steady gaze, looking forward, will never relax until he comes out of the mire, and it is only then that he takes a respite. O monks, remember that passions and sins are more than the filthy mire, and that you can escape misery only by earnestly and steadily thinking of the way.

The seeker has to go alone on the pilgrimage. Otherwise is not possible; it is not in the nature of things. Truth is not something outside you, otherwise you could go in company. It is within you. Truth is not objective, so it cannot be collective. It is subjective. Truth is subjectivity, it is your innermost core. Only you can penetrate it; nobody else can go with you. The path has to be traveled in tremendous aloneness. And a master knows that he is pushing you in a journey where you will be left alone – Buddha particularly is very much aware of it. He has not uttered a single word against this understanding. He has never said, "I can lead you to the ultimate." You will have to go alone. The tour is going to be absolutely unguided, with no maps, with no guide to show you the path.

Then of course you have to be prepared for it. You have to provide for all emergencies, all accidents on the way, all possibilities for your going astray. You have to carry provisions for the journey. Buddha has called these provisions *parmitas*.

The word is beautiful – *parmita* means that which can lead you beyond; the provisions for the other shore. The journey is going to be alone. The moment you leave this shore you will be left alone in a great and wild ocean, and you will have to fight the ocean and find the way absolutely on your own. No knowledge that you have gathered before is going to be of any help, because each person comes to truth in his own way. The perception of truth is absolutely unique and individual. No two persons have known truth in the same way, because no two persons are ever the same. They are different – their vision is different, their perception is different, their interpretation is different, their expression is different. So all that you have gathered about truth is not going to help you much. In fact it may hinder you, but it cannot help you. It can become an obstacle.

So, Buddha says, don't carry knowledge. Then what does one have to carry with oneself? If the journey is going to be alone, then you have to create some qualities, *parmitas*, which can follow you like a shadow. These ten *parmitas* have to be understood very deeply.

The first *parmita* is *dana* – generosity, sharing. Ordinarily the mind is a miser. It tries to hold, to possess. Mind is not generous. And if you go with this mind you will be lost – because a miser's mind is a very closed mind. Miserliness is a sort of closing in: you are not open to the world, you don't allow your windows and doors to bring more light from the outside, you don't allow your windows to bring new breezes from the outside – because you are constantly afraid that something you are holding inside may escape.

> Mulla Nasruddin was appearing in court, and he was saying, "Now it is too much, and I cannot tolerate any more. We have a small room to live in, only one room. I live there, my wife lives there, my twelve children live there, and my wife is obsessive. She has a few goats in the room and a dog also sleeps there. It is becoming so ugly and so dirty. It stinks! And I cannot live any more. So I have come to ask for a separation."

The magistrate said, "But don't you have any windows? Can't you open your windows?"

He said, "What! And let my pigeons out?"

When you are holding something you cannot open the windows, you cannot open the door; you will be afraid. And if you don't open the windows of the mind you will be in trouble – because when you are alone in the ocean, fighting with the waves, a closed mind will be a blind mind. You will need all openness there, because only out of openness can the response be right.

So Buddha says *dana*, generosity, sharing, has to be learned. While you are on this shore, learn as much sharing as possible. Share whatever you have to share, because nothing really belongs to you. Your possession is a crime. Whatever you possess or claim that you possess is a crime against the whole. You can, at the most, use things – but you cannot claim possession. Things have existed when you were not here, things will be here when you are gone and completely forgotten. Who is the possessor? We come empty-handed, and we go empty-handed. So while you are in the world, don't become like fists; remain open-handed. An open-handed person is an open-minded person too. In fact, the hand is nothing but an extension of the mind.

The right side of your mind is joined with your left hand, the left side of your mind is joined with your right hand. When you move your right hand your mind moves, when you move your left hand the other side of your mind moves. When your hand is like a closed fist, then your mind is also closed like a fist. Yes, this expression "open-handed" is beautiful: an open-handed person is also open-minded.

So Buddha says the first *parmita*, the quality that can take you beyond, is sharing. He does not mention what to share, because it is not important what you share. Whether you share a song or a dance, or you share your love, or you share your experience, your meditation, your money, your house, your clothes, your body, that is not the point. But sharing should become essential.

Ordinarily hoarding is essential. A hoarder will remain clinging to this shore; he cannot go to the other shore – because a hoarder, in the first place, cannot leave this shore. All his hoarding belongs to this shore. See the point of it. Somebody says, "Come, there is a bigger house," but you will say, "First I will have to pack up and bring the treasures I have hidden in this house. I cannot go right now. I have so much involvement with this house. My whole life's savings are here. I will have to take it with me; then only can I come." But the other shore is such that you cannot take anything from this shore.

This is a beautiful paradox – you cannot take anything from this shore but if you are sharing enough, and if you share all that you have on this shore, you can carry a sharing mind. You cannot carry your house, you cannot carry your money, but you can carry your love, your compassion. And that compassion will be helpful.

Buddha says that if you have love and compassion in your heart, existence also behaves in the same way. Existence always reflects you. If you share, existence shares with you. If you are hoarding, that means you are against existence. A hoarder is against, he's afraid, he does not trust – "Who knows what is going to happen tomorrow?" He does not trust existence, he trusts his own bank balance. His trust is in things that he has created or that he has accumulated. He is not trusting of the vast, of the infinite.

Buddha says if you trust, then the existence also responds in the same way. Existence is a mirror . . . it echoes you. If you go as a hoarder then you will be in trouble, because then everywhere you will see the enemy: in the waves of the ocean, in the infinite journey. A thousand and one problems will arise and you will be at a loss. There will be no guide, there will be no guidebook, and you will be alone, absolutely nude and alone, with no hoardings of your own, no securities, no insurance. It will be difficult for you to go.

Buddha says you can go only when you have already dispossessed all that you have. Now, you can dispossess in two ways. You can dispossess only as a means, so that you can possess on the other shore – but that is not true dispossession, that is again just a trick of the mind. That's what many Buddhist monks, Jaina monks, Catholics and others are doing. They are ready to renounce, but their renunciation is out of calculation. It is not out of love, it is out of calculation. They calculate that nothing can be saved on this shore, so why not renounce it and save something on the other shore, in the other world? Money cannot be saved, it is going to go, so why not have virtue in your possession?

But the possessiveness remains the same.

Buddha says be non-possessive; possess neither on this shore nor the other. Be always sharing. So there is a very specific teaching. Buddha has said to his disciples that when you meditate and you come to beautiful spaces in your being, immediately share them. If there is nobody, then just close your eyes and shower that blessing on the whole existence. But don't become a possessor of it – even of meditation, even of wisdom . . . don't become a possessor.

There is a beautiful anecdote.

A young man came to Buddha. He was attracted by Buddha's presence; by and by, he started meditating. But there was one problem. One day he came and he said, "There's only one problem – the problem is: you say that when meditation flowers, then you have to release all the fragrance to the whole world. I can do this with just one exception: I cannot shower it on my neighbor. I can do it on the whole of the world, but just give me permission not to shower it on my neighbor."

Buddha laughed and he said, "You fool, that is the whole point! You can shower it on the whole universe because you are indifferent to the whole universe. You cannot shower it on your neighbor because you have an enmity. Love knows no enmity. First you shower on your neighbor; only then will the universe receive it. There is no other way. First shower on your enemy, first befriend your enemy, then the whole universe will befriend you."

That's the meaning when Jesus says you should love your enemy. "Love thine enemy as thyself." Jesus also says, "Love thy neighbor as thyself." Maybe, in almost all cases, the enemy and the neighbor are the same person! They are not different people, the neighbor and the enemy are almost always the same person – because he who is very far away from you cannot be your enemy. To be your enemy somebody has to be very close to you. To be an enemy somebody has to be just on the boundary of your being, has to be your neighbor. Then he pinches you, then his very existence becomes an anxiety, then he interferes, then his very existence is non-acceptable.

Buddha says shower your meditation, otherwise you have missed. Now, this is a new teaching – Patanjali has not said it – this is a new insight. Buddha says if you attain to meditative states, shower it immediately. If you don't shower it, then you have not attained the space that you think you have attained. Then you are in a deception, you are in an illusion – because a meditative state is, by its very nature, sharing. If you cannot share, then you must be in a deception somewhere. Then the state is pseudo, then the space is not real. A real meditative space, by its very nature, wants to be shared. If your meditation does not become compassion, then somewhere, something has gone wrong.

This is his first *parmita*, the quality on which you can ride and go to the other shore.

But ordinarily we live very clinging, afraid. Our attachments are more to things than to persons, and our attachments to persons are also very self-motivated. There is no compassion in them.

So many people come to me and they say, "I am in love with this woman or with this man," and I look into them, and I see that they are in love only with themselves. Nobody seems to be in love with anybody else – hence so many problems. If you really love a woman or a man, love will be enough. There will be no problem out of it. Love knows no problems. If problems arise that simply shows that somewhere love is not true, or it is something else just pretending to be love. Everybody is trying to exploit the other. It is not a sharing thing, you are using the other as a means. Sooner or later the other starts feeling that too – that he or she is being used as a commodity. Then there is rebellion, reaction, revenge, conflict.

People you call lovers are continuously trying to dominate each other. We possess things, we possess people. And in this mad race for possessions, we lose our own selves; one is lost in his possessions. If you really want to know who you are, you will have to become a little loose from your possessions.

> A rabbi and a Catholic priest were fishing in separate boats some distance apart. The priest got a bite and was so nervous that he fell out of the boat. He sank twice, and as he was coming up the second time, the rabbi rowed over and called out, "Father, can I have your boat if you don't come up again?"

We may not be so direct, but this is how we are, just waiting – how can we possess more? Just waiting – how can our territory become a little bigger? Even if others suffer for it, even if they have to die for it, we are ready to sacrifice the whole world. For what? For things that you will not be able to carry to the other shore. Death will come and shatter all your arrangements.

Buddha said, before death takes things away from you, share them. At least there will remain some gratitude in people's hearts for you, at least they will remember you. Death will not be able to efface your memory completely. And by sharing you will become open. And by sharing you will become more trusting – and trust becomes the boat to the other shore. Trust people, because people are nothing but a manifestation of the universe, a manifestation of the universal soul. When you share with somebody, in fact you are sharing with the whole – because everybody is a manifestation of the whole. When you water a tree and the tree feels happy, and the leaves seem to be delighted, and the tree starts swaying and dancing in the breeze, it is the whole you have watered. The whole was thirsty in the tree; you have watered, and the whole is happy.

Whatsoever you do to people, to trees, to animals, you are doing to existence. And of course existence repays a thousandfold. When you are totally alone and there is nobody with you, only existence all around, it will repay you. Buddha says this is the first *parmita*.

> Oscar Muscovitz and Sidney Margolis had a profitable little business going, importing artificial flowers for the ladies' dress trade. Mainly, it was profitable due to their seldom, if ever, paying Uncle Sam taxes.

But to their loft came, as it must to all men, the agents of the Internal Revenue Service. Finding Oscar in charge, as Sidney was on a buying trip, the first agent tried to explain the nature of the visit.

"Mr. Oscar, you people are doing business and failing to report to the government."

Oscar turned purple: "Report? What report? What is to report?" he demanded.

"Well," the agent replied, "first of all, we would like to know about your dependents, that is, your family exemptions."

Oscar proceeded to tell them all about Harriet, his wife, dependent number one, and all the trouble and aggravations she had been giving him lately; then he got to his son and described in great detail how Freddie had gotten this girl in trouble, and the ensuing problems from that scene; dependent number three, his daughter Marjorie, a good girl, but no beauty, and how much she was costing.

Finally, after absorbing as much of the detail of Oscar's private life as he could stand, the agent said, "Mr. Oscar, let us forget all that for a moment and concentrate on the business itself."

Replied Oscar, "Like what, exactly?"

"Like how much business you are doing, what the assets are worth, how much profit you made . . ."

"What!" screamed Oscar, hysterically. "Are you crazy? I don't even tell my partner that!"

You don't give, even to those who are very intimate with you. You don't give, even to those who love you. You don't give to your father, your mother, your wife, your children; you simply don't give. You don't know the language of giving. You know only one language: how to get more, how to get more, how to get from everybody else. You know only one way of thinking, and that is get-think.

Buddha says learn give-think. Learn the ways of giving and you will flower. That flowering, that fragrance, will follow you. That will be one companion on the infinite pilgrimage.

The second is *shila*.

Shila means discipline, *shila* means grace in living. Buddhists have misinterpreted *shila* in many ways; they think *shila* means a rigid character. It does not mean that. The very word means a graceful life, a life that has grace in it, elegance. And what life can have grace in it? Only a life of compassion, love, gratitude; only a life that is responsible, a life that cares for others. Now, you can be non-violent but it is not necessary that your non-violence will have grace. I have seen so many Jaina monks . . . they are non-violent but very ungraceful; the beauty is missing. And the fruit is the proof of the tree, there is no other proof. If they were non-violent there would arise a tremendous beauty; their eyes would show it, their very vibe would show it. There would be a constant soundless music around them – but it is not there. Everything seems to be dull and dead. They are non-violent, but their non-violence is not graceful. It has not happened spontaneously, it has been forced. Their non-violence has a violent element in it; it has been violently forced. They have tried hard to become non-violent, they have managed somehow to become non-violent, but the non-violence is not like a natural flowering, it is cultivated.

The Buddhist word *shila* is very beautiful; it means graceful.

There can be two types of stillness. You can force yourself according to yoga methods, you can learn a certain posture. By and by, you can manage to force your body into that posture. First it will be uncomfortable; by and by the body adjusts. The body has tremendous capacity to adjust to any situation. Then you can force your body to sit unmoving. And if you go on doing it, by and by, after a few months you will become like a buddha statue. But that will be violence, and there will be no grace in it. Deep down you will be boiling; deep down there will be hellfire; deep down you have not changed. How can you change just by changing the body? The real phenomenon has to be just otherwise: the within has to change, then the outward thing follows. Then it has grace.

It is not a question of forcing the periphery – because the center will not be affected at all by forcing the periphery. You can keep quiet; that does not mean you are quiet. But if you *are* quiet that certainly means you can keep quiet. This difference has to be understood. This is one of the most vital distinctions in a person's religious life. The way is not from out to in, the way is from in to out. Don't force things from the outside, and don't think that by changing your body and your outward demeanor you can change your inner qualities. No, it doesn't happen that way. Change the inner and the outward follows. Then there is grace.

Buddha says the second *parmita* is grace in living, a discipline that has arisen out of understanding.

The word "discipline" is meaningful. It comes from the same root as "disciple". It means readiness to learn. "Disciple" means one who is ready to learn, open to learn. When one is open to learn that means one is aware, because learning is possible only when you are aware. When you are not aware you cannot learn anything. People who are aware can learn – everywhere, anywhere.

Just the other day I was reading about a Sufi mystic, Shibli. Shibli was asked, "Who guided you on the path? Who was your first master?" And the questioner was surprised, because Shibli said, "A dog. One day I saw him almost dead with thirst, standing by the water's edge. Every time he looked at his reflection in the water he was frightened and withdrew, because he thought it was another dog. Finally, such was his necessity that he cast away fear and leapt into the water, at which point the other dog vanished. The dog found that the obstacle, which was himself, the barrier between himself and that which he was seeking, melted away. In this same way my own obstacle vanished when I knew what I took to be my own self was just a reflection, not the reality. And my way was first shown to me by the behavior of a dog. He was my first master."

A man of understanding learns from everywhere. A man of understanding learns and becomes a disciple. A discipline arises.

And Buddha says: Unless you have discipline, the capacity to learn, to receive – the awareness – you will not be able to go to the other shore. Knowledge will not help, but the capacity to learn will help. And the difference is clear – knowledge is borrowed; the capacity to learn has to arise in you. It is your capacity. You cannot borrow the capacity to learn. You can borrow knowledge; knowledge is cheap. The capacity to learn means a great transformation in your being. You will have to drop the ego and you will have to drop accumulating. Knowledge you can accumulate, information you can accumulate; learning is not accumulation. You never accumulate learning, you simply remain learning. No treasure arises out of it. It is just like a mirror; something comes before it and it reflects. When the thing has moved it remains quiet – again a mirror, again simple, innocent. It does not collect. You cannot ask a mirror, "How many people have looked into you?" He does not collect, he is simply a mirror . . . he mirrors. Learning is like a mirror, and knowledge is like a photo-plate. It also mirrors, but only once. Then it is caught with the reflection, then it is destroyed.

Buddha says *shila* is the second *parmita*.

The third is *shanti*. *Shanti* means "patience". Of course, the journey is vast, and you cannot be in a hurry. If you are in a hurry you will never be able to move to the other shore. The journey is timeless; great patience is needed, infinite patience is needed. Nirvana cannot be something instant.

Sometimes people come – very foolish people – and they say, "I have come only for three days. Is meditation possible?" They don't know what they are asking! Even three lives are not enough. And when you are in such a hurry, even three hundred lives will not be enough because in such hurry your mind is very tense. Slow down, relax a little bit. Don't be impatient, and then it is possible.

Maybe it can happen in three days. You see the point? Try to see the point – it can happen in three days, it can happen in three seconds, it may happen in a split-second, but then you will need oceanic patience. How much time it takes will depend on how much patience you have. The more patience you have, the less time will be needed; the less patience you have, the more time will be needed. If you really want to have it, drop all impatience. Forget all about when it is going to happen. You simply enjoy the moment. Enjoying the moment, being totally in it, one day suddenly it is there. In fact, it has never left you; it was always there. But you were so much in a rush that you could not see it. The day you relax and sit silently in your room, suddenly you become aware of the presence. It is there, the whole room is full of it. The whole world is full of godliness; yes, every bush is afire.

The Jews have the beautiful story about Moses going to the mountain, Sinai, and there Moses saw a green bush afire. He was puzzled, he could not believe – because the bush was not burning and the fire was there. And then God spoke to him: "Don't be afraid, Moses. I am your God, your Lord. This fire is my fire." And, of course, how can God's fire burn a bush? The bush is also God's fire. Moses saw one bush afire on the mountain, and I would like to tell you that every bush is afire. There is no need to go to Sinai, just look in your garden – every bush is afire with godliness.

Patience . . . then suddenly you start feeling the divine is present. Impatient, and you are rushing madly, and in your mad rush you cannot see. It is almost as if you carry a beautiful camera, and running around you try to take some pictures, and you go on rushing and running. What is going to happen? – you won't have any pictures, you may have only a few destroyed plates. The whole film will be just a chaos. When you are taking a picture you have to hold the camera absolutely still; it should not be shaky. Then a clear-cut picture comes out of it.

When you are not rushing anywhere and your inner being is just still, here now, existence reflects. Then all chaos disappears, all questions disappear. Buddha says *shanti*, patience, is the third *parmita*.

The fourth is *vidya*. *Vidya* has many meanings – it means "energy", it means "courage". Certainly courage is needed, and certainly energy is needed. One has to be continuously aware that one's life energy should not be wasted unnecessarily. One should not have leakages. We are leaking; we are never a reservoir of energy. Infinite energy is given to you, but you are a leaking vessel. In every way, you dissipate energy, you never sit silently.

Buddha used to call his meditation *jhan*. *Jhan* is a Pali term for the Sanskrit *dhyan*. From *jhan* came the Chinese *chan* and the Japanese *zen*. In Japan, Zen became the crescendo; what Buddha had planted as a seed flowered in Japan, came to its climax. What Buddha had started came to a conclusion. And Zen people say: meditation is nothing but sitting silently, doing nothing. That's what Buddha was doing – doing nothing – when he attained. That's what he was doing sitting under the Bodhi Tree. What was he doing? – he was not doing anything; he was simply sitting so silently that there was no leakage of energy. That energy started rising higher and higher and higher – that energy was reaching peaks. And then the energy rushed and touched the *sahasrar*, the seventh chakra; it came to the ultimate. Suddenly there was a flowering; Buddha became a lotus flower.

You have the same energy but you go on throwing it. Whenever you have energy, a great desire to throw it away arises in you. You may call it "sexual urge" or you may call it something else; it makes no difference. But whenever you have energy a great desire arises to relieve oneself.

In the West, sex is thought of as a release. In the East we have taken the sexual energy in a totally different perspective. There is no need to release it, it is your energy – because you go on releasing it, you remain empty. If you allow it sometimes to gather, if you simply let it gather inside you, the sheer quantity comes to a point when there is a qualitative change. The gathered energy rises higher and higher, the level goes on becoming higher and higher, and you touch higher altitudes of your being. A point comes when the energy has touched to the climax of your being. That's what samadhi is.

And Buddha says *vidya* is the fourth *parmita*. One should learn how not to dissipate energy. Remember, he is not telling you to become a miser – because he has given you the first *parmita*, never be a miser. When he says, "Gather energy," he is not teaching you any miserliness, he is simply teaching you wisdom. He knows how it happened to him. Share whatsoever you have, but don't leak. Leaking is not sharing.

That's why I see that two persons can make love to each other, and still there may be no sharing. Both leaked. They use the other just as a help to leak, that's all. Sharing is totally different; it is not a leaking. And this has to be remembered: when you leak, you simply lose, nothing is gained out of it; when you share, you give something very ordinary and you gain something very extraordinary. In sharing you never lose.

The fifth, Buddha calls *dhyan* – meditation, silence, sitting, doing nothing.

Let that penetrate your life more and more. Whenever you have time, whenever you have nothing to do, don't create unnecessary, unneeded occupations. Just sit silently, watch life flow by. Look at the trees or at the stars, or just look at your nose, or at your navel. Or close your eyes and just look at the inner silence, or inner thoughts. Just be . . . and let things pass; you sit silently.

Buddha says if you can sit silently for even a few moments without doing anything, glimpses will start coming to you.

Now, modern psychologists also agree that if a person can be allowed just to sit silently, that's enough. Nothing else is needed. All else is just a help to sit. Somebody gives you a mantra and says, "Sit silently and do the mantra." Now there is much research work going on about Transcendental Meditation. And Mahesh Yogi thinks it is because of the mantra that things happen. That is not true. It is just because you sit silently for twenty minutes that things happen. The mantra is not relevant. You can sit without the mantra and the same thing will happen. Maybe the mantra gives you an excuse to sit – because you are so foolish that you cannot sit, you have to have something to do. So if somebody tells you, "Say, 'Rama, Rama, Rama,'" you have some excuse to sit silently for twenty minutes because you are doing "Rama, Rama, Rama". Whatever results come – your blood pressure goes lower, your breathing becomes more silent, there are changes in the oxygen content of your body, even your heart beats with a different rhythm, you feel very relaxed, the alpha waves are created, and out of those alpha waves you feel very quiet and refreshed – it has nothing to do with the mantra, or with any mantra in particular. You can say "Rama, Rama" or you can say "Aum, Aum" or you can say "Allah, Allah" or "Ave Maria" or anything. Or you can create your own mantra; you can repeat your own name, even that will do. In fact, it has nothing to do with any mantra; it has nothing to do with a mantra as such. If you can simply sit for twenty minutes without doing anything, the same will be the result. So whatever psychological investigations have revealed about TM, it is not about TM, it is simply about sitting silently.

Just sit silently and you will see that you are growing a new quality to your being; you are becoming more collected, more centered, more fulfilled. Your face will change, your eyes will change, you will have a serenity around you. Even others will start feeling your serenity. Even they will start feeling that something has happened to you – because wherever you move you will bring a certain cool breeze with you. And the situations you encounter will remain the same. Somebody will insult you – but now you will be able to laugh; no anger will arise. Not that you are controlling it; in fact, it is not arising. You can see the whole absurdity of it. You can see the point that the poor man who is angry and insulting you is in bad shape. It has nothing to do with you. You have to be more compassionate to him. You will feel compassion rather than being angry.

Rather than being destructive to him, you will feel much pity for him . . . a totally different quality.

Worries may be the same – they continue. Through your meditation the world is not going to change, the world will be the same. But through your meditation *you* will be different, and when you are different the world is different – because it is your world. It depends on your vision, on your interpretation. Everything will be the same, but nothing will be the same anymore – because you have changed.

Buddha says on this lonely journey to the other shore, you will need very much to learn how to sit silently.

Ordinarily we are almost obsessively occupied. You cannot sit silently, you have to do something. Doing is madness. If you have nothing to do you feel at a loss, you start boiling within. You start reading the same newspaper again, or you go and start gossiping to the neighbor. You have talked about these things a thousand and one times, and again you are there. You have to do something. You cannot remain quiet, you cannot remain unoccupied.

In the West you have a very absurd proverb: "The empty mind is the devil's workshop." This must have been invented by the devil himself – because the empty mind is a divine workshop! This proverb must have been invented by the devil so that nobody remains empty and the devil can continue his work. If you are really empty the devil cannot enter you, because thoughts function as horses for the devil. He cannot come otherwise. Without thought, evil cannot enter you. Without thought, there is no possibility of anything entering into you. All that enters into you from the outside enters through thought. When there is no thought the outside disappears; you are just an inside. That's what I said in the beginning: truth is subjectivity.

The sixth *parmita* Buddha calls *pragya*. *Pragya* means "wisdom". It is different from knowledge. Knowledge is that which is not based on your own experience, wisdom is that which is based on your own experience. Rely only on that which you have experienced. Don't rely on anything else – otherwise when you are left alone, all your knowledge will disappear and nothing will be left. That which has come from others is not going to be with you when others have left you. Only that which is yours will be yours.

> A disciple was leaving his master. It was a dark night and it had become late. The disciple was a little apprehensive because he had to pass five miles of dense forest to reach to his village. The master saw that fear. He said, "Are you afraid of the darkness?"
>
> The disciple said, "Yes, I am afraid, but I couldn't gather courage to say so."

The master said, "Don't be afraid." And the master lit a candle, gave the candle to the disciple, and said, "This will do. You go."

When the disciple was going out of the door, the master suddenly blew the candle out. The disciple said, "I don't understand what you have done. Just a moment before you lit the candle for me with such compassion. Now why are you so cruel? Why have you blown it out?"

The master laughed. He said, "My candle will not be of much use to you."

Buddha has said *appo deepo bhava* – "Be a light unto yourself."

"The night is dark, I know, and I would like to help you in every way; but I cannot do anything that is impossible. Only your light will help you in the dark night, so rely on yourself. Go with my blessings. Go into the dark night with my blessings. Rely on your own consciousness. Remain alert, let that be your light, because nobody else's light can help you."

This is a beautiful parable, of infinite significance.

Wisdom is that which is your own experience – remember it. And all that you have gathered from others, throw it, burn it! That which is yours is true; that which is not yours is untrue. A truth is truth only if you have experienced it. Even a truth becomes a lie when you have not experienced it. When I say a truth to you, it is truth when I say it. When you hear it it becomes a lie – because for you it will not be based on your experience. So drop all that luggage that you have been carrying. It is useless, it is not going to help.

Buddha says, in this journey to the other shore, you drop all the weight that you have gathered from others. Just take that much which is yours. Of course, you cannot drop it. You will have to take it; there is no way to drop it. Can you drop anything that you have known? Can you drop it? How can you un-know what you have known? There is no way. If you have experienced something in meditation, how can you drop it? You cannot drop it . . . because by experiencing it, it has become part of your being. That's what *pragya* is. *Pragya* is some experience that has become part of your being. It is no longer a possession, it is just your very being. And how can you carry that which you have not experienced? You cannot carry it. Only that is yours, which has been experienced by you.

Beliefs have to be dropped. Only wisdom can be of help.

There is a Hasidic story:

> Without telling his teacher anything of what he was doing, a disciple of Rabbi Baruch had inquired into the nature of God, and in his

thinking had penetrated further and further until he was tangled in doubts and what had been certain up to that point became uncertain. When Rabbi Baruch noticed that the young man no longer came to him as usual, he went to the city where he lived, entered his room unexpectedly and said to him, "I know what is hidden in your heart. You have passed through the fifty gates of reason. You begin with a question and think and think up an answer . . . and the first gate opens. And to a new question, and again you plummet, find the solution, fling open the second gate, and look into a new question. On and on like this, deeper and deeper, until you have forced open the fiftieth gate. There you stare at a question whose answer no man has ever found – for if there were one who knew it, there would no longer be any freedom of choice. But if you dare to probe still further, you plunge into the abyss."

"So I should go back all the way to the very beginning?" cried the disciple.

"If you turn, you will not be going back," said the rabbi. "You will be standing beyond the last gate. You will stand in faith."

That's what Buddha calls wisdom.

Belief is from others, faith is your own. Don't be deceived by dictionaries. Dictionaries say faith means belief, belief means faith. They don't mean that; they are not synonymous. They are really opposite to each other, antagonistic. Belief is just faith in appearance; deep down there is doubt, because you have not experienced – how can the doubt disappear? You are simply pretending that you know. Without knowing, the doubt will remain there deep inside your heart. One day or other you will have to face it. And the time that you wasted in repressing it is a sheer wastage. In the first place, you should have encountered it.

Doubt encountered, not repressed, disappears. Then arises faith. Faith is the Jewish term for the same thing that Buddha calls *pragya*, wisdom. Through belief you trust others, but others cannot go with you. Don't lean on others, that is Buddha's fundamental message. Lean on your own self, because you will be left alone in the final stage, and only your own eyes, your own wisdom, will be of help.

Another Hasid story I would like to share with you . . .

A woman came to Rabbi Israel, the Mazid of Kosnitz, and told him with many tears that she had been married a dozen years and still had not borne a son.

"What are you willing to do about it?" he asked her.

She did not know what to say.

"My mother," so the Mazid told her, "was ageing and still had no child. Then she heard that the holy Baal Shem was stopping over in the course of a journey. She hurried to his inn and bade him pray that she might bear a son. 'What are you willing to do about it?' Baal Shem asked her. 'My husband is a poor bookbinder,' she replied, 'but I have one fine thing that I shall give to the Rabbi.' She went home as fast as she could and fetched her good cap, her *katinka*, which was carefully stored away in a chest. But when she returned to the inn with it, she heard that Baal Shem had already left for Magditch. She immediately set out after him, and since she had no money to ride, she walked from town to town with her *katinka*, until she came to Magditch. The Baal Shem took the cap and hung it on the wall. 'It is well,' he said. 'My mother walked all the way back from town to town until she reached Ept. A year later, I was born.'"

"I too," cried the woman, "will bring you a good cap of mine so that I may get a son."

"That won't work," said the Mazid. "You heard the story; my mother had no story to go by."

Old answers won't help, others' answers won't help. You cannot repeat in life; life is unrepeatable. You can read the Vedas and the Koran and the Bible and it won't help. It may help the rishi who wrote the Veda, but it won't help you – because it is a borrowed thing to you. The rishi had never read any Veda, Mohammed had never read any Koran. You cannot have that which Mohammed gained, because he had never read any Koran. And you are trying to gain it by reading the Koran? No, it is not possible.

Remember, life is unrepeatable, truth is unrepeatable. Nobody else's answer is going to help; you have to find your answer. Depend on only your experience. Sort it out in your mind; all that is not yours, throw it out. Go and throw it in the river. Keep only that which you know, which you know on your own, and that will become a provision, a *parmita*.

The seventh is *upai*. *Upai* means "skillful means". Buddha emphasizes very much that all means are not good; only very skillful means have to be used. What does he mean by "skillful"? He means an *upai*, a method which can be dropped when its use is finished. Otherwise one can become too burdened by the method itself. He used to say, "You use a boat to go to the other shore, but then you leave it. You don't carry it on your head." You don't say, "This boat has brought me to this shore, so now how can I be so ungrateful and leave it here? I will carry it on my head for my whole life."

Buddha says use things, and drop them when their work is finished. When you have utilized them, go ahead. Leave them behind.

All methods have to be dropped by and by. Ultimately, finally, before you reach to the other shore, you have to drop all – meditations, disciplines, everything has to be dropped. So be very skillful, otherwise there is a tendency to be caught by the method.

I know people . . . even a person like Ramakrishna was in a difficulty. He used Mother Kali for his meditations, then he became obsessed with it. Then whenever he would close his eyes, Kali would be standing there. Her image would come . . . beautiful . . . but this was trouble. Now he could not be alone. Now there was no way to be totally silent; the Mother was always standing there, so there was always company. And when the Mother is standing there, of course Ramakrishna had to say something – to praise her, sing a song, pray, do something. He became very disturbed: "What to do about it?" And he himself had cultivated it. For years he had cultivated it, for years he had prayed before the image, saying, "Come into my dreams." For years he had been asking, crying and weeping, "Mother, when I close my eyes, why don't you come to me?" Then it started – not that the Mother heard; there is nobody to hear. Not that the Mother took compassion; there is nobody. But constantly asking, constantly remembering, he became hypnotized. It was an auto-hypnosis, but tremendously powerful; he was a powerful man. Now Kali was always standing there – in the night, in the day – it was difficult to have any privacy now. Even if he went in, Kali was there. His inner space also became occupied; he became burdened. But how to drop Kali? – even the idea to drop her was difficult. Then he asked a very great saint who was passing by. He told him, "Something has to be done now."

The saint could see the point. Ramakrishna had used a method but had used it unskillfully, so he had become too obsessed with the method. It was good, it could have been used, but one should always remember that every method has to be dropped one day, so don't become too attached. Now he had become too attached.

The saint told him, "You close your eyes and when Kali appears, take a sword from inside and cut her in two."

Ramakrishna said, "What are you saying? Have you gone mad? How can I cut Mother Kali? No, that is not possible. I cannot do it, I cannot even think about it!"

Then the saint said, "Then you will be always obsessed with this idea. You will never attain to real samadhi, because real samadhi is when consciousness is absolutely pure and there is no content in it. The mirror is absolutely pure, nothing reflects." He said, "Then it is for you to decide."

Now Ramakrishna was in much doubt about what to do. He wanted to attain to samadhi, but this attachment was coming in the way. Finally he decided: "Okay," he said, "I will do it. But from where to get the sword?"

And the saint laughed and said, "From where you have got your Mother Kali, from the same place! It is imagination, so imagine a sword – and imagination can cut imagination. This Mother Kali is your imagination, your sword is your imagination. The cutting, and Mother Kali falling apart, is also imagination. To destroy imagination a real sword is not needed. For an unreal thing, another unreal thing will do."

Ramakrishna tried many times, but would not succeed. The saint got fed up. He said, "Now tomorrow I am leaving. This is the last time. To help you I will do one thing. I'm going to bring a piece of glass, and when the Mother Kali arises," . . . because whenever the Mother Kali would be there, immediately you could see it from outside also; Ramakrishna would start swaying and tears of happiness would start rolling down his face . . . He said, "When I see that now you are in your hypnosis and the Mother Kali is there, I will cut you on your third-eye center with my piece of glass. Blood will flow. At that moment, it is to remind you not to forget the sword. As I am cutting you, you cut your Mother Kali. You try it, otherwise tomorrow I will go." He was threatening to go, and it was difficult to find a man like him. His name was Totapuri, a very rare man.

Ramakrishna tried, crying and weeping, and when Totapuri cut his third-eye center, Ramakrishna also took courage and cut the Mother inside. Suddenly, all disappeared, Mother and sword and all. He was in absolute silence.

Buddha says, use all means and methods in a very unattached way, so when the time is right to drop them, you can drop them. Everything has to be dropped.

The eighth is *pranihan*, "surrender". And Buddha says remember, you have to do much, but the ultimate always happens when you are not doing anything. It happens in a let-go. *Pranihan* is the state of let-go. You do all that you can do; it will help, it will prepare the ground, but it cannot cause the truth to happen. When you have done everything that you can do, then relax, then nothing more is left to be done. In that relaxing, in that let-go, the truth happens. Truth is not something that we can bring. It comes, it descends, it happens; it is nothing of your doing.

The ninth, *bala*, is "power". After surrender is power. Now, see the difference. At the fourth Buddha said *vidya*, energy. It was not power, it was simply

429

energy, human energy. Now after surrender there is *bala* – power, divine power. When you have surrendered and your ego is dropped, suddenly you are full of unknown power. You have become a receptacle.

And the tenth, *ghyana*, is seeing into the nature of things, or awareness. Buddha uses the word *ghyana* in a very specific way. It is seeing into the nature of things. When you have surrendered and the power of the divine or the power of the whole has descended on you, then there is that encounter, that vision, that realization – nirvana.

These ten are the *parmitas*. They have to be practiced.

Now, the sutra. The sutra is to remind you of how you have to work for these ten *parmitas*.

THE BUDDHA SAID:

Those who study the doctrine of the buddhas will do well to believe and observe all that is taught by them.

It is like unto honey; it is sweet within, it is sweet without, it is sweet throughout; so is the Buddha's teaching.

This is one of the things to be understood. This is very significant, and Buddha has repeated so many times, "My teaching is like honey – sweet within, sweet without, sweet throughout; sweet in the beginning, sweet in the middle, sweet in the end. My teaching is like honey." He has repeated that a thousand and one times. Why? There is a very significant message in it.

Ordinarily, whenever you feel happy, afterwards comes unhappiness. When you indulge you have a glimpse of happiness; then there is pain and frustration. So it is sweet in the beginning, but bitter in the end. Seeing this, many people have tried the reverse, the extreme opposite. That's what ascetics do. They say, "Fasting, austerities, discipline, are painful in the beginning, but very sweet in the end." These are the two ways in the world, the way of the worldly man who hankers for pleasure ... Even if in the end it brings pain, it's okay: "We will see. Right now, why miss?" Even if a drop of honey is there, he's ready to suffer for years for it. The worldly man thinks of the momentary and suffers for it.

The so-called religious man, seeing this absurdity, stands on his head. He turns the whole thing upside-down. He says, "If in the world this is experienced, if you enter into a blissful, peaceful, happy state, in the end you become frustrated. The happiness is for a moment, and for years afterwards you remain frustrated." He tries the other: he says, "First I will move into pain – I will fast, I will move away from all pleasure, I will go to the Himalayas, I will stand in the cold, or in the hot sun, I will move into pain on my own, voluntarily – and then comes pleasure." Yes, that's true. It happens because pain and pleasure are two aspects of the same coin. If first you look at one side, you will have to look at the other side later on.

Buddha says, "My teaching is totally different – it is neither of the worldly nor of the other-worldly; it is neither of one extreme or of another extreme; it is sweet in the beginning, it is sweet in the middle, it is sweet in the end." It is not a question of choosing between pain and pleasure. If you choose pleasure, pain will come; if you choose pain, pleasure will come. But on the whole both are there.

"My teaching," Buddha says, "is of choiceless awareness." You don't choose. You should not choose – neither pain nor pleasure; then the whole coin drops out of your hand. Then pleasure and pain both disappear, and that which is left behind is what bliss is, or peace, or serenity . . . but it is sweet.

It is like unto honey; sweet within, sweet without, sweet throughout; so is the Buddha's teaching.

THE BUDDHA SAID:

O monks, you must not walk on the way as the ox that is attached to a wheel. His body moves, but his heart is not willing.

If your heart is not willing then there is no need. Then the time has not come for you to move on the way or to go in search for the truth. Then you still need to live in the world and get a little more mature. But don't go against the heart, because that going is useless. If your heart goes with you into the search for truth, only then go.

His body moves, but his heart is not willing. But when your heart is in accord with the way, there is no need of troubling yourselves about your outward demeanor.

If your heart is ready, if you have experienced life and the pain of it, if you have suffered life and understood the frustration of it and your heart is ready to move to the other shore – you have experienced this shore and have found that it is just empty, just illusory – if you are ready to move to the other shore without looking backwards, not even a slight desire for this shore has remained in your being, then you are ready.

Then, Buddha says, you are free of all discipline. Then there is no need; then this much is enough, that your heart is in accord with the way. Discipline will come; this is enough. Discipline is needed because your heart is not in accord with the way. "But then," Buddha says, "that discipline is not of much use."

Remember, Buddha is not ready to take you on the way if you are immature. Maturity is a must. And what do I mean by maturity? By maturity I mean one who has looked into life and found that this is just a dream. When the reality that you think is real starts looking like a dream, you are mature. Then it is very simple to move to the other shore alone – there will be no difficulty; your heart will be in accord with the way. You can go dancing, you can go singing, you can go laughing . . . you can go joyous, cheerful. You will not go reluctantly, you will not go resistantly, you will not go against yourself. In fact, you will not be going; you will simply be moving with the stream, like timber.

THE BUDDHA SAID:

Those who practice the way might well follow the example of an ox that marches through the deep mire carrying a heavy load. He's tired, but his steady gaze, looking forward, will never relax until he comes out of the mire, and it is only then that he takes a respite. O monks, remember that passions and sins are more than the filthy mire, and that you can escape misery only by earnestly and steadily thinking of the way.

Buddha says that first, great effort is needed – and then great surrender, too. That is the meaning of the Zen people saying that "effortless effort" is needed. A great harmony is needed of effort and no-effort. If you rely on your effort, you will never reach; if you rely only on God's grace, you will never reach. The possibility to reach arises only when you have done all that you can do. Only at that moment does the universe shower on you, not before it. Then you can relax.

So Buddha says first do each thing that you can do. Never ask for help before that. Don't be lazy, don't be lethargic; bring all your energy into action. Become totally involved in the spiritual work. Of course, remember also that this is not going to give you the ultimate. A moment will come when you will have to surrender. But . . . you can surrender only when you have done all that you can do. Existence helps those who help themselves.

There are two types of people. The first type says, "If it is going to happen by grace, it will happen. When existence needs, or when it wants, it will happen. I will have to wait." Their waiting is impotent, their waiting is not of any worth. They have not earned it, they have not taken even a step. It is not going to happen. Then there are egoistic people; they say, "It is going to happen by my effort. There is no grace, there is no possibility of the universe helping me; the universe is absolutely indifferent to human beings. I have to do all that I can do, and it is going to happen only by my effort."

Buddha says these people also will never reach. They are too egoistic. The first type is too lethargic, the second type is too active, and the reality is just in the middle. Be active and yet ready to surrender.

These are the differences among the three religions in India. Hinduism is of the first type, Jainism is of the second type, Buddhism is of the third type. Hinduism believes it will happen by God's grace; that whenever God wills, it will happen: nothing can happen without his will. Not that what they say is wrong, but they don't earn it. Jainism says it will happen by our will, our power. There is no grace, no help coming from the universe, so we have to fight and struggle. So Jainism becomes a very egoistic trip.

Buddha says you have to do all that you can do. Be a Jaina first, and then be a Hindu. That is the greatest synthesis ever brought to the world: be a Jaina first, and then be a Hindu.

In Buddha the whole East came to a synthesis. Buddha's contribution to the world is unique. And that's my teaching too: be a Jaina first, and then be a Hindu. First make all the effort that you can, go to the very end that you can, and then relax. Then you have earned it; now the grace will be coming.

Effort plus surrender, struggle plus surrender, brings one home.

Enough for today.

Chapter 22:

Collecting Pebbles on the Seashore of Life

THE BUDDHA SAID:

I consider the dignities of kings and lords as a particle of dust that floats in the sunbeam. I consider the treasure of precious metals and stones as bricks and pebbles. I consider the gaudy dress of silks and brocades as a worn-out rag. I consider this universe as small as the holila fruit. I consider the lake of Anavatapta as a drop of oil with which one smears the feet. I consider the various methods of salvation taught by the buddhas as a treasure created by the imagination. I consider the transcendental doctrine of Buddhism as a precious metal or priceless fabric seen in a dream. I consider the teaching of buddhas as a sky flower before my eyes. I consider nirvana as awakening from a daydream or nightmare. I consider the struggle between heterodox and orthodox as the antics of the six [mythical] dragons. I consider the doctrine of sameness as the absolute ground of reality.

The Buddha is the greatest anarchist in human history. He does not believe in any rule from the outside. To help you become free from the outside, he teaches you an inner rule, an inner discipline. Once you have learned the ways of the inner discipline, he's there, ready to destroy that too – because either you are ruled from the outside or from the inside. You are a slave; freedom is only when there is no rule.

So the inner discipline is just a step to get out from the outer domination – of the society, of the state, of the masses, civilization, culture, etcetera. Once you are free of the outer domination, then Buddha starts destroying your inner discipline too. That's why I call him the greatest anarchist ever. There have been people who have taught that no outside rule should exist, but Buddha is alone in teaching that even the inside rule is a form of slavery, a subtle slavery. No-discipline is his discipline. And when a person is absolutely without any discipline, then there is beauty because then there is freedom. Then one acts spontaneously, not according to any rule imposed by others or imposed by oneself. Then one simply acts out of nothingness. Then the response is total; nothing is being held back, and there is no enforcement of any sort, there is no violence. There is tremendous grace, there is benediction – because now the actor has completely disappeared, the doer is no longer there. If you are trying to discipline yourself, the doer remains in a subtle way. If you are trying to discipline yourself, you remain schizophrenic, you remain divided. A part of you disciplines you, another part is being disciplined by you. So one part becomes the master and another part becomes the slave. Again there is division, again there is duality, again you are not one.

And there is bound to be conflict in this duality, because in reality you *are* one, and this duality is a fiction. Who is trying to rule whom? Who is there to be dominated by whom? There is only one existence inside, one being. To bring any sort of discipline means to divide that unity, and that division is misery, that division is hell.

So first Buddha says there is no God – because if there is a God and any belief in God, then man can never be free because then there is a dominator, a dictator. With a God in the world, there can be no democracy – impossible. If God has created man, then of course he is the ultimate power. If he's omnipotent, omnipresent, omniscient, then how can freedom exist? You are never left alone, he's everywhere. That's what the so-called religious people teach. They say, "He's looking at you wherever you are. In the most private situation also he's there, watching you constantly. His eyes follow you."

This seems to be a very dangerous teaching. It means you don't have any freedom, it means you don't have any privacy. God is like a universal peeping-tom; he's always there at the keyhole, you cannot escape from him. His very presence is destructive; his presence means that man has no freedom.

Nietzsche's declaration – that God is dead and now man is free – has a Buddhist tone to it. That's what Buddha has said: God is not, and there is freedom. Freedom means you are not created by anybody and you are not dominated by anybody and you are not manipulated by anybody.

To Buddha, freedom is God. Try to understand it. It is difficult, because Buddha uses such terminology that it becomes very difficult for childish minds to understand. The childish mind can always understand that there is a God dominating you, looking after you, compassionate, kind, great – the father, the mother. These are childish ways to understand the truth. Buddha says there is no God, and freedom is absolute. That absolute freedom is Buddha's God. Freedom is God. Freedom is divine.

So first he takes away all outer beliefs. There is no need to believe in a God. The belief itself will become the barrier. The ordinary religions have taught people that you become religious only when you believe. If you don't believe, you are irreligious. The West is completely unaware of a great religion that has existed in the East, which does not require any belief; in fact it says belief is a barrier. A religion without belief is very difficult for a Christian or a Mohammedan and a Jew to conceive. It was even difficult for Hindus and Jainas to conceive.

Buddha is a great revolution, he brings a very radical outlook. He says all beliefs are dangerous. You should not believe, you should see.

Doubt is better than belief. Doubt can never hinder you; doubt remains open. Belief is a closing of the mind – then the aperture is closed, then you don't look. In fact, a man who believes becomes afraid to look. Maybe the truth is against his belief, then what to do? He closes his eyes. It is easier to protect one's belief with closed eyes than with open eyes. Who knows? The truth may not coincide with your belief. The truth may shatter your belief, the truth may be against your belief. It may not be Christian, it may not be Hindu, it may not be Mohammedan. Then what will you do? So it is better to remain with closed eyes.

A man with belief becomes afraid. He does not seek and he does not inquire and he does not search. He never explores. He remains stuck with his belief. He holds his belief to his heart; this is out of fear.

Religion is not out of fear – at least *real* religion is not out of fear. At least it should not be out of fear. Real religion is fearlessness. And with a God, how can you be fearless?

The Jewish God says: "I'm very jealous. Don't worship any God other than me; I'm very jealous. And if you worship any other God, I will destroy you." Now, these words look very political, and very stupid. And to put these words into the mouth of God himself is sheer nonsense. God saying, "I am jealous" – then God seems very human, even below human because there have existed human beings who are not jealous. A Buddha has existed who is not jealous. Buddha seems to be in a better state of consciousness than the Jewish God.

Jealous? Forbidding his followers to worship anybody else, "Because I am jealous, and I will destroy you"? What the Jewish God says is simply unbelievable. He says. "If you commit something against me, for ten generations I will torture you. Not only you, ten generations of your children will be tortured. And if you worship me, for a hundred generations the rewards will be coming to you."

Now, what type of God is this? Your child has not done anything. You commit some crime, you disobey God, and for generations your children will suffer! And for a hundred generations your children will get the reward if you have done something good. This "something good" means, in Jewish terms, that you have obeyed the omnipotent God. If you disobey him it is sin; if you obey, it is virtue. There seems to be no real value. God may be saying something absurd, but if you obey it is virtue and if you disobey it is sin. And this threat . . . "For ten generations I will take revenge,'" and this bribery, that "For one hundred generations I will reward you," – look at what type of mind has worked out this concept of God! It cannot be very divine. It is not divine at all; it is, in fact, subhuman.

Buddha says, "There is no God. Don't be afraid." To make man fearless, Buddha says there is no God and to make man an explorer of truth he says there is no need for any belief. Belief is not a requirement, it is an obstacle. Be open. Explore. Doubt, think, meditate, experiment. And when a mind comes to experience truth without any belief, the mind itself becomes true – because then there is a communion between truth and the mind.

Be fearless. There is no need for anybody to dominate you; freedom is your very substratum.

First Buddha drops outer beliefs – in God, in hell, in heaven, because your hell and heaven are just your projections. If you knew about all the different hells and heavens you would understand. The Tibetan's hell does not have fire in it, because the Tibetan's hell has to have more cold, more ice. They know – they suffer from cold, so hell has no fire at all. Of course, the Hindu's hell has fire; they suffer from heat. The Hindu's concept of heaven is almost of an air-conditioned heaven. The sun is never hot, and cool breezes are always blowing, and shady trees, and the flowers are like diamonds . . . everything is cool. Of course, a hot country – suffering for centuries from heat – they have their dreams.

But these things are your projections. There are as many hells in the world – and as many heavens – as there are climates, because it will depend on the experience of your own climate. For a Tibetan, fire in hell will look almost like a heavenly gift. No, fire has no place in the Tibetan hell. It is absolutely cold;

you will be frozen to death by coldness. Fire exists in heaven. There, everything is warm.

Now, what do these concepts show? They show your mind, they don't show anything about heaven or hell. Man continues in his dreams, in his projections.

If you die, you may be dying as far as your body is concerned but your mind continues. In fact, the Buddhist approach is that the idea of heaven and hell has arisen because during his whole life a man projects, thinks about the afterlife. And if he has been committing many crimes and sins, he feels guilty, he feels that he is going to hell. He becomes very afraid. By the time he's dying the fear arises: "Now there is no time left to put things right." Now he is going into hell, and he has an idea of hell, of what hell is. So when a person dies, when he is free from the body, the projections become very real. He starts dreaming. So when a Hindu dies, certainly he dreams after death. Immediately he dreams either of heaven or hell; it depends. If he was a good man, virtuous, a worshipper, then of course he is very self-confident. When he dies, he knows that he is going to heaven. Immediately after death the mind starts dreaming. The time between one death and another birth is used in dreaming.

You live in a dream world, exactly as you live in the night. What happens when your body relaxes and you go to sleep? You start dreaming. You forget your body in your sleep. Sleep is a tiny death, a mini-death. You forget your body, you don't remember your body at all; you become just your mind, as if the mind is no longer burdened by the body and the reality of the body. The mind is freed. There is no pressure on the mind of bodily reality, of objective reality. Mind is freed and suddenly you start dreaming. Of course, your dream is *your* dream; it has nothing to do with any reality whatsoever.

When you die this is exactly what happens, and it happens in a bigger way. Once you die, all the pressure of bodily reality and objective reality disappears. The mind is free to dream. Even in sleep there is a burden, even in sleep you are connected with the body, but in death you are disconnected completely. Now the mind is completely free. Like a balloon it starts rising into its projections. So if you have lived a bad life . . . When I say, "If you have lived a bad life," I mean if you *think* your life has been bad, if you have been taught that this life is bad.

For example, if a Jaina has been eating meat, he will suffer hell after his death – but not a Mohammedan, not a Christian, not a non-vegetarian who has never thought about it. He will not suffer hell. But a Jaina is bound to suffer hell. If he has eaten meat, his idea will make him guilty; the guilt will be there and the guilt will project. He knows what hell is and the hell will be projected.

Between death and birth there is a great dreaming time, and you can live long in that dream time because the dream time is absolutely different from your waking time. Have you sometimes observed that you are just sitting in your chair and for a minute you fall asleep and you dream? And the dream is so long that it takes years – in dream time. Then suddenly you are awake and you look at the clock and only one minute has passed. Now you are puzzled. How, in one minute's dream, could you see a projection of many years? You were a child, then you become young, and then you went to the college and the university, and you fell in love and were married, and you were just coming out of the church – and the dream is broken. There is such an expanse of many years – how has it happened in a single minute?

Dream time is different from actual time; it can happen in a single minute. So maybe between death and birth there are only a few minutes, or a few days at the most, or a few hours. But they will look very long; you can dream infinite dreams. You can dream of hell, you can dream of heaven – but *you* continue. Your hell is your hell; your heaven is your heaven. It is your projection, it is your personality projected in dreams. These are not realities.

Buddha is tremendously existential. He's the first religious man who has said that there is no heaven and no hell; it is just in the dreams of humanity that heaven and hell exist. If you have stopped dreaming while alive, then there is no heaven and no hell. In fact, there is no sin and no virtue. He's the greatest iconoclast, the idol-breaker. He takes everything away from you because he knows that unless everything is taken away, the mind continues. Mind needs props. If all the props are taken away, the mind collapses. And in that collapse, reality arises in its true color, in its true tone.

The reality is only when the mind is not. Mind is a distorting faculty.

Now these are the last sutras – of tremendous import. Each sentence is like a sword, and it cuts the roots of the mind. And when it comes to cutting the roots of the mind, Buddha excludes nobody, not even himself. That's his authenticity. It is not that he is against other philosophies, he's against philosophy as such – against his own philosophy too.

That's the authenticity of the master. It is very easy to be against others' philosophies, but to be against one's own philosophy means the man has no philosophy of his own. He's simply asserting a truth – that philosophy is not the door to reality. He's against all methods, including his own.

You will be surprised – then why does he use methods? The methods are to be used only because of you, because you are not ready to take the jump. The jump is too big, and you take it in small doses. Hence, he has to invent methods. The same is true about me. I would like you to take the quantum jump without any methods, but you cannot take it. The abyss looks too big and fear possesses you. So I have to make small steps for you. Slowly, slowly, I persuade you. The more you become ready, the more I push you into no-method, into no-mind, into no-religion.

The essential religion is no-religion, and the greatest method is no-method. And to come to a state of no-mind is to come to awareness. Buddha has to talk to many categories of people, but these sutras are for those disciples who have come of age, who have become mature.

It happened once:

> I was chatting with Mulla Nasruddin, who was an avid fisherman. I told him, "I notice, Nasruddin, that when you tell about the fish you caught, you vary the size of it for different listeners."
>
> "Yes," he said, "I never tell a man more than I think he will believe."

And that's what Buddha is doing too. If you have come to him with a childish mind, he will give you some toys to play with. If you have come with a little better, a little more grown-up mind, a little more mature, he will not give you those toys. And if you are really mature enough to listen to truth, unafraid, then . . . then these sutras.

Today's sutras are the last. They are meant only for very grown-up people, so listen to them very attentively.

It is said that once Jesus' disciples asked him, "Have you brought a message of peace to the world?" He said, "No. I don't bring peace, I bring a sword."

A sword? And Christians have puzzled over it down through the centuries, because it doesn't look right. Jesus is the messenger of peace and he says, "No, I have not brought peace to you, but a sword." And he says, "I will teach you how to hate your mother and how to hate your father and how to hate your wife and how to hate your husband and how to hate your children. And unless you are ready to hate your father and your mother, you cannot follow me."

Now, these words coming from Jesus – who says God is love – look very contradictory, very inconsistent. It is difficult to sort out what he means. And it has been difficult for Christians; they avoid these sentences. But if you understand this sutra of Buddha, you will be able to understand Jesus too. By "sword" he means that each master brings a sword into the world to cut the roots of the mind. When he says, "Unless you hate your father and your mother and your family, you cannot follow me," what is he saying? He's saying that unless you drop the mind that has been given to you by your mother, by your father, by your family – unless you drop your past; unless you forget completely what the society has given to you, the idea of good and the idea of evil – unless you drop the whole conditioning that society has given to you, you cannot follow me.

These sutras are like swords. They cut, and they cut totally. Buddha is very hard because he has great compassion. He will not allow any loophole from where you can find your slavery again. So first, drop all outer discipline; and then, drop the inner discipline too. In that undisciplined state is freedom, is nirvana, is moksha. And out of that freedom, whatsoever happens is virtue. Out of slavery, whatsoever happens is sin.

THE BUDDHA SAID:

I consider the dignities of kings and lords as a particle of dust that floats in the sunbeam.

He says all political power, all power as such, is stupid. Don't rush after it; don't be ambitious because all ambition collects dust and only dust. If you are not disillusioned by dust, you will not be able to know what truth is. A man obsessed with ambition is not capable of knowing truth at all. Eyes full of ambition never see what is; they only see what they want to see. The ambitious mind is the wrong mind; the non-ambitious mind is the right mind.

To be non-ambitious – what does it mean? It means that you are not hankering for the future, that you are not hankering for the next moment, you are not hoping for the next moment, you have abandoned hope. You live in this moment, you don't have any future, the present is all that is. A non-ambitious mind becomes still, and that stillness comes of its own accord – not that you still yourself. A non-ambitious mind is still; there is nowhere to go, nothing to hanker after. Then reality is available.

For an ambitious mind, reality is not available – because reality is available only in the present and the ambitious mind is always somewhere else, always somewhere else. The ambitious mind is never content. Discontentedness is its very base. Buddha says, "For what are you desiring? Desiring for kingdoms? You want to become great kings and dignitaries?"

I consider the dignities of kings and lords as a particle of dust that floats in the sunbeam.

Why does he say "that floats in the sunbeam"? Have you seen sometimes . . . a sunbeam enters through the roof, the whole room is dim and dark and just one beam of sun enters into the room; then you can see dust floating, dust particles floating in it. They shine, they look like diamonds. They are ordinary dust. If the sunbeam were not there you would not even see them, but in a sunbeam they look like diamonds. They shine, they become radiant.

Buddha is saying that when you project an ambition, when the sunbeam of ambition is there, dust particles look very precious. They are not precious in themselves. And he should know, he was born a king and then he left those palaces. The day his ambition dropped, suddenly the sunbeam disappeared and he saw only dust and dust.

The night he left his palace and his kingdom and his newly-born child, the charioteer took him out of the kingdom not knowing where he was going. And the charioteer was not supposed to ask. But when Buddha got out of the chariot and told the charioteer, "Now you take my clothes back, and please give your dirty clothes to me," the charioteer could not understand what he meant. He said, "What are you doing? Have you gone crazy?" He was an old man, the age of Buddha's father, and he said, "I have watched you and I have loved you from your very childhood. What are you doing? I am just like your father – tell me, what is your agony? Why are you leaving these beautiful palaces, this kingdom? You are the happiest man in the kingdom. Where are you going?"

And Buddha said, "I look at those palaces and they are on fire. Everything is burning, the whole world is burning and I want to move into a cool shade." The charioteer, of course, was not able to understand what he was saying. He said, "What are you talking about? I don't see any fire anywhere. What are you talking about?"

And Buddha said, "You may not understand, but I have seen the fire. Everything is on fire, everything is burning because everything is moving towards death."

Just the day before, he had gone to the town, his capital town, to inaugurate a youth festival, and on the road he had come across a dead body. He had not seen a dead body up to that moment. He asked, "What has happened to this man?"

The story is beautiful. The story is told in an Eastern way, in a mythological way. The story says that the charioteer was prohibited by Buddha's father ever to talk about death, and ever to answer such questions – because the father had been forewarned when the Buddha was born that if ever he came to know about death, he would renounce the world. So the charioteer was not going to say anything. But the story says that one god, looking at this, entered into the charioteer's body. Seeing that the moment had come when Buddha was ready to renounce, and only through that renunciation was he going to realize, the rare moment of existence had arrived, the gods helped. They forced the charioteer to say the truth.

The charioteer said, "The man is dead, Sir."

And Buddha asked, "Is this going to happen to me too?" And the charioteer had to say, because the gods were forcing him, "Yes, this is going to happen to you too, sir."

Buddha said, "Then return home. Then there is no point in going to inaugurate the youth festival. I am no longer young. Seeing death, I have become old. Seeing death, I have died." A great glimpse, a great insight happened. And Buddha said the next day, "The whole world is on fire. I have seen death and when death is coming, then what is the point? I would like to find something which is beyond death."

I consider the dignities of kings and lords as a particle of dust that floats in the sunbeam.

But we don't see death; our ambition prevents us from seeing it. Even if death came right in front of you, you would not be able to see it because your ambition would function as a barrier. It won't allow you to see, it is like a blindfold.

I have heard:

A rich manufacturer from New York suffered a nervous breakdown.

"You must have a rest," advised his doctor. "Go to Florida, lie around under the sun, go swimming. You will be better in a month."

The businessman followed the doctor's advice and went to Miami, got into his swimming shorts and strolled the warm sandy beach. Then the water was too much to resist and he went for a dip. But he had overestimated all the years he had gone without exercise and before he realized it he was over his depth, and could not swim back.

"Help! Help!" yelled the businessman. "Save me! I'm drowning!" An alert lifeguard heard the cry, dived into the water, and towed him to safety.

The manufacturer's wife came running to the scene on the beach. "Irving, baby, are you alright? Speak to me!"

"I'm alright," wheezed Irving, dripping water, "but I've got to ask you something in private, please. Bend down."

The worried wife stooped over. "Yes, Irving, what is it that you want to ask me?"

"Tell me, how much do I tip for a thing like this?"

He had faced death . . . but he asks his wife, "Tell me, how much do I tip for a thing like this?" Life is not a problem; money is the problem: "How much do I have to tip?" Even facing death a man never realizes that the very existence of death makes his whole life meaningless. Money has no meaning when death is there. But the ambitious mind lives in a very different world. The sunbeam of his ambition makes dust particles shine like diamonds. Once the sunbeam disappears, once the ambition is not there, everything falls flat and you can see where you were going and what you were hankering for. If life is going to disappear – and it is going to disappear, it is going to move into the desert of death sooner or later, it is only a question of time – then ...? Then whatsoever you are hankering for is meaningless. Death will take everything away from you.

Buddha says: Seek something which death cannot destroy.

I consider the treasure of precious metals and stones as bricks and pebbles.

All your money, all your precious stones, all your bank balances, Buddha says, "I consider as pebbles." You are children playing on the seashore of life, collecting pebbles – colored of course, they look beautiful of course, but they are pebbles on the seashore – of no significance. And while you are collecting them life is rushing out of your hands, slipping by. You are taking a great risk. This opportunity is not to be destroyed in only collecting pebbles.

> A man who took his two little girls to the amusement park noticed that Mulla Nasruddin kept riding the merry-go-round all afternoon. Once, when the merry-go-round stopped, the Mulla rushed off, took a drink of water, and headed back again. As he passed near the girls, their father said to him, "Mulla, you certainly do like to ride on the merry-go-round, don't you?"
>
> "No, I don't. Rather, I hate it absolutely and am feeling very sick because of it," said Nasruddin. "But the fellow who owns this thing owes me a hundred dollars, and taking it out in trade is the only way I will ever collect from him."

Money seems to be the greatest obsession in the world. Money seems to be the greatest madness in the world. We go on selling our lives and collecting pebbles – we call it money. One day we simply disappear and the money is left behind. And the life that you wasted in collecting that money could have been used in a more creative way. It could have become a song, a dance; it could have become a prayer, a meditation; it could have become a realization of truth, freedom ... but you missed.

BUDDHA SAYS:

I consider the gaudy dress of silks and brocades as a worn-out rag.

All that you go on desiring seems foolish. There are people who live only to eat; there are people who live only to dress; there are people who go on playing with things – good when you are a child, but it seems that very few people ever become grown-ups. They certainly grow old, but very few people become grown-ups. To grow old is one thing, to become grown-up is quite another. A grown-up person is one who can see through things, can see what is a toy and what is not a toy. Small children playing – you laugh at them, but have you looked into your own life? Have you grown up at all? Maybe you have changed your toys – they are playing with toy cars and you are playing with real cars – but the play remains the same.

Once I was a professor in a university, and a professor used to live just across from me. He had a car but it was always sitting there, and he would clean it and wash it every day, religiously. I became puzzled, by and by, because it never came out of the driveway.

I inquired. He said, "You see, the traffic is such, and the car is so beautiful, and it is risky to take it to the university. You know the students; somebody may scratch it."

"Then why have you purchased this car?"

He said, "I love it."

Now, think of loving a car! But there are people who love cars, who love houses. It is not very difficult to see what has happened to them. These are the people who cannot love a person, they can only love a thing – because you can manipulate a thing, control a thing, better than a person. A person is always dangerous. If you love a woman it is always dangerous; if you love a man it is always dangerous – because a man or a woman is a freedom, intrinsic freedom. You cannot totally control them. Man has tried in every way to create marriage, and laws, and this and that, and create respectability around it, and punishment and rewards, and everything just to make one thing certain – that the woman is no longer a freedom, that the man is no longer a freedom. When a man is a "husband" he is no longer a person, and when a woman is a "wife" she is no longer a person. The freedom has been killed. Now, a husband is a thing, and a wife is a thing. They can be controlled more easily. If the wife does something, you can go to the court and the magistrate will help you. The police will help you to force the wife back into her "thinghood".

People love things . . . and people are afraid of persons.

Then people can go to absurd limits. Now, a car has a utility, certainly it has a utility – but to be in romantic love with a car is absurd. And this was romance! I would see that man washing it every day for half an hour, completely absorbed, and the car was never used. He went to the university on a bike and the car went on sitting there. But he felt very happy that the car was there. He looked at the car as if he were looking at his woman, he touched the car as if he were touching a human body. I watched him: his eyes would suddenly become aglow when he looked at his car; something great happened around the car. It is absurd – not only absurd, it is insane.

I consider this universe as small as the holila fruit.

I consider the lake of Anavatapta as a drop of oil with which one smears the feet

And Buddha says if you become aware, the whole universe looks very tiny – because awareness is bigger than the whole universe. Man is very tiny if you look at his body, man is very foolish if you look at his mind, and man is tremendously vast if you look at his consciousness. Three things meet in man. The vast, the infinite lies in his consciousness, in his awareness. That's what you become aware of when you meditate. Boundaries recede and disappear. The body does not contain you; in fact, you contain the body. Ordinarily you think, "I exist in the body." It is absolutely wrong. The body exists in you; you are vaster, you are bigger – not only bigger than the body, you are bigger than this whole universe. It is awareness that holds all. But if you look at the body you are very tiny. And then, if you go on getting identified with your body, a great desire arises to be big. That's what politics is, that's what the desire and ambition for money is, that's what you try when you use beautiful clothes to exhibit yourself. You try to hide the body, your tinyness, your smallness. You try to make it look beautiful, you try to make it precious.

> It is said that once Mulla Nasruddin was in his Turkish bath, and there came Tamerlane, the great murderer and the great emperor and the great conqueror. And only two persons were there, Mulla Nasruddin and Tamerlane. Tamerlane, as was his habit, asked Mulla Nasruddin, "I have heard that you are a very wise man. How much do you think is my cost, my price?" Of course, he must have been hoping that he would say, "You are priceless, sir. The whole universe is nothing before you."
>
> But Nasruddin looked at him, brooded over it and said, "Sixty rupees."
>
> Tamerlane was very angry and he said, "What do you mean? Sixty

rupees? Even this towel I am wearing is worth more than sixty rupees!"

Nasruddin said, "That's why I said sixty rupees. I am not counting you – you are nothing – only this towel. That's why I say sixty rupees."

If you are identified with the body, of course your value is not much – cannot be much. How much value do you think you can get out of your body if you go and sell it? If you ask the scientists they say, "Somewhere near around five rupees." Not even sixty rupees, somewhere nearer to five rupees. There is a certain amount of aluminum and iron and phosphorus and things like that; if they are all collected and sold in the market, they will cost about five rupees – and that's only true because the cost of things has gone so high.

And in the first place, nobody would be ready to purchase your body. Immediately, the moment you die, everybody is ready to dispose of you in some way or other: "Just finish it now."

It is said about the great Emperor Akbar that he used to go to see a Sufi mystic, Farid, and he used to touch his feet. Now, Akbar's court people became a little jealous: "Akbar, the great emperor, touching the feet of a poor beggar?" And they told Akbar one day, "This doesn't look good, it is humiliating. You need not touch that beggar's feet. Your head is an emperor's head and you put your head on his feet?"

Akbar said, "You do one thing: take the head of a dead man and try to sell it."

Because the emperor had said it, they had to try. Wherever they went with the head, people chased them out. They said, "Have you gone crazy! Get out of here! That head is stinking, and who wants it? Get out!" They tried in all the shops, in every market in Delhi, and from everywhere they were thrown out. They came back and they said, "Nobody is ready to purchase it – not only that, people don't even listen. They simply say, "Get out of here! Have you gone mad? What will we do with a human head?"

Akbar said, "Then what do you think? My head is just a human head; one day you will not get any price for it. So if I put this useless head at the feet of Farid, why do you think it is humiliating?"

It is said that once a great Sufi mystic was caught by a few people who wanted to sell him in a slave market. He was a very young, healthy man, radiant, so the kidnappers were very happy; they were going to get a good price. They took him. He said to them, "I know that you are going to sell me, but let me tell you one thing: if you listen to me, you can get the highest price possible. I know my price, you don't know, so whenever you are ready to sell, just ask me, 'Is it the right price?'"

After just a few hours they came across a king, and the king said, "The man looks good; I will purchase him. I will give five thousand rupees." It was a lot of money in those days, and they were ready to take it. But the mystic said, "Wait, this is nothing; let the right purchaser come and I will tell you. Don't be fools," – so they refused. A rich man came and he offered ten thousand rupees. Now they were ready; they were not even going to ask. But the mystic said, "Wait! Are you a fool? Have you not seen? The price is double now. Just wait." And then came another rich man and he offered fifteen thousand rupees. By now, those people had become aware that he was right: "We have a very precious man." And this continued the whole day. Many people offered, but the mystic was saying, "Wait." The last offer was for fifty thousand rupees but the mystic said, "Wait!" After that, people started going home, the market was becoming deserted. The last man came and he was carrying just a bundle of straw. That was the last man, and the kidnappers said, "Now there seems to be no purchaser, and we will again have to wait for eight days. Next week, again there will be a market."

The mystic said, "Wait, ask this man." They asked the man and he said, "I can give you this bundle of straw. I don't have anything else." And the mystic said, "That is the right price; sell it! This is exactly the right price. Now don't miss this opportunity." Those people started beating their heads. They said, "We have got a madman! We have lost fifty thousand rupees and now he says, "This is the right price!"

But he was indicating something: there is no price. The body is very tiny and very small. If you get identified with it, you are getting identified with straw, a bundle of straw – or as Buddha says, "A bag of skin, full of filth." If you get identified with the mind you have a little more freedom. But mind is foolish, mind is stupid, mind is mediocre. It does not know anything about truth. It simply goes on inferring about truth, guessing. Mind is guesswork.

Buddha says: If you get to really know yourself, then you are vast, infinite. Then you are God.

I consider this universe as small as the holila fruit. I consider the lake of Anavatapta as a drop of oil with which one smears the feet.

Buddha is saying if you know man in his true reality, he is so vast that the biggest lake is just an oil drop on his feet. He is so vast that the whole universe is smaller than him.

I consider the various methods of salvation taught by the buddhas as a treasure created by the imagination.

This is the sword – it cuts everything from the roots. Now he says: *I consider the various methods of salvation taught by the buddhas as a treasure created by the imagination.* All methods are created by the mind, so they cannot lead you beyond the mind. That which is created by the mind cannot lead you beyond it. To go beyond it you will have to leave all that is created by the mind. Methods are also created by mind – yoga, tantra, yantra, mantra, all methods are mind-creations, imagination. Beautiful imagination, sweet dreams, golden dreams, and of course, they are created by buddhas . . .

To bring you out of your body the mind is used. So there are a few techniques to bring you out of the identification with the body. Then, to bring you to the very boundary of the mind there are other methods, which take you to the very brink of where mind ends. Then you have to jump out of the mind – of course, by jumping out of all methods.

I consider the various methods of salvation taught by the buddhas as a treasure created by the imagination. I consider the transcendental doctrine of Buddhism as a precious metal or priceless fabric seen in a dream.

Buddha says: Even what I am saying to you . . . maybe it is very precious, but it is precious metal or precious stones seen in a dream. That's what I say to you always, that truth cannot be uttered. The moment you utter it, it becomes a lie. Truth cannot be said. The moment you say it, it is almost part of a dream now; no longer truth.

The Zen Buddhists say Buddha never was born, never walked on earth, never taught a single teaching, never initiated anybody to be his sannyasin. And still they go and worship Buddha! Rinzai used to say that it looks absurd.

One skeptical philosopher came and he heard Rinzai saying that Buddha was never born. And just behind Rinzai was a great statue of Buddha. The thinker waited, and Rinzai said that Buddha never taught anything; in fact, he never existed, so how could he teach? And then, when the sermon was over, he went to the statue, touched the feet and offered a few flowers. The skeptical thinker said, "Wait! Now, there is a limit to everything. This is too much! You say this man never walked on the earth; you say he never taught; you say in fact that he was never there. And now, whose feet are you touching? Whose feet are you touching, and to whom are these flowers offered?"

And Rinzai laughed and he said, "I am offering these flowers to this man because he taught and still he said, 'I have not taught you anything.' He was born and yet he said, 'That which is born is beyond birth and death.' He walked on the earth but still deep inside he remained immovable; he never walked. The wheel moved; the hub remained in its place, centered."

Buddha's teaching is tremendously contradictory. First he teaches you, "Do this, do that," and then he suddenly says, "Drop all. Now the boundary of the mind has come. Now drop this last dream too."

I consider the teaching of buddhas as a sky flower before my eyes.

Have you sometimes watched, sitting by the shore, on a beach? – look into the sky and you will see flowers moving in the sky. Now scientists say they are ions. Or if you ask Wilhelm Reich, he says that they are particles of orgone energy. If you ask the eye specialists, they say that there is nothing; just the movement inside your eye nerves creates the fallacy of something in the sky. You can press your eye with a finger and then you can see those flowers more. These are called sky flowers – they exist not, but you can see them. And if you move your eyes they will come down and they will go up; you can play with them like a yoyo. But they are not, they are not existential.

BUDDHA SAYS:

I consider the teaching of buddhas as a sky flower before my eyes.

All teaching is meaningless. Truth cannot be taught, it can only be caught. There is no way to teach it. By teaching you can transfer words, doctrines, beliefs; truth is never transferred that way. But being with a buddha, you can catch it . . . it is infectious. Hence the value of *satsang* – being with a buddha, being with a master, being with one who has become enlightened.

What does it mean to become "enlightened"? Buddha says it simply means:

I consider nirvana as awakening from a daydream or nightmare.

He says you are living in a dream – the dream of ambition, desire, a thousand and one types of greed, anger, lust, passion. You live in a dream. Nirvana, enlightenment, is nothing but coming out of the dream, just becoming awake. There is nothing occult in it, nothing esoteric in it. Buddha has no esoterics in his teachings; he is very simple. He says: This is all – the man who lives in the world, the worldly man, the "samsaric" man, is in a dream, that's all. And the Buddha is one who has come out of the dream. The difference is not in their consciousness, the difference is only that the worldly man has something more than Buddha. Buddha has only awareness and the worldly man has something more than the Buddha. Buddha has only awareness and the worldly man has awareness plus dreams. Because of those dreams, the awareness becomes clouded – as if the sun is clouded and you cannot see. Clouds disappear and the sun is there. But as far as the inner light is concerned, there is no difference between a buddha and an ignorant man. They are made of same stuff.

I consider the struggle between heterodox and orthodox as the antics of the six [mythical] dragons.

And Buddha says it is all nonsense – the traditional and the anti-traditional, the orthodox and the heterodox, the theist and atheist, and the thousand and one types of philosophies and systems fighting with each other, arguing, proving, disproving. He says it is just a game, a mind-game, mythological. It has no significance. Don't be too much entangled with theories and doctrines; they are part of the dream. Get out of the dreaming state, become more aware.

I consider the doctrine of sameness as the absolute ground of reality.

This is his ultimate assertion; meditate over it.

I consider the doctrine of sameness as the absolute ground of reality.

Buddha says things are not different, they are the same; they only look different, they only appear different. The tree there, and the rock, and you, and the animals and the stars, are not different. At the innermost core, reality is one and the same. Substance is one and the same, there are no distinctions. Distinctions are dreams.

Physicists call that one reality "electricity" or "energy". Materialists, Marxists, communists, call that reality "matter". Idealists call that reality "mind". Yogis call that reality "consciousness". Buddha calls that reality "nothingness".

Now, this word "nothingness" is very important. "Nothingness" means *no-thing-ness*. No thing is. All things are just forms, dreams. We are different only in form, and forms are just dreams. It is as if out of gold you can make many sorts of ornaments. Those forms, different ornaments, are just dreams – because the gold is the reality. Behind all the forms is gold; behind all the forms is one reality. Buddha says that sameness is the absolute ground of reality.

If you go in, you leave the form. First you leave the form of the body. Have you observed it? – these sayings can be understood only if you have certain insights of your own; otherwise, it is impossible to understand them. When you are meditating, many times it happens that you forget your form, your body. You don't know who you are and how you look. You forget your face. In fact, in deep meditation, you completely become oblivious of your body. When you close your eyes you are formless.

Your mind also has form – you are a Hindu, Christian, Mohammedan, Jaina, Buddhist. Then you have a form of the mind; you think in terms of being a

Christian, you have a certain identity, dogma defines you. But if you go still deeper, mind also disappears. Then you are no longer a Christian.

At the deepest core you are neither a body nor a mind. Then what are you?

Buddha says you are nothingness, no-thing-ness. Now you are not a thing, now you are universal. Now you are not confined in any idea, you are infinite. You are that which has always been there and will remain always. You are eternal. Then there is no birth to you and there is no death to you. You are like the sky – clouds come and go and the sky remains untouched by them. Millions of times clouds have come and gone, and the sky has remained pure and virgin. It has not been corrupted or polluted by them. You are the inner sky. And when all forms disappear, the inner and the outer also disappear because they are also forms. Then there is nothing inner and nothing outer . . . oneness, sameness.

Buddha does not call it God – because to call it "God" you may start thinking again of form. But that's exactly what the word "God" should mean – it should mean the sameness that exists in all. "God" should mean existence, isness. The tree is, the rock is, the cloud is, the man is – forms are different but isness is the same. As far as *isness* is concerned, a tree and you are the same. The form is different, the tree is green and you are not green, and the tree has flowers and you don't have any flowers, and the bird can fly into the sky and you cannot fly – but these are differences of the form. Isness is the same. To look into that isness is what meditation is all about. And to come to realize that isness is nirvana.

This is the last message, the last sutra of this "Sutra of Forty-Two Chapters". This is the forty-second sutra, Buddha's ultimate message. I don't think you will be able to understand it right now. Intellectually of course you can understand it, but the real understanding has to be existential. That will come only if you follow the path of inner discipline to the point where you can drop it. If you follow the path of meditation to the point where even meditation becomes a hindrance, and you drop it . . .

It is as if you move on a staircase from one floor to another, but when you have reached the next floor you get off the staircase. You don't cling to it. All methods are staircases – or in Buddha's terminology, all methods are like boats; you cross the river and then you leave the boat and you forget all about it. Methods have to be used and then dropped. It has to be remembered from the very beginning – because there is every possibility that you may become too attached to the method. You become so attached that the method becomes a clinging. You start possessing it and it starts possessing you. Then the medicine has become a disease. It happens that you are ill, you take medicine, then illness goes but you cannot leave the medicine now. You have become accustomed to the medicine, to the drug.

When the illness has gone, throw the medicine immediately. Meditation is a medicine – because you are ill you have to use it. When wellness has come, then drop it immediately. All devices have to be dropped one day, and all scriptures have to be dropped one day. This is the greatness of Buddha – that he says that even his teachings, his methods, have to be dropped.

When Zarathustra was saying goodbye to his disciples, the last thing that he said to his disciples has to be remembered. Keep it in your heart. This is what Buddha is saying in the last sutra. Said Zarathustra to his disciples, "Now I am going and this is my last message: Beware of Zarathustra!" And he left.

Beware of Zarathustra? Beware of the master . . . because you can fall in love too much. You can become too attached. The real master is one who helps you to fall in love and then helps you to stand on your own so that you can leave the master. A real master never becomes a crutch for you. Never! Before he sees that you are clinging too much, he starts getting out of your life – because the ultimate goal is freedom – freedom from all crutches, freedom from all props, freedom from every discipline, doctrine, method. Freedom from all – that's the goal.

Always remember that goal. Remembering that goal will help you not to go astray.

A small story and I will finish this discourse. It is a Hasid story called "The Three Prisoners".

> After the death of Rabbi Uri of Istalisk, who was called "The Seraph", one of the Hasidim came to Rabbi Birnham and wanted to become his disciple. Rabbi Birnham asked, "What was your teacher's way of instructing you to serve?"
>
> "His way," said the Hasid, "was to plant humanity in our hearts. That was why everyone who came to him, whether he was a nobleman or a scholar, had first to fill two large buckets at the well in the marketplace, or to do some other hard and menial labor in the street."
>
> Rabbi Birnham said, "I shall tell you a story . . .
>
> "Three men, two of them wise and one foolish, were once put in a dungeon black as night, and every day food and eating utensils were lowered down to them. The darkness and the misery of the imprisonment had deprived the fool of his last bit of sense, so that he no longer knew how to use the utensils; he could not see. One of his companions showed him, but the next day he had forgotten again. And so his wise companion had to teach him continually. But the third prisoner sat in silence and did not bother about the fool.

"Once, the second prisoner asked him why he never offered his help.

'Look,' said the other, 'you take infinite trouble and yet you never reach the goal because every day destroys your work. But I, sitting here, am not just sitting. I am trying to bore a hole in the wall so that the light and sun can enter, and all three of us can see everything.'"

Now, there are two types of masters in the world. The first type I call the teacher. He teaches you things – disciplines, virtue, character – but next day you forget. Again he teaches you the same, and next day you forget again. The second I call the master. He does not teach you virtue, he does not teach you character, he does not teach you ordinary humility, humbleness, poverty – no. He bores a hole into your being so that light can penetrate, and you can see yourself. He tries to make you aware, full of light. That's the real master. In the East we call him *satguru*, the right master. Teachers are many; *satgurus* are very few and far between. Remember this distinction.

If you are with a teacher you may become a good person, but you cannot become enlightened. And your goodness will always remain on top of a volcano; it can erupt any moment. If you are with a teacher he will teach you outward things – how to discipline yourself, how to be good, how to serve people, how to be non-violent, how to be loving, kind, compassionate. He will teach you a thousand and one things.

If you come to a master, he teaches only one thing – that is how to become aware, how to bore a hole into your being so light can enter into your imprisonment. And in that light, everything starts happening of its own accord.

And when things happen of their own accord, they have a beauty to them. Then there is great benediction.

Enough for today.

OSHO INTERNATIONAL MEDITATION RESORT

The Osho Meditation Resort is a place where people can have a direct personal experience of a new way of living with more alertness, relaxation, and fun. Located about 100 miles southeast of Mumbai in Pune, India, the resort offers a variety of programs to thousands of people who visit each year from more than one hundred countries around the world.

Originally developed as a summer retreat for Maharajas and wealthy British colonialists, Pune is now a thriving modern city that is home to a number of universities and high-tech industries. The Meditation Resort spreads over 40 acres in a tree-lined suburb known as Koregaon Park. The resort campus provides accommodation for a limited number of guests, and there is a plentiful variety of nearby hotels and private apartments available for stays of a few days up to several months.

Resort programs are all based in the Osho vision of a qualitatively new kind of human being who is able both to participate creatively in everyday life and to relax into silence and meditation. Most programs take place in modern, air-conditioned facilities and include a variety of individual sessions, courses and workshops covering everything from creative arts to holistic health treatments, personal transformation and therapy, esoteric sciences, the "Zen" approach to sports and recreation, relationship issues, and significant life transitions for men and women. Individual sessions and group workshops are offered throughout the year, alongside a full daily schedule of meditations.

Outdoor cafes and restaurants within the resort grounds serve both traditional Indian fare and a choice of international dishes, all made with organically grown vegetables from the commune's own farm. The campus has its own private supply of safe, filtered water.

See <www.osho.com/resort> for more information, including travel tips, course schedules and guest house bookings.

RESOURCES

For more information about Osho and his work, see:

<www.osho.com>

a comprehensive web site in several languages that includes an on-line tour of the Meditation Resort and a calendar of its course offerings, a catalog of books and tapes, a list of Osho information centers worldwide, and selections from Osho's talks.

Or contact:

Osho International
New York
email: <oshointernational@oshointernational.com>